BYRON

Peter Quennell, one of England's most distinguished men of letters, was born in 1905, educated at Berkhamsted and Balliol College, Oxford, and in 1930 accepted a professorship at a Japanese university. Having returned to London, he became a regular contributor in various literary periodicals. From 1944 to 1951 he edited the *Cornhill Magazine*, and from 1951 to 1979 *History Today*. Besides his acclaimed two-volume autobiography (*The Marble Foot* and *The Wanton Chase*) he has published biographical studies of Hogarth, Shakespeare, Pope, Ruskin and Samuel Johnson, amongst many other books. His most recent book is *A History of Happiness*.

PETER QUENNELL

BYRON

The Years of Fame
Byron in Italy

COLLINS
8 Grafton Street, London W1

William Collins Sons and Co Ltd
London · Glasgow · Sydney · Auckland
Toronto · Johannesburg

First published as a single volume in 1974.
Byron The Years of Fame was first published in 1935.
A new edition, here reprinted except for
the omission of the dedication, was issued in 1967.
Byron in Italy was first published in 1941.
The text has been considerably revised for this edition,
and the foreword and dedication omitted.

© in this revised edition, Peter Quennell 1974

BRITISH LIBRARY CATALOGUING IN PUBLICATION DATA
Quennell, Peter, 1905-
Byron, the years of fame; Byron in Italy.
1. Poetry in English. Byron, George
Gordon Byron, Baron, 1788-1824. Biographies
I. Title II. Quennell, Peter, 1905. Byron in Italy
821'.7

ISBN 0-00-215080-8

Made and printed in Great Britain by
Hartnolls Ltd, Bodmin, Cornwall

Oh! there is an organ playing in the street—a waltz too! I must leave off to listen. They are playing a waltz, which I have heard ten thousand times at the balls in London between 1812 and 1815. Music is a strange thing.

—1821

Contents

Contents

Chapter 6

Chapter 7

Chapter 8

Chapter 9

Chapter 10

Chapter 11

Contents

BYRON IN ITALY

Chapter 12

Byron at Six Mile Bottom—Byron and Scott—duns and dissipation—
Byron's despair—the birth of Ada—the Separation Drama—three personalities—social downfall—Claire Clairmont—Byron leaves England

Chapter 13

Polidori—Byron in the Low Countries—The Lake of Geneva—Friendship with Shelley—Ghost Stories and Sight-seeing—Claire Clairmont—
The Bernese Alps—On the Road to Italy

Chapter 14

Milan and Henri Beyle—Polidori Again—The Ambrosian Library—
Venice—The *besoin d'aimer*—Armenian Studies—Strange Contentment
—Birth of Allegra—Carnival—In Rome—The Fornarina—Dissipation—
Childe Harold Concluded

Chapter 15

England—Lady Byron and Augusta Leigh—The Palazzo Mocenigo—
Bohemianism—Margarita Cogni—Death of Lady Melbourne—Shelley in
Venice—"Spooney and Young Spooney"—A Dandy in Decline

Chapter 16

Poetical Plans and Prejudices—*Don Juan*—Illness—Expulsion of the Fornarina—A Mock Suicide—The Problem of the Future—Angelina—The
Cavaliere Servente

Chapter 17

Teresa Guiccioli—Summons to Ravenna—Teresa and Her Husband—
England or the New World—Separation and Reunion—News from
London—The Palazzo Guiccioli

Contents

Chapter 18

Chapter 19

Chapter 20

The Years of Fame

Author's Note

Here, as in the original edition of this book, I wish to express my gratitude to Sir John Murray and the late Sir Harold Nicolson—to Sir John for allowing me to examine the wonderful collection of Byroniana at 50 Albemarle Street; to Sir Harold, for placing at my disposal his copy of Thomas Moore's *Life*, annotated by John Cam Hobhouse. Since my book was first published in 1935, there have been many important additions to the great body of Byronic literature. Dr. Leslie A. Marchand, for instance, has produced an immensely informative three-volume work, *Byron: A Biography* (1957); Mrs. Langley Moore, her illuminating study of Byron's posthumous influence upon his circle, *The Late Lord Byron* (1961); and Mr. Malcolm Elwin, his valuable portrait of Lady Byron, *Lord Byron's Wife* (1962). Both Mrs. Langley Moore and Mr. Elwin had an opportunity of consulting the famous dragon's hoard of Lovelace Papers, which have now passed from the keeping of Lady Wentworth (who for many years discouraged researchers) to that of her son Lord Lytton. Thanks to his more liberal attitude, the whole collection will one day be published.

P. Q.

Chapter 1

AFTER A LAZY SUMMER ODYSSEY of several weeks, the frigate *Volage* lay becalmed outside Ushant harbour. On board was a young nobleman returning from the Near East, where he had spent the better part of two years, accompanied by a pair of middle-aged foreign servants and surrounded by a great deal of baggage, which included marbles, a silver funerary urn, four ancient Athenian skulls, some live tortoises and a phial of Attic hemlock. It was mid-July 1811 and he was writing home. Writing, indeed, had been one of his chief occupations since his ship left the coasts of the Mediterranean—letters to his mother, whom he addressed alternately, no doubt according to his mood, as "Dear Mother" and, briefly and firmly, "Dear Madam," and to friends of his own sex and his own age; but through every letter that he scribbled on the return journey ran a note of somewhat hysterical apprehension.

His immediate prospects, he considered, were "not very pleasant." Embarrassed, he wrote, "in my private affairs, indifferent to public, solitary, without the wish to be social, with a body a little enfeebled by a succession of fevers, but a spirit, I trust, yet unbroken, I am returning *home* without a hope, and almost without a desire. The first thing I shall have to encounter will be a lawyer, the next a creditor, then colliers, farmers, surveyors, and all the agreeable attachments to estates out of repair and contested coal-pits. In short, I am sick and sorry. . . ." He hated bustle, he had remarked elsewhere, as he hated a bishop; and it was not to be expected that a poet of twenty-three, a voluptuary who, as he was fond of observing, had drained life to the very dregs, would look forward with elation to the management of two large, impoverished and much-involved domains—Newstead, which enclosed his ancestral seat, and Rochdale, of which the coal-mines produced, at the moment, neither "coals nor comfort." Yet his mood seemed in excess of his real grievances; it was as if England itself, and all that his return to England symbolised, had risen up before him like the phantom of some destiny from which it was no longer within his power to escape. Thoughts of his destiny were already haunting him. Lord Byron presented the strange spectacle of a young man who, though gauche, inexperienced and immature, had been visited by presentiments—not perhaps of future greatness so much as of a destiny larger and more invidious than falls to the lot of ordinary mortals. Outwardly, he might be naïve and in-experienced; his intuitive grasp of experience was already firm.

For two years, however, he had lived by impulse. Of his foreign peregrinations, the second call at Athens, after Hobhouse—the devoted but censorious, even slightly patronising, John Cam Hob-house—had parted "sentimentally" from "this singular young person" on a little stone terrace that overlooked the harbour of Zea, leaving behind him part of a small nosegay of wild flowers, had been one of the most pleasant and most carefree. "Fooleries with the females of Athens" had beguiled his leisure; from Teresa Macri—the Maid of Athens—either on that occasion or during his previous sojourn, he had received a dark-red, beautifully braided tress; and this trophy, among many other trophies of the same kind, he was bringing back, to join the collection that enshrined a tress "about three feet in length" given him by a Spanish beauty, which he had sent home much earlier to Mrs. Byron.

Yes, in Athens there was no question of Byronic melancholy. Lodged in a Franciscan convent near the Acropolis, he had joked and romped with the Father Abbot and the youths whom the Abbot was instructing—"six 'Ragazzi,' all my most particular allies"—charming adolescents whose spontaneity recalled the little court, composed of good-looking children, that had surrounded him while he was still a boy at Harrow. "In short," he had declared, "what with the *women* and the *boys*"—the women being certain Albanian laundresses who teased his English valet, Fletcher—"we are very disorderly. But I am vastly happy and childish. . . ." An encounter with pirates had supplied romance. Between the Greece that we explore to-day, where on the loneliest mountain path a traveller may be greeted in the accents of a Chicago bootblack, and the Levant that Byron knew, stretches the great gulf that separates a "backward" and feudal from an industrial and "progressive" epoch. Turkish soldiery lounged on the Propylaea; Velly Pasha lorded it in the Peloponnesus; and Velly Pasha had told the yonug Englishman that he thought him an "eumorpho paidi"—a pretty stripling—and had honoured him with "squeezes and speeches," which Byron reported afterwards, rather slyly, for his friend Hobhouse's benefit. Byron had made him a present of a sporting gun. Greece was the land of friendship, of adventure; all his life it was to remain associated in Byron's mind with the idea of youth —that precious gift which, even at the age of twenty-three, seemed to be slipping away from him like a prodigal's fortune. Greece implied the absence of responsibilities; indolent and yet ambitious, burdened with a very keen sense of the consideration that was due to a man of title and ancient lineage, acutely apprehensive of the criticism to which life in the great world would expose him, he shrank from the prospect of existence in England. He did not pretend that he looked forward to seeing his mother, to whom his attitude at the best of times was frigidly dutiful.

He was returning, he had told Mrs. Byron, in a letter written at sea, "with much the same feelings which prevailed on my departure, viz. indifference"—an assertion in which, as in so many assertions made by the poet at different stages of his career, a certain obvious unreality is married to a very definite psychological truth. He was less unconcerned than he chose to imagine; and yet a conviction that he had "anticipated life" haunted him with the persistence peculiar to every conviction that it is difficult, or perhaps impossible, to explain. He had spent his "little all" and had "tasted of all sorts of pleasure." He had "seen the World, that is the most ancient of the ancient part," and now might bethink himself, he added, with a touch of exaggeration that may be excused when we remember that he was addressing a devoted but essentially prosaic Cambridge acquaintance, "of the most eligible way of walking out of it; probably I may find in England somebody inclined to save me the trouble."

Meanwhile, he lay immobilised off a French port. Becalmed in the doldrums of immaturity, he composed a last batch of letters to the friends who were awaiting his return in England; then the weather changed and he must confront the misty approach of England's threatening coastline, sunk in its grey-green waters, a country of privileges to which he had a right but in which he did not share, of men and women who had not yet learned to accept him, of encumbered and contested estates—still further encumbered by the after-effects of his own early dissipations—and of the rambling, dilapidated Gothic abbey with which the history of mad, bad, unhappy Byrons—particularly "the Wicked Lord," his grand-uncle—for many generations had been bound up.

Having landed, Byron drove to London, where he took rooms at Reddish's Hotel in St. James's Street. Hobhouse was not there to make him welcome; and among his first visitors was an uninspiring but well-intentioned personage, Robert Charles Dallas, more than thirty years Byron's senior and a very remote family connection, one of those colourless but serviceable busybodies whom Byron sometimes encouraged, perhaps because it was not necessary to meet them on equal terms. He had nursed Byron's satire through the press; and the poet, whose appearance and animated account of his travels quite contradicted the melancholy report already given in his letters, now observed that he considered satire his *forte* and that he had written a fresh satirical squib, a paraphrase of Horace's *Art of Poetry*, "which would be a good finish to *English Bards and Scotch Reviewers*. He seemed to promise himself additional fame from it. . . ." Dallas, obliging as always, promised his help and carried off the new manuscript. Their conversation had been brief and interrupted; but it was arranged that he should return for breakfast.

Eagerly he looked over the paraphrase. "Grievous" was Mr. Dallas's disappointment when, instead of a poem coloured by two years' residence in the most romantic of Near Eastern countries, he found himself face to face with *Hints from Horace*, a poem as unoriginal as its predecessor and considerably less entertaining. This first impression, however, he did not divulge. But had his noble friend nothing else to show him? he demanded a day later over the breakfast table. Surely, he ventured, this could not be all? To which Lord Byron replied that it was true that "he had occasionally written short poems, besides a great many stanzas in Spenser's measure," descriptive of the landscapes he had visited. "They are not worth troubling you with," he added negligently, "but you shall have them with you if you like"; and from a small trunk he produced a sheaf of papers, remarking that they had been read "but by one person, who had found very little to commend and much to condemn." Of *Hints from Horace*, on the other hand, he had great hopes. With the hapless Spenserian stanzas, of which an unknown critic—probably it was Lord Sligo, a peregrinatory Irish nobleman whom Byron had met in Athens—had spoken so severely, Dallas might do what he thought best. Let the satire be printed as soon as possible! Dallas promised to see to it and took his leave.

By this time, no doubt, he was a trifle dispirited. Many critics, among them John Cam Hobhouse, pencilling in later years his rather acid commentary on the margin of Moore's *Life*, have questioned the genuineness of Dallas's story, since Byron was seldom indifferent to the fate of his poems. But, if he was ambitious, he was also sensitive. In an earlier note, Hobhouse puts it on record that, when the *Edinburgh Review* published its savage criticism of *Hours of Idleness*, the poet was "very near destroying himself"; and, as satire was the medium through which he had both avenged his wounded vanity and achieved a foretaste of that wide and worldly renown which, subconsciously, his temperament always demanded, it was natural that he should prefer satire to romantic verse. Dallas, with all his faults, was not Lord Sligo. Hurrying home, he had plunged into the poem, a production, as he immediately discovered, unlike anything that had yet appeared in English literature; for not only was it picturesquely personal—the autobiographical saga of a young poet whom Dallas was perspicacious enough to recognise as a very unusual human being—but it possessed the added virtue of seeming to catch and concentrate an unresolved element in the life of the period, something to which no versifier or novelist had yet been able to give a literary shape. Emerging breathless, he dispatched an excited message: "You have written [he exclaimed] one of the most delightful poems I ever read. If I wrote this in flattery, I should deserve your contempt rather than your friendship. I have been so fascinated with *Childe Harold* that I have not been able to lay it down. I would almost pledge my life on its advancing the reputation of your poetical powers, and on its gaining you great honour and regard, if you will do me the credit and favour of attending to my suggestions. . . ."

Followed a cautious list of minor complaints. Dallas's letter reached Byron as he was leaving London, bound for Harrow, whither he went at the invitation of Henry Drury, a clergyman, son of Dr. Drury, the formidable headmaster of his youth. Dallas had first visited him on July 15th; and by the 23rd, having seen Drury and passed a few days in the company of Hobhouse, he was back again in London, addressing his mother from St. James's Street to announce that he had been detained but that he hoped to visit her at Newstead. . . . "With great respect [he signed himself], yours ever, Byron. P.S.—You will consider Newstead as your house, not mine; and me only as a visitor." This epistle, dictated by memories of an unhappy childhood and by the resolution he had formed that henceforward his obstreperous parent must be kept at arm's length, was the last he ever wrote to Mrs. Byron, and certainly one of the briefest and most unexpansive. During the next week his time was fully occupied. Hanson, the family attorney, was at his elbow, presenting legal papers to be signed; while Dallas, an indefatigable literary nursemaid, busied himself with the future of *Childe Harold*.

He had overcome Byron's reluctance and was in quest of a publisher. Cawthorn, who had published the satire, was not sufficiently well known; Longman, who had refused to publish it, was ruled out; and Miller of Albemarle Street, to whom it was offered, declined the manuscript because it contained an attack on Lord Elgin. John Murray was finally approached; but he had not yet signified his acceptance when a letter from the north sent Byron posting towards Nottingham. He had heard that Mrs. Byron was seriously ill; a day later he learned that she was dead, and that her death had been characteristic of her unhappy and tempestuous passage through life, since she had expired (so it was reported) of a violent fit of rage. brought on by opening an upholsterer's bill, one of the many bills, presumably, incurred during her son's restoration of the tumbledown Abbey, just before he left England on his way to Greece.

He had never loved his mother—that gross-featured, loud-voiced and ill-mannered woman. Her rages had clouded his childhood; by harping on his lameness she had warped his character; her vulgarity—of royal descent, she was provincial to the core—had played havoc with his adolescent nerves; and yet, after all, she was a part of himself. To no part of her personal background was he wholly insensitive. He might resent her violence; yet in his own composition was a kindred strain. It may be that he understood and could forgive her more easily than he would have cared to admit. She was the uncontrolled mother of an uncontrolled son; but there was this difference: that, whereas his mother inherited the spirit of the Gordons—itself a dangerous and disturbing heritage—her son added the spirit of the Byrons, of his father, a handsome, debauched spendthrift, and of a long line of good-looking, active, unprincipled men, with a knack of spending money and marrying heiresses. A short-lived, disastrous, dissolute family! Among his mother's relatives, two members of an older generation had committed suicide; while his grand-uncle, from whom he had inherited Newstead, after killing a neighbour in a duel, fought with swords by the light of a single candle in a locked room, had retired to the Abbey, stripped and despoiled the surrounding parklands, sold five thousand pounds' worth of ancient oaks, illegally disposed of Rochdale and settled down as a vindictive and embittered recluse, his only associates being a man-servant, a village concubine and the household crickets which he had domesticated and trained to leave their hiding-places if he called.

Such was the recent history of Newstead; but between his accession to the title in 1798 and his birth on January 22nd ten years earlier, Byron had lived the life of a shabby and undistinguished little boy, who travelled about England and Scotland in the wake of an eccentric widowed mother. They had quarrelled incessantly as he grew up; just as tumultuously had they disputed while he was at Cambridge; they had parted, when he was preparing to sail for Greece, with a particularly violent scene. Clearly, mutual tolerance was out of the question. "Am I"—he stormed to a friend of his youth—"am I to call this woman mother? . . . Am I to be goaded with insult, loaded with obloquy, and suffer my feelings to be outraged on the most trivial occasions? I owe her respect as a Son, but I renounce her as a Friend." Had she not called him a "lame brat"? Had her behaviour not alienated him from his guardian, the punctilious and snobbish Lord Carlisle? Many a time she had shamed him in front of his school-fellows. "Byron, your mother is a fool," remarked a blunt acquaintance in the class-room at Dulwich. It was a discovery he had already made on his own account. "I know it," he had responded with cold conviction.

Yet now she lay dead, and he had begun to regret her. The night after his arrival at Newstead, Mrs. Byron's waiting-woman, as she passed her room, heard a sound from within and, entering, saw Byron seated at the bedside in the dark. She spoke to him. "Oh, Mrs. By," he burst out, "I had but one friend in the world, and she is gone!" "Renounced as a Friend," Mrs. Byron, through the strange metamorphosis that overtakes those whom we have lost, before the shock of their disappearance has died away, was now his "one friend" in a world of enemies. For the moment, his sense of loss was deep and sincere; but it is perhaps not uncharitable to point out that when Boatswain, his big black-and-white Newfoundland dog, had died some three years earlier, he, too, had been Byron's "only friend"—a singularity that had not prevented his commissioning from a miniature-painter a whole gallery of beloved Harrow favourites when he embarked for Greece the following July.

"He thought little of the absent," Hobhouse recorded. Always on his guard against that admixture of literary humbug which (he could not help suspecting) played so important a rôle in the determination of the "dear fellow's" personal attitude, Hobhouse seems to have overshot the mark. Never was a man more obsessed by his memories. The little girls whom he had loved when he was a child, Mary Duff and Margaret Parker, "one of the most beautiful of evanescent beings": and that other Mary, "the Morning Star of Annesley", Mary Chaworth, whom he had pursued long, passionately but to no purpose: the handsome protégés who had surrounded him while he was at Harrow—every one of them lived in his recollection. They lived there, however, as a part of himself, involved in *his* legend, overcast by the menace of *his* destiny. Was it not strange, he would ask himself, that so many of those whom he had loved best should die early or achieve, like Mary Chaworth, a miserable and frustrated end? Death seemed to follow in his footsteps; and, if he needed a confirmation of this belief, on the heels of the first tragedy came a second and then the echo of a third, the announcement of three deaths crowded into the short period that had elapsed since his return to England.

Mrs. Byron had died on August 1st. At Newstead, Byron received a letter telling him that, on the second of the month, a great friend, Charles Skinner Matthews, had been drowned while bathing near Cambridge. Accounts of his death were particularly horrible: Matthews, like a hooked fish, had been seen to leap breast high from the water, in a mute and desperate attempt to free his arms and thighs from the thick ropes of water-weed that had imprisoned them and were dragging him down. Among Byron's intimates he had occupied a privileged place. Was not Matthews "an intellectual giant"? To no other human being could he look up as once to this gay and delightful companion, whose character presented just that balance of qualities—for, though he was a scholar, he was also a man of the world and, though a philosopher and sceptic, devoted like his friend to masculine sports: he boxed and swam valiantly if not very well—which Byron found attractive and reassuring. Few men had he loved more disinterestedly. In Byron's nature, as in that of so many avowed egotists, a tendency to unselfish admiration was qualified by the extreme difficulty of discovering an object on whom his admiration could alight. But Matthews was a friend after his own heart; more than nine years later he still remembered him—his jokes, which were usually of a sardonic and somewhat serious kind; how they had travelled to Newstead in the same carriage "talking all the way incessantly upon one single topic"; how, at the famous Newstead house-party, he had threatened to throw Hobhouse out of the window, a threat that the rather humourless and consequential Hobhouse much resented; and how, when the party had broken up, Matthews and Hobhouse had agreed to walk back to London, had quarrelled and separated, and had finished the expedition, "occasionally passing and repassing," always without the exchange of a word or nod, as far as Highgate, where Matthews, who had spent his remaining threepence-halfpenny on a pint of ale which he drank in front of a public-house, received the cut direct from Hobhouse for the last time.

Matthews's image belonged to the middle distance—to Byron's second year at Trinity, "a very idle period" of his life, and to the ensuing spell of London libertinism. Their friendship had been close but unsentimental; from a remoter and less unimpassioned past came John Wingfield, whose memory—he had died of fever, at Coimbra in Portugal, on May 14th—joined the other presences haunting Newstead about this time. It was true that he had loved Wingfield better than Matthews; "he was the earliest and the dearest, and one of the few one could never repent of having loved: but in ability [he wrote to Dallas]—ah! you did not know Matthews!" For Wingfield he had felt something akin to passion; for Matthews reverential friendship; for Mrs. Byron the strong yet grudging sympathy that unites us to creatures of our own blood; and through every tie his fate was slipping its shears. When he considered his dereliction, he grew almost frantic. "Some curse," he wailed in a letter to Scrope Davies, another Cambridge friend, written on August 7th, "hangs over me and mine. My mother lies a corpse in this house; one of my best friends is drowned in a ditch. What can I say, or think, or do? I received a letter from him the day before yesterday. My dear Scrope, if you can spare a moment, do come down to me—I want a friend. Matthews's last letter was written on *Friday*; on Saturday he was not. In ability, who was like Matthews? How did we all shrink before him? You do me but justice in saying I would have risked my paltry existence to have preserved him. This very evening did I mean to write, inviting him, as I invite you, my very dear friend, to visit me. . . . Come to me, Scrope, I am almost desolate—left almost alone in the world—I had but you, and H., and M., and let me enjoy the survivors whilst I can."

Thus summoned, Scrope Davies proceeded to Newstead. Having kept vigil beside his mother's body, occupied, as he sat there in the darkness, with odd thoughts of the mysterious interdependence of life and death, until he had begun to doubt (he told Hobhouse) "whether I *was*, or whether she *was not*," Byron had dismissed her to her grave. Himself, he had refused to accompany the coffin. From the steps of the Abbey, he had stood watching the procession recede, then turned to Robert Rushton, the young man-servant, who acted as his sparring-partner, and had bidden him fetch the gloves for their daily bout. He was silent and his blows fell harder than usual. Suddenly he paused, threw down the gloves and, a solitary unapproachable figure, moving with a slight limp which he concealed—or attempted to conceal—by walking with a curious sliding swiftness, had lunged away in the direction of his private rooms. One duty that affected his mother he had still to do. Among the many vexations of his return, not the least painful was an attack published in the March number of a paper entitled *The Scourge*, which had reached him soon after his arrival in London. It was the product of a journalist named Hewson Clarke. Stung by his review of *Hours of Idleness*, a copy of verses, "Lord B——n to his Bear," and a second review that, whether rightly or wrongly, he attributed to Clarke's facile malevolence, Byron had retorted in *English Bards*. Clarke was hit off as a mercenary backbiter:

A would-be satirist, a hired Buffoon,
A monthly scribbler of some low Lampoon . . .

and this retort had so put him on his mettle that he had responded with a long, virulent and ill-informed discursion upon the poet and his entire family:

"It may be reasonably asked [had demanded the satirist] whether to be a denizen of Berwick-upon-Tweed be more disgraceful than to be the illegitimate descendant of a murderer; whether to labour in an honourable profession for the peace and competence of maturer age be less worthy of praise than to waste the property of others in vulgar debauchery; whether to be the offspring of parents whose only crime is their want of title, be not as honourable as to be the son of a profligate father, and a mother whose days and nights are spent in the delirium of drunkenness; and, finally, whether to deserve the kindness of his own college, to obtain its prizes, and to prepare himself for any examination that might entitle him to share the highest honours which the university can bestow, be less indicative of talent and virtue than to be held up to derision and contempt of his fellow-students, as a scribbler of doggerel and a bear-leader; to be hated for malignity of temper and repulsiveness of manners, and shunned by every man who did not want to be considered a profligate without wit, and trifling without elegance."

Byron had sought the advice of the Attorney-General; and

although at his suggestion proceedings were abandoned—he pointed out that the libel had been provoked and that a considerable time had elapsed since its appearance—Clarke's victim for the moment was still bent on revenge. Disturbed by this invocation of his troubled ancestry, his mind hovered with greater readiness around thoughts of the "curse."

On August 12th he composed a will. Scrope Davies had not yet joined him; and, lonely and desperate, the young man sat down to vent his feelings in a document so outrageous, and so characteristic of the affectations that were afterwards to become inseparable from his literary legend, that the lawyers to whom he entrusted it were somewhat bewildered. He was to be buried in the garden-vault at Newstead—the vault that already enclosed Boatswain—"without any ceremony or burial service whatever . . . and it is my will [added the misanthrope] that my faithful dog may not be removed from the said vault." No inscription, save name and age, was to mark his resting-place—such was his "particular desire"; and when Bolton, the solicitor, wrote inquiring whether the "clause relative to the funeral had not better be omitted" and the substance of it embodied "in a letter from his Lordship to the executors," his Lordship replied haughtily that "it must stand." An accompanying letter was more emphatic: "With regard to the few and simple directions for the disposal of my *carcass*, I must have them implicitly fulfilled, as they will, at least, prevent trouble and expense; and (what would be of little consequence to me, but may quiet the conscience of the survivors) the garden is *consecrated* ground." In short, he was living up to his reputation; the word *carcass*, as applied by a young and titled client, addressing a stolid firm of provincial solicitors, and underlined by a capricious dash of the Byronic pen, is at once comic, pathetic and a little absurd. Behind a patrician disregard for the opinion of others lurks the literary disinclination to forgo an attitude.

Otherwise, his testament was unremarkable. The second clause, however—his first and largest personal bequest—stands out among smaller and less important legacies. "To Nicolo Giraud of Athens, subject of France, but born in Greece," he bequeathed "the sum of seven thousand pounds sterling, to be paid from the sale of such parts of Rochdale, Newstead or elsewhere, as may enable the said

Nicolo Giraud . . . to receive the above sum on his attaining the age of twenty-one years." Hobhouse and Davies were named executors; and Hobhouse, who, during a year passed in Byron's company far from the restraining influence of English life, had acquired a certain knowledge of his friend's temperament, might have been able to supply an explanatory footnote. There were aspects of Byron's conduct towards his social inferiors that, away from England, he had found a trifle disconcerting.

Take, for instance, his patronage of Nicolo Giraud. Hobhouse himself had not been at Harrow and, except by hearsay, knew nothing of a period that had been perhaps the least unquiet— emotionally the least unsatisfying—of his friend's entire life. There Byron had obtained the stimulus he needed; starved of admiration and affection at home, he had discovered both in the companionship of good-looking younger children—Clare, Wingfield and Dorset— whom he spoiled and made much of, and who disputed his interest with the jealousy of exacting feminine favourites. "My school friendships," he recorded, in the journal of *Detached Thoughts*, kept at Ravenna in 1821, "were with *me passions* (for I was always violent). . . . That with Lord Clare began one of the earliest and lasted longest. . . . I never hear the word '*Clare*' without a beating of the heart even *now*. . . ." Wingfield and Dorset died young; Lord Clare, who survived, he encountered many years later "on the road between Imola and Bologna. . . . This meeting annihilated for a moment all the years between the present time and the days of *Harrow*. It was a new and inexplicable feeling, like rising from the grave, to me. Clare, too, was much agitated—*more* in appearance than even myself; for I could feel his heart beat to his fingers' ends, unless, indeed, it was the pulse of my own which made me think so. . . . We were but five minutes together, and in the public road; but I hardly recollect an hour of my existence which could be weighed against them."

Clare—a position temporarily usurped by Wingfield on the occasion of his death—had been Byron's "earliest and dearest friend," whom he had loved "better than any *male* thing in the world"; and it is not surprising that, transferred from Harrow to Cambridge, from the microcosm of juvenile society to a sphere overshadowed by adult standards, Byron should have felt "so completely alone" in this new existence that it "half broke" his spirits—that it should have been "one of the deadliest and heaviest feelings" of his life that he was "no longer a boy." Had he not moped and pined through his first terms?—until, a sentimental habit reasserting itself, Edleston, the humbly born but talented chorister, had been promoted to stop the gap in his affections. In their friendship, it is true, there was an element of patronage; Byron had received from his protégé a cornelian heart and had contemplated settling down with him and forming a household that would put the "Ladies of Llangollen"[1] to the blush, and Pylades and Orestes "out of countenance." But other interests and other passions had come between them. Poor Edleston had relapsed into an obscurity from which he wrote, now and then, grateful, imploring, obsequiously phrased letters, to solicit his former patron's help and advice, and was finally carried off by consumption in his twenty-first year. He, too, had died in 1811. Byron's *almost constant* associate since October 1805," when "his *voice* first attracted my attention, his *countenance* fixed it, and his *manners* attached me to him for ever," he left Cambridge during the July of 1807, bound for "a *mercantile* house," leaving his friend (as Byron expressed it to Elizabeth Pigot) "with a bottle of claret in my *head* and *tears* in my *eyes*" and his mind in "a chaos of hope and sorrow." Byron's spirits, however, were naturally elastic; London and its dissipations—urban gossip of "routs, riots, balls and boxing-matches, cards and crim. cons., parliamentary discussion, political details, masquerades, mechanics, Argyle Street Institution and aquatic races, love and lotteries, Brookes's and Buonaparte, opera-singers and oratorios, wine, women, waxwork and weathercocks"—and, on his return to Cambridge, the companionship of Scrope Davies, Matthews and John Cam Hobhouse—"who, after hating me for two years, because I wore a *white hat*, and a *grey* coat, and rode a *grey* horse . . . took me into his good graces because I had written some poetry" —did something to efface the memory of a fair-haired chorister. His keepsake, bestowed casually on Elizabeth Pigot, was tardily reclaimed in the tragic autumn of 1811.

---

[1] These two "inseparable inimitables," Lady Eleanor Butler and Miss Sarah Ponsonby, since 1779 or thereabouts had been settled together at Plasnewdd, where they were visited by fashionable tourists as one of the curiosities of the countryside.

Nicolo Giraud was to share the fate of Edleston; his name is not mentioned in subsequent wills; but at this period when, gloomy and unbalanced, Byron's fancy was much occupied with friendship and death, it bulked large in the poet's imagination. The youth had protested eternal fidelity; he had declared that he would follow Byron, whom he considered "his 'Padrone' and his 'amico,' and the Lord knows what besides," across the globe, adding that "it was proper for us not only to live, but 'morire insieme.' " His attachment had amused and gratified Byron; but there is some evidence that Hobhouse, a budding man of the world, conventional alike in his pleasures and in his sense of propriety, was less affected by Nicolo's Levantine charm. Such, at least, is the inference to be drawn from his jottings. Moore had suggested, in his *Life*, that when they parted at the island of Zea, Byron was tired of his friend's company; and Hobhouse retorted with a certain sharpness that Tom had "not the remotest guess at the real reason, which induced Lord Byron to prefer having no Englishman immediately and constantly near him." That Byron, otherwise so conscious of his inherited rank, should adopt towards various obscure but intelligent and good-looking youths—towards Nicolo, for example, brother-in-law of Lusieri, the journeyman artist employed by Lord Elgin—a tone of sentimental and expansive patronage may well have puzzled and annoyed his fellow-traveller. True, Byron had engaged Nicolo to teach him Italian; but the ordinary language-master is less munificently rewarded.

Hobhouse, who would certainly have disapproved, was not in England. While Byron, alone at Newstead, was sitting down to issue instructions for the disposal of his body and estate, John Cam, having joined a militia regiment with the rank of captain, was already on his way to Enniscorthy, where he remained till the middle of February 1812. Only Davies was left of Byron's intimates— Davies, whose "dashing vivacity" and hard-headed, devil-may-care cynicism made an agreeable contrast to the strain of diffidence, of morbid, almost feminine, sensibility, that ran through and pervaded his own nature. He admired and envied such masculine recklessness. What in himself was often bravado, in Scrope Davies was a genuine and unself-conscious appreciation of the good things that the flesh and the devil could provide. He spoke with respect of Scrope's prowess at the gambling tables. There had been an occasion, some time before he came of age, when his friends, who had in vain begged Scrope Davies to return home, left him in the early hours at a gaming house, very drunk and losing heavily, and discovered him next day, fast asleep, "not particularly encumbered with bed-cloathes, without a night-cap," a chamber-pot *"brim-full* of— *Banknotes!* All won, God knows how," but "good legitimate notes . . . to the amount of some thousand pounds," standing on the carpet at his side. Thanks to Captain Gronow, who knew Davies as the friend of Brummell and a famous habitué of Crockford's, we can glean his opinion of Byron's character; for Davies invariably told him (records Gronow) "that he considered Lord Byron very agreeable and clever, but vain, overbearing, conceited, suspicious, and jealous." By the twenty-first of August he had come and gone —"a pleasant person, a 'facetious companion' . . . he laughs with the living, though he don't weep with the dead"—and Byron slipped back into the unhappy, unstable and generally unaccountable frame of mind that had been interrupted by his refreshing worldly appearance.

Bursts of "hysterical merriment" enlivened his solitude. He had "tried reading, and boxing, and swimming, and writing, and rising early, and sitting late, and water, and wine, with a number of ineffectual remedies"; and here he was, "wretched, but not 'melancholy or gentlemanlike,' " the weathercock of moods that alternated between extreme levity—the flippant cheerfulness with which he was apt to relieve his feelings—and moments of dark introspective gloom. "At three-and-twenty I am left alone, and what more [he asked Dallas] can we be at seventy? It is true I am young enough to begin again, but with whom can I retrace the laughing part of life? It is odd how few of my friends have died a quiet death . . ." *Childe Harold*, his hapless offspring, must wait its turn. In the meantime he had reopened a desultory corres-pondence with his half-sister, Augusta Leigh, at her house at Six Mile Bottom, near Newmarket; and only three days had passed since his letter to Dallas when he was addressing Augusta in a very different and, if less likeable, far more characteristic strain, observing that he must marry—to recoup his fortunes by marrying an heiress, *bien entendu*—or, should he be unable to "persuade some wealthy dowdy to ennoble the dirty puddle of her mercantile blood" by uniting it to the azure stream of the Byrons', decide to "leave England and all its clouds." He was already heartily sick of the one and the other and merely tarried till his affairs had had time to mend.

Moments of genuine gravity were not less common. Francis Hodgson, who, with Dallas, was acting as literary nursemaid to *Childe Harold*, had written to protest against the scepticism expressed in the opening lines of the Second Canto; and their author, never averse from religious argument, replied at some length, reasserting his reasoned lack of orthodoxy. Concern for his salvation always touched him; Dallas, too, was much concerned about his soul, and Byron responded that he was "very sensible" of Mr. Dallas's good wishes, of which he admitted that he stood in need. "My whole life (he confessed) has been at variance with propriety, not to say decency; my circumstances are involved; my friends are dead or estranged. . . ." His present existence was dull and blameless; and in perfect accord with the tenor of his days—one of "uniform indolence, and idle insipidity"—was the boring school-friend, John Claridge, who stayed with him and, according to Byron's own account, considerably outstayed his tepid welcome, during the closing weeks of that dreary summer. Life was "as still as the Lake before the Abbey," its leaden surface sometimes ruffled by the north wind, just as fits of passion ruffled the apathy of its owner's spirits. Fletcher or his Greek servants would break the crockery, and the cynic-philosopher suddenly forgot himself in an access of rage.

All around him was a deserted house and its resonant emptiness. "Boxing in a Turkish pelisse" to keep his weight down, chewing tobacco and gum-mastic because it helped him to allay the pangs of hunger, without horses—they had been sold on his departure from England—without sporting guns—he had distributed them during his travels to "Ali Pacha and other Turks"—he remembered "joyous unprofitable evenings" spent in this same house with friends now dead and scattered. Newstead at the best was a cheerless place; for there is something in the Nottinghamshire hill country, its long, gradually ascending gusty slopes, the wide upland prospects, which unfold and seem to enlarge themselves at every turn of the road—rolling hillsides, small coppices and heaths patched raggedly with yellow broom—that exerts a curious effect on the imagination. Space and light cannot dissipate a feeling of sadness. Towards Southwell, the red-brick market town where Byron and his mother, at a period when they were too hard pressed to occupy Newstead and it had been let to Lord Grey de Ruthyn, passed several years at a modest house near the village green, the country grows richer, softer and warmer. Towards Annesley and Hucknall Torkard, it is bleak and exposed; Annesley Hall, from which Mary Chaworth—pathetic Morning Star—had shed her delightful deceptive beams, until that never-forgotten occasion when her suitor had heard her describe him to her maid as the "lame boy," stands back on the crest of a naked eminence, surveying hill-pastures of singular poverty and desolation. Newstead itself is out of view. The Hall, between its terraces, stands high and lonely; while the Abbey crouches in the shelter of its hollow park. Perhaps it is the shivering expanse of lake and stew-pond that lends the Abbey its peculiar air of chilly quietude.

In Byron's day, a great portion of it was uninhabited. The repairs undertaken in 1809 had done little more than check the process of ruin and spoliation initiated by the Wicked Lord, and continued, after their mysterious quarrel, by his successor's tenant; and when Byron invited his Cambridge friends to Newstead, there to revel with him in monastic robes hired from a neighbouring theatrical warehouse and to pass round the celebrated skull-goblet, Matthews reported that every room of the Abbey, "save those which the present Lord has lately fitted up," showed signs of neglect and decay, and that "the old kitchen, with a long range of apartments, is reduced to a heap of rubbish." This air—as of a building only half reclaimed by the cheerful echo of human voices and footsteps—even the enthusiastic but tactless restorations of Colonel Wildman, who lined the mediæval hall with neo-Gothic panelling, executed in varnished Victorian woodwork, and hacked out a sumptuous staircase from the floor below, were unable, years later, quite to exorcise. In 1811 it was a ruin built on to a ruin. Wedded to the main façade of the Tudor mansion, the west front of the original Abbey Church, a screen of pinnacled and fretted masonry —with double-arched door and huge west window, its intricate ribbing broken and fallen—was all that remained of the chancel and the nave. Boatswain's tomb marked the site of the high altar. Before the house, an hexagonal fountain—removed from the cloisters, but reinstated there by Colonel Wildman—stood in the centre of an open courtyard; a flight of steps—Byron's position as he watched his mother's funeral leave Newstead—led up to a battlemented porch which entered the house on the first floor, the ground or basement floor being occupied by vaulted store-rooms, and gave access to the much dilapidated Hall. It was in this room that his friends had practised marksmanship, and Byron and Robert Rushton boxed or fenced.

Beyond the Hall lay a small chamber, called the Prior's Dining Room; it was Byron's dining-room, we are told, for ordinary occasions, and one of the least uncomfortable quarters of an otherwise draughty and uncomfortable house, with its panelled walls and gilded and painted chimneypiece which contained the arms of Sir John Byron—little Sir John "with the great beard"—among emblematic and decorative figures in high relief. Also opening out of the Hall was the panelled West Corridor, overlooking the cloister garden round which the house had been built and leading to that large but exceedingly formal apartment, the Great Drawing Room. From the gallery, a tortuous stone staircase, which must often have tried his lame foot, mounted to Byron's private lodgings. Once he had crossed the threshold he was undisturbed; there was the anteroom in which he dressed, and there his bedroom, commanding the entrance court and a view of the distant mere, a round table in the window alcove, at which he wrote his verses and letters, flanked by four ancient Athenian skulls, and, dominating the room, an impressive bed.

Over the chimneypiece hung a splendid baroque looking-glass. But if the glass suggests the intense and unremitting care of his own physical beauty that caused Byron so many anxious and distracted moments, it is towards the bed that the visitor's eyes return. For its length—barely six feet—seems out of all proportion to the height of its posts and domed canopy. From a double-tiered cornice of gilded bamboo are draped overcurtains of some dark olive-green stuff, looped up with black and red silk cords, while beneath them are curtains of a greenish Oriental chintz, its pattern full of pagodas and palm trees, all in a taste that would have suited the Brighton Pavilion. The crowning ornament is provided by four top-heavy gilded coronets, placed on the four corners of the silken tester.

No doubt the bed had been ordered by Byron himself. At a later period, it was just such a bed that shocked the susceptibilities of Lady Blessington when she visited him at his house near Genoa and noted with refined dismay the odd, foreign, unfashionable and outlandish appearance that he then presented. So "un-English" a parade of his title she did not expect; the boy whom his school-friends had nicknamed the "Old English Baron"—he was fond of maintaining the superiority of old English baronies, as opposed to the mushroom crop of dukedoms and earldoms—had grown up into a young man who wore his nobility with a romantic flourish. He enjoyed the consciousness that he had a privileged place in the universe. Newstead was his; and his, too, were its inmates, Robert Rushton, Joe Murray, the devoted old man-servant, and the cottage girls and housemaids from whose number (critics of Byron's biography have concluded after long and serious debate) was recruited that alluring "Paphian" band which "sang and smiled" at the time of the Newstead house-warming. His attitude towards his servants was patriarchal; and, although he could be stern enough when it came to reprimanding the bastard-getting operations of rustic Lotharios, his household usually included some pretty and spoiled young woman whose presumption often set it by the ears. "I am plucking up my spirits," he wrote at the end of September, "and have begun to gather my little sensual comforts together. Lucy is extracted from Warwickshire; some very bad faces have been warned off the premises, and more promising substituted in their stead. . . . My former flock were all scattered; some married, not before it was needful. As I am a great disciplinarian, I have just issued an edict for the abolition of caps; no hair to be cut on any pretext; stays permitted, but not too low before; full uniform always in the evening; Lucinda to be commander. . . ."

Of the various "makers and unmakers of beds" to whom their master at one period or another had tossed the handkerchief, a certain Susan had gained the most recent ascendancy. Meanwhile the tortoises were laying eggs, and he had provided a broody hen to hatch them out. Among less important domestic concerns, the disputed property at Rochdale claimed him for a brief visit; whence he retraced his steps to Newstead, arriving there on the 9th, only to find a letter from Ann Edleston that announced his Cambridge favourite's death.[1] Once more he unburdened his heart to Dallas. "I have been again shocked with a *death*, and have lost one very dear to me in happier times; but 'I have almost forgot the taste of grief,' and 'supped full of horrors' till I have become callous, nor have I a tear left for an event which, five years ago, would have bowed down my head to the earth. It seems as though I were to experience in my youth the greatest misery of age. My friends fall around me, and I shall be left a lonely tree before I am withered." No wonder that he complained of feeling nervous—"really, wretchedly, ridiculously, fine-ladically *nervous*"; but under the impulse of new grief his mind turned to a sudden melodramatic resolution, and in a copy of highly coloured verses, dashed off on the same day as that plaintive and despairing epistle, he emitted a significant and portentous hint:

> *I've seen my bride another's bride,—*
> *Have seen her seated by his side,—*
> *Have seen the infant which she bore*
> *Wear the sweet smile the mother wore,*
> *When she and I in youth have smiled*
> *As fond and faultless as her child. . . .*
> *But let this pass—I'll whine no more,*
> *Nor seek again an eastern shore;*
> *The world befits a busy brain,—*
> *I'll hie me to its haunts again.*
> *But if, in some succeeding year,*
> *When Britain's "May is in the sere,"*
> *Thou hear'st of one, whose deepening crimes*
> *Suit with the sablest of the times,*
> *Of one, whom Love nor Pity sways,*
> *Nor hope of fame, nor good men's praise . . .*

---

[1] Ann Edleston's letter, announcing her brother's death "on the 16th May last," is dated the 26th of September; but, judging by Byron's letter to Dallas on October 11th, it did not reach him till after his return from Lancashire.

Byron

One rank'd in some recording page
With the worst anarchs of the age,
Him wilt thou know—*and*, knowing, *pause,*
Nor with the effect *forget the cause.*

On the wings of this alarming resolution, he left Newstead, bound for London and his public duties.

Chapter 2

BETWEEN Newstead and London, he halted at Cambridge. There
he saw Hodgson; Davies, too, was in residence at King's; and,
after dining with Mr. Caldwell of Jesus, "Scrope finished himself,
as usual," and Byron helped to put him to bed "in a state of
outrageous intoxication. I think I never saw him so bad before."
Wine, he recorded sadly, had lost its power over him. This was on
the 22nd of October; on the 28th he travelled up to London, where
he took rooms at No. 8 St. James's Street. To that address Dallas
was promptly summoned. During August and September they
had been in constant correspondence on the subject of *Childe Harold*.
Murray, who had accepted the manuscript for publication towards
the end of August,[1] first ventured to hope that certain "political
and metaphysical" passages might be toned down; then, much
against the poet's wishes, showed his work to Gifford of the
Quarterly Review. Gifford spoke highly of *Childe Harold*, which he
considered equal to any poem "of the present age."

Byron's literary prospects were growing more brilliant. Another
flattering diversion that came his way was the series of "demi-hostile,
semi-amicable" epistles, culminating in a definite offer of friendship,
that reached him from one of the victims of his early satire. In
July 1806, Tom Moore, who had not yet discarded his pseudonym
"Thomas Little," having challenged Jeffrey of the *Edinburgh Review*,
had been arrested on the field of combat at Chalk Farm and haled
off to Bow Street, where it was discovered that of the two pistols
only Moore's was loaded with ball, though Horner, his opponent's
second, swore the contrary. The affair produced a journalistic

---

[1]Byron having handed the manuscript to Dallas to do with as he pleased, it was
Dallas who received the £600 that Murray paid for the copyright.

hubbub. Byron, in *English Bards*, had included a reference to "Little's leadless pistol," and when a second edition appeared, giving the author's name, Moore demanded satisfaction. The challenge, however, had miscarried. Hodgson did not forward it to his friend in Greece; by 1811 Moore had assumed the responsibility of a wife and household; and his next letter, to which Byron replied from Cambridge on October 27th, was composed in a more moderate and conciliatory tone. Under Scrope's auspices, the quarrel was patched up. Then, during the first week in November, an invitation arrived from Samuel Rogers to meet Moore at his house in St. James's Place. The appointment was fixed for a Monday evening; and Rogers, naturally somewhat apprehensive about the success of his dinner party, invited Thomas Campbell to make a fourth. It was arranged, to avoid an awkward moment, that Rogers should receive Byron alone in the drawing-room.

Thereupon Moore and Campbell returned and were duly introduced. Confronting them they saw a shy and rather haughty young man, who moved with a slight limp, spoke with a faint provincial burr, and whose attitude was both friendly and reserved and distant. He still wore mourning for Mrs. Byron; and it was the "pure spiritual" pallor of his skin, accentuated by his black coat and glossy reddish-brown curls, that impressed Moore and lingered in his memory; while Rogers, sharp and observant behind the dinner table, surveyed the newcomer with a dispassionate and ironic glance. Talented, maybe, but absurd and affected! It made a very good anecdote (afterwards recorded in *Table Talk*), Lord Byron's behaviour as soon as they sat down to dinner. Rogers inquired politely if he would take soup. No, said Byron; he never took soup. Fish? No, he never took fish. Presently Rogers asked him if he would eat some mutton. No, he never ate mutton. A glass of wine, then? No, he never tasted wine. It was now necessary to inquire, Rogers added, what he *did* eat; and one imagines Rogers putting this question with a somewhat quizzical pucker of his large, bald, dome-shaped, ivory-white forehead, his small blue eyes peering out cold and inquisitive beneath his bushy grey eyebrows. "Nothing but hard biscuits and soda-water," replied the stoic of Newstead, fresh from Cambridge and the convivial company of Scrope Davies, where he had drunk at least enough to discover that wine had no longer any power over him. "Unfortunately," says Rogers, "neither hard biscuits nor soda-water were at hand; and he dined upon potatoes bruised down on his plate and drenched with vinegar. My guests stayed till very late, discussing the merits of Walter Scott and Joanna Baillie. Some days after, meeting Hobhouse, I said to him, 'How long will Lord Byron persevere in his present diet?' He replied, 'Just as long as you continue to notice it.' I did not know then what I now know to be a fact—that Byron, after leaving my house, had gone to a club in St. James's Street and eaten a hearty meat-supper."

So much for his first steps in the great world. It is true that Rogers's was a literary gathering; but both Rogers and Moore were persons of consequence, accustomed to the "best" society of the period, Rogers the banker and Moore the ambitious and versatile son of a Dublin tradesman, who, beginning eleven years earlier with a volume of Odes, translated from Anacreon and dedicated to the Prince Regent, had rhymed and warbled his way into the strongholds of the Whig aristocracy. Against Byron its precincts were still closed. He had lived hitherto, not in the upper world of power, privilege and elegance to which he felt that he was entitled by his birth and rank, but in the society of hard-drinking Cambridge friends or in the dim provincial round of Southwell gaieties. Even the House of Lords was almost unknown to him; he had taken his seat in 1809 before going abroad, but, alienated by the behaviour of his guardian, Lord Carlisle, had lounged through the ceremony with an odd mixture of pride and indifference, making Lord Eldon, the Chancellor, a stiff bow, putting the tips of his fingers into the outstretched hand, and had then thrown himself down for a few minutes on one of the empty benches to the left of the throne usually reserved for the lords in opposition.

Well, Carlisle, in *English Bards*, had received his due. A laudatory couplet in which, after referring to the dearth of poetic talent among the upper classes, he made an exception for the efforts of his guardian:

> *On one alone Apollo deigns to smile*
> *And crowns a new Roscommon in Carlisle*

had been extensively re-written and emended:

Roscommon! Sheffield! with your spirits fled
No future laurels deck a noble head;
No Muse will cheer, with renovating smile,
The paralytic puling of Carlisle.
The puny schoolboy and his early lay
Men pardon, if his follies pass away;
But who forgives the Senior's ceaseless verse,
Whose hairs grow hoary as his rhymes grow worse?

And this retort, though it had salved his wounded pride, had
certainly not increased his chances of acquiring Lord Carlisle—
once an extravagant young man, the friend and adored protégé of
George Selwyn, who had grown up into a straitlaced Court
official—as the sponsor he needed for success in London.

He was solitary; but he told himself that he enjoyed solitude.
November and the early weeks of December were passed, obscurely
and soberly, either "munching vegetables" at his club, The Alfred,
a dull, quiet place, or at his rooms in St. James's Street, where he
read, wrote letters, yawned—"conjugating the cursed verb
s'ennuyer"—or entertained a few friends, Dallas, Wedderburn
Webster—"bold Webster," that scribbler and bore, all the worse
for being newly married—and one or two others of the same sort.
To his old haunts in London he did not return. No longer was he
the adolescent, fascinated by the rattle and dash of the dice-box,
who had alternated the sensations of high living with those of
high play, the rake who had visited Brighton—then enjoying its
first splendour—his mistress riding beside him dressed in boy's
clothes, or frequented those fashionable coffee-houses, Limmer's in
Conduit Street and Stevens's[1] in New Bond Street, at which he
had "taken his gradation in the vices." Sedately, he and Moore
—now firm allies—jogged down to Sydenham to call on Thomas
Campbell; but Moore was a little disconcerted when "the noble
poet," setting out at midday for their mild suburban expedition,
asked his servant whether he had remembered to put his pistols
into the carriage—an inquiry that impressed his companion as
somewhat singular.

He heard Kemble on the stage, and Coleridge in the lecture-
room, where the middle-aged poet was then delivering his second

[1] It is true, however, that he and Moore sometimes dined quietly at this resort.

and most succesful course. "Romeo" Coates, too, was a popular spectacle; the attempts of this eccentric and rather pathetic personage to distinguish himself in tragic parts, wearing a "pink silk vest and cloak, white satin breeches and stockings, Spanish hat, with a rich high plume of ostrich feathers" and numerous ornaments set with real diamonds, made him a favourite butt of Regency audiences, who greeted his agonised posturings with roars of derisive glee. It was on the 14th December that Byron saw Kemble and found him "glorious," noticing, among those who had been crowded into the back seats, Lord Clare and—another but less faithful intimate of his Harrow days—Lord De La Warr, the young nobleman who, asked to spend an hour with Byron the day before he left England, "to be absent for years, perhaps never to return," had excused himself, because forsooth (Byron told Dallas, "bursting with indignation" as he repeated the story) "he was engaged with his mother and some ladies to go shopping!"

The two friends, once so close to him, had been encountered "by accident." . . . On the 19th he set out again for Newstead, accompanied by Hodgson and William Harness, himself "a *Harrow* man" and the third of his friends to whom the titles of "earliest" and "dearest" were applied by their admirer at various periods. Moore had been invited, but could not accept. Both Harness and Hodgson were prospective clergymen. Hodgson, it is true, had just been involved in a slightly discreditable squabble with the Reverend Robert Bland over Bland's mistress, who had been entrusted by her lover to Hodgson's care; but Harness seems to have been a young man of the highest virtue and, in later years, wrote an edifying account of this Christmas visit. It had been cold and misty weather when they started from London; and, when they reached Newstead, snow lay on the ground, and the Abbey, under a dark and dreary sky, struck Harness as "a straggling, gloomy, depressive place." Indoors, however, the rooms that Byron had refurnished, with their new crimson hangings and large fires, were so cheerful "that one soon lost the melancholy feeling of being domiciled in the wing of an extensive ruin. Many tales [adds Harness primly] are related or fabled of the orgies which, in the poet's early youth, had made clamorous these ancient halls of the Byrons. I can only say that nothing in the shape of riot or excess occurred when I was there. . . . Nothing could be more quiet and regular than the course of our days." Byron had been reading Sir William Drummond's "profane" book on the Bible before he left London; religious argument was a pastime that he never outgrew; and his housemates, Hodgson "often speaking with tears in his eyes," did their best to cure him of an error that "appeared to be the only obstacle to his hearty acceptance of the Gospel"— a tendency, strengthened by his early Scottish education, "to identify the principles of Christianity with the extreme dogmas of Calvinism."

Byron, who a few weeks earlier had been called upon to arbitrate between Hodgson and Robert Bland, then at daggers drawn over the deluded affection of Bland's concubine, may have derived a certain sub-acid amusement from "the judicious zeal and affectionate earnestness . . . which Dr. Hodgson evinced in his advocacy of the truth." "You censure *my* life, Harness," he had grumbled, in a letter written on December 15th; "—when I compare myself with these men, my elders and my betters, I really begin to conceive myself a monument of prudence—a walking statue— without feeling or failing; and yet the world in general hath given me a proud pre-eminence over them in profligacy. Yet I like the men. . . . But I own I feel provoked when they dignify all this by the name of *love*—romantic attachments for things marketable for a dollar!"

Sentiment was the bane of mercenary love affairs. Somewhere in the background of his Newstead household, hidden away, no doubt, from the self-righteous gaze of Hodgson and Harness, lurked Susan[1]; but poor Susan's tenancy was already coming to an end. Soon after Byron's departure, she quarrelled with Robert Rushton. His master wrote to scold him; then, on the 28th of January, proof was furnished that the girl, who had written on the 11th to protest that she would never cease thinking of her "Dearest *and only friend*", had "forgotten *me* and *herself* too. Heigho!" scribbled Byron as he filed her note; and orders were dispatched for her prompt dismissal.

[1]Since this book was first published, Susan's identity has been established and a number of letters to Byron—some of them extremely entertaining—have been discovered. See *To Lord Byron*, Paston and Quennell:. Murray, 1939.

Of such intrigues, Byron's guests remained in ignorance. Hodgson was at work on the next number of the *Monthly Review*, a paper that he edited; Harness was reading for his degree; while Byron, correcting the proof sheets of *Childe Harold*, which had been "coming costively into the world" since the early days of November, observed with satisfaction its "vast margin," good paper and clear type. Copious notes had been added to the original poem. *Childe Harold* was now ready to meet the critics. Byron, however, was preoccupied, he told Hobhouse, by "weightier cares than authorship." His situation was "disordered in no small degree." Rochdale still caused him anxiety; he had been "dunning in Scotland" for his mother's money, which had not yet been paid, and, as a temporary measure of alleviation, the Newstead estate was to be doubled in rent.

By January 14th he was back at St. James's Street. On the 15th he went down and resumed his seat in the House of Lords; but, although political ambitions now engrossed a large share of his thoughts, the subject of his maiden speech was yet undecided. During the interval, Susan's duplicity was brought to light; for a few days he could think of nothing else and wrote to Tom Moore and Hodgson "in a state of ludicrous tribulation." Attendance at the Upper House distracted his mind. He had considered delivering a speech on the Catholic question, which was expected to come up next month; but during the first week of February he found a subject much nearer to his heart—the Frame-Breaking Bill, which was to be introduced by Lord Liverpool and would make the offence of frame-breaking punishable by death. The riots against which this savage measure was principally directed had occurred in a part of England that Byron knew very well and where he had been travelling only a few weeks earlier. It was in November that the unemployed stocking-weavers of Nottingham had begun to destroy the new and wider frames that threatened to deprive them of their livelihood. Bands of rioters spread through the surrounding country; on November 14th troops were called out, and, before long, a small army of regular soldiers—nine hundred cavalry and a thousand infantry—was picketed in Nottingham, a display of force strengthened on January 8th by the arrival of two further regiments.

Byron had seen something of industrial England; visits to Nottingham and, northwards, to his own coal-pits in Lancashire had shown him industrialism at work, propagating new industries, building its new, haphazard, insanitary barrack-towns, where it housed the vast influx of cheap unskilled labour. Primarily, the Luddite riots were an expression of the widespread misery caused among hand-labourers, accustomed to the old family system, by the introduction of modern machines; but these troubles had a broader aspect. "It was not the introduction of power-loom weaving [write the Hammonds in their classic volume, *The Town Labourer*] that ruined the hand-loom weavers, and the revolt of the framework knitters in Nottinghamshire is mistakenly conceived, if it is conceived as an uprising against machinery. The real conflict of the time is the struggle of these various classes, some working in factories, some working in their homes, to maintain a standard of life. This struggle was not so much against machinery as against the power behind the machinery, the power of capital. . . . The whole working-class world came under it. The miner, who had never been a domestic worker, and the hand-loom weaver, who remained a domestic worker, were just as sensible of this power as the spinner who went into the factory to watch a machine do the work that had been done in the cottage, or the shearman who tried unavailingly to keep out of the gig-mill."

A new ruling caste had emerged from the community. Many representatives of the old dispensation, including, of course, Byron himself, and such mighty territorial magnates as Lord Londonderry, Lord Durham, Lord Fitzwilliam and the Duke of Portland, had inherited and even worked coal-mines in different parts of England; but, as a general rule, owners leased out their collieries; and, here as elsewhere, capital was represented not by men born to power but by men who had risen to it from the shopkeeping and labouring classes. On the one hand, we have the elegant irresponsibility of aristocrats who, like Lord Melbourne, considered the sufferings of the factory children entirely outside their province—men brought up in Olympian ignorance of the "lower orders"—and, on the other hand, the grinding and inhuman discipline imposed by masters who had themselves known what it was to pinch and slave, "uneducated, of coarse habits, sensual in their enjoyments, partaking of the rude revelry of their dependents, overwhelmed by success, but yet, paradoxical as it may sound, industrious men, and active and far-sighted tradesmen."[1]

To these new employers, it was but natural that, as an aristocrat —and a self-conscious aristocrat into the bargain—the lord of Newstead should feel a decided antipathy. He admitted, nevertheless, that he thought the manufacturers "a much injured body of men, sacrificed to the views of certain individuals who have enriched themselves by those practices which have deprived the frame-workers of employment. . . . The maintenance and well-doing of the industrious poor is an object of greater consequence to the community than the enrichment of a few monopolists. . . . My own motive for opposing the bill is founded on its palpable injustice, and its certain inefficacy. I have seen the state of these miserable men, and it is a disgrace to a civilised country. Their excesses may be condemned, but cannot be a subject of wonder." By disposition and political preference Byron was a liberal; and it angered him that the methods he had observed in use throughout the Turkish Empire should be directed against the inhabitants of an English town, and that the first care of the government should be to suppress evidences of misery rather than attempt to remedy its underlying cause. On the 27th of February he rose to speak. His address had been carefully committed to memory; but, although energetic and effective, sharpened by all the devices of indignant sarcasm, his delivery of it was too theatrical to be very good. He spoke in an histrionic sing-song:

"I have traversed the seat of war in the Peninsula; I have been in some of the most oppressed provinces of Turkey; but never, under the most despotic of infidel governments, did I behold such squalid wretchedness as I have seen since my return, in the very heart of a Christian country. And what are your remedies? After months of inaction and months of action worse than inactivity, at length comes forth the grand specific, the never-failing nostrum of all state physicians from Draco to the present time. After feeling the pulse, and shaking the head over the patient, prescribing the usual course of warm water and bleeding—the warm water of your mawkish police and the lancets of your military—these convulsions

---

[1]Gaskell: *The Manufacturing Population of England*, quoted by Hammond.

must terminate in death, the sure consummation of the prescriptions of all political Sangrados. Setting aside the palpable injustice and the certain inefficacy of the bill, are there not capital punishments sufficient on your statutes? Is there not blood enough upon your penal code, that more must be poured forth to ascend to heaven and testify against you? How will you carry this bill into effect? Can you commit a whole country to their own prisons? . . . Or will you proceed (as you must to bring this measure into effect) by decimation; place the country under martial law; depopulate and lay waste all around you, and restore Sherwood Forest as an acceptable gift to the crown in its former condition of a royal chase and an asylum for outlaws? Are these the remedies for a starving and desperate populace? . . . With all due deference to the noble lords opposite, I think a little investigation, some previous inquiry, would induce even them to change their purpose. That most favourite state measure, so marvellously efficacious in many and recent instances, *temporising*, would not be without its advantage in this. When a proposal is made to emancipate or relieve, you hesitate, you deliberate for years, you temporise and tamper with the minds of men; but a death-bill must be passed off-hand, without a thought of the consequences."

The reception of this speech was extremely flattering. It was referred to in subsequent speeches by Lords Holland and Grenville, and replied to for the Government by Lord Harrowby and the Lord Chancellor himself. Praise, both from members of the opposition and from "divers persons *ministerial*—yea, *ministerial!*" came to his ears. "Marvellous eulogies . . ." He left the chamber, "glowing," with triumph, "much agitated;" and the faithful Dallas ran up to meet him in the passage. Byron thrust out his right hand, but Dallas, encumbered with an umbrella, extended his left. "What!" cried Byron emotionally, "give your friend your left hand upon such an occasion?" Apologising and fumbling, Mr. Dallas disengaged himself from his umbrella, and the two shook hands warmly, while Byron rehearsed for Dallas's benefit "some of the compliments which had been paid to him, and mentioned one or two of the peers who had desired to be introduced to him. He concluded with saying that he had, by his speech, given me the best advertisement for *Childe Harold's Pilgrimage*."

Of the fellow-peers who had praised his maiden speech, Lord Holland, as Recorder of Nottingham, had already approached him, through Samuel Rogers, at a time when it had not yet been written and memorised. Behind Lord Holland loomed his wife, autocratic mistress of Holland House, one of the most important intellectual and social strongholds of the Whig party. Byron had attacked the Hollands and their troop of servile reviewers in *English Bards*; and on March 5th, anxious to make amends, he dispatched Lord Holland an advance copy of his poem, accompanying it with a diffident and conciliatory letter: ". . . Your Lordship, I am sorry to observe to-day, is troubled with the gout; if my book can produce a *laugh* against itself or the author, it will be of some service. If it can set you to *sleep*, the benefit will be yet greater; and as some facetious personage observed half a century ago, that 'poetry is a mere drug,' I offer you mine as a humble assistant to the *eau médicinale*." A second copy, affectionately inscribed, went to Augusta. Meanwhile John Murray, who had announced that he would issue *Childe Harold* at the beginning of the month, had decided to postpone the date of publication; and it was not until the morning of March 10th that Byron opened his eyes to a world that had changed overnight out of all knowledge. Suddenly he found himself famous, the most celebrated young man in the whole of London, the cynosure of admiring and inquisitive glances, the subject of endless excited talk. The months that succeeded his return to England had formed a dim and disappointing prologue. Now the curtain rose on the main drama; a hidden orchestra burst into music; and, as a crowd of supporting actors entered from the wings, the stage was flooded with a powerful light.

The first edition of *Childe Harold*—five hundred quarto copies— had been exhausted in the course of three days; and almost every reader of the poem—certainly every feminine reader—aspired to meet the poet face to face. Wherever he went, his admirers surrounded him. They saw a small man, carefully but rather too elaborately dressed, who stood apart, often frowning with a sharp contraction between the brows, the victim, as they imagined, of some mysterious secret sorrow. But this melancholy was tempered by an air of underlying gentleness. His voice was musical and engaging; and, although his movements were apt to be awkward and constrained, and now and then he seemed both shy and sulky, in some aspects he had an almost feminine distinction His hands, for instance, were unusually small and white; and both of his hands and of the fine reddish-brown ringlets that clustered on his forehead Byron was immoderately proud. We are told that he retired to bed in curl-papers. Davies, at least, claimed to have discovered him in bed thus prepared for his day's exertions and to have roused him with stuttered cries of "S-s-sleeping Beauty"; at which Byron admitted drowsily that it was a foolish habit. He was also proud of the texture of his skin; throughout his life he made unsparing use of purgatives, and the practice may have accounted for his strange "ethereal" pallor, which, combined with his look of melancholy self-absorption, gave him the appearance of a brooding visitant from some other plane.

Good or bad angel? his admirers asked themselves. Byron perplexed as well as dazzled. Even in the cast of his features there was something subtly disturbing; "the forehead clear and open, the brow boldly prominent, the eyes bright and *dissimilar*, the nose finely cut and the nostril *acutely* formed—the mouth well-formed, but wide, and contemptuous even in its smile, falling singularly at the corners, and its vindictive and disdainful expression heightened by the massive firmness of the chin." This description was composed by Sir Thomas Lawrence; it accords with the descriptions of other observers, yet passes over a striking peculiarity, omitted in Phillips's famous portrait but illustrated in Westall's picture and Thorwaldsen's equally famous bust—the fact that Byron had no ear-lobes. The upper part of his face was the more impressive. From a smooth, magnificent forehead, his nose ran down in a straight classical line; but whereas his forehead was open, large and tranquil, surmounted by thickly growing locks, his mouth and the lower half of his physiognomy (as Lawrence and Thorwaldsen alike noticed) suggested a temperament neither accommodating nor at ease. The mouth was apt to seem loose and the chin heavy; rebellious pride and injured sensitiveness might produce a dark forbidding scowl.

Five feet eight inches was his full height. Privately he chose to assume a further half-inch; and, since lameness obliged him to walk upon his toes, his compact and muscular body, developed by

46

exercise—by the boxing, swimming and fencing in which he satisfied his love of masculine sports—appeared a little taller than dimensions warranted. There was always a danger that he might grow fat; during his adolescence he had been described as "a fat, bashful boy," and his mother, in her later years, had grown into a cumbrous, short-winded personage whose only traces of handsomeness were her fine eyes. Her son fought off the hereditary trait; strict dieting, exercise, hot baths, purgatives and many other expedients were invoked to enable him to retain his figure, and this penitential discipline, though often suspended, was persevered in, with an almost monastic severity, over long periods of his adult life. Naturally he had somewhat ascetic leanings. At a first glance, it might have been supposed, by the worldly and critical observers among whom he now found himself, that Lord Byron was merely a very handsome and exceedingly vain young man; but closer examination would have shown that, while he spared no pains to present his beauty to the best advantage and was intensely conscious of the magnetism that it exerted, his self-love was more than counterbalanced by self-disgust. He may have loved, but he certainly hated, his own image; he knew that he was beautiful, but he could not forget that he was also lame.

This obsession he transferred to those who encountered him. Did we need a proof of the intimate and indissoluble bond that exists between soul and body, we could perhaps discover it in the effect produced by any physical shortcomings on the spiritual or intellectual part of the human organism. Whole existences are determined by some bodily accident; very short men derive from their lack of height a stimulus that nothing else could have afforded them, since to look up in the flesh becomes an incentive to look down in the spirit, and the mind puts forth its most valuable efforts in an attempt to console its fretful and despondent coadjutor. The effect of a definite deformity is yet more insidious. That Byron was lame we know too well; but as the poet himself was incapable of discussing his lameness with restraint, lucidity or resignation, and as Byron's attitude inevitably coloured that of his friends, the entire subject is still enveloped in obscurity. It is difficult to gauge the extent of his lameness; its origin and precise character have not yet been diagnosed.

In London it was rumoured that he was club-footed. Melancholy, wicked, endowed with genius, of ancient lineage, as handsome as Apollo—yet marked from birth by a hopeless and humiliating disfigurement: the conclusion was too dramatic to be missed. He was watched in the street or at a party; on tiptoe, gliding along with a gait that almost amounted to a shamble, he would enter a room "running rather than walking" and come to rest by planting his sound foot on the floor. But here again there is an element of mystery; some observers confine his lameness to his left foot; Hobhouse and his mother locate it in the right, and their assertion is confirmed by other evidence. It has been suggested that both feet were slightly deformed; but it is clear that one foot was more seriously crippled than its fellow.

What, then, was the nature of his defect? A foreign doctor, a quack osteopath and that queer ruffian and inveterate legend-monger, Edward John Trelawny, all claimed to have handled the deformed foot; and of these witnesses, Trelawny contradicts himself in two editions of his reminiscences, published at an interval of twenty years, with unexampled shamelessness. Was his first account a piece of revolting fantasy? "Both feet [wrote Trelawny in 1858, after a description of the successful ruse by which he persuaded Fletcher to leave him alone with the dead body] were clubbed and his legs were withered to the knee—the form and features of an Apollo, with the feet and legs of a sylvan satyr." In 1878, preparing for death, Trelawny revised this passage, explaining that when he uncovered Byron's feet he saw that they were normal and perfectly shaped, but that a contraction of the Tendon Achilles, behind the ankle, made it impossible to rest his heels upon the ground. With this last account, neither the doctor nor the quack agrees. Dr. Millingen, who attended Byron at Missolonghi, reported that the lame foot was "deformed and turned inwards" and that his lame leg was "shorter and smaller" than the sound one. On the testimony of Sheldrake, whose article, an obvious essay in professional self-advertisement, was published in *The Lancet* for 1827,[1] too much

[1]"Mr. Sheldrake on distortions of the feet," *The Lancet*, 1827-28, vol. ii, p. 779. The writer wishes to make it clear that he is not to be confused with "Sheldrake the truss-maker," who treated Byron in childhood.

reliance need not be placed. He appends a couple of crude woodcuts —both of the left leg—showing a hideously deformed club-foot, which (he alleges) were made from casts of the member, taken when Byron visited him before leaving England. In the absence of artificial support (writes Sheldrake), "he stood upon the outside of his foot. . . . The leg was much smaller than the other leg. By making the inside of the shoe of a peculiar form . . . and by placing additional substances upon the smallest leg, they made it appear equal in size to the other."

From this, and similar evidence, a modern authority[1] has deduced that Byron's lameness was caused by "congenital club-foot of the Talips Equino-varus type," which affected the right foot only, *equinus* deformity being a condition in which the foot is thrown forward on to the toes, *varus* a condition in which it is bent inwards, and *equino-varus* a combination of the two. But such a diagnosis, though learnedly argued, is difficult to reconcile with the existence of a pair of surgical boots, designed for the right foot, which, according to another critic, show that the limb was "not clubbed, but was long and very slender." Our first authority replies that these boots were intended to cover the foot after it had been reduced to a normal shape by various artificial means; and a biographer must fall back on the reflection that human observers have an invincible aptitude for seeing what they want, or expect, to see, and that we live less in a world of fact and reality than in a shifting world of appearances and dreams, dictated by prejudice and irrational belief.

There remains an extremely interesting hypothesis that Byron suffered from an affection know as "Little's disease,"[2] which is "caused by haemorrhage on to the surface of the infant's brain, the result of some delay in the establishment of respiration at the moment of birth. That part of the cerebral cortex which presides over the voluntary movements of the legs is damaged. A child so injured walks clumsily and with difficulty, though the legs and feet are well formed. . . . The sufferer walks with a curious running gait, with a great appearance of effort, though only slow progress may be achieved. The body rises upon the toes and the knees are

[1]James Kemble, *The Quarterly*, October, 1931.
[2]Otherwise spastic paraplegia.

kept tightly pressed one against the other."[1] Epileptiform attacks, of the kind that Byron experienced at Missolonghi, are a "not uncommon result of the cortical damage in Little's disease." Undoubtedly there is a great deal to be said for the suggestion that Byron's deformity had a nervous and deep-seated, rather than a localised and merely structural, origin; and it must be remembered that he himself always attributed his lameness to some natal or pre-natal misadventure. Hence his life-long animus against Mrs. Byron. "Out, Hunchback!" cries Bertha, in the first line of *The Deformed Transformed*; and "I was born so, mother!" retorts her son. The whole drama, Moore notes, was founded on Byron's recollections of his mother's treatment. At a later period, he told Hobhouse "that he reproved Lady Holland for speaking to Henry Fox[2] about his lameness in an angry tone"; since he remembered the exquisite sufferings of his own childhood. Nor could he forget the clumsy and degrading instruments with which the "experts" had attempted to straighten his foot.

All they had done was to increase his sense of solitude. It is possible that in 1809 he still hoped that his deformity could be alleviated, if not entirely removed; but by 1811 he seems to have accepted it as an inescapable condition of his life—one of the many signs by which his fate had distinguished him from the rest of mankind and sent him forth on a lonely and ominous journey. Loneliness was the background of his existence; and mere celebrity, much as he enjoyed it, could not satisfy the craving for affection and esteem—thwarted in childhood, sharpened by constant reminders of his physical shortcoming—that was to haunt him at every stage of his career. His vanity was omnivorous and insatiable. No advantage, he felt—a feeling peculiar to human beings in Byron's predicament—neither fame nor beauty nor the love of women, could quite outweigh the disadvantage with which he had been born, though these were palliatives he did not cease to value. The admiration he might arouse while he remained

[1]"The Mystery of Lord Byron's Lameness," by H. Charles Cameron, *The Lancet*, March 31st, 1923.

[2]Henry Edward Fox and his mother did not agree. Byron seems to have been very fond of him; and it was this young man, oddly enough, who soon after Byron's death was inveigled into a love affair with the Countess Guiccioli (see his *Journal*, edited by the Earl of Ilchester, 1923).

stationary must vanish, he felt sure, when he began to cross the room.

From this belief came his habit of composing a portrait. As he leant upon one elbow, his small white hand clenched beneath his cheek, meditative, immobile—like Chateaubriand, among the fallen columns and crumbling architraves of the ancient world, or in the anteroom of some brilliant London party—melancholy and sullen detachment pervaded his attitude. To move entailed an humiliating and awkward effort. He developed, therefore, a proclivity for standing still; and, since the young man who stands still must do so for some very good reason—other than the exertion it would cost him to walk or dance—his looks suggested that he remained motionless through force of ennui.

Moods of expansion, however, were reserved for his intimates; with companions of his own sex he was often ebullient and talkative. His closest friends found the discrepancy between the Byron of *Childe Harold* and the Byron whom they had known at Cambridge, Brighton and Newstead, and in London coffee-houses and clubs, highly perplexing and, now and then, exasperating. Moore supposed that he was genuinely melancholy; Hobhouse suspected literary artifice—the dear fellow always relished mystification, and the big stupid public (as distinct from John Cam Hobhouse, that rising politician and man of affairs) was only too ready to swallow the romantic bait. In fact, both attitudes were sincere. Byron was at his happiest with men of the world—cheerful Moore, loyal, dogmatic Hobhouse, sardonic, hard-drinking Scrope Davies—for their self-sufficiency put him at his ease; but there was a *malaise* against which their friendship could not prevail. The trials of celebrity seemed to intensify rather than to lighten it. Instead of releasing him, they drove him back upon himself.

Chapter 3

Social triumphs – the contemporary background – London – the fascination of *Childe Harold* – Byron as showman of the Romantic Movement

BYRON was ill qualified for social success; and the society into which he was precipitated during the giddy spring months of 1812 was in itself ill qualified to understand him. Like our own, it was a period of transition; and its confused prospects and baffled aspirations, with riots at home and wars abroad, combined to produce an atmosphere of deep anxiety and restlessness. Poverty was growing, and wealth was accumulating; squalid misery, such as Byron had observed in the industrial north, where towns had begun to spread over the country, each resembling some enormous murky stain, existed side by side with the rapid development of commerce and with the introduction of new luxuries and standards of living. The untrained labouring populace thickened and multiplied; before dawn the cobblestones of many blackened, narrow streets resounded to the clogs of innumerable children, who would not emerge from factory, mine or sweat-shop until dusk had once again descended, working, some of them underground and in complete darkness, for twelve or fourteen hours. Labourers were still forbidden to join a union; the invention of new machinery had upset the equilibrium and had curtailed the livelihood of the earlier industrial classes; and throughout the year of 1812 "frightful" reports—rumours of discontent and civil disturbance—continued to arrive from Lancashire and Yorkshire. The Frame-Breaking Bill, which had reached the statute book, showed an apprehensive government attempting to regain and reinforce its hold.

The task of administration, moreover, was not eased by the royal family. Hypochondriac, lachrymose, perverse, bad-tempered, disloyal, the Prince Regent, though still supported by his stays, dragged himself through existence, a paunchy, ridiculous figure, the source of embarrassment alike to his friends and to his enemies.[1] His brothers' conduct was scarcely more reassuring. Some years had elapsed since the scandal of the Duke of York and Mary Anne Clarke, a lady who had profited by her relationship with the commander-in-chief to sell commissions; but the Duke of York was a respectable and well-liked personage compared with the Duke of Cumberland, a prince whom all parties and all classes— including his brothers, who detested him—agreed to make the worst-hated man in the realm. Frequent quarrels destroyed the peace of the royal family. "The conduct of these illustrious personages [wrote a politician of the time, referring to a violent quarrel that had broken out between the Dukes of Cumberland and Clarence, over the distressing affair of Mrs. Jordan, the latter's recently discarded mistress] is a most melancholy and alarming feature in the difficulties which every hour increase upon us; and it is not without great forbearance one can impute it to any other ground by an affection of the same nature as that under which the King labours."

All hope of George III's recovery having at length been abandoned, 1811 had seen the virtual succession of the Prince Regent; but it was soon discovered by his former allies of the Whig party that the liberal principles he had exhibited as a young man had been adopted with the sole purpose of annoying his father and that no change of government could be expected. "Prinny" became the target of Liberal critics. "Eminently characteristic of its princely designer," noted one of them, was the superb banquet he had given at Carlton House during the summer of 1811; for "there were still left in the Kingdom many persons, who bitterly compared the Prince's professions of filial devotion on accepting the Regency only a few months back, with this ill-timed display of regal magnificence and prodigal rejoicing." Yet more bitterly, another—Sir Samuel Romilly—contrasted "the great expense of this entertainment" with "the misery of the starving weavers of Lancashire and

[1] See the verses with which William Mackworth Praed anticipated the news of the Regent's death:

A noble nasty course he ran!
Superbly filthy and fastidious.
He was the world's first gentleman
And made the appellation hideous.

Glasgow." "The grand table [we learn] extended the whole length of the conservatory, and across Carlton House to the length of two hundred feet. Along the centre of the table, about six inches above the surface, a canal of pure water continued flowing from a silver fountain, beautifully constructed at the head of the table. Its banks were covered with green moss and aquatic flowers; gold and silver fish swam and disported through the bubbling current, which produced a pleasing murmur where it fell, and formed a cascade at the outlet. At the head of the table, above the fountain, sat his Royal Highness, the Prince Regent, on a plain mahogany chair with a feather back. The most particular friends of the Prince were arranged on each side." Among the plush and scarlet of sixty footmen moved an attendant clad—for no ascertainable reason—in a complete suit of mediæval armour; while behind the Prince's chair stood tables draped in crimson, supporting "a profusion of the most exquisitely wrought silver-gilt plate," and, above this display, "a Royal Crown, and his Majesty's cypher, G.R., splendidly illumined."

Besides liberal statesmen, others voiced their disgust. Shelley, lately sent down from Oxford, and then living a somewhat solitary and precarious life in London lodgings, caught sight of a newspaper account of the Regent's festivity and dashed off a doggerel address. He had the satire printed as a pamphlet; and callers at Carlton House were surprised to notice an untidy, enthusiastic young man who, while their carriages approached the majestic Corinthian portico of the Regent's official residence, tossed a broadsheet through the window. Republicanism as fervid as Shelley's was still exceptional; but there were not a few observers to whom the revolution appeared close at hand.[1] The disorders of 1811 were repeated all over the north of England during the year 1812. Authority took alarm; militia regiments were hurried up to Yorkshire; and a special commission was appointed to try the rioters at Stockport. In London, although the Opposition had lost the support of the Prince Regent, it gained an ally and tool in his wife, Princess Caroline, who had a separate establishment and main-

[1]Some years later, in 1816, a secret committee was appointed to investigmarede ten of the rapid spread of revolutionary feeling among the working classes. It recoemsptdr o the suspension of the Habeas Corpus Act.

tained a rival court at Kensington Palace and Blackheath. Her
wrongs and grievances were loudly canvassed. Altogether, four
royal establishments—Windsor, where the old King languished
in hopeless insanity, relieved from time to time by the strains
of Handel's music, Carlton House, Kensington Palace and
Warwick House, the residence of Princess Charlotte, the
Regent's daughter—gave variety to the pattern of domestic
intrigue. It was notorious that wife and husband were sworn
enemies, and that father and daughter were very often on explosive
terms.

Their differences provided an endless source of gossip; the
indiscretions and vagaries of Princess Caroline were common
knowledge, while "the strange histories of Carlton House [remarked
a domestic chronicler] supply the appetite of the town with daily
anecdotes more or less interesting." Already once liquidated, the
Prince's debts were calculated now to exceed a hundred thousand
pounds. Neurotic and easily moved to tears, as when Brummell
had denounced the cut of his coat, he was inclined to escape from
any difficult or unpleasant situation by retiring to bed—"shamming,"
the Duke of Cumberland called it—there to lie on his stomach and
absorb soporific draughts of laudanum. Such a régime at Carlton
House indicated storms in the political hemisphere. The prospects
of Catholic Emancipation—a measure the Prince had formerly
supported—seemed now almost as distant as in the past, and the
reform group, though powerful and ambitious, was reduced to a
long and difficult guerrilla campaign.

Discontent, then, was characteristic of the period—among the
starving workmen of the grimy industrial north; in London drawing-
rooms and in the great country houses where the leaders of the
Opposition kept up their prosperous round of dinner-parties, balls
and leisurely visits. London itself was extremely animated. As
yet it had changed very little since the closing decades of the eighteenth century; but there was much talk of "improvements in the
metropolis"; and it was said that the Prince was "to have a villa on
Primrose Hill and a fine street leading direct to it from Carlton
House," which would be named after him at the suggestion of his
Prime Minister.[1] The boundaries of urban life were still restricted.

[1]Regent Street, however, was not begun till 1813.

No. 20 Devonshire Place, Marylebone, was the last house northwards; beyond Portland Place were meadows that gave pasture to a thousand cows; while, from Gower Street, one walked down a short lane, through an archery ground, and thence across open fields to Hampstead and Highgate. On the west, London ended at Tyburn Turnpike; Bayswater, among its nursery gardens, was a pleasant country village, and the haymakers whetted their scythes near the Paddington canal. Chiswick and Hammersmith were entirely rustic; farther south, the ranks of houses came to a full stop at Hyde Park Corner. Behind the Abbey, from Tothill Fields, the resort of Westminster schoolboys, ran the Willow Walk, which extended to Halfpenny Hatch at Millbank, bordered by swampy gardens and small cottages. Pimlico was a remote but agreeable hamlet, which contained the public-house and tea-grounds called "Jenny's Whim."

Even the inhabitants of the Strand were not far from the country; and Mrs. Inchbold, who lived there six years earlier, had congratulated herself on "an enchanting view of the Thames, the Surrey Hills" and of three windmills peacefully at work. Yet London contrived to shelter a million inhabitants. Round the Abbey were rookeries, dense conglomerations of dark, ancient buildings where the poor lived and pullulated in a world of their own. Perhaps the most dreadful of all these slums was Clare Market, situated between St. Clement Danes and Temple Bar. In the City, near Billingsgate, streets existed that had survived quite intact from a period before the Great Fire, decrepit reminders of Elizabethan and Caroline London. The tall houses bulged and toppled above the alleyways, still rich with the rusted iron of their swinging signs.

Wealth had flowed steadily northwards and westwards. Lawyers and rich merchants, forsaking their original homes, had now removed themselves to the dignified quietude of Bloomsbury streets and squares. Portland Place, Harley Street and Langham Place were inhabited by Nabobs, plump with the spoils of India, by ship-owners, and by Russian and East- and West-Indian merchants. Grosvenor, Berkeley, Cavendish, Portman, Hanover and Bryanston Squares were the preserves of the aristocracy. Belgrave Square was not to arise in the open ground that separated London proper from the outskirts of rural Chelsea until 1825; and the

Regent's residence, with its crimson and gold saloons and gigantic cast-iron Gothic conservatory, occupied the whole site of Carlton House Terrace. The extent of fashionable London was not large; Bond Street was the chief thoroughfare for shoppers and idlers; but London, then as now, was very far from being a democratic city, and privilege spent a great part of its life in resorts to which poverty and obscurity could not obtain an entrance—in private houses, at Almack's, in the clubs and new hotels.

Of fashionable hotels and coffee-houses there were no less than five. Limmer's and Stevens's have already been mentioned; and Gronow tells us that, should a stranger present himself at Stevens's and ask for dinner, he was "very solemnly assured" by disapproving and wide-eyed waiters that there was not a single table to be had. Limmer's was the dirtiest hotel in London; but its "gloomy and comfortless coffee-room" was frequented by members of the rich squirearchy, who came up from their estates during the sporting season. "It was a midnight Tattersall's, where you heard nothing but the language of the turf, and where men with not very clean hands used to make up their books." Other hotels were Fladong's, Ibbetson's, Grillon's and the Clarendon; and this last was "the only public hotel where you could get a genuine French dinner . . . for which you seldom paid less than three or four pounds." Among clubs, White's, Brooks's, Boodle's and Watier's were the most celebrated. Bankers and merchants—"My tradesmen," a gambler of the period, Lord Allen, was accustomed to call them—had not yet been permitted to set foot there; and from the balcony of White's dandyism reigned supreme. Brummell nodded down at a favoured acquaintance, and praised, or contemptuously dismissed, a passing coat or beaver hat.

Hyde Park was the parade-ground of urban modes. Something of the sober and exacting elegance that Brummell had prescribed in every detail of masculine dress and deportment was to be distinguished in the design of the carriages, the perfection of harness and general turn-out, and in the symmetry and beauty of spirited carriage-horses. A well-appointed four-in-hand was a work of art. Lord Sefton, the wealthy Whig magnate, would appear at five o'clock, accompanied by his two daughters, driving splendid bays; while "Tommy" Onslow, perched in his sable-painted phaeton, drove four black horses—reputed to be the finest blacks in England —with an immense gravity that still emerges from a caricature. "A sort of tacit understanding," Captain Gronow informs us, reserved Hyde Park for "persons of rank and fashion;" and "a hundred years of triumphant aristocracy," heightened by that long isolation from the Continent which was an effect of the Napoleonic wars, had produced, in the men and women lucky enough to be members of one of the great territorial ruling families, a type that may never be repeated. It was less noticeable among the women than among the men; Lady Cowper and Lady Granville in their correspondence retain something of the wit and delicacy of an earlier time; but to examine the letters and portraits of the politicians, dandies and men of pleasure who moved in the same circle is to understand that a profound change was taking place. It was a change that gave the Regency its special character and modelled the strange society that Byron knew.

By comparison, the eighteenth century seems lackadaisical. Lord Chesterfield and Horace Walpole were good Englishmen; but they were also good Europeans, at home in foreign courts, conversant with cosmopolitan manners and literature. Napoleon and his armies had shattered this background. Taking advantage of a lull in hostilities, Englishmen might still travel; but they travelled with less freedom than in the past, and visited Paris rather as critics than as admirers. The harmonious framework of "polite society" had been broken up. Perhaps almost for the first time, Englishmen of the upper classes became distinctively—even self-consciously— insular, until the "milor anglais," his red hair and his raucous voice, thickened by "many a monstrous *goddam*," found their way into the Continental imagination. Literacy, it is true, was to die hard; but although there were noblemen of the nineteenth, as of the eighteenth, century who possessed fine taste and a wide knowledge of classical authors, the titled æsthete and dilettante grew more uncommon. At least in their own eyes and the eyes of their followers, the Regency magnates were essentially practical and forthright men.

One need only glance at a selection of portraits. Here, registered by the sharp needle of Richard Dighton, comes Lord Alvanley, "going to White's," stepping along brisk, stocky and matter-of-fact, his plump bewhiskered jowl half lost in a starched cravat and high-collared coat, yellow-gloved fists swinging masterfully on either side.[1] Here, too, is the crooked profile of Lord Sefton. With spurs on the high heels of his varnished boots, here is the Duke of York, ponderous, majestic and good-natured, his whole inflated presence seeming to exhale an air of guttural geniality; while the tail of the procession is brought up by such minor exquisites as Tom Raikes, "Kangaroo" Cooke—amiable and snub-nosed, with ginger whiskers —by Ball Hughes, "The Golden Ball", and "Poodle" Byng. Each flourished in the second decade of the nineteenth century. Gamblers, lovers of good food, heroes of the green room, devotees of racing, boxing and the Four-in-Hand Club, even to their manner of walking, fists carried well forward and elbows flexed, they have a masculine, self-assured and possessive swagger—solid personages, firmly planted on the pavement of St. James's Street, sanguine and healthy, with not a touch of the "man of feeling."

Like most artists, Byron was incurably imitative. Ever since that fatal occasion, thirteen years ago, when his schoolmaster had called him from his desk and, after giving him "some cake and wine," had told him "that his great-uncle was dead and that he was now a Lord," he had been haunted by thoughts of his patrician rank. The attitude of his informant he had never forgotten; describing the incident to John Cam Hobhouse, "Byron added that the little treat and the respectful manner of the master gave him at once high notions of his new dignity;" and these notions had become stronger and more definite during a boyhood when he had been alternately flattered and abused, reminded that he was the inheritor of an estate and title, and stigmatised as a lame and ungrateful brat. No wonder that his dignity was a prized possession. He preferred to be considered, Lady Blessington noticed in 1823, "more an *homme de société* than a poet;" and there is no doubt that, among other men of fashion, Byron did his utmost to assume a character that was not really his—to play a part for which his sensitiveness scarcely fitted him. By nature he was shy, moody and reserved; a young man who aims at general acceptance must

[1] "Lord Alvanley [Byron told Lady Blessington] is a delightful companion, brilliant, witty and playful; he can be irresistibly comic when he pleases. But what could he not be if he pleased? For he has talents to be anything."

develop a certain equanimity, of which Byron, as it happened, was completely devoid. His spirits plunged or skyrocketed, and clouded or cleared, with a rapidity that it was often hard to follow.

Even a fellow Romantic found him inscrutable. Lady Hester Stanhope, one of the most romantic and "Byronic" personalities of an earlier generation, had taken a very unsympathetic view of the young Englishman whom she had seen dive from the mole of the Piræus as her ship entered the harbour in 1810. ". . . A strange character," she told the faithful Dr. Meryon; "his generosity was for a motive, his avarice for a motive; one time he was mopish, and nobody was to speak to him; another, he was for being jocular with everybody. Then he was a sort of Don Quixote, fighting with the police for a woman of the town; and then he wanted to make himself something great. . . . At Athens I saw nothing in him but a well-bred man, like many others. . . . He had a great deal of vice in his looks—his eyes set close together and a contracted brow. . . . The only good thing about his looks was this part"—she illustrated her words by drawing a finger under the cheek and down the front of her neck—"and the curl on his forehead."

"Oh, Lord!" Lady Hester summed him up, "I am sure he was not a liberal man, whatever else he might be;" and the impression that Byron was in some way crafty and calculating, and that for everything he did he possessed some sinister and illiberal motive, seems to have been shared by other women who had resisted his charm. He was dangerous, they felt, and undependable. At a very early stage of his social career, Lady Granville, a plain and prudent young matron, devotedly attached to a husband who had the reputation of being the best-looking and most captivating man of his day, commented that, although she thought him "agreeable," she had "no wish for any further intimacy. His countenance is fine when it is in repose, but the moment it is in play, suspicious, malignant, and consequently repulsive. His manner is either remarkably gracious and conciliatory, with a tinge of affectation, or irritable and impetuous, and then I am afraid perfectly natural."

The personality that had left so disconcerting an impression on all whom he encountered, when he was celebrated only as the author of an amusing satirical squib and a book of elegant juvenilia, such as any other young nobleman might have produced, seemed even darker, stranger and more imposing when it was reinforced by the legend of *Childe Harold*. With amazement and apprehension, the world at large—particularly the feminine half of it—assumed that Childe Harold and his creator were necessarily the same being. Byron himself might deny the resemblance; but the suspicions of his credulous admirers were not entirely ill-founded; for in manuscript drafts of the poem Childe Harold figures as "Childe Burun" —the last an archaic version of the Byron name—while the personal aspect of the narrative was undisguised. Thus *Childe Harold* had the fascination of an autobiography. In an age not yet sated with autobiographical revelations, the frankness with which the poet referred to his own youthful delinquencies struck a thrill of horror and delight through susceptible breasts. Romantic libertinism was not yet the vogue. Childe Harold was no cheerful voluptuary; he looked back on the memory of his "sins" with a cynical, saddened, embittered eye, but he did not repent of them, regarding them rather with a certain detachment, not wholly devoid of literary self-esteem, since to break social bounds and infringe moral laws was the proper expression of a fiery spirit. The responsibility for his offence belonged to his destiny; and that destiny was something he could not control.

As a mere boy he had been thwarted and disappointed. Among masculine friends, Byron would speak of Mary Chaworth and of her marriage to Jack Musters—

Who soon had left her charms for vulgar bliss,
  And spoil'd her goodly lands to gild his waste

—in a dispassionate, indeed in an almost ribald and irreverent, strain. Yet a conviction persisted that, had his early love been returned, had the estates of Annesley and Newstead been joined by the union of two ancient families—Montagues and Capulets of Nottinghamshire—the furies that dogged the Byrons might have been laid to rest. It was a Chaworth who had been killed by the Wicked Lord. The literary origins of *Childe Harold* must be discussed elsewhere; but the Wicked Lord, that ferocious and eccentric recluse, shunned by his neighbours, hated and feared by the surrounding peasantry, has not yet received his due. His legend and that of his successor have much in common. The stories told of him, Moore observes, "were of a nature . . . to arrest the fancy

of the young poet;" they aroused "a sort of boyish admiration";
and, little by little, Byron came to identify himself with a forebear
of whose misanthropic existence Newstead, its desecrated chapel,
its ruinous cloisters and the naked hills beyond, had constantly
reminded him at a very impressionable period of his own life.
Childe Harold is a tribute to his gift of showmanship. Absurd,
trumpery, affected—and yet, as in everything Byron did, the
affectation is hard to distinguish from sincerity; in affectation, the
writer seems often more sincere than when submitted to conventional standards. On his contemporaries the effect was irresistible.
A love of Gothic and Oriental bric-à-brac was by no means new;
Horace Walpole had announced that he was building himself "a
little Gothick castle" as early as 1750; and in 1812 the author of
Vathek, a gaunt and lonely figure, lost in the echoing immensity of
Fonthill, amid his bronzes, precious stones, gold plate, porcelain,
"fine medals, gems, enamell'd miniatures, drawings old and
modern, curios, prints and manuscripts," was already a man of
fifty-three. The word "Romantic" had long outlived the critical
and slightly derogatory significance that had once attached to it;
René and Werther had taken their appointed place in the imagination of mankind; but, great as was the influence exercised by Goethe
and Chateaubriand, their effect was less instantaneous and far-
reaching than that of *Childe Harold*. Byron's triumph, it may be
argued, was personal rather than poetic. From time to time the
vague aspirations, the restlessness and nostalgia of an entire period
appear to be summed up in the pages of a book; but very seldom is
this crystallisation of feeling associated with a single human
personality—so intimately associated that we cannot discuss one
without proceeding to discuss the other; and such was the miracle
that the author of *Childe Harold* had accomplished.

Henceforward he was the showman of the Romantic movement.
The movement itself had existed for more than half a century, but
its character remained indeterminate; it floated and hovered; and
Byron's function—a function, incidentally, that he neither quite
understood nor found particularly sympathetic—was to display it in
a popular and dramatic guise. Byron was too inveterate and brilliant
an opportunist to refuse any striking or advantageous rôle for which
his destiny had cast him; but it must be remembered that, though

by temperament a Romantic, his literary preferences were those of an earlier period, and that Alexander Pope was his poetic hero. In his work, as in his life, he was a creature of instinct. Few men have gone through existence with less faith in the authority of the human will; and this lack of faith lent his rhetoric its peculiar strength and gravity. Sincere and yet compact of affectations—even in his own eyes he remained mysterious.

Chapter 4

The year of the Waltz – Lady Caroline Lamb – her family – Byron visits Melbourne House – *un homme à bonnes fortunes* – sexual snobbery – Byron as an amorist – the penalties of being loved

THE YEAR of Byron's apotheosis was the year of the Waltz. "Language can hardly exaggerate," says a contemporary, "the folly that prevailed" in 1812—year of calamity, distress, of social and political upheaval, year that saw the destruction of the Napoleonic *Grande Armée*, horribly prolonged across the frozen marches of Russia, and heard the waltz strike up in London ballrooms for the first time. By some hostesses waltzing was not countenanced; as to the propriety of this intoxicating modern measure, a dance that entailed the closest and most provocative physical contact and was said to produce among its devotees a state of exhilaration highly dangerous alike to the virginity of débutantes and to the constancy of sober married women, opinion in the fashionable world was sharply divided. Even at Almack's, that "exclusive temple of the *beau monde*," for which not more than half a dozen of the three hundred officers of the Foot Guards had been able to obtain vouchers of admission, it was still practised only by the most self-confident. Lord Palmerston, "describing an infinite number of circles," the Baron de Neumann, whirling with Princess Esterhazy, were figures of a slightly later period.

Waltzing, nevertheless, had become the rage. "In certain noble mansions," Gronow tells us, the new dance was practised every morning "with unparalleled assiduity;" and nowhere was it more popular than at Melbourne House. By some standards the Melbourne family might be considered *parvenus*; Sir Peniston Lamb, the possessor of great wealth, founded, it was thought, on the plunder of the Earls of Salisbury, to whom his father had played the part of confidential adviser, had received his title as late as 1770; but, thanks to his wife, a charming and accommodating woman, the sister of Sir Ralph Milbanke in the county of York, he had since risen to the forefront of the fashionable London world. Their eldest son, Peniston, had died unmarried; William, his mother's favourite, was an indolent but gifted youth, good-looking, well read; and, when the time came for him to choose a wife, he had fallen in love with Caroline Ponsonby, daughter of Lady Bessborough, niece to Georgiana Duchess of Devonshire, and, like himself, the scion of an important Whiggish clan.

He enjoyed her unaccountable vivacity. Of all the "Devonshire House girls," he noted, Caroline was the one for him, imaginative, capricious, headstrong and emotional, pretty, too, though in a manner that was provocative rather than voluptuous, with her thin, graceful body, her large, dark but somewhat unduly prominent eyes and her dishevelled short-clipped curls, which are described as of a "fawn-flaxen" hue. Her education had been strange and desultory; abroad, under the charge of her mother's maid, at home, among the chaotic splendours of her aunt's great London house, where the little Cavendishes and Ponsonbys lived a life of aristocratic bohemianism, dining off silver plate or running in and out of the enormous kitchens in search of their own food—innocents who knew of no social grade between duke or marquess and the barefooted beggars of the streets—she had grown up with a reputation for cleverness and queerness.

From her mother she had inherited the warmth of her temperament. Lady Bessborough's devotion to Lord Granville Leveson-Gower, afterwards Lord Granville, who married her niece, Harriet Cavendish, had been the joy and sorrow of her existence for almost a quarter of a century; and it was to this ambassadorial Adonis—a man much younger than herself, who made her the confidante of the innumerable liaisons and intrigues imposed on him at various stages of his career—that she had written, and was, indeed, still writing, one of the most delightful, pathetic and perplexing series of letters ever penned. She pursued Granville, and was herself pursued by Sheridan and the Prince of Wales. As he lay dying, Sheridan had declared that he would haunt her when he was a disembodied spirit; his eyes would always be looking up at her through the lid of his coffin. . . . As recently as 1809, the Prince—an "immense, grotesque figure flouncing about half on the couch, half on the ground"—had treated her to a violent and tearful scene, had implored her to become his mistress, "sometimes struggling with me, sometimes sobbing and crying," until his victim was reduced to the verge of collapse.

No less stormy and unconventional was the life of Caroline's aunt, the celebrated Duchess of Devonshire; and numerous were the stories of the strange three-cornered household that she maintained with her husband and her husband's mistress—also her greatest friend—Lady Elizabeth Foster, one of the Herveys, daughter of the "Building Bishop," that sumptuous prelate whose journeys about Europe have left an Hotel Bristol in so many French and Italian towns. The Duchess had a passion for high play; apparently the most fortunate of women, she had been made wretched by gambling debts that she dared not confess to her husband, the perfect type of phlegmatic English *grand seigneur*. In 1806, a year after her niece's marriage to William Lamb—during the same year as her constant admirer, Charles James Fox—the Duchess had died. Her disappearance seemed to prelude a new epoch. Caroline Lamb was to run a course even more passionate and impetuous than that of her mother; but, in her composition, the ballast of good sense, that had been inherited by Lady Bessborough from the eighteenth century, was replaced by a kind of hysterical bravado. Lady Bessborough might have dared everything for the sake of love; Lady Caroline would love and dare—for the sake of daring.

William Lamb was cynical and good-natured. In him, at least, the tradition of good sense and good manners was not yet dead. Disappointed, perhaps; but his disappointment only deepened the air of negligence and dandyism, the habits of carelessness and studious sloth, that had distinguished him ever since he had entered the world. His coats *happened* to fit him to perfection. . . . It was this attitude, no doubt—his faculty of "letting things alone," his refusal to be "bothered"—that allowed him, as Queen Victoria's Prime Minister, a cultured, mild-spoken, middle-aged statesman, to continue to draw his revenues from collieries where children worked from six o'clock in the morning to eight o'clock at night. Caroline had charmed him at Devonshire House; their son, Augustus Frederick, born in 1807, had proved a backward child and presently developed into a harmless but hopeless imbecile; and now, in 1812, when the lessons of cynicism he had taught her at Brocket Hall during their honeymoon began to have a definite effect upon his wife's behaviour, he shrugged his shoulders and met her vagaries with a tolerant smile. His mother and his sister frowned and remonstrated; William Lamb thought that there was little that he could say or do.

Poor Caroline! After all, she was an exceptional being. Marriage had not tempered her volatility; and three months later, she was described by Lady Elisabeth Foster, writing to her son, as entirely unchanged, "the same wild, delicate, odd, delightful person. . . ." Unfortunately, no one was more conscious of her odd and delightful singularity than Lady Caroline herself. She envisaged her existence in appealing diminutive. A commonplace book, kept during the early stages of her married life, includes a list of the nicknames she had been awarded by admiring members of the Devonshire House circle; and though these pet names—Ariel, Young Savage, Squirrel, Her Lavishship and others—afford an indication of the charm that even so negligent and unromantic a dandy as William Lamb had found it hard to resist, we cannot but feel that they were enumerated with a certain self-complacent gusto. Among women she was naturally less popular. "The little Fairy Queen," a wayward Titania, attended by pages whose livery she sometimes borrowed, with whom she quarrelled or played at ball in the spacious upper apartments of Melbourne House, when viewed through the critical eyes of Lady Melbourne, of her cousin, Harriet Cavendish, and of her sharp-tongued intelligent sister-in-law, Lady Cowper, seemed merely a little nuisance or a little plague. A young woman of follies, if not of passions, she was already beginning to create a stir.

Thus, she had started a flirtation with Sir Godfrey Webster.[1] It was unwise to accept a bracelet; in the light of subsequent happenings, it was almost criminal to accept a dog. For the dog had flown at and bitten Augustus Frederick. Was it mad? By her heartless inadvertence, had she not perhaps endangered her child's life? Desperate and hysterical, she begged the forgiveness of her "dear, her dearest Lady Melbourne, who had been more than a

[1]The son of Lady Holland by her first marriage.

mother to her," promising amendment, vowing that Sir Godfrey should be dismissed—all protestations that the elder woman received with scepticism or demolished in some brief and chilly reply.

Lady Caroline relapsed into self-pity. William was the best and most indulgent of husbands. Again, it was William who had undermined the strict and self-denying principles with which she had been brought up—"that horror of vice, of deceit, of anything that was the least improper." The religious faith of her childhood he had been "pleased to call superstitious enthusiasm. . . . He called me Prudish, said I was strait-laced—amused himself with instructing me in things I need never have heard or known, and the disgust I at first felt to the world's wickedness . . . in a very short time gave way to the general laxity of principles which, little by little, unperceived by you all, has been undermining the few virtues I ever possessed." William himself, she understood, was strong in the possession of an "excellent heart, sight, head and superior mind;" weaker and more sensitive, she needed the restraints that he had subtly, if half carelessly, taken away. "Some heads may bear perfect happiness and perfect liberty . . ." Her own was at the mercy of every impulse.

By 1812 the situation had become unbearable. Behind the classic façade of Melbourne House (nowadays the Scottish Office), with its sober brick frontage and elegantly pillared portico bestriding the pavement of Whitehall, dwelt the two households, each established on a separate floor, Lady Melbourne and her husband, a man as conventional and inconspicuous as his wife was brilliant, clear headed and shrewd, and above them William Lamb's distracted ménage. Outwardly life continued in the usual fashion; callers— Miss Berry dragged upstairs by Lady Caroline to see the baby; the Prince, still faithful to one of the objects of his early love, stepping out of his carriage to visit Lady Melbourne—and parties; a great supper party, prolonged till six o'clock in the morning, which Sheridan and the Prince Regent had both attended and at which Sheridan, as usual, grew exceedingly drunk.

Something more was needed by Lady Caroline—some violent, self-justificatory explosion, some crisis in which she could gather up the spasmodic and ill-directed energies that drove her from repentance to folly, from folly to tears. The fever of Romanticism was in her blood. She admired—there were occasions when she believed that she adored—her husband; but his tolerance, his stoical detachment—"Caroline! Caroline!" he would murmur, confronted with the evidence of a new and humiliating escapade—were not calculated to check the extravagance of her career. If he were tolerant, then surely he must be indifferent? He could not love her, since he allowed her to go her way. And attention, of one kind or another, was the desiderium of this incorrigible exhibitionist.

Her voice rose to a scream at crowded dinner parties. Always must she lead the movement, plunge headlong into the latest craze; and, when the Waltz reached London from the Rhineland, Lady Caroline—"dressed, or rather *not* dressed, so as to excite universal attention, and authorise every boldness of staring"—was among the first to succumb to the spell of that giddy measure. It would seem that she was among the first to read *Childe Harold*. Instantly she decided that she would meet the poet; for she herself had written verses, and was the author of a rambling unpublished story, in which, against a wild romantic background, she had described the seduction by an infidel nobleman of an innocent girl.

Lord Byron's reputed history was of the darkest. Mr. Rogers, to whom she applied for an introduction, looked doubtful. The poet, he warned her, had a club foot; moreover, he bit his nails. She must see him, Lady Caroline persisted; but when, a few days later, at the house of Lady Westmorland, whom Byron had met at Algeciras, she found herself being led by her hostess towards that ominous attractive figure and saw the other women "throwing up their heads at him," she hesitated and abruptly turned aside.

The poet had noticed her change of purpose. It is characteristic of human beings with Byron's mentality that one rebuff—a single failure to charm—outweighs a dozen triumphs; and from the centre of an admiring and dazzled circle he had seen Lady Caroline approach, had seen her hesitate and, decisively and dramatically, turn away. Henceforward his vanity was up in arms. She had refused a presentation. . . . The little scene was the most effective, incidentally the most calamitous, that Lady Caroline had ever staged; and that evening she confided to her journal a string of epithets so famous that they scarcely deserve resurrection, yet so apt and so picturesque that no biographer can resist the temptation of transcribing them for the hundredth time. *"Mad, bad and dangerous to know . . ."* It was not until later that she completed the sentence, adding *"That beautiful pale face is my fate,"* and during the interim their encounter had had a sequel. On this occasion the scene of their meeting was Holland House, where Byron was now privileged to pay his respects.

He was announced while Lady Caroline was with Lady Holland. "This offer [he observed piercingly, as soon as he had been introduced] was made to you the other day—may I ask why you declined it?" The frontal attack he followed up by asking if he might call on her at her mother-in-law's house. Lady Caroline agreed; apparently, she did not fix a day; but next morning, just after she had returned from her ride and was sitting on the sofa between Rogers and Moore, hot and untidy—or, as she herself preferred to describe it, "filthy and heated"—a message came that Lord Byron was downstairs. Immediately she flew to change her habit. "Lord Byron, you are a lucky man," said Rogers when she returned. "Here has Lady Caroline been sitting in all her dirt with us, but as soon as you were announced, she fled to make herself beautiful."

Before leaving, her visitor asked if he might see her alone. In his attentions there was still a shade of aggressiveness; and, when he appeared one day carrying an early rose and a carnation, he put them into her hands with a sardonic smile. "Your Ladyship, I am told [he observed stiffly], likes all that is new and rare—for a moment." Lady Caroline's reply has not been recorded; but the letter that she sent him about this time—a long, intemperate effusion written on a blue-bordered sheet, embossed at the corners with a design of scallop shells—was as encouraging a document as any lover could hope to receive. "The Rose Lord Byron gave Lady Caroline Lamb [she scribbled, with the lavish and inconsequent sentimentality that was one of the distinguishing features of her epistolary style] died in despight of every effort to save it; probably from regret at its fallen Fortunes. Hume, at least, who is no great believer in most things, says that many more die of broken hearts than is supposed. . . ." In the next sentence she promises that, as soon as she returns from Brocket Hall, she will send him, "the Flower she wishes most of all others to resemble, as, however deficient its beauty and even use, it has a noble and aspiring mind, and, having once beheld in its full lustre the bright and unclouded sun that for one moment condescended to shine upon it, never while it exists could it think any lower object worthy of its worship and Admiration."

The letter concludes with a request that Lord Byron will "eat and drink like an Englishman" until Lady Caroline sees him again. It is fair to assume that when a woman begins to interest herself in a man's diet she is already a little in love with him, and that Lady Caroline was more than a little—was, indeed, desperately and deliberately—enamoured, the fervour of her floral imagery could leave no doubt. At last she had the excuse she needed. From that time Byron's stumbling and hesitant footstep was heard almost every day upon the staircase of Melbourne House; and, as Byron approached, so did the other familiars of Lady Caroline's existence diminish and recede. No longer were there waltzing parties in the Great Drawing Room. Looking back across an interval of many years to the life she had enjoyed while *Childe Harold* was yet unread and its author yet unencountered, Lady Caroline forgot the quarrels and the scenes, the angry notes that had passed to and fro between her own and her mother-in-law's apartments, remembering only the gaiety and hubbub occasioned by "forty and fifty people," all young, all cheerful and all noisy, who had practised waltzes and quadrilles from noon till night.

She saw herself as "the happiest and gayest of human beings" . . . Lord Byron had banished the musicians and dancers. He could not dance; naturally puritanical—at least when it was a question of pleasures in which he was unable to take a direct and demonstrative share—possessed, moreover, of a somewhat Mohammedan attitude towards the public exhibition of feminine beauty, he resented and ridiculed the new fashion. At his command the morning waltzing parties were given up. He preferred solitude; "he liked to read with me and stay with me out of the crowd. Not but what we went about together everywhere, and were at last invited as if we had been married. . . ." His manners were still ingratiating and gentle. Byron could be very gentle when he chose; and the adoration of this young, distinguished, cultivated and charming woman, obedient to his every mood and his every wish, soothed his vanity and calmed his nerves.

Vanity counted for much in their relationship. ". . . It was not vanity misled me," protested Lady Caroline, writing her own pathetic narrative, after the appearance of Tom Medwin's *Recollections*. "I grew to love him better than virtue, Religion—all prospects here." Byron's memories of the episode were less poetic; he was flattered, gratified. . . . Women had never proved inaccessible; but Lady Caroline, one of the most brilliant luminaries of the Devonshire House set—a little world in itself to which but a few short months ago he scarcely dreamed that he would ever obtain the *entrée*—was a conquest not to be compared with lowlier, more venal loves. Her first reception of him had presented a challenge. While their friendship was still in the platonic stage, Lady Bessborough—hoping, possibly, that she might thus persuade her daughter's cavalier to relax his all-too-successful and speedy pursuit —had assured him that Lady Caroline's heart was already occupied; and her motherly ruse had served to quicken his interest. The young man who, as he had written in *Childe Harold,*

> *Was not unskilful in the spoiler's art,*
> *And spread its snares licentious far and wide;*
> *Nor from the base pursuit had turned aside,*
> *As long as aught was worthy to pursue*

found his feather-headed admirer easy game. In fact, he had hardly troubled to set his snares; his prey had rushed out at him, inviting capture.

Rumour and legend are potent aphrodisiacs. More powerful, perhaps, than beauty or riches, certainly more powerful than intelligence, is the reputation of being dangerous and irresistible; and by now this was Byron's reputation in the London social world. Women schemed and squabbled to be presented to him. Samuel Rogers, as one of the first denizens of inner Whig circles to meet the new lion, was "frequently amused at the manœuvres of certain noble ladies to get acquainted with him by means of me: for instance, I would receive a note from Lady —— requesting the pleasure of my company on a particular evening, with the postscript, 'Pray, could you not contrive to bring Lord Byron with you?'—Once, at a great party given by Lady Jersey, Mrs. Sheridan ran up to me and

said, 'Do, as a favour, try if you can place Lord Byron beside me
at supper.' " Around the dinner-table, when he was not present,
Byron's name (we are told) occurred so often, and was mentioned
in such rapt and excited tones, that the repetition of it—*Byr'n-Byr'n-*
Byr'n—sank into a low continuous murmur, until the whole
assemblage seemed to be talking of nothing else. His rudeness
was as attractive as his amiability. Had she noticed his expression?
one lady would ask another His "*under* look"? The sudden penetrat-
ing scrutiny, before which the heart fluttered and the senses began
to reel? Encountering this *under* look on the threshold of a ballroom,
Lady Rosebery had quailed and almost fainted; and Lady Rosebery's
experience was by no means exceptional. It would have needed a
stronger head than Lady Caroline's to resist the paralysing influence
of Byron's celebrity.

"About this period," he remarked to Medwin, in Italy, reviewing
the incidents of his London career, "I became *un homme à bonnes*
fortunes . . " With a frankness that must have delighted Shelley's
Eton friend, that "perplexing simpleton," who loved to hear a man
of genius gossip, he proceeded to speak of his earliest triumphs.
"The lady [he explained] had scarcely any personal attractions. Her
figure, though genteel, was too thin to be good, and wanted that
roundness which elegance would vainly supply." All his life he
abominated thin women; when they were young, he said, they
reminded him of dried butterflies and, when they had grown old,
of spiders. Lady Caroline's fragile and angular body, lavishly
revealed at the dictates of a fashion that, in time past, had been
carried to heroic and preposterous lengths by Madame Tallien,
Madame Beauharnais and other distinguished *sans-chemises* of the
Directoire, did not appeal to an exacting modern amorist whose
criterion of feminine beauty was derived from his residence in the
Near East, and who liked women supple, sensuous and uncompli-
cated. His ideal was that of a Turkish voluptuary; he was fond of
imagining, he informed Lady Blessington, the little feet of some
seraphic odalisque, the Leila, Zuleika, Gulnare or Medora of his
own poems, well shaped but "small to diminutiveness, peeping
from beneath the drapery that half conceals it, or moving in the
mazes of the dance." He liked "*roundness* of contour accompanied
by lightness. . . ."

Such ideal graces were not to be found in the thin, graceful, expressive, perpetually agitated person of poor Lady Caroline, for all her white teeth, big eyes and soft, drawling, prettily affected voice, which slurred and lisped in the manner of Devonshire House society. Lady Caroline was conscious of her own shortcomings. ". . . As he and you justly observe [she wrote to Medwin] I had few personal attractions." Had she been a famous beauty, she remarked elsewhere, with the insight that is sometimes a reward of deep and prolonged unhappiness, Byron might very well have loved her. Sexual snobism is often a by-product of physical deformity; and snobism—the pleasures of sexual *amour propre* and of gratified social self-esteem—had influenced his attitude from the very outset. Lady Caroline was "young and of the first connexions. *Au reste* [he added] she possessed an infinite vivacity of mind, and an imagination heated by novel-reading. . . . I was soon congratulated by my friends on the conquest I had made, and did my utmost to show that I was not insensible to the partiality I could not but perceive. I made every effort to be in love, expressed as much ardour as I could muster, and kept feeding the flame with a constant supply of *billets doux* and amatory verses. . . ."

In fact, he had sustained the comedy as long as he could; Byron was nothing if not plastic. It is true that the grandeur of Lady Caroline's "connexions" weighed with him more heavily than he might have been prepared to admit; true that his reputation as spoiler and seducer had preceded him into the world where he now moved, and that his vanity had been piqued by the initial difficulty; but it is also true that he himself was at the mercy of a designing victim. In a short time their rôles had been reversed. For a man who complained bitterly, and not without reason, of the inconvenience to which he was subjected by turbulent and over-enthusiastic women, Byron showed an uncommon readiness to accept every adventure that came his way, although the last chapter of these romances, he knew, was customarily disastrous. The explanation, like everything about him, is paradoxical. Had Byron been a less good-natured lover—had his gratitude for affection been less immediate—it is probable that he would have caused infinitely less suffering. As it was, he found it difficult to say "No"—at least, at the beginning of a relationship; until desperation obliged him to snap his chains. The brutality he sometimes displayed, when he struck for freedom, was directly proportioned by the indulgent facility with which he lost it.

Sexually, his character remains ambiguous. "No man is so easily led [declared Medwin] but he is not to be driven." Almost any lady could manage his Lordship, said Fletcher, the foolish, faithful valet, who had seen many ladies come and go, from the kept women of his Cambridge and London days, those—

> . . . *Laughing dames in whom he did delight,*
> *Whose large blue eyes, fair locks, and snowy hands,*
> *Might shake the saintship of an anchorite,*
> *And long had fed his youthful appetite*

to the more disturbing cohort of fashionable females. His heart, Byron confessed, always alighted on the nearest perch. He boasted that he had never seduced a woman; and, indeed, the arts of seduction were seldom necessary, for he himself was very often the pursued. Vanity or gallantry might induce him to open the battle; thereafter he was hard put to it to beat a retreat.

Anything for peace and a quiet life! "You know I hate women," he had reminded Hobhouse; and yet—perhaps because his own nature included a decidedly feminine strain—he appreciated their company and conversation. He despised women, but he could not do without them. "There is something to me very softening in the presence of a woman—some strange influence, even if one is not in love with them—which I cannot at all account for. . . ." The trend of his desires was oddly domestic; a sentimental philanderer rather than the "marble-hearted" debauchee portrayed in *Childe Harold*, a sensationalist rather than a determined and brutal sensualist, he valued the velleities of amorous intercouse, the small change of a calmly conducted love-affair and the opportunity it afforded him of settling down. But to settle down, alas, was rarely practicable. . . . Discussing any aspect of Byron's existence, we are at once brought face to face with a number of startling and perplexing contradictions. Thus, the Romantic poet would have preferred to model his work on the classical achievement of the eighteenth century; the gloomy wanderer proves, in congenial society, to have been a garrulous and cheerful young man; while the great lover and unscrupulous seducer, presented by legend, lacked many essential qualities of the inveterate rake.

Byron was no Casanova or Maréchal de Saxe. When we examine his character a little more closely, we ask ourselves—as some of his friends and of the women with whom he came into brief and painful contact may perhaps have asked themselves—whether his taste for women was really profound. Was he as susceptible as he was attractive? That Byron—still more the Byronic legend—possessed an extraordinary magnetic power we cannot doubt; but the man who attracts women is not necessarily attracted in his turn; or he exploits his fascination from motives—opportunism, vanity, the wish to impress his fellow men—that have nothing to do with desire and love. In his sexual life, as in many other things, Byron was an opportunist. Opportunity had made the rake; but if we assume that the typical rake exists—a human being dominated by the pursuit of the opposite sex, whose whole life is devoted to amatory carnage, whose greatest joy is the satisfaction of sexual inquisitiveness—Byron's temperament falls short of the requisite standard.

He was too lazy; he was, incidentally, too soft-hearted. "I would not [he announced] give the tithe of a Birmingham farthing for any woman who could or would be purchased, nor indeed for any *woman quoad mere woman*; that is to say, unless I loved for something more than her sex." He grew sentimental in his relationship with women; but sentimentalism is never far from cynicism; and it was only in his relationship with men that the more romantic and idealistic side of his nature was allowed to emerge; for among men alone did he recognise his equals. Of what woman (barring, perhaps, one tragic and momentous episode, which has not yet found its place in the story of Byron's career) could he say, on encountering her after an interval of seven or eight years, that he hardly recollected an hour of his existence worthy to be weighed against five minutes spent in her company, and that their meeting was like a resurrection from the grave? Lord Clare had been dearer to him than any mistress. The summer months of 1806, engrossed by a "violent, though *pure*, love and passion," when he had had serious thoughts of settling down with John Edleston and forming a household of which the prototype was provided by those "two

dear inseparable inimitables" Lady Eleanor Butler and her friend
Miss Sarah Ponsonby, had been (as he remembered it) "the most
romantic period" of a life in which "romantic" interests, usually of a
more meretricious and less platonic kind, were so plentiful that no
biographer can keep track of them.

I have already touched on his friendship with Nicolo Giraud.
At the very end of his life, in the squalor of Missolonghi, where
opportunities of playing the part of Byronic amorist were few or
none, his adoption of a second Levantine youth, Loukas Chalan-
dritsanos, a good-looking boy whom Byron had promoted to the
rôle of his page and personal attendant, once filled by Robert
Rushton, caused some stir among the members of his suite. His
conduct on their Grecian tour had fluttered Hobhouse; and at this
juncture it may be opportune to transcribe yet another of Hobhouse's marginal notes, in which he refers to Byron's intimacy with
Lord Grey de Ruthyn, the young nobleman who had occupied
Newstead while Byron and his mother were domiciled at Burbage
Green. Byron (Moore tells us) often visited Newstead and lodged
at a small outlying cottage known as The Hut. Grey offered him
more comfortable accommodation in the Abbey itself; "and a
circumstance occurred during this intimacy [Hobhouse notes]
which certainly had much effect on his future morals."

An unexplained, yet bitter, feud was the next development.
Byron refused to disclose the subject on which the two friends had
fallen out; but he assured Augusta that, were his reasons known,
his indignation would seem to be perfectly justified. . . . Beyond
this point the historian cannot venture. It is obvious, at least, that
Hobhouse's view of Byron's emotional life was not entirely orthodox, and that there were aspects of his friend's biography he neither
cared to illuminate nor (stung by the stupidity and poetic mis-
representation that he thought he detected in Moore's narrative)
was content to leave discreetly behind the veil. Thus, with regard
to the "passions" of his Harrow days, he wrote that "M. knows
nothing, or will tell nothing, of the principal cause and motive of
all these boyish friendships;" from which we assume that Hobhouse
himself was better informed. Byron was supremely erratic in his
bestowal of confidences; and John Cam, though sober and ponderous,
had received his full share.

To Hobhouse he spoke of his earliest sexual adventures. Moore
had heard the story of the little girl whom Byron had loved when
he was nine years old, and quotes him as having said that he was
"bewildered to assign any cause for his precocity of affection;"
whereat Hobhouse remarks that he is "acquainted with a singular
fact, scarcely fit for narration but much less romantic and more
satisfactory than the amour with Mary Duff." Continuing his notes,
it was at Southwell, Hobhouse informs us, Byron's home from 1804,
that he "learnt not only his first lessons in sensuality, but had an
opportunity of seeing to what base expedients self-interest will
resort—One of the families he mentions winked at an intercourse
between him and one of the daughters in hopes of entangling him
in an unequal marriage." So much, concludes Hobhouse triumphantly, for the "silly romance of T. M. respecting the purity of
Southwell." . . . When Byron went up to Cambridge, during
October 1805, he was already—at least, in his own eyes—a man of
the world, armed with a cynicism that befitted the part. His opinion
of the opposite sex had never been high; implanted originally by his
mother, in whom all the most detestable peculiarities of woman-
hood seemed to have been realised, strengthened by his experiences
among the mercenary and provocative young ladies of a small
northern country town, it was confirmed by a course of urban
dissipation. He had learned how to exploit his natural charm and,
with feminine insight, to canalise the outpourings of feminine
folly.

He "hated" women because he had hated and resented his
mother; he pursued them because affection and admiration never
came amiss, and because he himself was sufficiently feminine to
find in their society—much as he despised it—a "strange influence"
that he could not at all account for. Among men, his social
faculties were keyed up; he was at his best; but there are moments
when we prefer not to be stimulated, when a man—even a professed
rake—wishes to talk nonsense, to be simple and make foolish jokes,
to feel that there is no need for him to shine. In every writer, says
a French critic, there is a man and a woman; genius is bisexual;
and in Byron's nature this division was strongly marked, an aggressive and, to some extent, factitious masculinity being counter-
balanced by a softer, more susceptible and romantic self, which,

though rarely seen, always quivered beneath the surface. It is the union of these two contrasted personalities that makes the essence of his character so hard to discern.

He would approach the same episode, for instance, from completely different angles. To Hobhouse he talked of Mary Chaworth "without the slightest appearance of regret or feeling of any kind;" yet he had moods when the whole lost delightful land-scape of that early passion—"*le vert paradis des amours enfantines*"—began to blossom anew and the image of the beloved, still fresh and faultless but unapproachable, returned to torment him as in the past. Not a shade of that unhappy love affair had he forgotten. At fifteen he had been one of a party that visited a cavern in Derbyshire, where there is a stream "which flows under a rock, with the rock so close upon the water" that the ferryman, "a sort of Charon," was obliged to push a boat through, wading behind it and stooping at the stern. Only two people could lie safely inside the skiff, and in the darkness he had lain there with Mary Chaworth. He recollected his sensations, he wrote at Ravenna; but he could not describe them—"and it is as well."

"*My* M. A. C."—she had never been his. "Our Union would have healed feuds . . . it would have joined lands broad and rich; it would have joined . . . two persons not ill-matched in years . . . and—and—and—what has been the result?" Half the per-manence of Mary Chaworth's image depended on Byron's convic-tion that she was his "destiny," or rather that the alliance of the Chaworths and the Byrons offered a solution to the Byronic destiny, a fateful process in which he was involved and from which hence-forward he would never be able to find an issue. The pattern was dreadfully conclusive. I have referred to Byron's opportunism; but his opportunism might also be called fatalism. I have suggested that his nature included a pronounced strain of homosexual feeling; but, as in so many bisexual temperaments, the emotion was curiously narcissistic. We love only ourselves, declares Paul Valéry; in love, it is the self that we desire, the self that we long to encounter; and of Byron it is certainly true that a passionate preoccupation with himself—a personage both loved and abominated—ran more deeply than any normal passion.

Passion and passions are frequently confused. In Byron,

passion was strong. He was full of the electric energy that excites and disorganises the emotions of other human beings; but, although at bottom he was hard to change, superficially he was easily influenced, and the love affairs in which he indulged were very often trifling. Thus, his bond with Lady Caroline was of the weakest and vaguest. Patiently, at first not unkindly, he played his part in the comedy of letters, verses and love tokens. "He was very good," said Lady Caroline, "to what he grew afterwards." His health was delicate; with his pale face, set off by his dark clothes, his beautiful voice and his pathetic gliding or shambling carriage, he evoked at the same moment desire and pity. That he could be harsh, Lady Caroline soon discovered. From a *passade*, tolerated by her husband and her mother-in-law, their relationship rapidly developed into a source of public scandal. Lady Caroline's infatuation was undisguised. On May 4th the Duchess of Devonshire, writing to her son, announces that Lord Byron "continues to be made the greatest fuss with. . . . Your little friend, Caro William, as usual, is doing all sorts of imprudent things for him and with him;" while, six days later, Lady Granville—Lady Caroline's cousin, Harriet Cavendish—observes that "Lord Byron is still upon a pedestal and Caroline William doing homage."

Her conduct was more than ordinarily "wild and imprudent." Lady Caroline was no stranger to disgrace; but, for lack of an object, she had not yet disgraced herself so thoroughly as during the months of April and May 1812. At any cost, she seemed determined to produce a crisis. Lord Byron, writes the Duchess on May 10th, "continues to be the great attraction at all parties and suppers. . . . He is going back to Naxos, and then the husbands may sleep in peace. I should not be surprised if Caro William were to go with him. . . ." Byron did not retire to Naxos. He himself gives the term of his extreme celebrity as six weeks; but in the middle of May he was still a focus of gossip and would appear night after night, at supper parties, under the lustres of a London ballroom, Lady Caroline following him like his shadow.

He had expressly forbidden her to waltz. He was at least jealous enough to deny her a pleasure in which his lameness made it impossible for him to participate. Often the lovers quarrelled. Coming home to his house in St. James's Place, Samuel Rogers, an emaciated bachelor who lived only for society, for his bibelots, his caged nightingales and the pretty verses that he composed—they were "all sentiment and sago and sugar," whereas his conversation was remarkably caustic—would hear that Lady Caroline was in the garden and would find her walking up and down, "waiting for me to beg that I would reconcile them." An odd scene, and Rogers must have appreciated it: the sleepy servant at the door, who announced that her Ladyship had called and said that she would wait; the dark garden, and, beneath the soft obscurity of a summer sky at two or three o'clock in the morning, the young woman, a light scarf of Indian muslin thrown over her shoulders, who paced backwards and forwards as she explained that there had been another quarrel—Lord Byron was very angry—and dear Mr. Rogers, her oldest friend, must please hurry round to Lord Byron's lodgings and make it up!

Otherwise. . . . Her threats were always terrific. So were her protestations. According to Rogers, in her very first letter—which Byron, unkindly but characteristically, gave him to read—"she assured him that, if he was in any want of money, 'all her jewels were at his service.' " As a romantic, she refused to stoop to the harmless but necessary subterfuges that her mother and her mother-in-law, both experienced and passionate women, would have considered indispensable. If she and Byron attended a party together, she would insist on driving back with him in his carriage; if she herself had not been invited, "such was the insanity of her passion [Rogers records] that sometimes she would wait for him in the street till it was over! One night, after a great party at Devonshire House . . . I saw her—yes, saw her—talking to Byron, with half her body thrust into the carriage which he had just entered. In spite of all this absurdity, my firm belief is that there was nothing criminal between them."

This firm belief was not shared by Rogers's contemporaries. It is obvious that Lady Caroline's emotions worked primarily through her head; but Byron had no use for platonic dalliance and, about this time, added to his collection of sentimental relics a token not readily associated with a bookish love affair. She was, moreover, desperately possessive and jealous. Disguised as a page or as a carman, she would burst into his rooms at moments when Byron had given strict orders that she was not to be admitted. Scenes "worthy of Faublas" were apt to occur. Byron was far from faithful; he could forgive much; but, if vanity and indolence had facilitated his capture, the same qualities proved Lady Caroline's undoing. He understood that she made him look ridiculous. Although he acknowledged her talents—"greater and more pleasing" than he had met in any other woman—he could not but regret that they were "unfortunately coupled with a total want of common conduct. . . . Then your heart, my poor Caro (what a little volcano!) that pours *lava* through your veins. . . . You know I have always thought you the cleverest, most agreeable, absurd, amiable, perplexing, dangerous, fascinating little being that lives now, or ought to have lived 2,000 years ago." Prudence, nevertheless, *must* be maintained; and Lady Caroline borrowed the stratagems of comic opera.[1] Hating scenes, he had submitted to the thraldom as long as he could; a day was coming when he would be obliged to snap it "rather rudely."

[1]"While I was with him the lady's page brought him a new letter. He was a fair-faced delicate boy of thirteen or fourteen years old, whom one might have taken for the lady herself. He was dressed in a scarlet huzzar jacket and pantaloons, trimmed in front in much the same manner, with silver buttons and twisted silver lace, with which the narrow slit cuffs of his jacket were also embroidered. He had light hair curling about his face; and held a feathered fancy hat in his hand, which completed the scenic appearance of this urchin Pandarus. I could not but suspect at the time that it was a disguise . . ." R. C. Dallas: *Recollections of the Life of Lord Byron.*

Chapter 5

THOUGH a distracting influence, Lady Caroline had failed to
monopolise him. Celebrity produced many new acquaintances;
and in Lady Caroline's immediate circle Byron had struck up a
warm friendship with Lady Melbourne, an intelligent, cynical,
sharp-tongued woman, known to Lady Bessborough as "The
Thorn," and had been charmed by the singing of Mrs. George
Lamb—"Caroline George," so nicknamed to distinguish her from
her temperamental sister-in-law "Caroline William." It was at
Melbourne House, too, before the waltzing parties were discontinued that he had first set eyes on Caroline's cousin, Miss Anne
Isabella Milbanke. A strange girl; heiress and only child of Sir
Ralph Milbanke of Seaham, Lady Melbourne's brother, she brought
with her into the Great Drawing Room of Melbourne House an
air of idealism and high-minded feminine pedantry, somewhat
surprising in a young woman who had large expectations and would
eventually become a peeress in her own right. "Good, amiable, and
sensible," as the Duchess of Devonshire wrote to her son Augustus,
a rejected suitor, "but cold, prudent, and reflecting," Annabella
Milbanke was the exact antithesis of her cousin-by-marriage, Lady
Caroline Lamb, of whom in the letters that she sent back to her
parents at Seaham, she had many severe and amusing things to
say. "Lady Caroline," she noted, "baa-a-a-a's till she makes me
sick." During her residence in London, Miss Milbanke herself had
taken the opportunity of hearing lectures on mnemonics and
geology, had visited the British Museum and had attended Campbell's course on poetry at the Royal Institution; and she considered
that "Lady C. Lamb does not do justice to her own understanding"
and "seems clever in everything that is not within the province
of common sense." William Lamb she thought conceited and self-

sufficient. It was on March 22nd that Annabella opened *Childe Harold* for the first time; and by the 24th she had discovered that its author was "rather too much of a mannerist," but excelled "in the delineation of deep feeling, and in reflections relative to human nature." Next day she saw Byron at Melbourne House. "His mouth," she observed, "continually betrays the acrimony of his spirit." For her part, she declined to seek an introduction; "all the women were absurdly courting him. . . . I really thought that Lady Caroline had bit half the company and communicated the *Nonsense-mania.*" Yet she added that, although she could neither "worship talents that are unconnected with the love of man, nor be captivated by that Genius which is barren of blessings," she would not refuse the acquaintance if it came her way.

They met, on the 14th of April, at Lady Cowper's; and even in that earliest conversation, which revolved mostly round Joseph Blacket, a shoe-making poet whom Miss Milbanke had befriended, she recognised "much evidence of his goodness." Byron "played up" with his usual docility. Of "Cobbler Joe" and his "Orphan Daughter (pathetic Pratt!)," who "will, certes, turn out a shoe-making Sappho," he had previously written to Murray in a far less indulgent vein. But, face to face with the patroness of obscure merit, he was adroit and well mannered enough to allow the "humanity of his feelings" the fullest possible expansion; so that Miss Milbanke reported herself relieved and pleased. He threw out, moreover, hints of repentance. In her diary she noted that she was now "additionally convinced that he is sincerely repentant for the evil he has done, though he has not resolution (without aid) to adopt a new course of conduct. . . ." Who was to supply the aid that he needed? Lady Caroline, affected, fashionable, crack-brained, hiding her erratic cleverness beneath the "childish manner" that annoyed Miss Milbanke to the extent of almost making her physically sick, was scarcely qualified to undertake the reformation of this "very bad, very good man;" while the majority of his other companions were either foolish and frivolous or downright wicked. He disdained them, she felt, yet he endured. He was "restlessly thoughtful," his upper lip being "drawn towards the nose with an expression of impatient disgust," shy, moody and prone to sudden satirical outbursts. "Do you think there is one person here who dares look into himself?" was his abrupt question, fired off at a party where Annabella had already decided that he was the most attractive person within sight. "But I was not *bound* to him by any strong feeling of sympathy till he uttered these words . . . in my hearing—'I have not a friend in the world!' "

"I vowed in secret to be a devoted friend to this lone being"— The sentence belongs to a period, later and more unhappily introspective, when Annabella was attempting to take stock of the confused emotions that had passed through her mind during the tumultuous summer months of 1812. In the meantime their friendship progressed slowly. For the young woman, it was an adventure, perhaps the most stirring and exciting experience she had ever enjoyed; at last she had found a rôle worthy of those incontestable talents and virtues which she owed to the care and love lavished on her education by an adoring mother and father, and to the immense pains that she had lavished on herself. The point of view of the "lone being" was comparatively prosaic. *Hommes à bonnes fortunes*, literary lion and spoiled hero of half a dozen London houses, in Miss Milbanke he saw primarily Lady Melbourne's niece, the débutante who would one day inherit the estates and title of her rich uncle Lord Wentworth. After the worldliness and corruption of urban society, which, although it stimulated his senses, shocked the unconscious puritanism of his nature, there was something pleasantly reassuring in the interest—tinged by disapproval—of this modest, sensible, well-informed and well-conducted girl, who charmed him without provoking his desire. On his side, at least, the friendship was humdrum. "Lord Byron" (wrote the Duchess of Devonshire, to the inconsolable Augustus, who still hoped that Miss Milbanke might favour his suit) "makes up to her a little, but she don't seem to admire him except as a poet, nor he her, except for a wife." Through Lady Caroline, she sent him her verses to criticise; and, sending them back, Byron observed that they showed fancy and feeling, and that "a little practice would soon induce facility of expression. . . . She certainly is a very extraordinary girl; who would imagine so much strength and variety of thought under that placid Countenance? . . . She is too good for a fallen spirit to know, and I should like her more if she were less perfect."

With the end of the season, the débutante retired to the country.

Miss Milbanke, however, like her cousin, had been but a single episode in the crowded and exhausting life to which Byron was now condemned. He had other admirers, and there were other heiresses. Miss Mercer Elphinstone—she became comtesse de Flahaut and is thus connected with the history of an almost equally romantic adventurer, Louis Napoléon—had given him very decided encouragement; while, during the last few weeks, he had gained the *entrée* to every great Whig house in the metropolis and moved between Holland House and the drawing-room of Lady Jersey with as much ease as, a few months earlier, he had moved backwards and forwards between his solitary lodgings and the dull club where he consumed his abstemious vegetarian meals. Lady Jersey was a patroness of Almack's; supported by the Ladies Castlereagh, Cowper and Sefton, Mrs. Drummond Burrell, Princess Esterhazy and Princess Lieven, she exercised a censorship that even the Duke of Wellington could not resist; and it was reported that on one occasion he had been sent away because he appeared at Willis's Rooms in King Street, St. James's, clad in black trousers, when a ukase had gone forth that only knee breeches, white cravat and *chapeau bras* were to be worn. To her character of social dragon, Lady Jersey added a touch of histrionic haughtiness that suggested the tragedy queen. She was elegant and personable, with her dazzlingly white skin and dark curling hair; but Byron used to tell her (he informed Lady Blessington) that "she spoiled her looks by her excessive animation; for eyes, tongue, head and arms were all in movement at once, and were only relieved from their active service by want of respiration." Creevey, staying at Middleton in 1820, noted the same abundant and rather bewildering flow of fashionable high spirits. . . . "Shall I tell you [he wrote to his step-daughter] what Lady Jersey is like? She is like one of her numerous gold and silver musical dickey birds, that are in all the show rooms of this house. She begins to sing at eleven o'clock, and, with the interval of the hour she retires to her cage to rest, she sings till 12 at night without a moment's interruption. She changes her feathers for dinner, and her plumage both morning and evening is the happiest and most beautiful I ever saw. . . . This morning her ladyship condescended to give me two fingers to shake."

If Lady Jersey had something in common with Oriane de

Guermantes, Lady Holland—who represented the intellectual apex
of Whig society, while Lady Jersey shone from its social zenith—
bore a certain resemblance to another and yet more famous Proustian
personage, Madame Verdurin, and the coterie among whom she
passed her life to *"le petit noyau,"* as described in *Sodome et Gomorrhe*
and *Un Amour de Swann.* She exercised the same capricious tyranny.
Lady Holland, however, was more powerful than *la patronne*; and,
though few of her intimates really loved her, and though the
resentment and criticism she aroused grumble on for several decades
through the letters and memoirs of her acquaintances, it was a
brave man or an exceptional woman who defied her wrath. Like
Madame Verdurin, she was tyrannous for its own sake, a virtuoso
in the art of obtaining submission, even from her proudest and
apparently least tractable guests; and nowhere, perhaps, does her
character appear more distinctly than in an anecdote related by the
haughty and formidable Madame de Lieven to Lady Granville. *"Ma
chère,"* began Madame de Lieven, *"j'étais chez elle. . . . On annonce
Pasquier. Elle a l'air tout charmé, tout flatté. Elle me dit: 'Restez, je vous
supplie; causez avec le Chancelier.' Je résiste; elle m'implore de ne pas
l'abandonner. Je cède. Pas plutôt assise avec tout cet entourage qui nous
regarde, qu'elle laisse tomber son sac. Elle me tape sur l'épaule:* 'Pick it
up, my dear; pick it up'*—et moi, tout étonnée en bonne bête, me plongeant
sur le tapis pour ramasser ses chiffons."* Was not this, continued Lady
Granville, the acuteness of whose observations would have delighted
Marcel Proust, "a true and incomparable Holly-ism, taking out of
Lieven's mouth the taste of the little flutter at the visits, and the
besoin of her support . . . and showing off, what I believe never
was seen before, Mme. de Lieven as a humble companion?"

It seems possible that the flavour of deliberate impertinence
that distinguished Lady Holland's manners may have been
sharpened by the fact that, owing to a somewhat unconventional
early life, her social position was very largely self-made and that
she was never on visiting terms with the more puritanical English
ladies. A rich West-Indian heiress and the divorced wife of Sir
Godfrey Webster (father of the Sir Godfrey whose flirtation with
Lady Caroline was to cause so much domestic hubbub), she had
married Lord Holland in 1797. The Hollands' first son was illegitimate; until 1805 they had lived much abroad; but despite these

tempestuous beginnings, Lady Holland had raised herself to an eminence where she levied contributions, promulgated laws and retained—while constantly exasperating, snubbing and humiliating —the army of admirers she had gathered at Holland House. Here assembled both writers and politicians. Within easy riding or driving distance of the centre of London, Holland House, the big Elizabethan mansion built by Sir Walter Cope, a protégé of one of the Cecils, was still a pleasant country seat, situated far beyond the turnpike and surrounded by the park and gardens that Charles James Fox had known as a boy. The library was large and the dinners were excellent. Lord Holland, "a great grig and a great love," made up in sweetness and smoothness of disposition for all the virtues that his wife conspicuously lacked, and bore her despotism with invariable good temper. The characters of husband and wife were complementary; the hostess aroused storms which the host pacified.

Altogether it was a stimulating house to visit. From his uncle, Lord Holland had inherited not only his thick, dark eyebrows, but that breadth and cultivated catholicity of learning which had made Charles James Fox so extraordinary and refreshing a portent in English public life. Painting, it is true, gave him no pleasure, and music (noted Rogers) "absolute pain;" but of books he had a very wide knowledge; and to his uncle he owed his sound yet conservative literary taste—standards that laid special emphasis on "freedom of manner," "easy grace" of diction, but admitted the immense superiority of Homer to Virgil, and of Shakespeare and Chaucer ("What a genius Chaucer was!") to the more polished and fluent writers of the Augustan Age. Both the Hollands, moreover, were accomplished *gourmets*; and the schoolboy who, asked what he would prefer for dinner, chose duck and green peas, to be followed by apricot tart, was gravely congratulated by Lord Holland and assured that, if in all the important questions of his life he decided as wisely, he would be a great and good man.

The chief drawback of dinner parties at Holland House was that the guests were usually overcrowded, and that Lady Holland had a habit of rearranging them, of squeezing in new guests at the last moment, and of perpetually dropping her fan or bag, which the nearest gentleman was obliged to grope for and return. Sometimes

Lord Holland was her victim. Now it was his white waistcoat. . . .
Expanded over his vast stomach, it gave him the look, Luttrell
suggested, of a turbot standing on its tail; and Lady Holland
refused to sit down to dinner until he had consented to change it.
Now it was the crutches with which he supported his ponderous
gouty frame. . . . "Put away your nasty crutches, Lord Holland;
you look as if you were in prison." "Oh, dear woman, pray let me
have them; I like to have them near me." "Impossible. Mary, take
away your papa's crutches. . . ." In the drawing-room she was
equally abrupt. "Have the goodness, sir, to stir the fire!" was the
command, uttered in tones of extreme sharpness, with which she
dislodged any guest presumptuous enough to occupy the rug
between herself and the fireside. The fire-screen was never arranged
to her liking; at dinner it was very often so placed as to shut off all
warmth from the rest of the company, who sat in patient wretchedness, almost petrified with cold, looking "as if they were just
unpacked, like salmon from an ice-basket, and set down to table
for that day only."

Such were the cruder aspects of her dictatorship. Yet, from the
beginning of the century until the year 1845 when, an agnostic to
the last, she faced death without the smallest sign of religious
feeling but with "a very philosophical calmness and resolution and
perfect good-humour," she had been a rallying point for some of the
best brains of the period; and it was at her house that the common
sense, worldly charm and picturesque, yet restrained, imagination
of Sydney Smith, Lady Holland's especial favourite, were confronted
by the incessant verbosity of a talker who (according to Sydney
Smith) "not only overflowed with learning but stood in the slop"—
Macaulay, an apostle of the Victorian spirit. At Holland House
two periods converged; representatives of the temperate and aristocratic liberalism that preceded the Reform Bill of 1832, Lord
Holland and his friends had little in common with an age of which
some of the chief actors had already begun to make an appearance,
though this new age was to realise many of their dreams. Meanwhile
they formed a brilliant opposition. Rather oddly intertwined with
the hatred of "tyranny" that characterised Lord Holland's conduct
in questions of domestic politics was Lady Holland's worship of
the Emperor Napoleon, whose exile she afterwards consoled by

regular offerings. The "poor dear man," as she usually called him, looked forward to "*les pruneaux de Madame Holland.*"

Politics, however, were not the sole—nor, indeed, were they the chief—preoccupation of the parties that gathered in the big cheerful dining-room, with its crimson damask walls, its sideboard "glittering with venerable family plate," its huge looking-glass and its china closet, filled with the bright and delicate colours of Oriental porcelain; or explored the long panelled library, where the ceiling was painted blue and powdered with golden stars. Besides the politicians, there were authors, reviewers and journalists, and, among professional writers, men who dabbled in literature, society and the arts of good living—Rogers, of whom it was said that, if one borrowed five hundred pounds from him, he would control his natural spitefulness until one came to pay it back; and the wealthy Radical, "Conversation" Sharp. Henry Luttrell was celebrated as a talker and wit. The tone of humour is always hard to preserve; but, while Rogers's witticisms, uttered in a faint and expiring voice, were uncommonly savage, Luttrell's were distinguished by a certain bonhomie. It was hardly possible, declared Greville, to live with a more agreeable man. He was the "most epigrammatic conversationist" Byron had ever encountered; "there is a terseness, and wit, mingled with fancy, in his observations, that no one else possesses. . . . Then, unlike all, or most, other wits, Luttrell is never obtrusive; even the choicest *bons mots* are only brought forth when perfectly applicable, and then are given in a tone of good breeding which enhances their value."

Curran, too, aroused Byron's admiration. An Irish patriot who had moved to Westminster when the ill-fated Irish parliament ceased to exist, he was a fine orator whose native ability more than counterbalanced the effect of his Irish accent and uncouth gestures. As he developed his theme (we read in Holland's *Memoirs of the Whig Party*) "Mr. Pitt beat time to the artificial but harmonious cadence of his periods, and Mr. Canning's countenance kindled at the brightness of a fancy which in glitter fully equalled and in real warmth far exceeded his own." Curran's interest in Catholic Emancipation naturally brought him into touch with Lord Holland, the champion of every liberal measure. Byron heard him talk at Holland House. "Curran! [he wrote in his journal of "Detached

Thoughts"] Curran's the Man who struck me most. Such imagination . . . His *published* life, his published speeches, give you *no* idea of the Man—none at all. He was a *Machine* of Imagination. . . . I did not see a great deal of Curran—only in 1813; but I met him at home (for he used to call on me) and in society . . . and he was wonderful, even to me, who had seen many remarkable men of the time."

Curran, however, was not an habitué. With his "fifty faces and twice as many voices," a person of irrepressible gaiety which afterwards degenerated into profound melancholy, he was a rare but delightful apparition. Other members of the circle were regular inmates. Luttrell and an Eton friend of Lord Holland, Hookham Frere, might supply surface brilliance; but John Allen, a large, white-headed figure, concealing very bright eyes behind a pair of gigantic silver-rimmed spectacles, who lived at Holland House as librarian, steward and general factotum for more than twenty devoted and laborious years, provided the solid groundwork of exact scholarship. Illustrative of the scope of conversation is the account of a debate, held after Byron's death, in which Allen engaged William Lamb—then Lord Melbourne—on the subject of the Christian Church. "Allen spoke of the early reformers, the Catharists. . . ." Not to be outdone, Melbourne quoted Vigilantius's letter to Jerome, and asked Allen about the 11th of Henry IV, an act passed by the Commons against the Church, and mentioned the dialogue between the Archbishop of Canterbury and the Bishop of Ely at the beginning of Shakespeare's *Henry V*, "which Lord Holland sent for and read, Melbourne knowing it all by heart. . . . About etymologies Melbourne quoted Tooke's *Diversions of Purley*, which he seemed to have at his fingers' ends." On a different occasion, talk of women writers prompted the discussion of Madame de Sévigné, Madame de Staël, Sappho, Mrs. Somerville and the admirable novels of Miss Austen; when conversation strayed to English history and Klopstock.

Shakespeare—German mysticism—English novelists—the grave political questions of the day: at Holland House statesmen discussed literature as if literature were at least as real to them as politics. Byron's own learning was a trifle sketchy; his literary explorations, Hobhouse assures us, had been considerably more unadventurous than he himself chose to believe; he "could not repeat twenty lines of poetry in any language" and was no match for the lightly carried scholarship of Allen, Lord Holland or William Lamb. Nevertheless, he appreciated their society; he enjoyed conversation, the battle of wits, general argument, so long as it was carried on under the rules of good manners. Sydney Smith alone seems to have offended him. Smith's exuberance, no doubt—"the loudest wit I e'er was deafened with"—struck Byron, always self-conscious in questions of rank, as ill adapted to the character of a poor parson who had been known to arrive by hackney coach and to change his outdoor shoes in the hall. His fellow writers Byron treated with a circumspection that arose partly from his dislike of literary gatherings—the idea that to scribble was undignified—partly from mere professional uneasiness. But Moore and Rogers he now accounted old friends. Southey was an infrequent visitor at Holland House; and Byron, who admired his "very *epic* appearance" and "fine head" as heartily as he detested his political apostasy, did not meet him with the Hollands until 1813. Thomas Campbell he had already encountered at Sydenham; after a "somewhat awful meeting" with Lady Holland in 1808, when Campbell had decided—not without reason—that his hostess was a "formidable woman . . . cleverer by several degrees than Buonaparte," the poetaster had very quickly recovered his poise. "Dressed to sprucery," in a blue coat and a smart wig, he "really looked as if Apollo had sent him a birthday suit."

Popular novelists were not excluded. "Monk" Lewis had known Lord Holland since they were both at Christ Church. A small, melancholy-faced, rather tedious and sentimental man, he had projecting eyes that reminded Sir Walter Scott of those of an insect; and it was difficult to imagine him as the author of the macabre and sadistic story to which he owed his nickname and reputation. "A damned bore," Byron dubbed him in a moment of impatience. . . . But no picture of life at Holland House would be complete without a glimpse of Sheridan—"poor dear Sherry"—the genius who "got drunk very thoroughly and very soon," charming, incorrigible, easily moved to tears, dishonest in small things, in other and more important matters surprisingly and disastrously upright. Byron made his acquaintance during 1812. "He had a sort of liking for me, and never attacked me—at least to my face.

. . . It occasionally fell to my lot to convoy him home—no sinecure, for he was so tipsy that I was obliged to put on his cock'd hat for him: to be sure it tumbled off again, and I was not myself so sober as to be able to pick it up. . . ."

In his new circle of acquaintances, it will be noticed that the men of whom Byron spoke with most admiration were politicians, talkers, men of the world—men in whose life action predominated over introspection, who shone without the necessity of scribbling. For he still clung to his dream of public eminence. Meanwhile, pliable as ever, he followed the course that his destiny seemed to have laid down. Hobhouse was once more at his side, Tom Moore an unfailing source of comfort; and, released from the constraint imposed by a crowd, the poet would gossip and chatter "with the bursting gaiety of a boy let loose from school. . . ." Nowadays he and Moore had the same friends; "our visits," Moore writes, "were mostly to the same places, and, in the gay and giddy round of a London spring, we were generally (as in one of his own letters he expresses it) 'embarked in the same Ship of Fools together.' "

The landscape of his old life had been left behind. Few young men, at the age of twenty-four, are able so thoroughly to change their entire existence; but the transformation might have been more effective had Byron's character not contained an element that it was almost impossible to change; since, try as he might, he could not jettison himself. The awareness of his fate perpetually pursued him. Having admitted that he was morbidly superstitious, we must also admit that circumstances were continually conspiring to give his superstitions fresh colour. Not the least extraordinary event of the year 1812 was the death of Spencer Perceval—the first English Prime Minister to meet a fate that many English Prime Ministers have deserved—shot down in the lobby of the House of Commons by Bellingham, a crazy timber merchant who had lost money at Archangel and fancied that he had a grievance against the Russian government and the British Ambassador at Petersburg, Lady Bessborough's friend Lord Granville Leveson-Gower. Perceval was murdered on May 11th; a week later Bellingham was hanged in front of Newgate Gaol. Byron had taken a window for the execution; like other abnormally sensitive men, he found in the spectacle of sudden death a certain horrid curiosity, a frigid and masochistic thrill, that is sometimes reflected in the imagery of his verse. On this occasion he was accompanied by two school-friends, Baillie and John Madocks. After spending the night at a party, they arrived at Newgate about three o'clock. The house from which they were to watch the execution was still bolted and barred; and, while Madocks did his best to rouse the inhabitants, Byron and Baillie walked arm in arm up the deserted street. On a door-step Byron caught sight of a homeless woman. With an expression of sympathy, he bent down and offered her a few shillings; but instead of accepting them, the stranger thrust away his hand, tumbled to her feet with a wild scream of laughter and, hobbling alongside, began to mimic his awkward limping movements. Byron said nothing and they moved off, leaving the beggar-woman to her inexplicable and hideous parody. But as they rejoined Madocks, Baillie recorded, "I could feel his arm trembling within mine." . . .

Byron himself makes no mention of the incident. In a letter to Moore, written on the 20th, he announces that "on Monday, after sitting up all night, I saw Bellingham launched into eternity, and at three the same day I saw —— launched into the country." The name omitted was probably that of Caroline Lamb. During the early days of June, the Duchess of Devonshire had remarked that Caroline William is at Brocket, "thank Heaven!"; for it was quite clear that, were she to remain in London, nothing could avert a serious crisis. Byron's friends were equally relieved. Hobhouse, he told Moore, "is endeavouring like you and everybody else, to keep me out of scrapes." A difficult task! He was still very far from having broken through the entanglement in which he had been involved by Lady Caroline; he had not yet been able to harden his heart; and it may have been about this critical period of their relationship that he wrote her an epistle so soothing and so affectionate that many biographers have concluded that it is a forgery[1]; "My Dearest Caroline [he began] If tears which you saw and know I am not apt to shed—if the agitation in which I parted from you—agitation which you must have perceived through the *whole* of this most *nervous* affair, did not commence until the moment of leaving you approached—if all I have said and done . . . have not sufficiently proved what my real feelings are, and must ever be

[1] This letter, however, is usually dated the beginning of August.

towards you, my love, I have no other proof to offer. God knows, I wish you happy, and when I quit you, or rather you, from a sense of duty to your husband and mother, quit me, you shall acknowledge the truth of what I again promise and vow, that no other in word or deed, shall ever hold the place in my affections, which is, and shall be, most sacred to you . . ."

To deny Byron's authorship of this production, because it is inconsistent with what we learn elsewhere of his attitude towards Lady Caroline and reveals an unexpected generosity, is to forget that Byron was a creature of moods, and unscrupulous or compunctious as his mood dictated. Easy to lead, he would not be driven. Affectionate, when affection was not demanded of him, magnanimous when he was not pressed for magnanimity, until he was exasperated he had no desire to wound. Peace with honour was the policy he would have preferred. Had Lady Caroline resigned herself to going in peace, "this most *nervous* affair" might have faded into oblivion and left behind it only a sentimental memory. His declarations, then, seem to offer a means of escape. He had loved her. Here was his letter to prove that his passion had been genuine and still persisted. Was not that enough? Would she not take the opportunity of preserving what little self-respect she still retained by accepting the gesture at its face—or face-saving —value, and agree to shake hands and end the drama?

Lady Caroline refused to go quietly. March and April had been tiring and exciting months; May and June provided an even more distracting alternation of adventures in high and low life, as brisk a procession of balls, dinner parties and transitory love affairs. His correspondents were already becoming a burden. The letters of young and old, the letters of admirers, of stern critics who wished to take him to task for the voluptuous and atheistical heresies expressed in *Childe Harold*—Byron may or may not have thought it worth his while to answer these obscure or anonymous effusions; but they were seldom destroyed; and, among the pompous and long-winded reproofs administered by some writers and the hyperbolical enthusiasm of others, a far-away echo of real emotion can still be distinguished. Absent or present, he was a focus of storms. Scenes and situations he abhorred; but scenes and situations continued to pursue him; for not only on those who knew him well, but on his chance acquaintances, on men and women who had no knowledge of him except through his legend, his temperament had a curiously heightening effect. Thus, impulsive girls would commit themselves to the rake's protection. Such was Miss Isabella Lanchester, whose letter, headed *Strawberry Cottage, Fulham, May 6th* 1812, affords an odd hint both of the catholicity of Byron's pursuits and of the generosity by which his libertinism was often accompanied.

Her mother, she announces, has been "extremely unfortunate in business as well as in the choice of friends. . . . A person that I believe you are not unacquainted with has persuaded her to sacrifice her Daughter. . . . That mother who would six months ago have rather seen me in my grave than in a dishonourable way of life is trying to undermine that virtue of which she formed the basis. It is not my wish, my Lord, to appear romantic or falsely virtuous, but merely to undeceive you. When I did consent to your coming it was with an intention to claim that protection which my Friendless Situation requires. The proposal that was made to me will never be effaced from my memory. . . ."

The story behind this letter seems plain enough. The mother, perhaps a small and struggling shopkeeper, the wily *entremetteuse*— one of many who then carried on a more or less clandestine business round the west end of London—the young nobleman with whom the clever and accommodating old lady was "not unacquainted" and who, at her suggestion, had driven out to Strawberry Cottage. Tears and indignation met his proposal. . . . Notwithstanding certain discrepancies, this would appear to have been the episode that Byron had in mind when he told Medwin that a woman had once written, offering to let him have her daughter for a hundred pounds and adding the "excellent" postscript: "With *dilicaci* everything may be made *asy*." The same post brought him "a letter from the young one deprecating my taking advantage of their necessities, and ending with saying that she prized her virtue. I respected it too, and sent her some money."

From the tragedies of a remote and leafy suburb, it is a long journey back to the scenes of boredom, grandeur and dissipation where Byron's fate had temporarily come to rest. Even the Prince Regent now recognised him. Towards the end of June, finding himself at the same party as the most celebrated and notorious young writer of the age, the Prince gave orders that he should be presented; and an interview took place that gratified Byron's susceptible vanity, though his loyalty proved more difficult to capture. For the moment, nevertheless, he was flattered and charmed. On occasions, the Prince could be very gracious; the fascination of his youth, when he was the spoiled darling of the Whig party—the royal hope of Brooks's and Devonshire House—had not entirely deserted the middle-aged man, and there was yet a shadow of dignity in those puffy features. "After some sayings peculiarly pleasing from royal lips, as to my own attempts," he went on to speak of Sir Walter Scott, whom he "preferred to every bard past and present," discussing poetry with a "tone and taste" that gave Byron "a very high idea of his abilities and accomplishments, which I had hitherto considered as confined to manners. . . ."

Byron must have received these attentions with a somewhat uneasy conscience if he remembered, as no doubt he did, the unsigned but vitriolic satire, "Stanzas to a Lady Weeping" (otherwise "Sympathetic *Address* to a Young Lady") that he had published in the *Morning Chronicle* for March 7th. The young lady addressed was the Princess Charlotte. The Regent's heiress, who was now growing up and was reported to be "extremely spread for her age," had inherited her mother's concern with domestic politics. Hearing her father, who had "drunk immoderately," deliver an impassioned onslaught against his former Whig friends at a Carlton House banquet, she had burst into tears. ". . . It was just after the course - was removed. The Princess [Hobhouse learned from Miss Mercer Elphinstone] began to sob violently, and in spite of pushing round the dessert and other efforts, her emotion became sensible, so that the Prince said, 'You had better retire,' with which the ladies all rose; and the Prince, laying hold of Miss Mercer's arm, dragged her into an inner drawing-room, and sat there for half an hour. In consequence, Miss Mercer was forbidden, for eight months, the *entrée* of Warwick House."[1] The Prince's enemies had made much capital of this *contretemps*; but the virulence of Byron's anonymous attack had outdone them all. Feeling, conceivably, some need of justification, he was careful to explain both to Scott and to Tom

[1] The Princess's residence in Cockspur Street.

Medwin, describing his interview with the Regent many years
later, that, his politics being as perverse as his rhymes and his
curiosity "sufficiently allayed," he had never troubled to attend
the Prince's levée. Dallas, on the other hand, remembered finding
him "in a full-dress court suit, with his fine black[1] hair in powder,"
prepared for a levée that was afterwards postponed. The publication
of the "Stanzas" under his name made it impossible for him to
repeat his act of homage.

Meanwhile he wished himself out of London. To Professor
Clarke, author of six volumes of *Travels* which appeared between
1810 and 1823, whom he had met and with whom he had discussed
the landscape and inhabitants of Greece at Cambridge in 1811, he
wrote that he still sighed for the Aegean, "the bluest of all waves
and the brightest of all skies," and that he longed "to be restless
again and wandering." Financial miseries tormented him as of old.
The interest on loans contracted during his minority absorbed a
large part of his income; and, as the business of Rochdale was no
nearer solution, he had decided regretfully that Newstead must be
sacrificed. Hobhouse was sympathetic, but he could give no help.
". . . If I had but £5,000 a year," confided Hobhouse to the pages
of his well-filled diary, "life might then be a little tolerable. . . ."
Back from Ireland, penniless and unoccupied, at the mercy of a
father with whom he did not agree, it really seemed as if John Cam,
staunch and self-sufficient though he was, might fall a victim to
the disturbing influence that Byron radiated. Ennui and melancholy
cloud his journal. "Danced—" he wrote miserably; "nothing more
dull than the *beau monde*." "What is the use of reading or writing?"
he inquired elsewhere, and followed up this candid interrogation
by an extended analysis of the woes of human life.

His mention of political changes was comparatively cursory.
After the murder of Perceval, the Whigs had some hopes—soon
disappointed—of returning to office. "Lord Moira sent for. Whigs
coming in at last," Hobhouse noted on May 27th. "Whigs not
coming in," he added on the 2nd of June. Two days later, in the
company of Byron and Captain George Byron, his friend's cousin
and heir presumptive, Hobhouse left London for Newstead, there

---

[1]Byron's hair was not black; but he was accustomed to darken it by a liberal use of
macassar oil.

to spend what he described as "a week of delirium." Byron might never return to the Abbey. Perhaps it was his farewell visit to scenes so deeply entrenched both in his own past and in the past of his whole family that, beside them, the scenery of his new life appeared crude and insubstantial as a painted back-cloth; for Newstead was seldom absent from his mind. But the demands of London pursued him to the country. On the 10th, one of Lady Caroline's pages arrived, bearing a letter; and by the middle of the month he was back at St. James's Street. His "nervous" and distressful love affair resumed its course; Lady Caroline's volcanic heart was again in eruption.

Even Hobhouse could not escape the havoc it caused. Coming home on the 30th, he found "an odd note," written by Lady Bessborough, waiting for him at his lodgings; and, on July 2nd, having called at Cavendish Square, participated in "a very curious scene." A second note assailed him the following day. "Went to Byron [he adds] who agrees to go out of town." If Byron kept this promise, it is clear from subsequent entries in Hobhouse's journal that he did not remain in the country for more than a short visit. "Most strange letters from Melbourne House" reached his friend on the 8th; and on the 16th Hobhouse "walked, by desire, to Lady Bessborough's," where in the midst of an anxious conference Lady Caroline entered the room and, with her usual flighty humour, "talked of Lady Bessborough and myself looking guilty. Here's a pass for the world to come to!" exclaims the diarist, shocked by the wantonness of a feminine imagination.

A week earlier Hobhouse had visited Hanson, Byron's man of business, and "had a full account of Lord Byron's affairs. Poor Newstead! Things are bad enough in that quarter;" and, to make Byron's troubles yet more grievous, the storm that had been gathering presently burst over his head. The relief experienced by Byron's well-wishers and by her own friends, when they learned that Lady Caroline had retired to Brocket Hall, had been of very short duration. At the beginning of August it again seemed advisable to remove her from London; and Lady Bessborough, perhaps not the most tactful though certainly one of the most affectionate of mothers, drove down to Whitehall on the morning of the 12th and tried to persuade Lady Caroline to come with her to

Roehampton. William Lamb would join them the following Friday; and the whole party would then leave England, to spend what remained of the summer at the Bessboroughs' Irish country house. She found Lady Caroline in a bad temper. Lord Melbourne appeared while they were talking and "reproach'd her for some of the strange things she does;" and Lady Caroline "answer'd so rudely, so disrespectfully," that Lady Bessborough "was frighten'd and ran to call Lady Mel."

In her absence, Lady Caroline threatened to elope with Lord Byron. Her indignant father-in-law told her to go and be damned, but that he doubted if Lord Byron would have her; whereat the young woman whisked wildly out of his presence. Hurrying back, the two ladies met Lord Melbourne on the staircase, "pale as death, screaming to the porter to stop Caroline." It was of no avail. Darting downstairs and through the front door, she had vanished in an instant, "too quick for the servants who ran out after her to guess which way she had turned." There was an agitated consultation; and Lady Bessborough got into her carriage and drove backwards and forwards "in every direction I thought she could have gone." When she returned to Melbourne House, Lord Melbourne had so far collected his dishevelled faculties as to remember the original cause of the rumpus. Probably she was to be found at Lord Byron's lodgings. But, in the rooms at St. James's Street, whither Lady Bessborough and Lady Melbourne immediately resorted, they saw a man as puzzled, frightened and irritated as they were themselves. No, he assured them, he had heard nothing. It was not until much later in the day that a hackney coachman knocked at the door with a message for Byron's servant, asking him to tell his master that he would find a note from Lady Caroline at her mother's house in Cavendish Square. Byron followed this messenger and, with the help of threats and bribes, persuaded him to divulge the lady's hiding place. She had taken refuge, it transpired, at a surgeon's house in Kensington. From Whitehall, she had run along Pall Mall, had secreted herself in a chemist's shop, and, emerging when she supposed that the pursuit must be nearly over, had hailed a hackney coach and had ordered it to carry her beyond "the first turnpike off the stones."

The coachman had driven her to Kensington. "Think of the

bad look to the lacquais employ'd at Holland House," wailed Lady Bessborough, pouring out the whole sorry story to Lord Granville. At Kensington she had obtained twenty guineas by pledging a fine opal ring. Her plan was to go to Portsmouth and take a passage on the very next ship that sailed, "wherever it might happen to be bound for." *N'importe où hors du monde!* But she had not counted on the common sense and determination of which her lover now gave unexpected yet characteristic proof. Thrusting his way into the surgeon's house—"for she had refus'd to see him or any one, having told the people that she had run away from her friends and never would return to them"—he announced that she was his sister and, "almost by force," prevailed on her to accompany him to Cavendish Square. Summoned from a dinner party at the Duke of Devonshire's, Lady Bessborough joined her remonstrances and pleas to those of Lord Byron; and she was mortified to have to record that "it was more by his persuasions than mine, and almost reproaches at her bearing to see me suffer so much, that she was induc'd to return with me to Whitehall." Lady Bessborough went in first to prepare the way. The Melbournes, however, were "very good"; William "most kindly promised to receive and forgive her;" and Lady Caroline seemed moved and softened by their reception.

"I never saw so distressing a creature . . ." Remorse was soon followed by threats, talk of suicide by the declaration that she was with child and that, if she were obliged to leave London, she would certainly miscarry. Outburst followed outburst; and, to make the domestic tragi-comedy more complete, Lady Bessborough's housekeeper, one Mrs. Peterson, took the privilege of an old retainer and spoke her mind. "Cruel and unnatural as you have behaved [she wrote to Lady Caroline on Monday, the escapade having occurred the previous Wednesday] you surely do not wish to be the Death of your Mother. I am sorry to say you last night nearly succeeded in doing so." Lady Bessborough, it appears, had fallen in a fit at the bottom of her carriage. Could Lady Caroline have seen her at that moment, remarked Mrs. Peterson, she would have been convinced how wickedly she was going on; "she was perfectly senseless and her poor mouth Drawn all on one side and cold as marble. We was all distracted. Even her footman cryed out *Shame* on you, for alas you have exposed yourself to all London.

. . ." A few months ago, added Mrs. Peterson, it was Sir Godfrey; now another had turned her head and made her forget what a husband she had and what an angel child, besides torturing her indulgent friends and relatives.

The butt, according to her mother's servant, of "every Groom and footman about Town," Lady Caroline's behaviour was also the subject of conversation in far more exalted circles; and the Prince Regent, meeting his old friend Lady Bessborough at a party, told her that Lord Melbourne had been with him, "very much out of humour," complaining that the young woman drove him distracted and that "*we* were almost as bad," that Lord Byron had bewitched the whole family, "Mothers and daughter and all, and that nothing would satisfy us but making a fool of him as well as of ourselves. . . ." The Prince delivered his tirade in a loud and excited voice, interrupting himself now and then to exclaim: "I never heard such a thing in my life—taking the Mothers for confidantes! What would you have thought of my going to Lady Spencer[1] in former times?"; and Lady Bessborough, despite the occasion, came near to laughing.

Impossible not to sympathise with Lady Bessborough! But for Byron, the man who hated scenes, who valued more than all else the peace and quietude that were so seldom and so precariously his, the sympathy one feels is at least as profound. He was the centre of endless bustle and consultation. Would Caroline go? On the pretext that she was *enceinte*, would she refuse to leave England? Lady Melbourne was affectionate and understanding; but Caroline's mother—"Lady Blarney" as he called her—a woman who combined real intelligence in some questions with effusive sentimentality in others, seems to have brought out his most unamiable traits. Her he horrified by confidences or mock confidences. She had not been able to get away from Lord Byron, she reported, once he started talking to her. Part of the time he had talked of other matters; "but he did tell me some things so terrifying and so extraordinary! To be sure if he does mean to deceive he takes the strangest way of doing it I ever knew—unless a shocking notion the P. has, can be true—but I do think it impossible. It is too diabolick."

[1]Mother of Lady Bessborough and Georgiana, Duchess of Devonshire.

The only inference we can draw from this passage is that Byron, ostensibly with the purpose of convincing Lady Bessborough that he had no serious intention of upsetting her daughter's married life, either admitted to some relationship of a more scandalous kind or hinted that his real tastes were more esoteric. Was that the shocking notion the Prince had conceived? The passage is doubly provocative of thought since here, almost for the first time, we see Byron as the enemy of his own reputation, the master of auto-biographical innuendo, into which he afterwards developed. We must remember that his nerves were strained to breaking-point. Lady Caroline had fled from home on the 12th; and on August 14th Newstead was put up for sale at Garroway's Coffee House, a sacrifice to which he had resigned himself with the utmost bitterness. Hobhouse, though he had then one pound one shilling and sixpence in the whole world, helped to increase the price by bidding a dozen times. Whatever the morality of his manœuvre, it was unsuccessful. The reserve price was not reached; Hobhouse left off bidding at 113,000 guineas for the large lot; and the two lots, large and small, were bought in at 113,500 and 13,000 guineas respectively.

The autumn, however, produced a respite—if not from money troubles, at any rate from the cares of love. Lady Caroline had finally left London. She had promised not to see him again, to obey her mother, to do all that she could to make up for past faults; and by the first week in September he had the satisfaction of knowing that she was safely established upon the opposite side of the Irish Channel, with her husband and Lady Bessborough both in attendance. Not unreasonably, Byron felt that he had deserved a rest. He would go to Cheltenham. There is a strange contrast between this journey and the expedition that he had made to another watering-place, during the same month, in the year 1806. Then his companion had been an unpretentious Southwell crony, John Pigot. "We lived retired and made few acquaintances [Pigot wrote], for he was naturally shy, *very* shy;" and, after dinner, they had retreated quietly to their private room. Since those days his superficial shyness had vanished, to be replaced by a more fundamental sense of solitude.

Chapter 6

As ALWAYS, the "lone being" fell among friends. Lady Holland was at Cheltenham when he arrived; and although her departure left him, he protested, writing to her husband, in a state of philosophic isolation, he did not remain solitary for very long. During September he was surrounded by fashionable acquaintances, "a very pleasant set . . . Jerseys, Melbournes, Cowpers . . ." He had some ideas of continuing *Childe Harold*; meanwhile, at Lord Holland's special request, he was at work on a prologue for the reopening of Drury Lane Theatre, which had been closed since the disastrous fire of 1809. Its preparation would appear to have occupied several weeks. Byron's methods of versifying were usually slipshod; and it was perhaps the prospect of public recitation that induced him to write to Lord Holland no less than fourteen times, including suggestions, emendations and meticulous after-thoughts. But, notwithstanding the care and patience that it received, there is little that can be said in the poem's favour.

His task was finished; his acquaintances scattered. September glided away into October; but Byron still delayed at his lodgings in Cheltenham. "The only persons I know," he told William Bankes, "are the Rawdons and the Oxfords. . . ." Discretion required that he should give the Oxfords a second place; but to Lady Oxford he was indebted both for his immobility and for the comparative tranquillity of mind that had succeeded the nervous restlessness of the summer months. Once again his volatile heart had alighted on the nearest perch. Over his spirits had stolen the almost maternal charm of a woman as calm, accomplished and experienced as Lady Caroline was feverish and crack-brained, a mistress able to satisfy both mind and body. Between them was a gulf of two decades. It was in 1794, when Byron was six years old, that the Reverend James Scott, the vicar of Itchin in Hampshire, had married his pretty daughter, Jane Elizabeth, to Edward Harley, fifth Earl of Oxford, a personage "whose mind and body [Byron remarked] were equally contemptible in the scale of creation." Sacrificed when she was little more than a child, Lady Oxford had revenged herself by bestowing on her husband "a numerous family to which the law"—and the law alone—"gave him the right to be called father." Incidentally, she had a taste for classical scholarship; and her *libertinage* and her erudition went hand in hand. "Most uncommon in her talk, and licentious," she was also, Hobhouse found, "uncommonly civil."

It may have been with Lady Holland that she encountered Byron. Not until he reached Cheltenham, however, did the new love—at first somewhat obscured by his liking for a young actress and for a married Italian lady, against whom his chief complaint was the size of her appetite: she devoured enormous quantities of supper—begin to preoccupy him to the exclusion of all else. Happy is the love affair that has no history! Towards the end of October, Byron left Cheltenham for Eywood, Lord Oxford's house in Herefordshire; and it was there, either as an inmate of the Oxfords' household or as the tenant of Kinsham Court, the family dower house, which he had taken in order to be near his friends, that he remained, sober and contented, throughout the winter.

At last he could enjoy the semblance of domestic quietude. Hopes of settling down had not yet been abandoned; and with this design, some weeks before he left Cheltenham, he had written to Lady Melbourne, now one of his closest and most trusted friends, expressing a guarded interest in her niece. He had decided that he was "attached" to Annabella. He had never met a woman whom he esteemed so much; the effect of that placid countenance, those reserved and distinguished manners, had but increased during the storms of July and August; and her whole temperament, as he recollected it, was a promise of harmony. Love, after all, was beside the point. He was not in love with Miss Milbanke; but then, love was an emotion of which he had begun to doubt the real existence. He respected, he admired her. "She is a clever woman, an amiable woman, and of high blood. . . . Whomever I *may* marry, that is the woman I would wish to *have married*." It would give him a particular pleasure to become his dear Lady M.'s nephew; and he begged that his prospective aunt-in-law would do her best. Finally, after an animated correspondence, Lady Melbourne agreed to forward a proposal of marriage.

Miss Milbanke was neither startled nor unprepared. Characteristically, she had immediate recourse to pen and ink and paper; and, in the attempt to resolve her feelings, she not only set forth her views on marriage at some length but composed an ambitious portrait of her suitor. It reaffirms the impressions she had gathered in London. Among his tendencies, she announced, were many that deserved to be associated with Christian principles: "his love of goodness in its chastest form, and his abhorrence of all that degrades human nature, prove the uncorrupted purity of his moral sense." Yet, "from the strangest perversion that pride ever created," he attempted to conceal his own good points; while indignation and disgust had warped his outlook. Very different was the partner she demanded. A list of the qualities she would look for in a husband—which included "consistent principles of Duty," "strong and *generous* feelings," "an equal tenor of affection," adequate fortune, respectable connections and the manners and education of a gentleman, but did not include beauty, genius or rank—was posted to Lady Melbourne for her further enlightenment. Byron's proposal was definitely declined on October 12th; and the embassy closed with protestations of mutual esteem.

She feared, Annabella had written, that Lord Byron could never become the "object of that strong affection which would make me happy in domestic life;" and Byron's response was good-humoured to the verge of flippancy. ". . . She deserves a better heart than mine. What shall I do—shall I advertise?" he asked Lady Melbourne. But any hankerings after the haven of marriage that still remained had evaporated in the course of the next week; for it was then that he had definitely arranged to join the Oxfords. Of Annabella, he wrote, "I never was enamoured." Towards Lady Oxford, on the other hand, his attraction had grown steadily more and more pronounced; and when, over detestable roads, he had

driven down to Herefordshire, the haven that he found awaiting
him was far more satisfactory than any remote matrimonial refuge
promised by Miss Milbanke's "innocent eyes." Yet the two episodes
cannot be dissociated. Having grown up without a settled home,
with a mother for whom he had nothing but contempt, and a half-
sister of whom he was very proud but whom he rarely saw, Byron
had preserved such pictures of domestic happiness as usually form
themselves in the mind of a lonely or neglected child; and these
pictures still haunted the background of his imagination. Lady
Oxford was old enough to be his mother. There was something in
the mere fact of her maturity that appealed both to the more perverse
side of Byron's sexual temperament and to the love of peace and
order that oddly accompanied it. He had discovered the paradise
of which so many neurotics have dreamed, where mistress and
mother blend into the same person.

An autumnal paradise, voluptuous and calm. No tempests
raged here, as they had raged around Lady Caroline; no lava-streams
flowed; but a warm, restful sensuality pervaded the "bowers of
Armida," the Circean halls and groves, in which he now dwelt.
The enchantress herself was kind and seductive. Hoppner's portrait
shows us Lady Oxford as a young woman, pouting, pretty, with
soft, dimpled arms. And how much better that kind of beauty
suited her lover's somewhat Oriental taste than Lady Caroline's
exquisite angularity! He remembered her "with more than admiration;" the autumn of a beauty like Lady Oxford's, he informed
Medwin, was preferable to the spring in others. "She resembled,"
he observed to Lady Blessington, "a landscape by Claude Lorraine,
with a setting sun, her beauties enhanced by the knowledge that
they were shedding their last dying beams," but casting all about
them a diffused radiance. A woman, he continued, was grateful
only for her first and for her last conquest. "The first of poor dear
Lady ——'s was achieved before I entered on this world of care;
but the *last*, I do flatter myself, was reserved for me, and a *bonne
bouche* it was." She told him that she had not been in love till she
was thirty; "and I thought myself so with her when she was forty.
I never felt a stronger passion; which she returned with equal
ardour. I was as fond of, indeed more attached than I ought to
have been, to one who had bestowed her favours on many; but I was

flattered at a preference that had led her to discard another, who in personal attractions and fashion was far my superior."

Besides his memories of Lady Oxford, Byron kept in later life a medallion-portrait, carved in white shell, and a ringlet of soft brown hair tied with black silk. The hair was accompanied by four lines of doggerel:

> *Yes, Yes my Byron by this curl I swear*
> *Which never more shall join its kindred hair*
> *How much my panting heart will always prove*
> *Of faith in friendship and of truth in love.*

Signed ASPASIA, in Greek characters, these verses are a somewhat unkind reflection on Lady Oxford's poetical gift[1]; but there is no doubt that her contemporaries thought of her as a bluestocking, and that she was generally credited with a wide knowledge of the classics. Certainly her erudition impressed Byron. Feminine cleverness—in spite of his declaration that, give any woman a looking-glass and a box of sweets, and she would be happy—never failed to attract him, particularly when it was allied to good looks and did not preclude the more natural exercise of a woman's talents. Lady Oxford's children he adored. Nicknamed "the Harleian Miscellany," since their origins on the paternal side were vague and various, to Byron they seemed all of them "perfect angels." But Lady Charlotte Harley he loved best. The Ianthe celebrated in *Childe Harold*[2]:

> *Love's image upon earth without his wing,*
> *And guileless beyond Hope's imagining!*

this little girl left upon his mind an imprint of which the freshness and fineness recalled the faint yet never quite obliterated image of his cousin Margaret Parker—"one of the most beautiful of evanescent beings"—and his early recollections of Mary Chaworth.

Two curls—childish dark-blond tresses, labelled in Byron's handwriting *Charlotte H—— Nov. 10th 1812 and C. Hy. 1812-13* —found their way into his sentimental archives; and if, at a later and more unbalanced period of his life, he gave it out that he had attempted to seduce his mistress's thirteen-year-old daughter, the

[1] See *The Rape of the Lock*, Canto IV, line 133.
[2] In the Introduction to Canto I, which, although not published till February 1814, in the seventh edition, was written during the autumn of 1812.

suggestion was perhaps a kind of indirect and perverse tribute—conveyed with typically Byronic bravado—to the emotion that her charm and innocence had once inspired. That period, luckily, was far ahead. Delighted with his new family, he was genuinely devoted to Lady Oxford; and his only misadventure, during the first months spent among the "wild and beautiful" landscape around Eywood, was an incident that occurred when they were visiting the site of a Roman camp, and a stone, thrown by one of the children, struck him beneath the eye. Providentially the eye itself was not damaged. He was "a little laid up;" but, except for a slight scar, no real harm was done and, indeed, possibly some good, since, after the accident, his headaches disappeared.

"Sick of scenes," he wrote to Lady Melbourne, he had "imbibed a taste for something like *quiet*." ". . . *We* are very quiet," he added, during November, "and wish to remain so as much as C. and *others* may permit. . . ." It was Lady Oxford who summed up their happiness. Had they not spent the last two months, she exclaimed, like the Gods in Lucretius?—deities of whom it was written that they took no account of human life but dwelt, blissful and self-absorbed, on a plane far removed from mortal miseries and agitations. Such was the tenor of existence at Eywood. Distantly sounded the shrill grief, the endless teasing prayers, the shrewish recriminations of Lady Caroline; for, though in Ireland, she was not yet reconciled to a complete separation; and her letters, supplemented by Lady Bessborough's flurried and "hyperbolical" missives, still arrived with desperate regularity. Their recipient countered them as well as he could. He scolded, pacified and, buckling on the cardboard trappings of a Romantic lover, sat down to compose epistles that, he declared, were "worthy of the Grand Cyrus or the Duke of York,"[1] full of "the greatest absurdities." . . . There was always a danger that she might carry out her threat and return to England by the next packet-boat that sailed.

Lady Melbourne was his confidante and adviser. Their friendship, at least—the half-cynical, half-sentimental intimacy that had

---

[1] One of the most striking features of the parliamentary investigation of the Duke of York's conduct as commander-in-chief in the year 1809 had been the production of a number of extremely effusive love-letters to his mistress, Mary Anne Clarke

sprung up between the woman of sixty-two and the young man of twenty-four—was a pleasant by-product of his intervention, otherwise so prolific of woes and calamities, in the distressful affairs of Melbourne House. "If she had been a few years younger," he reflected afterwards, "what a fool she would have made of me had she thought it worth her while—and I should have lost a most valuable and agreeable friend." As it was, Lady Melbourne's mind and heart being "as fresh as if only sixteen summers had flown over her, instead of four times that number," their attachment hovered around, and yet never quite transgressed, the boundaries that divide friendship from carnal love and remained on the delicate footing of an *amitié amoureuse*.[1] And yet there were moments when it threatened to cross the line. Among the practical or humorous discussions of Caroline's vagaries, Byron would insert some phrase expressive of his own deep admiration for "dear Lady M." which drew from her a pleased but deprecatory response. His "high-flown compliments," she assured him, were undeserved. "I happen fortunately to be gifted with a fund of good nature and cheerfulness, and very good spirits—and have a little more *tact* than my neighbours, . . ." Byron had written that he admired her "as much as you were ever admired." She was duly flattered; but she could not understand, she replied, "why you should wish that you had not known me. It cannot lead to any regrets and if circumstances should not stop it entirely our Friendship will be very pleasant to both as any sentiment must be where all is sunshine—and where love does not intrude itself, there can be no jealousys, torments and quarrels."

In this atmosphere—one of friendship coloured with love, and of an almost filial respect tempered with sentimental familiarity—Lady Caroline's behaviour was discussed and analysed. Byron forwarded her letters, described the stratagems that he had employed to prevent her returning to England, and made fun of "poor Lady Bessborough" and "her hopes and her fears." Caroline, both correspondents agreed, was "no novice." They had come to regard her with something like hatred—Lady Melbourne because William

[1] Lady Melbourne, who might have been my mother, excited an interest in my feelings that few young women have been able to awaken."—Byron to Lady Blessington.

Lamb was her favourite son, and his wife did not conform to the rules of matrimonial infidelity as they had been understood by women of her generation; Byron because she was the enemy of his peace and quiet. In the last resort, that was Caroline's worst offence. Slowly but inevitably, she had begun to arouse the cold cruel strain—his heritage, it may be, from some Gordon or Byron ancestor, the Wicked Lord or another of the same breed—that lay concealed beneath the indolence of his disposition. Much effort was required to bring it to light. For several months Byron's attitude had been patient and conciliatory. He had reproved, expostulated, squandered his entire stock of "amatory tropes and figures;" but all this scheming and scribbling was of no avail. Having tried the effect of a somewhat exaggerated mildness, he now had recourse to an equally exaggerated brutality.

Lady Caroline was sent her dismissal during November. "One of the kindest letters he ever wrote" had been followed by a silence that persisted for ten days. Then Mamma received a "very gay" epistle from Cheltenham. He was angry, Lady Caroline knew, "at one I wrote—a very improper one, no doubt;" but she had heard "such things, such double things of his saying and doing," that with her "usual violence" she had burst into recriminations. The reply that she evoked was brief but crushing. "Correct your vanity which is ridiculous and proverbial," he had advised her, "exert your Caprices on your new conquests and leave me in peace, yours, Byron." At the moment Lady Caroline knew or suspected nothing of her lover's latest intrigue; and it was an unhappy chance that led her to confide in Lady Oxford. "My dearest Aspasia," she wrote— for Lady Oxford and Lady Caroline were old acquaintances— "only think Byron is angry with me!" Would Lady Oxford write to him and intercede on her behalf? She had done nothing to displease him; she was miserable; she had written a cross letter, it was true; but for that she had already begged his forgiveness a thousand times. . . .

The reply was a letter that, at the first glance, she imagined to have come from Lady Oxford; but, when she opened it, she discovered a note, written in Byron's hand, even more crushing and telegraphic than the first. "Lady Caroline," she read, "—our affections are not in our power—mine are engaged." Were he inclined to reproach her, he went on, he might do so for twenty thousand things. But he would not; and the letter concluded with some reference to "levity," "caprice" and the "mean subterfuges" with which she had attempted to persuade him that she was inconsolable, when, in fact, her life had been "wildly gay." Headed *Presteign*, this communication was sealed with Lady Oxford's private signet—"one I had myself shown him and laughed with him about" —the pretty classical intaglio, representing Cupid in a two-horse chariot, of which the impression may still be admired among Byron's papers. Afterwards, when the recollection of her woes and wrongs bubbled up into the narrative of her celebrated autobiographical romance, these two epistles formed the basis of the notorious *"Glenarvon* letter," sent to Lady Avondale at the instigation of her lover's unscrupulous mistress.[1] The actual letter, according to contemporary gossip, was "really dictated" by Lady Oxford; and she is reported to have been very much offended that Lady Caroline "treated the matter so lightly as to introduce it into her book."

For Lady Caroline, her dismissal seemed the end of all things. In Ireland her life had been one of irresponsible gaiety, alternating with sudden outbursts of rage and despair; and the new blow precipitated a crisis. Her mental equilibrium never had been sound; Byron's letter, she told Lady Morgan, temporarily deprived her of her reason, and she returned to England ill, nervous and distraught. It was in this state that she visited her cousin.[2] Contented herself, happy with her fascinating husband, delightful children and a country house which she loved "beyond expression"—particularly during the summer months, when she had described it as "in radiant beauty, all over roses, rain, sunshine"—Harriet Granville had little patience to spare for a young woman whose behaviour was so extraordinary and whose reputation was already so bad.

[1] In addition to a glimpse of Lady Oxford, *Glenarvon*—otherwise almost entirely unreadable—contains an amusing portrait of Lady Holland as the Princess of Madagascar.

[2] In the collection of Lady Granville's letters, edited by her son, the letter describing Lady Caroline's arrival is dated *September* 12th. It is obvious from Byron's letters to Lady Melbourne that Lady Caroline was "safely deposited" in Ireland by this date; it seems probable, therefore, that the visit was paid when the Bessboroughs were on their way home from Ireland.

She hated "her character, her feelings, and herself" when she was away from her; but "she interests me when I am with her," and to see "her poor careworn face," worn to the bone, pale as death, her eyes starting out of their orbits, was indeed dismal. Caroline appeared to be in a condition "very short of insanity, and my aunt describes it as at times having been decidedly so." Her spirits, while they lasted, were "as ungovernable as her grief." At supper on the day of her arrival she was "excessively entertaining;" Lady Bessborough, who, despite the anxieties she had gone through, looked stout and well, was "very gay and amiable;" and William Lamb laughed and ate like a trooper.

Here, in this strange gathering, flanked by William Lamb's philosophic indifference and her mother's sentimental resignation, beneath her cousin's part disapproving, part understanding and sympathetic gaze, a novelist might end Lady Caroline's story. Lady Caroline, alas, was irrepressible. She must have a final interview with Lord Byron. Her guardians gave way; but, when Lady Melbourne advised that a third person should be present, the witness Byron chose was Lady Oxford. As it happened, Lady Oxford refused to play the rôle to which she had been allotted; and the interview did not take place until the following spring. Byron "looked sorry for me," Caroline remembered. "I adored him still, but I felt as passionless as the dead. . . ."

Meanwhile, she had burnt her lover in effigy. It was during December, when she was alone at Brocket Hall. Village girls, dressed all in ghostly white, danced around the pyre; and Lady Caroline herself, clad in the livery of one of her own pages, committed to the flames Byron's book, his ring and chain, and copies of his letters, the original letters being carefully preserved. Against the background of a wintry park, where the cold damp mists of Hertfordshire lay low among the beech trees, Byron's waxen effigy shrivelled, melted and slowly collapsed into the flames. Hand in hand, the village maidens—apparelled, presumably, with the help of her Ladyship's maid, in cast-off dresses or muslin frocks run up for the occasion—performed their embarrassed and hesitating dance, as Lady Caroline thrust her relics on to the blaze:

See here are locks and braids of coloured hair
Worn oft by me, to make the people stare;

Byron

Rouge, feathers, flowers, and all those tawdry things,
Besides those Pictures, letters, chains, and rings . . .
Burn, fire, burn, while wondering Boys exclaim,
And gold and trinkets glitter in the flame.

Her next thought was for the open-mouthed rustic audience:

Ah! look not thus on me, so grave, so sad;
Shake not your heads, nor say the Lady's mad . . .
Upon my youthful faults few censures cast.
Look to the future—and forgive the past.

London, farewell! . . . she concluded triumphantly.

Young tho' I seem, I quit the world for ever . . .

Learning of these fooleries in his Olympian retirement at Eywood, Byron may have hoped that she would keep her resolution, while doubting if she had the necessary strength of mind. In practice, though her importunities grew more spasmodic, for several years they would continue to exasperate him.

Thus, in January, she executed a daring *coup*. Having burned Byron's effigy, she began to regret apparently that she had no likeness of him, and forging his hand, wrote a letter to John Murray, installed in his new offices at Albemarle Street, requesting him to deliver up a miniature portrait. The ruse was impudent, but completely successful. Lady Caroline presented the letter, abstracted the portrait and wrote to Byron, describing what she had done. Between laughter and rage, Byron reported the whole transaction to Lady Melbourne; this, he observed, was "flat Burglary." If he had any tenderness left for Lady Caroline, the story of the Brocket *auto-da-fé*, her own information that she was amusing herself by having her pages' buttons inscribed with a parody of his family motto: "*Ne* Crede Byron," her threats of vengeance, and now this latest and wildest idiocy—involving, as it did, a member of a different social class—confirmed him in his attitude of savage contempt.

Except for a brief visit to London, by way of Cheltenham and Middleton, where he stayed with his friend Lady Jersey, he had enjoyed an almost unbroken, but entirely contented, seclusion since his arrival at Eywood more than two months earlier. January brought heavy falls of snow; but, some time at the beginning of February, he drove up to London, accompanied by Lady Oxford, and took rooms, not far from his old lodgings, at No. 4 Bennet

114

Street, St. James's. As soon as the spring came, it had been arranged that he should join the Oxfords in an expedition to Sicily. The idyll of the autumn and winter was to be prolonged among the flowers and ruins of the ancient world. Unfortunately he had very little money. Just after the failure of his attempt to sell Newstead by auction, a prospective purchaser—one Mr. Claughton—had made a private bid; but it now transpired that he was unable to complete the purchase price; and the ensuing negotiations dragged on through 1813 and 1814.[1]

Byron, however, was determined to go abroad. At first, April was fixed, then May; but, instead of crossing the Channel, he returned to Eywood, and there spent the greater part of April, "on the water and in the woods, scrambling and splashing about with the children," by himself or in the absorbing society of his mistress. Lady Charlotte he continued to adore. A pity that she must one day grow up! Yet he would probably marry her, he informed Lady Melbourne, when she was "old enough, and bad enough to be made into a modern wife." As always, there was the inclination to settle down; but those few weeks at Eywood—its reading, music, blind-man's buff, the children, Lord Oxford's old aunts who had lived in aristocratic retirement since the days of Owen Glendower, his bedroom decorated, most appropriately, with a picture of Rinaldo and Armida—were his last glimpse of the possibility of Lucretian happiness. Here, too, there were hints of an approaching storm. Lady Oxford had withstood the attacks of Lady Caroline—otherwise "Phryne" and "Little Mania"—unruffled and unalarmed; but once the lovers had parted, and Armida was in Cheltenham while Rinaldo braved the perils and perplexities of London, she broke a small blood vessel and complained of being weak, worried and ill—"all of which she attributes to 'me and my friends in town!' "

At a later period he spoke of her inconstancy. Even for a woman as experienced as Lady Oxford, Byron was a difficult, despotic and, now and then, an exceedingly disagreeable lover; and it was no doubt after their return to London, during February 1813, that they visited the Princess of Wales (whose cause Lady Oxford had championed) and that her antechamber was the scene

[1]Towards the end of 1814, Claughton forfeited £25,000.

of a painful *contretemps*. "Lady Oxford, poor soul [wrote the loquacious Princess, to her confidante, Lady Charlotte Campbell] is more in love this time than she has ever been before. She was with me the other evening, and Lord Byron was so cross to her—his Lordship not being in a very good mood—that she was crying in the anteroom." Elsewhere she remarks that "Lady Oxford has no thought but for Lord Byron. . . ." Both letters are undated; and judging by the fact that the Princess wondered if Lady Oxford would succeed in captivating him—"she *can* be very agreeable when she pleases"—it would appear that she was singularly ill-informed. What she took for the birth-pangs of a love affair were really signs of its impending dissolution.

Besides mentioning the various "civilities" for which he was indebted, a party, at which "a man with a flute played a solemn and somewhat tedious piece of music," and an occasion when the Princess, visiting Lady Oxford, tripped over a domestic utensil on her dressing-room floor—"a minute sooner, she might have stumbled on something still more awkward"—Byron's letters contain no references to his intimacy with this eccentric, blowsy, indiscreet, yet not unsympathetic, royal personage whom an unkind fate had thrust into the Regent's arms. During the year 1806, a commission, appointed to examine her conduct, had acquitted her of the charge of having given birth to an illegitimate son; but, notwithstanding their criticism of her general behaviour, Caroline of Brunswick-Wolfenbüttel remained the free-spoken, loud-laughing, irremediably undignified German princess whose vulgar manners and dirty petticoats had once offended Lord Malmesbury. The court she kept was nothing if not bohemian; and she wore out the ladies and gentlemen who composed her household by "pro-longed rambles over the heavy fields and impassable lanes" of Blackheath—a form of amusement that was voted only one degree less improper than "her scrambles through the streets of London, when going to a public masquerade in disguise."

As a good Whig, Byron owed her his support; and it was in the same capacity that, during May, he visited Leigh Hunt, then enjoy-ing a not uncomfortable term of imprisonment in Surrey Gaol, whither he had been relegated for an attack on the Princess's husband. Hunt had already once escaped from the law; but when the *Examiner*, in March 1812, exasperated by the almost Oriental eulogies of the *Morning Post*, stigmatised this "Glory of the People" and "Adonis in Loveliness" as "a corpulent man of fifty . . . a violator of his word, a libertine over head and ears in disgrace, a despiser of domestic ties, the companion of gamblers and demireps, a man who had just closed half a century without one single claim on the gratitude of his country or the respect of posterity," Leigh Hunt and his brother had been convicted, fined and each sentenced to two years' imprisonment. Hunt's spirits, however, were indomitable. There was something in the reformer's mercurial temperament both engaging and, more than often, a trifle repulsive, since he combined genuine sincerity with the worst type of journalistic facility, and poetic feeling with the exuberant mannerisms of a Cockney poetaster. Yet it is difficult, after all, not to like and admire him. He had entered gaol in February 1813; and it was not long before books, flowers and busts, a piano and a ceiling painted to represent the sky, had transformed the cell of the modern Hampden into as pretty a suburban parlour as had ever embowered the puns and arguments of his literary friends. Mrs. Hunt and his children were soon installed. Altogether "the wit in the dungeon" was one of the blithest of political prisoners; but his acquaintanceship with Byron might have been more productive had he been able to forget that "the compact, energetic, curly-headed person" who arrived with Tom Moore was by birth a lord, and had his snobbery—which he was inclined to reveal by a somewhat distressing parade of manly independence—not transferred itself to his notably self-conscious visitor.

Politically the two writers were much in accord. Hunt's martyrdom, though not very onerous, was a dramatic proof of the tyranny exercised by Lord Liverpool's government; while Byron's advocacy of "freedom" had made its mark. He had not yet abandoned his political interests. His second speech, supporting the Catholic claims, which was delivered on April 21st, 1812, had "kept the House in a roar of laughter"; and these early triumphs were to be followed up by a petition, presented on the 1st of June, 1813, that "gave rise to some debate" and evoked hostile notices from *The Times* and the *Herald*. But, although lively, his enthusiasm was not very deep. "He was totally ignorant," wrote his acidulous friend

John Cam, "of the points in dispute . . . in any . . . question of politics"; and Moore relates how the orator called on him, after presenting the petition and, while his host dressed for dinner, strode backwards and forwards in the next room "spouting in a sort of mock heroic voice, detached sentences" of the speech he had just delivered. "I told them," he declared, "that it was a most flagrant violation of the Constitution—that, if such things were permitted, there was an end of English freedom, and that——" "But what," Moore mildly interrupted, "was this dreadful grievance?" "The grievance?" echoed Byron, halting as if to take thought. "Oh, *that* I forget."

No wonder Hobhouse (who professed, by the way, to have had a considerable share in composing Byron's parliamentary speeches) regarded his political pretensions with a certain scepticism. Dear fellow, of course, he was on the right side! But, as to why he was on the right side, an old friend might be pardoned for doubting if, at the best of times, he was always very clear. Not unnaturally, Hobhouse was apt to resent such brilliant but superficial expeditions into a field that he hoped himself one day to conquer; and Hobhouse's judgment, however prejudiced, seems to have been accurate. Byron was not—nor, granted the nature of his genius, could he ever expect to become—a man primarily concerned with the welfare of his fellow human beings, a liberator driven by a sense of social injustice or a *doctrinaire* politician impelled by a theory. For Byron there could be no escape from his destiny in the mass excitement of political life. Ambition had consumed him since his boyhood; but it was a passionately self-centred craving; and none of his previous achievements had brought him any real solace. What have I done? he would ask. What am I? The author of *Childe Harold.* . . . But *Childe Harold*, though he had now come to value it at its proper worth, was perhaps nothing more than a freak of fortune. Was versifying his real *métier*? True, with the help of pen and ink, he could give vent to some of his dammed-up energy; but for the youth who had pictured himself as the scourge or saviour of the realm, destined to write his name large in letters of blood and fire—

One rank'd in some recording page
With the worst anarchs of the age

it was an odd and unexpected termination—this life that he was condemned to lead, surrounded by hysterical women, importuned by admiring correspondents, a hero whose celebrity was due not to his rank, not to the distinction of his intellect, but to a fictitious personage with whom his credulous readers had chosen to identify him.

Yet, being an inveterate fatalist, Byron slipped easily and almost painlessly into a resigned acceptance of his lot. He spoke in the House of Lords; but, although he had enjoyed his triumphs, he decided that "parliamentary schemes are not much to my taste." He had "no intention," he said, "to 'strut another hour' on that stage." And so (he continued) he wasted the best part of his life, "daily repenting and never amending." What else was there for him to do? Fate had cast him for the rôle of poet; and, obedient to a vocation with which he was by no means in entire sympathy, he published during the spring of 1813 *The Giaour* (an Eastern tale, which must be described in conjunction with its successor, *The Bride of Abydos*) and *The Waltz*, an anonymous satire, the fruit of long and acrimonious vigils in London ballrooms where he had observed the "whirling propensities" of more agile friends.

What he needed for his personal happiness was an equally perplexing problem; but it was plainly affection of a kind that had already been foreshadowed by the months of Olympian retirement passed with Lady Oxford—some love that, although warm and sensuous, should not be exclusively sexual in its character and should draw its strength from its quasi-domestic origin. He had thought that he could be happy with a woman whom he respected but whom he did not love. Lady Oxford had shown that the woman who made him happy might very well be older than himself, and combine the attractions of a mistress with the charm of a member of his own family, and that, besides arousing his passion, she must calm and comfort him. Lady Oxford had united these diverse functions; but even Aspasia, as we have noticed, could not withstand the somewhat shattering nervous effect of Byron's society, and wrote from Cheltenham in an unusually distracted mood. His voyage to Sicily had now been postponed until the early summer. Claughton's delays were never-ending; and in an attempt to ease his situation Byron ordered John Hanson, his man of business, to sell horses,

books (except for one or two improper volumes, which he wished
burned), plate, linen, pictures—"every moveable that is mine, and
can be converted into cash." All he wanted, he told his patient
underling, was a few thousand pounds; "and then adieu. You
shan't be troubled with me these ten years, if ever."

Once again he would launch into the void. Pending her
departure, he spent ten days with Lady Oxford at Salthill, near
Maidenhead. But that sojourn—an effort, it may be, to re-evoke
the fabulous and unforgettable blisses they had tasted at Eywood—
would appear to have been productive of fatal results; for, although
he went down to Portsmouth to see his friends off[1] and promised
that, later, he would try to join them, he himself gave up the
projected journey. Lady Oxford sailed on June 29th, and Byron
returned to his London rooms alone.

---

[1]Though Byron went down to Portsmouth, he seems to have returned to London
before their ship set sail.

Chapter 7

"TO TELL THE TRUTH," Byron remarked to Lady Melbourne, writing with the information that Lady Oxford had sailed yesterday, he felt "more *Carolinish*" about her than he had expected. The love affair that had "continued without interruption"—with few scenes and almost without a single yawn—"for eight months" was now dead and buried, and he was free to resume his restless life. So far as London was concerned, the Byron Fever of 1812 showed signs of dying down. London had a new object of curiosity; and on June 21st Byron dined out to meet the author of *Corinne*, who had lately arrived in the metropolis, accompanied by her eldest son, her daughter and her unacknowledged second husband, M. de Rocca, the good-looking young officer whom she had married in 1811. Although not the most agreeable, Madame de Staël was "certainly the cleverest" woman whom Byron had encountered. But she talked too much; instead of conversing, she declaimed; and English audiences, at first puzzled and impressed, were afterwards amused by the thick, coarse-featured foreign bluestocking whose face—to which "one or two irregularly prominent teeth" gave an air of "habitual gaiety"—grew animated and floridly handsome as she unfolded her dramatic monologue. No one evinced so little tact. On the supposition that she was a Liberal, Madame de Staël was invited to certain Whig gatherings; but, since her exile by Napoleon, her politics, Byron found, were "sadly changed;" she was all "for the Lord of Israel and the Lord of Liverpool," and emitted these heterodox preferences at the top of her voice.

Sheridan made fun of her; and the Dandies—Brummell, Mildmay, Alvanley and others—who disliked literary persons in general (though, it was gratifying for Byron to be able to record, "they were always very civil to *me*") "persecuted and mystified" Madame de Staël, told her that Alvanley, who was deep in debt, had an hundred thousand pounds a year, until she complimented that very ugly exquisite on his beauty and did her best to capture him for her daughter Albertine, "and a hundred other fooleries besides." But, if Madame de Staël was conscious of these snubs and humiliations, she did not allow them to daunt her; and from her house in George Street, Cavendish Square,[1] she proceeded to carve herself out a large and important niche in London society, and to collect friends and admirers in both political camps. Even Byron forgot his dislike of her views; and they became very good friends. Yet, belonging as she did to a nation that lays it down that any woman, provided she takes pains, should have the privilege of quickening the pulses and exciting the interest, amatory or intellectual, of almost any man she meets, Madame de Staël was somewhat exasperated by the poet's sleepy and supercilious manners, his habit of sitting at dinner with his eyes half shut, and the dreadful blasphemies he presumed to utter against love. He was "totally *in*sensible to *la belle passion*," she declared, in the course of a vociferous attack delivered over a dinner table, and *had* been all his life. He had "no right to make love . . ." "*C'est un démon!*" she cried; and, her interlocutor being Lady Caroline Lamb, no doubt she received a confirmation of her theory. "True enough," noted the demon, "but rather premature;" for as yet she had no opportunity of finding out.

It was not unflattering to be compared to a bad angel; and, describing his own character, "fallen spirit" was an expression that Byron had already used. Among his male friends, however, he was anything but diabolic. John Cam, a staunch defender of his friend's wholesome humanity, had recently gone abroad; but Tom Moore was again in London; and it was during the spring or summer of 1813 that they passed a hilarious evening at Rogers's house. Very different was this occasion from the famous dinner party, held less than two years before, in November 1811. Byron was now sure of himself and of his company. After a supper of bread and cheese,

[1]Madame de Staël eventually moved to a house at Richmond, chosen for the view, which she found "*calme et animée: ce qu'il faut être, et ce que je ne suis pas.*"

The Years of Fame

Byron and Moore, notwithstanding Rogers's decorous protests, appropriated a presentation copy of Lord Thurlow's poems and began to hunt through the volume in search of absurdities. Byron discovered some verses addressed to their host, "On the Poem of Mr. Rogers entitled 'An Epistle to a Friend' ":

When Rogers o'er this labour bent,
Their purest fire the Muses lent,
T'illustrate this sweet argument.

But, although Byron made several efforts to read them aloud, he could not get beyond the first two words. "When Rogers . . ." he would begin and then break down. Moore, too, was overcome by the demoralising influence of Lord Thurlow's solemn congratulations; Rogers himself gave way; and the three poets were soon reduced to "a state of inextinguishable laughter."

Remembering such episodes, Byron's intimates would ask themselves if this were the behaviour of a "demonic" being, perverse, melancholy, embittered by the recollection of past sins. To laugh with him was a sure road to his heart. Byron's requirements, like those of many over-complicated characters, were, on the whole, extremely simple. He needed—he felt that he deserved—a family; and it was during June, soon after Lady Oxford's disappearance, that his half-sister—the only relation nearer than a cousin whom the fate that seemed to pursue all Byrons had left alive—came up to join him from the country. Brother and sister had corresponded in 1811; an advance copy of *Childe Harold* had been dispatched to Augusta in 1812; but afterwards some coldness had supervened; and it was not until March 1813, when he was yet in the thick of his affair with Lady Oxford, that Mrs. Leigh had written again, this time asking for financial help. Byron had delayed answering because he still hoped that Claughton would pay the price agreed, and that any day would bring information "that might enable me to reply better than by apologies." But Claughton, alas, would not, or could not, pay, with the result (he told Mrs. Leigh, writing to her, finally, on March 26th) that he was "not less embarrassed than ever," and in no position to alleviate her troubles.

He would like to see her, nevertheless, before going abroad. He wished (he added pensively) that she was "not always buried in that bleak common near Newmarket". Byron has his fame, the love of women at whose mention he imagined his sister putting on a slightly *"demure"* look—"which is very becoming and matronly in you;" while Augusta, at her house at Six Mile Bottom, was engrossed by the cares of a large family—children who fell sick and must be nursed, bills that clamoured for payment but that there was no means of paying, and Colonel Leigh, "that very helpless gentleman," one of Lord Darlington's horsy friends, the member of a fast and bibulous racing set.

Fortunately, Colonel Leigh was seldom at home. Having left his regiment under a cloud, Augusta's husband (who was also her first cousin) moved from race meeting to race meeting, from country house to country house, as he went borrowing, staking and losing considerable sums of money; and, although Augusta had prosperous connections—the Duke of Leeds, her half-brother by Lady Carmarthen's early marriage; Lady Chichester, her half-sister, and various others—the Leighs themselves were never out of debt. Only Newmarket races brought the colonel home. In Byron's story he was to take little direct share; yet, as a figure in the background— a personified problem, the source of endless worry and vexation— he emerges clearly enough, shifty, feckless, improvident, the type of military gentleman with a past to which his friends are careful not to refer, who has a strong head, no luck and a fund of blusterous bonhomie. . . .

A character not seen at his best in family life. But Mrs. Leigh, beset by difficulties, surrounded by ailing children, accepted her lot with a resignation that was part Christian—for she had inherited the pious phrases of a devout grandmother, and gave away prayer books when she was in the mood—part pagan and the natural product of her volatile temperament. Above all, she was an easy-going woman. Neither intelligent nor stupid, she belonged (says Lord Lovelace) to "that great family—often very lovable—which is vague about facts, unconscious of duties, impulsive in conduct." That Augusta *was* lovable, we cannot doubt. The "kind of moral idiotcy," declared by one of her severest critics to have distinguished her behaviour since birth, might equally well—and perhaps with greater justice—have been described as an elasticity that knew no bounds. She was childish, good-natured, muddle-headed. In March she had written to her brother, appealing for the help that

Byron was unable to give; and by the summer of 1813 the creditors who besieged Six Mile Bottom had grown so obstreperous that even Augusta's optimism was daunted. She was constrained to disband her Newmarket household and take refuge in London at her brother's side.

She had arrived on June 26th. Since the death, in 1801, of Lady Holderness, Augusta's grandmother, who detested Mrs. Byron, brother and sister had corresponded but had very rarely met; and it was a comparative stranger—a somewhat blasé yet extremely fascinating young man of twenty-five—who welcomed her between one and two that afternoon. Augusta herself was twenty-nine. The mother of several children, she had never been considered a beauty; and, in the discussions that raged many years later, there were those who asserted that Mrs. Leigh had not the smallest pretension to good looks, that she was a dowdy personage, motherly and unprepossessing. This account does not agree with her portraits. No offspring of "Handsome Jack" Byron's could have been entirely plain; and Hayter's pencil portrait, executed in 1812, shows us graceful shoulders, a long elegantly moulded neck and a head that suggests some touches of charm and distinction. Holmes's miniature is far more realistic; painted during the third decade of the century, it reveals a serious face, dark expressive eyes beneath dark, rather heavy eyebrows, a sentimental mouth, a broad forehead and, over it all, dark glossy hair piled, looped and ringleted in the fashionable taste of the period. Like Byron's, Augusta's features were better seen from above—from the forehead and eyes—than from below. Round her wrist is fastened an elaborate bangle; and one feels sure that Mrs. Leigh was the sort of woman who favours small inconsequent scraps of finery, and that, if she was "smart," it was in a capricious and untidy style. One pictures her attractive but slightly dishevelled, laughing at, yet also a little flustered by, her want of proper neatness.

She always enjoyed a joke at her own expense. What a relief, after Six Mile Bottom, the tradesmen, the moneylenders, Colonel Leigh either away on his travels or at home demanding that she should help him prepare his racing correspondence, to find herself in London, laughing with her brother at trifles of which they—and they alone—seemed to appreciate the comic point! They discovered that their sympathies and antipathies were strangely the same. "Baby B.," the somewhat pathetic product of her father's second marriage, the boy at Harrow who had written her so many angry and tempestuous scrawls, lamenting the dullness of Southwell and the intractability and violence of his mother's character, was now an *homme à bonnes fortunes*, his life full of secrets, his drawers and portfolios full of the feverish letters, the curls, verses and portraits that devoted women sent him. Only Augusta remembered his early life. She knew the darker aspect of the Byron heritage; but it was her greatest charm that, whereas other women might be convinced that he was a demon—the destructive, and self-destructive spirit that in his more sanguine moments he felt sure that he was not—Augusta regarded him with endearing simplicity. Her companionship helped him to forget the Byronic doom. Only Augusta could reconcile him to himself.

During the next few days they were much together. It was a "new *sensation*" indeed, arranging for Augusta to be invited to a party given by Lady Davy, bluestocking wife of the famous chemist, or escorting her, more fashionably, to Almack's Masque. Her society, he told Moore, was a great comfort. And, as if to emphasise his good fortune, on July 6th he was the unwilling object of one of the most violent and ridiculous scenes in which he had so far been involved. Superfluous to add that its author was Lady Caroline. Throughout June the desperate young woman had been "quiet to a degree of *awful* calmness;" but during the week that preceded Lady Heathcote's ball she had been "in a dreadful bad humour;" and, with Lady Caroline (as her mother-in-law observed), once the process of fermentation had begun, there was no arresting it until it had at length burst forth. Presumably she suspected that she would meet Byron. She must have gone to Lady Heathcote's (decided Lady Melbourne) "determined to pique you by her waltzing;" and when their hostess, anxious to get her party under way, begged Lady Caroline to take the floor, she had agreed, though she protested that she was not in the mood. Then she leant towards Byron, who was standing near her. "I presume I may waltz *now*," she murmured dramatically.

"With everybody in turn," Byron replied. "You always did it better than any one. I shall have a pleasure in seeing you." "I have been admiring your dexterity," he added a little later as he met her with Lady Rancliffe at the entrance to a small inner room where supper had been laid. Lady Caroline's response was to seize his hand and press "some sharp instrument" into the palm. "I mean to use this," she whispered. "Against me, I presume," Byron said, and turned to follow Lady Rancliffe, whom he was taking in to supper. "Byron!" cried Lady Caroline and rushed away. . . . What happened during the next few minutes she scarcely knew. She had grasped a knife (she explained afterwards) but she had not intended to make use of it. The other women had screamed. People had pushed and struggled. She had been terrified; and, in the confusion, "my hand got cut, and the blood came over my gown." According to Lady Melbourne, the knife was imaginary; she had broken a glass and scratched herself, whereat Lady Ossulstone and Lady Heathcote, instead of taking it from her, had lifted up their voices in shrill alarm. Lady Melbourne, however, had flown to the rescue; and she had "just left off holding her for two minutes," when she returned to find Lady Caroline wounding herself, "but not deeply," with a pair of scissors.

Meanwhile the cause of the trouble was quietly at supper. Politeness (he excused himself to Lady Melbourne) had not permitted him to desert Lady Rancliffe; besides, he had imagined that the whispered threat—delivered in so staccato a stage-whisper that he had trembled lest it should be overheard by "Ld. Y. or Ly. R."—was merely a piece of the usual rodomontade. It was not until four o'clock in the morning that Lady Ossulstone," looking angry (and, at that moment, ugly)," had given him some kind of confused message from Lady Melbourne, concluding, with feminine absence of logic, that to have provoked such a scene Lord Byron must surely have behaved very ill. Other female friends were of the same opinion, Lady Westmorland asserting that he "must have done something;" between people in that delicate situation a word or a glance were apt to go a long way.

For his part, he was exasperated and aggrieved. He had said nothing, done nothing; and, if he was to be "haunted with hysterics" wherever he appeared and whatever he did, Lady Caroline (he considered) was not the only person who deserved pity. Even Lady M. seemed disapproving. Back at Melbourne House, a draggled mænad, her ball dress, and the few shreds of reputation she yet retained, spattered and soiled beyond repair, Lady Caroline had been hurried off to bed. As always, William Lamb was mild and forgiving. But the scandal was enormous. "I never held my head up after—never could," Lady Caroline declared; and while friends wrote to commiserate with Lady Melbourne, enquiring parenthetically if it were really true that "poor Ly. C. L.," besides wounding herself in several places, "at last was carried out by several people actually in a strait waistcoat," the newspapers gave their version of the episode. It made a splendid theme for journalistic enterprise —*Scandalum Magnatum!* And under a quotation borrowed from *Rejected Addresses,*

> *With horn-handled knife*
> *To kill a tender lamb as dead as mutton*

The Satirist offered its readers a facetious and highly flavoured account of how Lord B——n, who was a great favourite with Lady C. L——b, at Lady H's ball had "seemed to lavish his attention on another fair object. This preference so enraged Lady C. L. that, in a paroxysm of jealousy, she took up a dessert knife, and stabbed herself. The gay circle was, of course, immediately plunged in confusion and dismay, which, however, was soon succeeded by levity and scandal. . . ."

Even worse was a reference to his lame foot. Once before Byron had escaped from the devastating effect of Lady Caroline's passions and follies into the quasi-maternal society of Lady Oxford; and it was now Augusta who provided consolation. Augusta invariably made him laugh. Childish she might be, foolish, muddle-headed, full of inappropriate pieties and of evasive speeches, couched in that odd vocabulary of hers which Byron afterwards described as Augusta's "damned crinkum-crankum." . . . But, though he respected intelligence, Byron's temperament had stronger and more fundamental needs; and mere cleverness was incapable of solving his problems. He was both simpler and more complicated than he at first appeared. "His character is a labyrinth; but no clue would ever find the way to his *heart.*" Yet whereas the woman who wrote these words—a clever woman, one who knew him well and suffered all the power of his attraction—groped patiently but in vain for the mysterious clue, Augusta by some miracle had picked up the thread. In part, she owed it to the accident that they were brother and sister; in part, to the very simplicity of her pagan spirit.

Simplicity suits with complication. Had Augusta been doubly related to him but, instead of the "Goose" he was coming to know and love, a woman proud of her intelligence and, like Miss Milbanke, of her ability to take an intellectual, rather than uncritical and instinctive, view of men and things, she might have failed as deplorably as her successors and her predecessors. Gifted with equal virtues, but unrelated to him, she might also have failed; and it was the combination of these two unconnected factors—consanguinity and a strong natural sympathy—that formed the strength of her peculiar and lasting influence. As maternal, as comfortably a pagan, as Lady Oxford, she had the romantic charm of being united to him by ties of blood.

His family formed the basis of his romantic attitude. Classicism implies an acceptance of the present; but Romanticism, alike on its revolutionary and on its picturesque and archæological side, looks to the future or to the past[1]—to the future where dreams of liberty and equality seem to be rising; to the past when men were nobler, their passions more violent and their lives more brightly, variously and dramatically coloured than they are to-day. For all his early hankering after public distinction, Byron's romanticism was of a private, retrospective and essentially egocentric type. In common with many Romantics, he raised ghosts; and the phantoms he evoked were those of the unhappy, tempestuous, tormented families whose blood had met in his—Stuart sovereigns; the mad Gordon line that had produced his mother; his grand-uncle the Wicked Lord, and his grandfather the Admiral, known to shipmates as "Foul-Weather Jack," since a hurricane sprang up whenever he sailed. Such was his "inheritance of storms," such the ancestral load that made it impossible to steer the innocuous and unadventurous course reserved for ordinary human beings. Only a Byron could understand a Byron; and it was with a sort of pride that, in a poem written to Augusta after he had left England, he dwelt on the burden of their descent:

[1] "What is Poetry?—the feeling of a Former world and Future."—Note in Byron's Ravenna Journal.

Byron

A strange doom is thy father's son's, and past
Recalling, as it lies beyond redress;
Reversed for him our grandsire's fate of yore:
He had no rest at sea, nor I on shore.

Augusta herself partook of the Byronic heritage; but her response was as rudimentary as his was romantic. It gave perhaps an additional potency to Augusta's spell that she remained so gaily impervious to the fate they shared.

As a matter of course, Byron dramatised the situation. Self-dramatisation came naturally to him; but to say that Byron's temperament was histrionic is not to suggest that he was a charlatan, or that the emotion aroused in him by everything that pertained to his own destiny, and to the general destiny of his race, was false, affected or insincere. At best, his character was a pattern of opposites; indeed, there is scarcely a quality, moral or intellectual, to be discerned in Byron's make-up that cannot, at one time or another, be balanced by its exact antithesis. Thus, he was impetuous but cautious; devoted to his friends and yet, in many respects, an extremely untrustworthy intimate; soft-hearted, yet distinguished, now and then, by a streak of deliberate and cold-hearted cruelty; a lover of quiet and yet a perpetual focus of storms; generous and open-handed, yet, at all events in his later period, the "damned close calculating fellow" of whom his Italian acquaintances often complained; puritanical but promiscuous; a person of rare common sense, a man of the world blessed with a sceptical and disbelieving irony, and yet the prey of superstitions without end. He was the Romantic and Wanderer *malgré lui*. Fate, he would have said, or the Goddess Fortune, for whom, like Sulla (he noted in his *Detached Thoughts*), he had a particular regard, had portioned out the good and the bad, had made him a public figure—angel or demon— when what he most desired was the quietude of private life. "I have always believed," he announced, "that all things depend upon Fortune, and nothing upon ourselves." And, when he looked back, as even at the age of twenty-five he was frequently prone to do, the inevitability of his career confirmed this notion.

Who could have predicted his extraordinary rise? Brought up as a Calvinist, Byron retained the Calvinist dogma of predestination, though he had outgrown its framework of Christianity. He was a

Calvinist with leanings towards agnosticism. The little boy, frightened by his Scottish nurse, had become the adolescent who mused upon the legend of his wicked and passionate forebears. It had seemed improbable, when he was born, that he would inherit Newstead; and yet his destiny, by a series of unexpected turns, had raised him to the semblance, if not to the reality, of power and wealth. His story had something in common with that of Œdipus, a descendant of kings, reared amid humble surroundings, yet marked by signs of greatness from his earliest days—Œdipus the lame-footed, who returned to his birthright only to involve those who were nearest to him in death and disaster. If Œdipus was a predestined being, so was Byron. He did not act of himself; it was his fate always that appeared to be working through him, that had beckoned him home from Greece (where he might have passed his whole life in contented indolence), thrust *Childe Harold* into Robert Dallas's eager, officious grasp, given him fame and love (usually in the shape in which these gifts were most unwelcome), kept him at work on the treadmill of fashionable celebrity, and now, at a moment when he had intended to go abroad—Claughton's shufflings alone had held him back—brought Augusta to his side in London.

She had found him in a restless and unsatisfied mood. . . . But, at this point, the historian of Byron's life is obliged to make a pause, for he is standing on the brink of one of the most formidable biographical controversies that have ever shaken the peace of English letters, a question that has been discussed, quarrelled over, interred, raised again from the dead, since the spring of the year 1816. During July 1813 an event occurred that changed the whole course of Byron's personal life. It was an event that those whom it concerned did their best to envelop in the deepest secrecy; though Byron himself could not forbear hinting, both in his correspondence and in the diary he afterwards wrote, that a secret there was, that it tormented him, that it was seldom out of his thoughts, but that there were weighty and terrible reasons why it could never be unfolded.

There seems nowadays little doubt that the secret concerned his relationship with Augusta Leigh. When controversialists of the last century sought to exculpate Mrs. Leigh by asserting that her attitude towards Byron was that of a mother, they stumbled,

I think, quite unawares on a very important aspect of Byron's temperament. Lady Oxford, too, had been maternal; and for an amorist so passionately self-centred there was a special charm in the thought that this woman, who supplied the domestic affection for which he had always longed, was no stranger but a part of his own background, and that her existence was complementary to his. Again one remembers his Calvinist upbringing. Doomed at birth, the wicked are as powerless to escape damnation as is the hero of classical tragedy to free himself from the mechanism of fate. It was not good, believed the ancients, that a man should exist on a more grandiloquent emotional plane than the majority of his fellows. Perils surround a man who leaves the herd. A single misstep, a moment of thoughtless arrogance, of impious curiosity; and the act of *hubris* has been committed; from which *ate*—infatuation—must soon result. Caught up in the consequences of an impious gesture, the hero moves on rapidly to his predestined fall.

Levity prepares the way for tragedy. That Byron envisaged the disaster as very largely of his own making is sufficiently proved by a couplet in the verses *To Augusta*, from which I have already quoted:

> *I have been cunning in mine overthrow,*
> *The careful pilot of my proper woe*

and by a passage in a letter to Lady Melbourne, written at the end of April 1814, in which he refers to his mysterious preoccupation. They have both of them, he declares, but more particularly himself, done "*my* A" (so called to distinguish her from "*your* A," Annabella Milbanke) a grave injustice. ". . . Really and truly—as I hope mercy and happiness for her—by that God who made me for my own misery, and not much for the good of others, *she* was not to blame one thousandth part in comparison." She had not been conscious of her own peril till it was too late to draw back; "and I can only account for her subsequent '*abandon*' by an observation which I think is not unjust, that women are much more *attached* than men if they are treated with anything like fairness or tenderness."

It was Augusta's simple belief—the practical philosophy with which she had supplemented her grandmother's rigid ethical precepts—that what one did was of very small consequence provided one made nobody else unhappy. Augusta, in spite of her training, was amoral; Byron, in spite of his antecedents, an immoralist acquainted with the sense of sin. Had Byron been an unreflecting pagan, it is possible that the act that caused so much misery might never have been precipitated—for then it would have lost the charm of the unlawful—or, if precipitated, that the havoc it caused would have been relatively slight. Byron, however, was an immoralist, a man who sins with a consciousness of wrong-doing, and sins again because the sense of guilt demands always fresh fuel. From his earliest youth he had brooded on his misdemeanours.

> *For he through Sin's long labyrinth had run*
> *Nor made atonement when he did amiss . . .*

wrote the Romantic versifier of 1811; but at that period, notwithstanding the "Paphian girls" of Newstead, and the "laughing dames" of London and Brighton, the beauties of Seville and the *beaux yeux* of Mrs. Spencer Smith, Byron was at least as innocent as most of his friends; and, before 1809, when, according to Robert Dallas, the poet "broke up his harams"—"oriental luxuries" (noted Tom Moore) which "the narrowness of Lord Byron's means would alone have prevented"—we have the word of his companion in travel and pleasure that there had been "no debauchery save a little . . . or a good deal of drinking." Such was the harmless record of *Childe Harold*. Few aspects of Byron's life are more interesting than the relationship between the man and his legend, between the gay companion, whom Hobhouse and Moore loved, and the Childe, his gloomy *alter ego*, a personage he might disown but from whose shadow he was never able to escape. For, although in many respects false and absurd, *Childe Harold*—so nearly *Childe Burun*—expressed a very important side of its author's temperament. At the time when the poem was composed, this side was only half discovered; and, besides being autobiographical, the image created was prophetic of features that had not yet come to light but were implicit in the young man's character. Once launched on the painful process of self-discovery, regardless of suffering it was his destiny to work it out.

Certainly, whatever the spirit in which his new adventure had been begun—whether it was in a spirit of idle experimentalism, of bravado or of genuine overwhelming passion—it was continued in no light-hearted mood. There was "a mixture of the terrible" (he confided to Lady Melbourne, at the beginning of the following year) about the feelings that had recently preoccupied him, which rendered all other feelings—"even passion (pour les autres)"— uninteresting and insipid. In his journal, mentioning a portrait for which he had sat during the summer, he observed that it was dark and stern—"even black as the mood in which my mind was scorching last July . . .;" while to Tom Moore, on August 22nd, he wrote of "a far more serious, and entirely new, scrape than any of the last twelve months, and that is saying a great deal."[1] Elsewhere this serious scrape is described—again to Moore—as "a strange summer adventure which I don't like to think of." But the thoughts he dreaded were hard to subdue. As distinct from every previous escapade—transitory affairs dictated by opportunism, vanity or the all-absorbing need of human affection—this new love troubled the deepest springs of his nature. There is no doubt that his attachment was profound—the more profound, one may surmise, because it was associated inevitably with feelings of dread and remorse, and threatened lover and beloved with common ruin. He declared afterwards that it had satisfied him as nothing else could. For once the whole range of his emotions was brought into play—from the simple and domestic to the demonic and the perverse—and there ensued a wild turmoil of conflicting impulses. The dark and sulphurous mood of the summer months left an indelible trace on the colours of his imagination.

Turning back to the controversial literature that has sprung up round the events of July and August 1813, and their sequel, the events of 1815 and 1816, one observes that commentators who have gone to heroic, and in certain instances, slightly fantastic lengths to rebut the charges against Byron and Augusta, have left the ethical side of the question almost undisturbed. Byron must be defended because incest *per se* is disgraceful, abhorrent and flagitious; yet the same commentators accept the irregularity of Byron's life in London, and the squalid and discontented debauchery of his career in Venice, with an understanding smile or shrug. Byron the rake is a popular figure. On the other hand, if moral standards are to be

[1] In a footnote to his edition of Byron's letters, Lord Ernle suggests that this passage refers to Lady Frances Webster. The subsequent publication of the Letters to Lady Melbourne has made it clear that Byron and Lady Frances were not yet acquainted.

invoked (which, when we are dealing with Byron, proves very often an awkward and ineffectual business), as much disgrace attaches to escapades entered without love, affection and, in many instances, without real desire, as to a passion that engrosses the faculties of mind and heart. Never was Byron less the cynic, the opportunist, the casual or calculating philanderer, than in a *liaison* of which he subsequently wrote that it had left him "utterly incapable of *real* love for any other human being—for what could they be to me after *you?*" His love might well annihilate its object; but that, he believed, was always the property of his devotion.

Outwardly, his life went on as before. Wretchedness, he told Lady Melbourne, had the effect of making him relax the strict diet to which he usually adhered; with the result that, by the end of July, his head ached "with the vintage of many cellars" and his brain was "as muddled as their dregs." When he was miserable, he could grow fat without showing it. . . . We have his own authority for the suggestion that during July he was in an exceptionally dark and tormented frame of mind; and, Byron's life being a drama in which the chief actors never miss the opportunity of providing an effective contrast, it was at this moment that the clear, cool tones of Annabella Milbanke were again heard—the voice of the "extraordinary girl" who had never forgotten him. Since his proposal she had encountered her suitor but once. During the spring they had met at a London party; and, as he pressed her fingers, she noticed that he seemed shaken and was deathly pale. From that time she had done her best to avoid another meeting; but when a story reached her that Lord Byron had behaved harshly and unfairly towards the young man who had purchased Newstead, she wrote to Lady Melbourne, expressing a hope that the report was untrue. Byron was able to contradict the rumour,[1] and Annabella, relieved and flattered, sent her thanks.

Described by her biographer as "one of the longest letters in the world, containing some of the longest words in the English language," Miss Milbanke's opening epistle was not composed

[1] He pointed out, in his reply to Lady Melbourne, that Claughton was not a young man, that he had made his original offer after due consideration and that, although he had tried to avoid his obligations and had driven him (Byron) to Chancery, he had not himself complained of ill-treatment.

until August 22nd; and meanwhile there had been many changes of mood at Bennet Street—Byron desperate; Byron flippant; Byron the sentimentalist, temporarily so happy in his own affairs that he could afford to be charitable to Lady Caroline when she wrote him "a most rational letter, full of good resolves," and "a most tempting basket" from Hertfordshire, full of grapes and gooseberries; Byron the *homme du monde*, intervening to prevent a duel between Lord Foley and Scrope Davies; finally, the Byron whose hints or revelations gave his confidante cause for serious anxiety. He had announced that he was going abroad with his sister. It was a wild scheme, a dreadful, an impossible project; and Lady Melbourne (we learn) warned him that he was on the verge of taking a fatal step, that he stood on the brink of a moral precipice. It was a crime, she said, for which there was no salvation in this world, "whatever there might be in the next."

Evidently she had been drawn into the Byronic web—into the network of confidences, half-confidences, hints and autobiographical innuendo—that the poet was inclined to weave around his friends. Amusing to be able to shock dear Lady M.! In the earlier stages of their acquaintanceship it was Lady Melbourne, no doubt, the cynical *grande dame*, who had shocked the comparatively inexperienced and naturally somewhat puritanical worldling; and her pupil now repaid her with compound interest. Lady Melbourne must be a good woman after all, he remarked jocularly, "for there are things she will stop at." Nevertheless, her expostulations did not pass unheard. Her kind letter, he wrote on August 31st, was "*unanswerable.*" He was still in London, "so that it has as yet had all the effect you wish;" and there was no further talk of the proposed journey. Towards the end of August Mrs. Leigh returned to Newmarket, and left Byron to the dubious comfort of his own reflections.

Chapter 8

Lady Frances – a new scrape – platonism in peril – "my little *white* penitent" – Byron's journal – headaches and nightmares – Byron's correspondence – his relations with the middle-class public

WHEN Augusta returned to her small and uncomfortable house at Six Mile Bottom, not far from the famous Heath and but a stone's throw from the main London-Newmarket road, she took with her, among other memories and tokens, a portrait of Byron that had once belonged to Lady Caroline Lamb[1] and a seal—the classical intaglio of Eros driving a two-horse chariot—that had been bequeathed to her brother by Lady Oxford.[2] It was doubtful if Byron himself would follow. Lady Melbourne, horrified by a situation in which, for all her worldly *sang froid*, she must have felt that she was hopelessly out of her depth, appeared to have urged him to remain in London; but on the 8th he announced that, come what might, he was determined to go down to the country for a few days, and that, as he was sure Lady Melbourne would get the better of his resolution, he had decided not to see her in the meantime.

He would write, he added, providing "nothing very particular" occurred. If it did—well, she would probably hear *of*, "but not *from*, me (of course) again." Adieu! he closed dramatically; whatever he was, whatever and wherever he might be, he was still most truly her obliged and faithful Byron. . . . Then the Romantic mood suddenly and swiftly dropped. Byron's "stay at Cambridge," he told Lady Melbourne on September 21st—and for "Cambridge," presumably, we must read "Newmarket"—had been very short. It

---

[1] "To the picture I plead guilty. I thought I had already said to you as I did to C. that it was for Augusta, who took it with her, I believe, into the country." Byron to Lady Melbourne.

[2] There is an impression of this seal on a copy of verses from Lady Oxford. A drawing of the same seal appears on the title page of Lord Lovelace's *Astarte*, where it is described as "Augusta's Seal from a Letter to Byron of December 1814."

was long enough, however, to unsettle him. Back in London, he felt "feverish and restless;" and in this mood he accepted the invitation of an old friend, James Wedderburn Webster, whom he joined at Aston Hall, Rotherham. By an odd coincidence, his father had once lived at this very house, which had come to him through Augusta's mother, Lady Carmarthen; but Byron had temporarily thrown off the dark preoccupations that had held him captive during July and August, and glanced around him with a sharp and critical eye. His hostess was "a pretty, pleasing woman." Married to Wedderburn Webster since 1810, she was in delicate health; and her husband, a verbose and self-important personage, took an early opportunity of preaching his guest a sermon on his wife's virtues, winding up with the assertion that "in all moral and mental qualities, she was very like 'Christ'!!!"; at which Byron laughed so much that his friend began to grow peevish. The Virgin Mary, hazarded Byron, would have been more appropriate; for Lady Frances seemed innocent, devout and retiring.

On his side, he was perfectly content that she should remain so. Lady Melbourne (we are informed), summoning all her worldly ruses, had advised him to start a new love affair and had even gone to the length of providing him with "most minute" instructions as to the technique he should adopt; but the seducer's was never a rôle that suited Byron's natural laziness; and during his first visit, which lasted until, towards the end of September, the Doncaster races drove him back to London, he regarded Aston merely as a house where he could snatch a few days of comparative quiet—the Websters' children, he noted, only screamed "in a low voice"— and pass his time in not uncongenial company. He was happy to leave love-making to others. Webster, who had a passion for seeing his wife admired, was also preposterously jealous; and when Lord Petersham[1] arrived, as he was expected to do within the next week—a dandy who had a snuff-box for every day of the year, a lisp, "a particularly winning smile," a habit of never venturing

[1]Gronow has left an account of this extraordinary personage: "I was then taken to Lord Petersham's apartments, where we found his lordship . . . employed in making a particular sort of blacking, which he said would eventually supersede every other. The room . . . was more like a shop than a gentleman's sitting room: all round the walls were shelves, upon which were placed tea-canisters, containing Congou, Pekoe, Souchong, Bohea, Gunpowder, Russian, and many other teas, all the best of the kind;

out till six o'clock at night, magnificent carriage-horses and a
fondness for brown which was attributed to his "having been
desperately in love with a very beautiful widow bearing that name"
—Byron looked forward, he wrote, to "some comic Iagonism
with our little Othello."

Against Petersham, he subjoined modestly, he himself would
have no chance; but, "in an innocent way," he believed that a
better-dressed, handsomer and more lively person might make
some impression on this dutiful, but pensive, Desdemona. He really
believed that Lady Frances was "a very good, well-disposed wife,"
who would do excellently if she were not carried off by consumption
or teased and bothered by her husband into downright hatred.
At all events, it was none of his affair. "The *Astonian* family" had
asked him to repeat his visit; but, once he had returned to London,
where he dined at Holland House, was "electrified" and "delighted"
by Curran, and observed that Lady Holland had "grown thin and
gracious," he was prevailed on to travel north again, not so much
for the sake of the Websters themselves as to collect a poodle with
which they had presented him, and which for some reason he had
left behind.

He was at Aston on October 5th. But his interest in Lady
Frances was now becoming vivid. Petersham, it transpired, had
excused himself; and, since there was no stray dandy to distract her
thoughts, the young woman's imagination was still unoccupied.
Byron's reputation as a roué had preceded him. She expected to be
attacked, he had noted in an earlier letter, and seemed prepared to
put up a brilliant defence. Byron's quiet and casual behaviour was
extremely disconcerting; and she had begun to think herself ugly
and her husband's friend "blind—if not worse." It remained for
Webster to supply a leaven of absurdity; *Il Marito* boasted about his
bonnes fortunes, about the foreign countess to whom he was just then

---

on the other side of the room were beautiful jars, with names, in gilt letters, of innumerable kinds of snuff, and all the necessary apparatus for moistening and mixing. . . .
Other shelves and many of the tables were covered with a great number of magnificent
snuff-boxes, for Lord Petersham had perhaps the finest collection in England, and was
supposed to have a fresh box for every day in the year. I heard him, on the occasion
of a delightful old light-blue Sèvres box he was using being admired, say, in his lisping
way—'Yes, it is a nice summer box, but would not do for winter wear.' "

laying an obstinate siege, about his wife's principles—"she can't go wrong, and therefore I may"—all in the same pompous and blustering vein. Byron suffered him, with an inward smile. Calm and malicious, he watched the husband, in one of those sudden bursts of fondness that were almost as embarrassing as his fits of jealousy, seize and kiss her hand before his guests, and note her expression of lifeless indifference—a symptom that struck him more forcibly "than if she had appeared pleased, or annoyed."

There was "a something interesting enough in her manner and figure." Pretty yet "not surpassing," graceful but "too thin and not very animated," Lady Frances had married to escape a bad-tempered family—had been "killed in covert" when she had not been out two months—and breathed an air of mild sentiment and resignation. She was the very "Soul of melancholy gentleness." Slender, fair, with long dark eyelashes, she moved through life fragile, acquiescent and subdued. When Moore encountered Lady Frances a few years later, he observed that, although "she must have been very pretty when she had more of the freshness of youth," at five or six and twenty she was already faded; and Byron had appeared at a critical moment. Would she slip unappreciated into middle age? Was she to remain always the faithful wife and chattel of an unfaithful and ridiculous busybody? It was Byron's task to introduce her to herself. With his fatal aptitude for arousing in the lives of others the same atmospheric disturbances that ravaged his own, he drew out all her power of passionate feeling. Whereupon, a little perturbed by the extent of his triumph, he gazed incredulously at the wild spirit he had set free.

Odd, he reflected, how women changed! The transformation undergone by Lady Frances proceeded at a rapid pace; and the pretty, pious young woman of October 5th—his gentle, retiring hostess, somewhat apprehensive in the proximity of a notorious London rake—in three days' time was a very different person. Taking his cue from her hypothetical query: what should a woman do, if she liked a man and he was not aware of it? Byron had ventured a declaration. His opportunity was a game of billiards. He had "made a speech," he informed Lady Melbourne, and the speech had been well received. Next, he had written her a letter; and, the letter having been conveyed to Lady Frances at considerable risk, he had had the satisfaction of seeing it deposited not very far from her heart. At this instant, who should enter the room but "the *Marito!*" Nevertheless, the billet had prospered and had produced an answer, "a very unequivocal one," though couched in excessively platonic language. Still, lovers generally *began* and *ended* with platonism; and "my proselyte," being but twenty, would no doubt improve.

He trusted, however, that "this spiritual system" would not last long; and, in a postscript to his letter of the 8th, written at six o'clock that evening, he was able to record that the affair was growing serious; that platonism had been "in some peril;" that there had been a stolen meeting, fresh protestations, a consolatory embrace—all of which, he supposed, must end in the usual way, and would have done so then, "had 'l'occasion' been *not* wanting." A second postscript described dinner in Webster's company. While he sat writing to Lady Melbourne, Webster would run into the room to ask his friend's opinion on a political pamphlet he had just composed; and these interruptions gave the correspondence an added gusto. Never had his letters been more diverting. If August had shown Lady Melbourne a Byron she did not know, and at whom she scarcely dared to look, during October she was comforted and reassured. At length they were back upon familiar ground. In a style reminiscent of, and perhaps suggested by, *Les Liaisons Dangereuses*, they exchanged their long, detailed, cynical, amusing letters; and, whereas Lady Melbourne assumed the rôle of Madame de Merteuil, wise, witty, machiavellian, Byron played the part of the crafty Valmont, calculating, disillusioned, the man who sat at dinner with the husband, listened to him as he prated of his conquests or proposed a bet "that *he*, for a certain sum, wins any given *woman*, against any given *homme*, including *all friends* present," then limped off to pursue the seduction of the wife.

Such was the picture that his letters drew. But although carefully cultivated, the Byronic *fanfaronnade des vices* never quite carries conviction. He was less the seducer, we have reason to suspect, than the sensationalist who tampered with emotions that he could not help arousing; less the frigid and calculating roué than the opportunist who, in a lonely and inhospitable world, must

warm himself at every chance-lit fire. Lady Frances had presented
an absorbing study. Anything delighted him, he remarked to Lady
Melbourne, that confirmed or extended his observations on life
and character; and from curiosity he proceeded to practical experiment. With the exception of a brief visit to "the melancholy mansion
of my fathers," accompanied by his garrulous and amorous friend,
Byron remained at Aston until the middle of the month, when he
invited the whole party—husband, wife and wife's sister, Lady
Catherine Annesley—to join him as his guests at Newstead. Once
more the situation had a spice of absurdity, Webster still sighing for
his obdurate countess, Lady Frances displaying unexpected guile,
Lady Catherine, the spectator, suspicious and inquisitive. Their
host himself was moody and preoccupied. After dinner, among
bottles of red and white champagne, burgundy, two sorts of claret
and lighter vintages, the gentlemen sat up late; and on one occasion
Byron was imprudent enough to drain his silver-mounted skull-cup,
which held rather more than a bottle, at a single draught; with the
result that he was obliged to retire to bed, where he was first
"convulsed" and presently lost consciousness.

His love affair, meanwhile, had reached a climax. Characteristic
in its inception, the episode was equally characteristic in its closing
stage. Byron had hoped much from the visit to Newstead. The
house was large, ancient, rambling and romantic; there were gardens,
cloisters, passages. An occasion soon presented itself. The lovers
were undisturbed; two o'clock in the morning was the hour; and
Lady Frances cast herself on Childe Harold's mercy. Let him do
with her what he pleased! She was not cold, she exclaimed, however
she might appear to others; but she knew that she could not endure
the remorse that a complete surrender must entail. That was the
truth; and now he might act as he chose. . . . In her words and
attitude there was a desperate calmness, "a kind of mild decision,"
that Byron, deeply versed though he was in all the stratagems and
vagaries of love, found very "peculiar." No struggle, no scene.
It was not the reluctant refusal that is the prelude to rapturous self-
abandonment, not the politic negative that he had heard so many
times before. In the silence, the Devil whispered that it was
"mere *verbiage*;" but the Devil had not counted on his disciple's
temperament—on its strange interludes of heartfelt tenderness and

pity. Half regretfully, he resigned the conquest when it was within his grasp; and platonism—despised platonism—regained the day.

"My little proselyte" became "my little *white* penitent," bewildered, shattered by her experience, happy in her escape, unhappy in the grasp of a love that she admitted she could not control. On the 19th the lovers bade good-bye. It was a restrained parting; for Lady Frances, "a moment of torture," and, when she felt his hand—that soft expressive hand—locked in hers "and stole a look at that *too dearly cherished countenance*," she suffered "the true horror of separation." Webster was also making the journey. "Seized with a sudden fit of friendship," he had announced that he was anxious to go to London; but the fact was that Byron, in a burst of compunction or generosity, had arranged to lend him a thousand pounds. Away rolled the carriage towards Nottingham. "Silent for hours, with the most ferocious expression possible on his countenance," Byron sat, his loaded pistols at his side. After a time, his *vis-à-vis* grew restive. "For God's sake, my dear B.," he expostulated, "what are you thinking of? Are you about to commit murder? or what other dreadful thing are you meditating?" Woken from his reverie, Byron replied that he had always had a presentiment that his life would be attacked, and this fear induced him to travel fully armed; "it was . . . the subject of his thoughts at that moment." Yet it seems likely, had Webster been capable of guessing it, that the subject of Byron's thoughts was considerably nearer home.

He was still prepared to go to any length—a duel, an elopement. . . . Although he regretted that he had failed to take advantage of "the best opportunity that ever was wasted upon a spoiled child," and that he had left Aston and Newstead having reaped only a harvest of "foolish trophies," he was now ready and willing to fly to the end of the earth. Foolish trophies, indeed, but oddly pathetic! Modern research[1] has brought to light the notes that were smuggled to Byron at Newstead or posted to him after his return to London; and Lady Frances's rapture and misery have been laid bare. Her letters were long, passionate and beautifully written.

[1]See the article based on hitherto unpublished letters by George Paston in the volume entitled *To Lord Byron:* Paston & Quennell: Murray, 1939.

She loved dearly (wrote Lady Frances), she more than loved—but never, never would she survive her *fall*. She had scribbled to him last night—this was at Newstead; but next morning she was ashamed of her guilty confession. She sent him two ringlets from her blonde head. Once he left the house, she had sat a whole hour in the window, tears slowly running down her cheeks.

Was the consciousness of having behaved well a little irksome? It was not a sensation to which Byron was much accustomed, or to which he ever took kindly; as a general rule, he preferred to remain a reprobate. The third week of October found him in London; and, his periods of activity being usually followed by spells of lethargy, ennui and introspection when he took refuge from his thoughts in verse, a new poem was soon ready for the printers. Having finished it, he immediately began a journal. Written, with many interruptions, between November 14th, 1813, and April 19th, 1814, this diary—a loose stringing together of reflections, memories and day-to-day records—was one of the most fascinating, revelatory and highly characteristic documents that Byron had yet composed. In his verses, naturalness was out of the question; spontaneous as were the brilliant descriptive gifts displayed by his letters, he was well aware of the effect that they produced; only his journal shows us Byron behind the scenes. Not that he was entirely unself-conscious; but here he wrote with the self-consciousness of an actor in the seclusion of his dressing-room.

His first sentences set the tone of the ensuing pages: "If this had been begun ten years ago, and faithfully kept!!!—heigho! there are too many things I wish never to have remembered, as it is. Well,—I have had my share of what are called the pleasures of this life, and have seen more of the European and Asiatic world than I have made a good use of. . . . At five-and-twenty, when the better part of life is over, one should be *something*;—and what am I? nothing but five-and-twenty—and the odd months." What had he seen? "The same man all over the world,—ay, and woman too. Give me a Mussulman who never asks questions, and a she of the same race who saves one the trouble of putting them." Had circumstances not disposed otherwise, by now he might be basking in the obscurity and voluptuous freedom of some Near-Eastern land. He might yet escape—provided, of course, that he neither married himself nor unmarried any one else during the interval. He wished . . . "I don't know what I wish. It is odd I never set myself seriously to wishing without attaining it—and repenting."

How different is the personality that suddenly appears before us in these jottings from the desperate, lachrymose young man who had endured the loneliness of Newstead, haunted as it then was by the ghosts of three lately vanished friends, during the tragic autumn months of 1811! He was still bored, still troubled by his memories, vexed by shadows of the past and future; but now there was "a mixture of the terrible" in the thoughts that obsessed him. ". . . Last night," he records on November 14th, "I finished *Zuleika*, my second Turkish Tale. I believe the composition of it kept me alive—for it was written to drive my thoughts from the recollection of—

Dear sacred name, rest ever unreveal'd.

At least, even here, my hand would tremble to write it." *Zuleika*, afterwards renamed *The Bride of Abydos*, describes the mutual passion of a boy and girl who believe themselves, though mistakenly, to be brother and sister, and whose love is eventually crowned by death. "All convulsions end with me in rhyme;" but, though it soothed him, rhyme was powerless to recall the past; and the past, like some enormous invisible burden, seemed to accumulate at every listless step he took.

Yet flippancy was perpetually creeping in. *Heigho!* half sigh, half yawn, the word is continually breaking through the restless and uneven surface of Byron's recorded meditations; and we imagine him, a more elegant prototype of the discontented dandy whom Shelley was to meet in Venice, rising from his table and lounging towards the window, where he would bite his nails and gaze down into the murky expanse of Bennet Street—"I will go out of doors, and see what will the fog do for me"—before he wandered back to the half-finished page. Nightfall brought the usual choice of amusements. Now he was dining at Holland House; now in a masculine company that included Canning, Hookham Frere and "Conversation" Sharp; now planning to attend a party where he hoped to meet "that blue-winged Kashmirian butterfly of book-learning, Lady Charlemont," whose head and shoulders, he thought,

were the most beautiful he had ever seen.[1] Then the fashionable
world was deserted for the pleasures of low life. During November
he was invited by Jackson, "The Emperor of Pugilism"—his
professor in boxing, who had also been employed, Hobhouse
assures us, in other and less creditable capacities—to the King's
Arms in Duke Street, St. James's, which was kept by a famous
ex-bruiser, Tom Cribb.[2] They had the champion up when the
cloth was removed. "A great man!" He liked energy, Byron
remarked—even animal energy—of all kinds; and Cribb, a coal-
heaver and sailor, who had made his name in some of the most
sanguinary bare-fisted encounters of the last decade, at a time when
huge ox-like pugilists hammered one another into insensibility for
as many as seventy-six rounds, though facetious and prolix, talked
well, assuring Byron that the young person with whom he lived
was the "truest of women;" from which Byron inferred—quite
correctly as it turned out—that she could not be his legal consort.

He came away, having drunk "three bottles of very fair claret."
But between the champagne and sturgeon of Holland House and
convivial evenings passed with Scrope Davies, there were periods
when hard biscuits, washed down by soda-water or tea, were
consumed in philosophic solitude. It is clear, however, that these
crises of asceticism rarely lasted longer than a few days. We
know, at least, that during August Byron had run up a bill with
M. Richold, the celebrated *restaurateur*, for twenty-six pounds; and
the complete account, which has been preserved among his archives
and extends from August 9th to November 21st, testifies to a respectable number of dinners or suppers. "When I *do* dine," he noted,
"I gorge like an Arab or a Boa snake. . . ." Caught in a vicious
circle of indulgence and abstinence, he would devour a heavy meal,
generally of vegetables and fish, only to be visited by one of those
hideous nightmares that left him sweating and shaken—wild
dreams in which the dead returned to pursue—or open his eyes to

[1]"How beautiful Lady Charlemont was! She had no great variety of expression, but
the predominant ones were purity, calmness and abstraction. She looked as if she had
never *caused* an unhallowed sentiment, or felt one,—a sort of 'moonbeam on the snow,'
as our friend Moore would describe her, that was lovely to look on."—Byron to Lady
Blessington.
[2]Cribb had won his title by twice defeating Molineaux, the coloured pugilist, in
December 1810 and September 1811. Byron had seen some of his best fights.

the agonies of a bilious headache. It is not surprising that his liver was often recalcitrant,[1] that he suffered from fits of spleen and depression, and complained that his life was "monotonous, and yet desultory," or that he was "*ennuyé* beyond my usual tense of that yawning verb. . . ." Next January, he remembered, he would be twenty-six. More and more rapidly, his youth—the gift to which he attached an almost superstitious value—seemed to be dissolving and disappearing; and there was nothing that he could do to arrest its rapid flight. "Past events," he wrote, "have unnerved me; and all I can do now is to make life an amusement. . . ."

Up an hour before he was called, he would dawdle three hours in dressing. "When one subtracts from life infancy (which is vegetation)," he mused, "—sleep, eating, and swilling—buttoning and unbuttoning—how much remains of downright existence? The summer of a dormouse." Outwardly his life was that of the fashionable "Bond Street lounger." "My afternoons," he told Medwin, "were passed in visits, luncheons, lounging and boxing —not to mention drinking." But, if his diversions were commonplace, his inward life, which drove him to take refuge in a hackneyed round of pleasures, was very far from ordinary; while his correspondents became more and more demanding. First, there was Lady Melbourne—but her letters, the wise, gay, cynical productions of a woman who (so he declared) had twice already prevented his plunging into irreparable folly, never came amiss. Augusta, too, was a welcome correspondent. More disquieting were the voluminous, romantic, heart-broken epistles of Lady Frances—"Fanny" or "Ph."—who had now been transported by her husband to Scotland, whence she wrote reiterating eternal love. Byron's replies were often behindhand. Ph. was very angry with him for not writing, he informed Lady Melbourne. Encouraged by the husband, he had discovered a slight matrimonial interest in her sister, Lady Catherine Annesley; and this project, although it failed to materialise, so distressed Lady Frances that she threatened to "burst the bonds of prudence" and remonstrated in a strain of jealous passion.

Lady Melbourne was the confidante of Byron's perplexity. Ph.'s letters were forwarded to receive her criticism; and she answered in

[1] *The liver is the lazaret of bile,*
But very rarely executes its function—Don Juan.

a letter of mild reproof. She felt that her friend's attitude was unduly cynical; it was true, she admitted, that Lady Frances was "a little childish and now and then tiresome;" yet she believed that her devotion was perfectly genuine, and that she loved Byron with a simplicity and sincerity that in his amatory existence he had never known before. Such constancy, nevertheless, was a trifle embarrassing. It was unfortunate that, whereas Byron himself counter-balanced an extremely retentive memory by the possession of an extraordinary elusive heart, no woman who had once loved him could forget his powerful influence. To them, his personality was a kind of drug. Even Miss Milbanke could not resist it. Good, sensible and prudent, she had met Byron, and she had refused him; yet their brief meeting, followed by that curiously off-handed proposal of marriage, had not failed to leave its mark; and her opening letter, written on August 22nd, paved the way for a course of epistolary dalliance. On paper wings, she danced around the flame. He had noted the placidity of her face, she wrote in her first letter. Well, she begged leave to assure him that hers was not the serenity of "one who is a stranger to care, nor are the propects of my future years untroubled." It was her nature "to feel long, deeply, and secretly;" in fact, she loved—another—but she loved without hope; and she disclosed this secret love (concealed hitherto from her nearest and dearest) "because it will be the surest basis of that unreserved friendship which I wish to establish between us. . . ."

She herself had suffered as he had suffered. In vain did Lord Byron protest that, although during "a very useless and unregulated life" he had "encountered events which have left a deep *impression*," he was not habitually despondent, but, on the contrary, regarded himself as "a very facetious personage. . . . Nobody laughs more." Humour was not Miss Milbanke's *forte*; and Byron was vastly entertained by her suggestion that, excepting always Mamma and Papa, no one else should be let into the secret of their correspondence. It was an odd suggestion, he thought, to come from so innocent a virgin. Needless to say, he made no attempt to respect her wishes and among the other feminine problems retailed for Lady Melbourne's consideration was that of her niece—"your A.," alias "the mathematician," alias "the Princess of Parallelograms," "the strictest of St. Ursula's 11,000 what do you call 'ems? a wit, a moralist, and religionist," who had entered into a clandestine correspondence "with a personage generally presumed to be a great roué, and drags her aged parents into this secret treaty."

On September 5th he had returned Annabella's carefully compiled catalogue of the virtues she would require in a husband if she were to be happy in the married state. His commentary on this effusion was short but cutting. Miss Milbanke, he wrote to her aunt, seemed to have been spoiled "—not as children usually are—but systematically Clarissa Harlowed into an awkward kind of correctness, with a dependence upon her own infallibility which will or may lead her into some egregious blunder." She would find exactly what she wanted, "and then discover that it is much more dignified than entertaining." But Byron had an unaccountable taste for sermons. They might annoy him; and yet he was strangely touched by the information, given with such solemn self-assurance, that he was not happy, and that he had dwelt upon a lonely and desolate height, "surrounded by admirers who could not value you, and by friends to whom you were not dear." At the end of October the correspondence languished; and Byron told Lady Melbourne that he did not intend to renew it. Annabella, on her side, was more persistent; and November brought an involved, pompous, ill-punctuated communication, full of high-sounding phraseology, laced with a dash of feminine *dépit*. Now she presumed to administer a rousing snub. She had not as good an opinion, she explained, of his powers of reasoning as he had of his powers of imagination. He had joked about her proclivity for mathematics. "At your age," she reminded him—Annabella herself was twenty-one—this science "is not to be commenced." Finally, she requested that he would warn her when her letters became unacceptable, that she might discontinue them.

Byron replied a week later. "A variety of circumstances and movements from place to place," he wrote "—none of which would be very amusing in detail, nor indeed pleasing to any one who (I may flatter myself) is my friend—have hitherto prevented me from answering your last two letters." Would she accept a copy of *The Bride of Abydos*? He hoped that when they met she would not take fright and imagine that he intended to add to the number of her thousand-and-one suitors: "I have taken exquisite care to prevent the possibility of that." In the closing phrase one may glimpse a reference, not only to Lady Frances, a phantom fast receding, whose claims would certainly not have prevented his seeking Miss Milbanke's hand in lawful wedlock, but to Annabella's mysterious counterpart, the "Other A." Perhaps it was the very "exquisiteness" of his preoccupations that lent this diffuse and prosy, but blameless and reassuring, correspondence the charm that saved it from an early demise. Annabella was so sensible, so firmly good. . . . "The best of life" (he was to declare afterwards) "is but intoxication;" and for a man who had swallowed heady drams of feeling—of desire, of passion, of remorse—until his palate had begun to lose its edge, there was a certain stimulus to be found in the lectures of a maiden prude. He was easily moved by any display of interest; and Miss Milbanke was attractive and sensible, virtuous and well born.

At the end of November he summarised the situation. "A very pretty letter from Annabella" had just arrived. "What an odd situation and friendship is ours!—without one spark of love on either side, and produced by circumstances which in general lead to coldness on one side, and aversion on the other. She is a very superior woman, and very little spoiled, which is strange in an heiress—a girl of twenty—a peeress that is to be, in her own right— an only child, and a *savante*, who has always had her own way. She is a poetess—a mathematician—a metaphysician, and yet, withal, very kind, generous, and gentle, with very little pretension. Any other head would be turned with half her acquisitions, and a tenth of her advantages." He ended on a note of admiration; but Miss Milbanke's letters were a single strand of the complicated epistolary web that ran through Byron's fingers during the autumn and winter months of 1813. Reading his journal, with its plentiful sprinkling of asterisks, we perceive that, although Lady Frances accounts for some and Augusta Leigh, no doubt, for others, whole tracts of his experience remain obscure. There are some episodes that have vanished beyond all guessing; nor does it much signify which of many ringleted or turbaned beauties, clad in the high-waisted, softly clinging dresses of the period that gave an ideal length of limb, a look of statuesque or nymphean grace, to all but the most squat and intractable figures, engrossed his restless attention for a week or for a day. More interesting is his relationship with the middle-class public. The greater part of Byron's correspondence, as it has hitherto been printed—the letters that he wrote and the miscellaneous letters that he received—is concerned with the doings of a very small section of English society, the world of aristocrats, of landed gentlemen, rich publishers, successful authors and critics, perched high above the drab level of the bourgeois universe.

Yet the middle class was steadily gaining ground—and not merely the rich middle class of merchants and bankers that had flourished in England since the fourteenth century, but the lower middle class, small capitalists consumed by an overwhelming desire for self-improvement, small tradesmen, modest employees of every kind. It would not be many years now before, all around London, streets, crescents, diminutive stucco houses planted in pleasant gardens, began to creep out into the regions of park and pasture. Suburban civilisation was under way; and, when the hubbub of Byron's fashionable celebrity had died down, his influence continued to spread through wider and ever wider circles, making fresh conquests as it proceeded. Childe Harold's shadow grew longer and longer; for Childe Harold—with what flattering and exciting differences!—was the personification, the grand exemplar, of every young man or young woman to whom fate had been unkind, who was conscious of wasted or thwarted talents. The humble curate lost in the depths of the country, the ambitious clerk buried in some gloomy counting-house, the despairing girl unappreciated by mother and sisters, the distraught maiden lady, even the impressed sailor and the debtor in gaol—no reader was so obscure that he or she did not feel qualified to write to Lord Byron and, after some prefatory apologies, mentioning that the correspondent had not the honour of his lordship's acquaintance, to sympathise, admonish or extol. Some set forth their problems at great length. Byron was the first English writer whose personal life, opinions and alleged private habits evoked a degree of curiosity nowadays reserved for film actors, popular musicians, famous athletes and other heroes of the popular daily press. He was one of the earliest victims of the modern technique of publicity; but it must be conceded that, although the poet often boggled at the part he was obliged to play, his presentation revealed an instinctive grasp of showmanship. The gifts he had shown in his private legend-making soon extended to the conduct of his public career.

The letters that he received were seldom destroyed.[1] In the pertinacity with which Byron collected letters, notes, bills—any scrap of writing that constituted a link, however fragile, between himself and the dead, unforgotten past—a psychologist might find an indication of his temperament. Certainly it worked to our advantage. The enormous post-bag that reached Byron during his stay in England can still be opened and examined; and, as we stir these drifts of fallen paper, sheet upon sheet, covered now with a beautiful copperplate handwriting, now with a wild erratic scrawl, we seem to be digging into the farthest recesses of the poet's public life. Faint, yet acrid, are the perfumes they disengage. Musty, desiccated, old-fashioned—and yet here and there, among these diffuse and excited outpourings, there is a letter that, despite time and oblivion, retains the sharpness of an individual personality. Not a few are the product of impassioned women. Already, during the early months of 1813, Byron had been subjected to the importunities of a distracted female—Lady Falkland, the widow of an old school friend[2]—whom he had never met but who fancied that he wished to marry her; and Lady Falkland was not the only woman who taxed his forbearance. There were others who had even less excuse—women in search of adventure, of sensation; grasping women who made a wild bid for the interest of one of the most famous and notorious young men of his day; women humbly but hopelessly enamoured. All contributed their quota of blackened pages. Some were impudent; and typical of the bravado they evinced is this anonymous letter, written in an uneducated, but neat and determined, hand:

> Should curiosity prompt you, and should you not be afraid of gratifying it, by trusting yourself *alone* in the Green Park at seven o'clock this evening, you will see *Echo*. If this evening

[1] "Byron says that the number of anonymous amatory letters and portraits he has received, and all from English ladies, would fill a large volume. He says he has never noticed any of them; but it is evident he recurs to them with complacency."—Lady Blessington: *Conversations with Lord Byron*.

[2] Lord Falkland was killed in a duel on the 28th of February, 1809, and Byron had befriended his children and widow. A lock of Falkland's hair was preserved in Byron's archives.

prove inconvenient, the same chance shall still await you to-morrow evening at the same hour. Be on that side of the Green Park that has the gate opening into Piccadilly and leave the rest to   ECHO
Should *apathy* or *indifference* prevent your coming, adieu for ever!

Judging by a copy of verses that refer to the sweetness of Byron's voice—a trait that particularly impressed those who encountered him for the first time[1]—it seems possible that he may have overcome his natural apathy or indifference and trusted himself to the chances of a romantic encounter among the dusky hillocks of the Green Park:

> *Who talks of loving in a voice so sweet?*
> *Yet says his heart can never love again.*
> *Who bids the heart with wildest throbbing beat?*
> *Yet gives no balsam to assuage its pain.*
>
> *Is it for thee blooming in youthful prime*
> *The sweets of love for ever to forego?*
> *And wand'ring thus alone from clime to clime,*
> *Abjure all joy but the joy of woe? . . .*

Many correspondents, however, did not aspire—or professed not to aspire—to direct acquaintance. That they should be allowed to write, and that the poet should deign to answer them, was satisfaction enough. Such was the gist of a communication that he received in September 1814:

A young lady of *deservedly unsullied fame* who to use Ld. Byron's discriptive lines is

> *The wither'd frame, the ruined mind,*
> *The wrack by misery* [not passion or guilt] *left behind*
> *A shrivelled scroll, a scattered leaf*
> *Sear'd by the autumn blast of grief*

has been led not from any motive but an irristible inclination to address a man whose character as far as she has learnt from public report (and she knows Ld. Byron from no other) she

---

[1]According to Mrs. Opie, "his voice was such a voice as the devil tempted Eve with; you feared its fascination the moment you heard it."

dares not admire and whom *she never saw* but she cannot read his works with the attention she has done, without believing his mind would sympathize with her own, and feeling herself strongly interested in his sorrows and early disappointments.

She suggests the following questions to be answered with truth from his own heart and *only to himself*.

Does he regret an error of his youth? . . .

and here the young lady proposes a long list of moral questions and, having fulfilled her task, prepares to retire into the shadows of heart-broken anonymity:

To Ld. Byron she must ever remain concealed; yet that some notice was taken of this address, and it did not meet with the silent contempt it may appear to deserve, may cast a gleam of sunshine over the almost broken heart of   ROSALIE

Never, one feels, save perhaps during the heyday of the French Romantic Revival, were heart-broken and frustrated girls quite so numerous as in that brief period, when Lord Byron's latest poem was snatched from hand to hand, and when Childe Harold's griefs were yet fresh and strong. Tiny fragments of feminine heart-break littered his correspondence. Take, for example, another anonymous votary—

. . ."One whose deeply wounded spirit has occasioned in early youth, for several years past, to shun all society as an intolerable annoyance . . . and who is alternately commiserated or condemned by the very few epistolary correspondents who are still retained for wasting the fairest part of Life, in what they designated as an unnatural solitude . . ." Or the admirer who, having described herself as a young woman—"certainly young" and, she trusts, "not disagreeable" —explains that she had been "deemed cold and insensible by everyone" until "I began to be myself convinced that I was never to experience any emotions more tender than the warmest attachment towards my own family. . . . Upon perusing *Childe Harold* and its accompanying poems I became as it were animated by a new soul, alive to wholly novel sensations . . ."

Some worshippers were passionate and straightforward. "I adore you," proclaimed Miss Baldry, who gave her address as the Post Office, Pimlico. "How can I convince you that love is my only motive for writing? . . ." Some dreaded the ignominy to which they exposed themselves, but could not resist the temptation of declaring their passion:

". . . For *two Years* I have lived but in your image . . . I am descended from parents *well-known* in the path of Honor and Integrity;—wound not, I beseech you, their Feelings, nor tinge their cheeks with a blush of shame through the consciousness of their Child's imprudence!"

In most of these appeals the jargon of passion, borrowed from popular novelists of the time, seems at least as important as the reality; and there is therefore a peculiar charm about two letters, written by a servant girl or, more improbably, a governess, domiciled at Gloster Row, Clifton:

My dear Lord Byron,

I am a poor country girl that has not the happiness of knowing you. I am afraid you will think me very impertinent in writing to you without the slightest claim in the world to your attention. But I admire you so very, very much that you must excuse this madness—I cannot help thinking that you have much feeling; you can now make one happy—! Oh, I speak from my heart when I say nothing could give me more joy on earth than a lock of your hair. Let me have it I entreat you by all you ever loved, and then when you see anybody in extasies think of your eternally devoted

SOPHIA LOUISA MACDONALD

If you feel a great deal of contempt, my dearest Lord Byron, pray tear this but do not show it anyone—Pray forgive my folly but give me the Lock.

A week later the lock had not arrived; and Miss Macdonald thereupon wrote a second epistle, couched in a strain even more pathetic and despairing than the first:

My dearest Lord Byron,

Your picture does not look very cruel, but I am afraid the talisman by which you fascinate the hearts of others charms away all sensibility from your own. . . . I have set my heart on but one lock. Do not be inexorable, Lord Byron, for the world says you will soon be married and then I dare not ask you. Excuse this letter. It is desperate, but I am obliged to write on the Down . . .

With those final glimpses of poor Sophia Louisa, her writing-paper across her knee, perched on a windy hillside behind Clifton; of a girl who signed herself "your young admirer and enthusiastic friend—Eliza;" and of a group of "several young ladies" who wrote to request that Lord Byron would arbitrate in a literary competition, we revert to the more public side of his correspondence. ". . . The moments of delight" his poems occasioned, a reader told him, were "not unmixed with regret that one, who speaks 'so sweetly and so well,' should not be *all* he might be." "Hear me, my Lord," besought an earnest evangelist, discharging his moral message at point-blank range, "*there is an hereafter* . . ." "Turn not from this address," pleaded a sympathetic unknown, writing in an exquisitely neat script, and in a strain of pompous commiseration worthy of the Princess of Parallelograms herself. ". . . You are unhappy—a being feared and mistrusted, even by those whom the fashion of the hour leads to flatter you—you are 'alone on earth.' " It was characteristic of Byron's feminine genius that, between the author and his readers, it should set up a relation so peculiarly personal that every man or woman who succumbed to his verse enjoyed the pleasing belief that he or she alone had the privilege of under-standing Childe Harold's sorrows, and that only the force of circumstance had kept them apart. Some claimed that they had anticipated his sufferings. Conspicuous among these was "your Lordship's real Christian friend, Thomas Mulock," a devout but insolvent gentleman, temporarily established at Boulogne-sur-Mer, who informed Byron that he was "one of the few things on earth who can understand the breadth and depth, and length and height, of your intellectual woes—one who had mourned and maddened where you now weep and writhe. . . ."

Comparatively modest were the pretensions of a clerk at Woodbridge, Suffolk, who, "during the few leisure hours allotted to me from the service of my employers", had amused himself "in the composition of some *Verses*, expressive of the feelings of the moment . . . now published solely at the request of a few friends, and for their perusal . . .;" or those of a "humble *Country Curate* . . . who, in his earlier and better days, was wont occasionally to cull a few flowers at the *foot* of *Parnassus!*" But, bold or unassuming, all these correspondents had fallen victim to the same spell—a magnetism that seems the more extraordinary when we remember that it was radiated by a very young man whose celebrity, at the time most of these letters were composed, was barely two years old, and whose finest work was not yet in contemplation. For his personality, rather than his verse, contained his secret. Unpolished, carelessly constructed, his poems presented, nevertheless, some reflection of the strength of personality—as distinct from strength of intellect or will—that gave his life its heroic or demonic colouring. The hero might be prosaic, the demon an opportunist. But then, demons, good or bad, are exceedingly rare.

Chapter 9

ALL through the winter he remained at Bennet Street; and, as the year drew in, so did the mood of splenetic ennui grow more and more acute. During January, or the latter part of December, Mrs. Leigh returned to London; and when, on January 17th, he set off for Newstead Augusta accompanied him north. Meanwhile a new thread had been added to the tangled skein of his correspondence. From a cottage near Nottingham, where she was living with a faithful but (Byron believed) mischievous and ill-natured female companion, Mary Chaworth—now Mary Chaworth Musters —wrote begging that, if he came to Nottinghamshire and wished to see "*a very old and sincere friend*," he would visit her in her retirement. Her love-match with Jack Musters had gone awry. They were separated. Her husband, Byron informed Lady Melbourne, had been behaving very ill and "playing the Devil with all kinds of vulgar mistresses." She was much changed, she told him in a subsequent letter. He would hardly recognise the happy creature he once knew; "I am grown so thin, pale, and gloomy."

Byron did not welcome her reappearance. Too clearly, in the efforts that she made to invest their renewed friendship with an air of mystery and secrecy that he himself had done nothing to encourage, could he recognise the tactics of yet another disconsolate and possessive woman, anxious to recapture, now that he was celebrated, the young man whose adoration she had neglected when he was an obscure and undistinguished boy. He replied—but lightly, guardedly, coolly. Perhaps he would visit her from Newstead. But no sooner had he reached Newstead than the snow came down—deep snow, blocking the roads, smothering the wind-swept and treeless park, isolating the huge, melancholy, ancient mansion.

Indoors gaiety and good humour prevailed. "I mentioned yesterday," he wrote to Lady Melbourne, with somewhat unconvincing casualness, in the last paragraph of his long letter of the 29th, "that Augusta was here. . . ." Her companionship, he added, rendered life in the Abbey "much more pleasant;" they never yawned or disagreed, and laughed far more than was suitable to the solidity and gravity of their surroundings. ". . . The family shyness makes us more amusing companions to each other than we could be to anyone else." They were happy; they were alone; and during this period Byron wrote fewer letters than had been his habit when he was living in London, while the journal that he had begun in November was temporarily put aside.

On Byron the combination of Newstead and Augusta—each the focus of so many dreams and memories—may well have had a disturbing, yet intoxicating and inspiriting, effect. Newstead, however, must be sold; and at the end of their sojourn Claughton, the defaulting purchaser, arrived and stayed two nights, preparatory, as Byron then hoped, to an amicable arrangement of the business. By February 10th he himself was back in London. Mary Chaworth he had not visited; and illustrative of his faculty of self-deception are two letters, one to Lady Melbourne in which he says that Augusta has been "urging me repeatedly to call before I left the country," one, written from Genoa in 1823, to Monsieur J. J. Coulmann, in which he asserts that he had been upon the point of paying his old love a visit, "when my sister, who has always had more influence over me than any one else, persuaded me not to do it. 'For,' said she, 'if you go, you will fall in love again, and then there will be a scene; one step will lead to another, *et cela fera un éclat.*' "

At Bennet Street more serious concerns awaited him. During his absence *The Corsair* had been published; and attached to the poem were his vitriolic "Stanzas to a Lady Weeping,"[1] which had been printed anonymously the year before. Their republication, under Byron's name, drew an outburst of embittered abuse from the entire Tory press. "Such a clash of paragraphs, and a conflict of

[1]See page 97.

newspapers. . . . The Regent (as reported) wroth; Ld. Carlisle in a fury; the *Morning Post* in hysterics; and the *Courier* in convulsions of criticism and contention." The *Courier* was particularly tenacious. Between February 1st and March 13th it devoted no less than nine articles—many of considerable length—to Lord Byron, his character and antecedents; and with not unnatural glee the paper reminded its readers that certain of Lord Byron's present friends—notably the Hollands and Tom Moore—had been satirised in the early editions of *English Bards*. Wounding references, since suppressed, were maliciously brought to light again—a sneer at Lady Holland's character and past life:

> *Blest be the banquets spread at Holland House,*
> *Where Scotchmen feed, and Critics may carouse!*
> *Long, long, beneath that hospitable roof*
> *Shall* Grub-street *dine, while duns are kept aloof . . .*
> *That lest when heated with the unusual grape,*
> *Some* glowing *thoughts should to the press escape,*
> *And tinge with red the* female *reader's cheek,*
> *MY LADY skims the* cream *of each critique;*
> *Breathes o'er each page* her purity *of soul,*
> *Reforms each error, and refines the whole.*

and the pleasantry about Moore's ill-fated duel. "We have, we should hope [remarked the *Courier*] sufficiently exposed the audacious levity and waywardness of Lord Byron's mind;" but it could not forbear including a mention of Melbourne House and the Lambs, derived from the same satire, that "must be amusing to those who know anything of Lord Byron in the circles of London."

Although more unsystematic than the animadversion of the *Courier*, the attacks of the *Morning Post* were even more personal. As in a previous fracas, his lameness was not spared; and contributors took him to task with varying degrees of severity, one likening him to the harpies of legend who bespattered friend and foe, and fed upon what they had already defiled; another to a baneful planet:

> *BYRON! thy dark, unhallow'd mind,*
> *Stor'd as it is with Atheist writ,*
> *Will surely, never, never find,*
> *One convert to admire its wit!*

The Years of Fame

Thou art a planet boding woe,
Attractive for thy novel mien—
A calm, but yet a deadly foe,
Most baneful when thou'rt most serene!

while a third attempted a facetious portrait:

Bard of the pallid front, and curling hair,
To London taste, and northern critics dear,
Friend of the dog, companion of the bear,
APOLLO drest in trimmest Turkish gear . . .

There was talk of a motion in the Upper Chamber. Coming, "at a time when peace and war, and Emperors and Napoleons, and the destinies of the things they have made of mankind," were trembling in the balance, this journalistic hubbub, excited by eight lines, written two years ago, seemed doubly strange. "I really begin to think myself a most important personage . . . I think you must allow [he observed to Lady Melbourne] that mine has been an odd destiny."

It was fortunate that Hobhouse should have returned to London. He arrived while Byron was still at Newstead; but on February 10th, after a call at Holland House where, beneath the autocratic eye of Lady Holland as she dominated her little court from the sofa, John Cam grew "foolishly embarrassed" and dropped his hat, he had occasion to visit Drury Lane and caught sight of his friend in a private box. Rushing upstairs, he joined "my dearest Byron . . ." Many were the days since he had been so happy; and from Drury Lane they drove home to Bennet Street and sat up talking until four o'clock. Byron himself was equally delighted. Hobhouse was his "best friend," he declared, "the most lively, and a man of the most sterling talents extant;" and again, when Hobhouse had regaled him with "ten thousand anecdotes of Napoleon, all good and true," that his friend H. was "the most entertaining of companions, and a fine fellow to boot." Henceforward Byron and Hobhouse were much together; Hobhouse dined with Byron at the Cocoa Tree, spent an entire evening listening to his confessions, and grumbled that, during his absence, Byron had become more and more unsociable—John Cam had recovered his taste for

the *beau monde*—that he was "a *loup garou*—a solitary hobgoblin."
Both friends had a passion for the theatre. On February 19th
they saw Kean in *Richard III*, and on March 12th the same actor in
Hamlet. When Hamlet fell, the pit rose to its feet, and a tempest of
emotion surged through the whole house. As Richard, Kean was
even more successful. A small man "with a piercing black eye," he
gave to the character "a sportive ferocity" that electrified his
audience; while his speech to Stanley: "*What do they in the
north?*" was delivered in "a loud, shrill, taunting interrogatory"
that produced "an extraordinary effect." His scene with Lady Anne
was "highly finished." Later—it was during May—Byron, Hobhouse and Tom Moore watched Kean in *Othello*.[1] "For two acts
and a half [reported Hobhouse] the play was tame, but from the
sentence: 'Not a jot,' he displayed his extraordinary powers, and,
as Byron said, 'threw a sort of Levant fury of expression into his
actions and face, to which we Orientalists had been accustomed,
and which we could appreciate.' His stabbing himself was a
masterpiece . . ."

"By Jove," commented Byron, returning home after his first
glimpse of Kean in *Richard*, "he is a soul! Life—nature—truth
without exaggeration or diminution." Energy, whether it was
displayed in the burly person of Tom Cribb or in the short dynamic
figure of Edmund Kean, never failed to kindle his respect. The
more lethargic he himself became, the greater was the admiration
that he felt for men whose courage and enterprise enabled them to
confront the difficulties of an active career. He was miserably
conscious of his own impotence; and it was in this spirit, while he
dined out or drank soda-water, gossiped with Hobhouse or attended
a London party, that he continued to brood over happenings on the
heroic European scale.

Napoleon was retreating inch by inch. During February,
attended by the prayers of the English Whigs, the Emperor was
still expected to hurl back the Allied armies; and it was not until
April 9th that the news of his abdication reached Byron. He had
been away—with Augusta at Newmarket. "On my return, found
my poor little pagod, Napoleon, pushed off his pedestal;—the

---

[1] "I am acquainted with no *im*material sensuality so delightful as good acting . . ."
—Byron to Moore, after seeing Kean in *Othello*.

thieves are in Paris." He had already voiced his abhorrence of "the dull, stupid old system—balance of Europe—poising straws upon kings' noses instead of wringing them off!" And now legitimacy had triumphed, and the representatives of the old system had been once again restored to power. For himself, he wrote, he had no ambition, "I shall never be anything [he confided to his journal], or rather always be nothing." Had he an ambition, "it would be *aut Cæsar aut nihil*." As it was, his hopes were limited to the arrangement of his affairs—to the achievement of financial security which would enable him to retire to Italy or the Near East. How different from his bustling friend Hobhouse! For, though shy and awkward—so shy that, at a party given by Lady Jersey, whither he had accompanied Byron, he describes himself as having "stood in terror at the doorway a long time," cut two or three good friends out of sheer nervousness, and been "quite cool with several others out of pure despair"—John Cam was beginning to enjoy society. On the news of the Restoration, he dashed over to Paris. Byron had promised that he would join him; but at the last moment he announced that he had changed his plans. "He is a difficult person to live with," lamented Hobhouse, as he prepared for three weeks of assiduous sightseeing.

On April 12th Hobhouse noted in his diary that "Byron goes not to Paris;" and, on April 15th, at Newmarket, Augusta Leigh was delivered of a child—Elizabeth Medora Leigh, a young girl destined to run through many vicissitudes, cause great scandal and endure much unhappiness before she eventually expired in poverty and obscurity in the year 1849. Colonel Leigh was away in Yorkshire when she was born; and on April 25th Byron informed Lady Melbourne that it was "*not* an '*Ape*'" (a reference, presumably, to the mediæval superstition that the children of incest were born monsters), "and if it is, that must be my fault; however, I will positively reform. You must however allow that it is utterly impossible that I can ever be half so well liked elsewhere, and I have been all my life trying to make someone love me, and never got the sort that I preferred before. But positively she and I will grow good and all that, and so we are *now* and shall be these three weeks and more too."

Fresh hints to trouble Lady Melbourne! But Lady Melbourne

was not the only intimate to whom Byron had given matter for grave anxiety during the last six months. Even Tom Moore, a friend who saw Byron in his most "facetious" and least demonic mood, was perplexed and alarmed by his innuendoes. In the world, his conduct was far from discreet. Lord Holland had advised against the publication of *The Bride of Abydos*; and his fears had been justified by an outbreak of gossip. Within certain circles the rumours were widespread; and at Eton (we are told) Mrs. Leigh's nephew was questioned by schoolfellows about his aunt and enlightened as to the stories that were then circulating. By temperament the poet was a daring talker; he loved to advance outrageous notions; and in the Holland House circle (according to Mrs. Villiers, an early and close friend of Mrs. Leigh, who subsequently convinced herself of Augusta's "guilt") he had not hesitated to put forward "extraordinary theories." We also learn—though here, it is true, we are on undependable ground—that, during the close of 1813 and the beginning of the year 1814, more than one woman was taken into his confidence. He had never known (he would say) what it was before. There was a woman he loved passionately; she was pregnant and, if the child were a girl, it should be called Medora. By nature he was incapable of keeping a secret; and, if he needed a listener, he took the first that came to hand.[1]

How are we to explain his indiscretion? "Diabolick" were the hints with which he had already overwhelmed the unfortunate "Lady Blarney;" and it is not surprising that, two years later, at a period when the physician whom he consulted described him as "horribly restless and irritable," and spoke of his "having lived excessively 'out of all compass' some time or other," the confidences he proffered should have been yet more dangerous. Must we put it down to pathological vanity? To mere levity? To the nervous aberrations of a man who often displayed an unusual degree of shrewdness in his attitude towards the world at large, but showed as conspicuous a lack of foresight in every problem that directly concerned his private existence? It is possible, I believe, that we should look deeper. There are exceptional human beings in whose

---

[1] "He is an extraordinary person, *indiscreet* to a degree that is surprising. . . . He is, I am persuaded, incapable of keeping any secret, however it may concern his own honour or that of another."—Lady Blessington: *Conversations with Lord Byron.*

lives the instinct of self-destruction outweighs the instinct of self-preservation—individuals who feel the need to suffer just as acutely as they may imagine that they feel the need to enjoy, who constitute themselves the patient architects of their own ruin. In this context one thinks of Oscar Wilde. For, like Byron, Wilde was a gifted and intelligent man who courted disaster as though disaster would bring fulfilment of some need that might otherwise never find expression. Like Byron, Wilde showed a streak of arrogance; but, whereas Wilde's nature was shallow and sparkling—witness the almost complete collapse that overtook his later years—at his most cynical, Byron's nature had a sluggish intensity. If he drifted, as all his youth he had been glad to do, it was in obedience to strong currents running deep beneath the surface.

His early life had been haunted by a sense of guilt. So much is obvious; but to determine the origin of his obsession is considerably more difficult. Was it derived from his relationship with Mrs. Byron? Had it been implanted at Aberdeen by his Scottish nurse, a pious, though ill-conducted, young woman, who not only aroused her charge's native sensuality—she is said to have been detected and dismissed—but spoke to him of death and hell and doom? Were its roots in some struggle waged against impulses that conventional moral precepts had taught him it was his duty to deny? Byron was an immoralist; but, in common with many other immoralists, he had very decided leanings towards asceticism; and Walter Scott (whom Byron did not encounter till the spring of 1815) was perspicacious enough to point out his moral bent. Scott had hazarded that Byron's opinions on religion and politics would change within the next few years. "I suppose," said Byron, rather sharply, "you are one of those who prophesy I will turn Methodist." "No," replied Scott, "I don't expect your conversion to be of such an ordinary kind. I would rather look to see you retreat upon the Catholic faith, and distinguish yourself by the austerity of your penances. The species of religion to which you must, or may, one day attach yourself must exercise a strong power on the imagination." Byron smiled gravely, and seemed to admit it might be true.

In this connection, it is interesting to learn, from a letter hitherto unpublished, that when, at the end of March 1814, Byron moved from Bennet Street into Albany, where he occupied a spacious flat on the left of the main entrance, the decorations of his sitting-room—besides his beautiful but savage macaw, the silver urns he had brought back with him from Greece, his screen pasted with scraps of boxers and actresses, and the long table before the fireplace heaped with a mass of books and papers—included a large crucifix conspicuously hung. That symbol of suffering was perhaps the chance acquisition of a dandy who loved to surround himself with strange objects put to an inappropriate use. It is indicative, nevertheless, of the trend of his mind; for, though Byron never accepted the dogmas of Christianity, he never rejected the spirit of a gospel that contains so many promises to the heavily laden, to men who bear burdens that they cannot understand. Christianity demands expiation; and we can only explain the remarkable lack of prudence with which he acted between 1813 and 1814 by suggesting that, far from shunning disaster, his sense of guilt enjoined that he should go out in search of it. The anxious man creates subjects of anxiety. Does not the guilty man prepare the way for his ultimate fall?

He was to declare that he had been "cunning in his overthrow;" but we must not assume that Byron was ever fully conscious of the inward schism that made it impossible for him to achieve that humdrum happiness—that calm and contented domestic obscurity —which was the goal he had always most desired. Goethe, who observed his career at a distance, remarked that, living from passion to passion and hour to hour, Byron understood himself but dimly, yet possessed "a high degree of that demonic instinct and attraction which influences others independently of reason, effort or affection, which sometimes succeeds in guiding where the understanding fails." Byron's genius, in short, was instinctive; and to this it may be added that his mental equipment was of the feminine and intuitive, rather than of the masculine and more strictly intellectual, type. He was neither deeply read nor highly educated. A list printed in the index of his collected correspondence enumerates a hundred and fifty writers to whom Byron was indebted for quotations; but, although the scope of his reading was wide, Byron's knowledge of literature, ancient and modern, seems remarkably limited when it is compared, for example, with that of Shelley. His curiosity was confined to a single plane. Men, their passions and habits, their memories of the past and their hopes of the future, he never ceased to find fascinating. He would have given the world (he wrote) "to pass a month with Sheridan, or any lady or gentleman of the old school, and hear them talk every day, and all day of themselves, and acquaintance, and all they have heard and seen in their lives." His interest was that of the *homme du monde*; and against architecture, sculpture, painting—forms of activity in which human beings transcend the ordinary social barriers—Byron's mind remained obstinately shut. For music, however, he had a certain affection; at a later period he was to annoy Leigh Hunt by singing snatches from one of Rossini's operas in an inaccurate and "swaggering" style as he bathed and dressed; but beyond a pretty tune his enthusiasm did not extend. He enjoyed the soothing influence of a mellifluous feminine voice. To other branches of art he was frankly indifferent.

Few writers have had less general æsthetic sensibility. But then few writers have held the profession that they followed in greater contempt. As a critic of modern literature, Byron's limitations may be gauged by the fact that he preferred Rogers, most insipid of versifiers, to Coleridge, Wordsworth and Keats, and that he had a considerable regard for the productions of Mrs. Hemans.[1] For "Johnny Keats's *p—ss a bed poetry*," the friend and admirer of Moore, Rogers and Scott had an especial abhorrence. Keats had presumed to criticise the achievement of Pope; and Byron, rallying to the support of "the most *faultless* of Poets, and almost of men," voiced his disgust in such rabelaisian imagery that certain phrases do not bear republication. Keats, he declared, was a "miserable Self-polluter of the human Mind;" his verse, "drivelling idiotism." To the author of *Childe Harold*, the author of *Endymion* was merely the pretentious and ill-bred poetaster whose knowledge of the world was circumscribed by the bricks and mortar of a London suburb; whose experience of love was derived from books; who was no gentleman and showed it in every line. A Cockney mannikin! A "tadpole of the Lakes!" Never is the evidence of vulgarity

[1]"As a woman, I felt proud of the homage he paid to the genius of Mrs. Hemans and, as a passionate admirer of her poetry, I felt flattered at finding that Lord Byron fully sympathised with my admiration."—Lady Blessington: *Conversations with Lord Byron*.

received in a more unsympathetic spirit than by a critic whose character itself encloses an element of vulgarity, clothed in some entirely different guise. But, whereas Keats's "vulgarity" was of the surface—a symptom of extreme sensitiveness and immaturity, of his openness to each impression that came his way—Byron's criticism was often vulgar because his range was small. In the human sphere his intelligence had a quickness and strength that in the literary sphere proved singularly lacking.

An unaccountable figure to stand at the head of a literary movement! Yet Romanticism was to become identified with Byronism; and Byronism may be defined as a personal presentation —to some extent a vulgarisation—of a movement that Byron himself scarcely understood, that had embodied itself in his personality very largely against his will and certainly ran counter to most of his tastes. But there was no escaping his enormous popularity. Despite the journalistic hubbub caused by "Stanzas to a Lady Weeping," *The Corsair* was more successful than any poem he had so far produced.[1] On the day of publication alone, it had sold ten thousand copies—"a thing perfectly unprecedented"— and thirty purchasers, reported Mr. Murray, had returned "to tell the people in the Shop how much they had been delighted and satisfied." Gifford, a severe critic, gave warm approval; while Moore, to whom the poem had been dedicated, wrote that he heard that it was "liked beyond measure. . . . I may, perhaps, as God-father, be suspected of undue partiality for the child; but . . . anything more fearfully interesting, more wild, touching, and 'negligently grand,' I never read from *your* pen. You are careless, but you can afford to be so, and, whenever you slumber, it is like the albatross, *high in the air and on the wing.*"

Alas for Moore's elegant hyperbole! A hundred years have passed; and the albatross, planing on negligent wings over the dark and troubled expanse of Byron's imagination, has been relegated to the obscurity of museum shelves, whence it fixes the student with a bright but glassy eye. Indeed, if we separate them from their place in Byron's life, it is nowadays extremely difficult to arrive at any definite critical opinion of the six long poems, *The Giaour, The*

[1]By November 1814 there had been nominally ten editions of *Childe Harold* I and II but, actually, only six reprints and a sale of 23,000 copies.

The Years of Fame

Bride of Abydos, The Corsair, Lara, The Siege of Corinth and *Parisina*, written and published between the years 1812 and 1816. Their interest is historical rather than literary; they belong to the story of Byron's existence; and, as we read them, we visualise not the self-denying artist—a Milton or a Pope—who balances the music of his words as carefully as the scientist works out a chemical formula, not the industrious literary craftsman who makes versifying his business and brings to it the same sober application as he would bring to any form of activity, but the young man, passionate, histrionic, whose custom it was to write verse when he returned home, excited and feverish, after supper. One imagines him writing as he undressed. Fletcher would be sent for a glass of brandy. Byron's mind was on flame; and, rapidly, impetuously, in a script so crabbed and ill-formed that it reminded Harriette Wilson of that of a washerwoman requesting the loan of a one-pound bill to enable her to "set up a *Mangle*," line after line would rush from his pen:

> *Unlike the heroes of each ancient race,*
> *Demons in act, but Gods at least in face,*
> *In Conrad's form seems little to admire,*
> *Though his dark eyebrow shades a glance of fire:*
> *Robust but not Herculean—to the sight*
> *No giant frame sets forth his common height;*
> *Yet, in the whole, who paused to look again,*
> *Saw more than marks the crowd of vulgar men . . .*
> *Sun-burnt his cheek, his forehead high and pale*
> *The sable curls in wild profusion veil;*
> *And oft perforce his rising lip reveals*
> *The haughtier thought it curbs, but scarce conceals . . .*
> *His features' deepening lines and varying hue*
> *At times attracted, yet perplex'd the view,*
> *As if within that murkiness of mind*
> *Work'd feelings fearful, and yet undefined . . .*

Such were the conditions in which he wrote those typical, but extremely disappointing, poems that followed the first two cantos of *Childe Harold* and preceded their continuation and the poem in which his genius found its most satisfactory vehicle, *Don Juan*. They are not the conditions in which great works of art are produced; and, whatever the merits of his earlier and later work, it must be admitted that, between 1812 and 1816, Byron's output, if we except various short lyrical poems, themselves imperfect and incomplete, was almost entirely devoid of literary value. Never had the absence of music been more conspicuous. Though he had a fine sense of rhetoric and a gift of magniloquent diction that he employed now and then to splendid purpose, Byron was not blessed with a sensitive ear. He was strangely insensitive, moreover, to the beauty of words. In his letters, Byron's knack of finding the right epithets, or the right conjunction of phrases, very seldom failed him; and yet, in his verse, it was the expected qualification, the jaded and shop-worn image, that he invariably chose. Keats may have written of women as if he were describing confectionery; but at least he wrote of them with the gusto of an inexperienced and voluptuous boy; whereas the houris of Byron's verse, the Gulnares, Leilas and Zuleikas, are dolls—tinselled and spangled puppet-shapes—whose charms are celebrated in neat, lifeless phraseology:

> *Fair, as the first that fell of womankind,*
> *When on that dread yet lovely serpent smiling,*
> *Whose image then was stamp'd upon her mind—*
> *But once beguil'd—and ever more beguiling;*
> *Dazzling, as that, oh! too transcendent vision*
> *To Sorrow's phantom-peopled slumber given,*
> *When heart meets heart again in dreams Elysian,*
> *And paints the lost on Earth revived in Heaven;*
> *Soft, as the memory of buried love;*
> *Pure, as the prayer which childhood wafts above,*
> *Was she—the daughter of that rude old Chief,*
> *Who met the maid with tears—but not of grief.*

Couched in the rollicking rhythm that Byron loved, his Eastern tales have all the disadvantages of unreality, with none of the advantages of downright fantasy. His conception of the poet's rôle was very simple. Poetry was a recurrent fever, an afflatus. In certain circumstances—usually during the aftermath of some more than commonly exacting passion—it "bit" you; the poet gave way; and the result was a torrent of unbridled verse. He had little aptitude for correction or revision. That poetry might be produced in the struggle between the poet and the recalcitrant verbal medium, against which he had pitted all his strength and ingenuity, did not occur to a poet whose poems were a projection of the personal legend he had been spinning since his boyhood. Byron's view of poetry, and of his own function as a poet, was very similar to that of his enormous middle-class public. Seen through their eyes, he was a poet *par excellence*; divine frenzy, dark moods—not a single detail had been omitted from the portrait; he was a poet and he belonged to a life apart. Poetry was an incalculable and enigmatic gift, not a normal function of the civilised human mind.

The drawbacks of this attitude require no emphasis. In happier periods the poet was also student, scholar, courtier, or man of affairs; and it remained for Byron (a writer whose greatest ambition was to mingle with his fellow men on equal terms) to relegate him to the position of divine outcast. Hence the more futile aspect of Romantic literature. Hence that peculiar and distressing confusion between life and art which we owe to a generation of writers who treated the poetic faculty as a kind of sacred disease. Because Byron was an imperfect artist who realised his genius through the vicissitudes of his life, many versifiers, less magnetic, have set themselves to do the same. Byronism at second hand is a sorry mixture. Byron's influence was salutary and invigorating; but there is no doubt that his example did much to relax poetic standards and had a share in the general decline of taste that became manifest during the course of the nineteenth century. One has sometimes heard it suggested that the utilitarian spirit of the new age was largely responsible for the rapid and appalling decay of æsthetic intelligence that culminated in the Great Exhibition of 1851. It is a curious fact, however, that the ills with which the Victorian age was chiefly afflicted were caused by the very excess of Romanticism, and by the Victorian susceptibility to exotic influences. In 1822 the aspidistra (a plant that has the gruesome peculiarity of being fertilised by slugs) was introduced from the Far East; and a great deal of the exquisitely excruciating ugliness, symbolised by the aspidistra's bouquet of liverish-hued, dust-collecting leaves, had its origin in our ancestors' cult of the strange and foreign. Only Romantics could have exchanged the eminently reasonable domestic architecture of Georgian England for the peculiarly unreasonable and uncomfortable buildings in which our grandmothers and grandfathers were condemned to pass their lives. A sideboard of Gothic or debased Renaissance form is not more practical or prosaic than a side-table designed by Hepplewhite. Indeed, while the latter is prosaic (though convenient and beautiful), the former is an object recommended by its Romantic appeal, by its lack of modernity and by a richness of convoluted ornament scarcely to be paralleled save in the bas-reliefs of a Hindu shrine. The cult of the exotic did not begin with Byron; but the popularity of Byron's verse gave it a very powerful impetus. Moorish or sham-baronial knick-knacks were proper to a generation that delighted in *The Corsair*, *The Bride of Abydos* and *Childe Harold*. Just as Byron's effects were often showily successful, rather than produced with the patience and love that an Augustan poet would have devoted to his work, so Victorian taste aimed at an immediate effect. This effect is often sumptuous and romantic, but, examined closely, proves mechanical and mean.

It is true that, during Byron's lifetime, the process of deterioration had already gone far. To the Regency we owe some of the most charming small houses that England has produced; but the Brighton Pavilion, particularly when this excrescence of royal taste is set alongside the Chinese fantasies of an earlier epoch, affords a gloomy premonition of future ills. Outwardly, bathed in the pink or green of modern flood-lighting, the onion domes of the Pavilion seem to have descended straight from Cloud Cuckoo Land and to be just coming to earth—big coloured architectural bubbles—amid a fantastic region of dusky lawns and glow-worm lamps. Yet, inwardly, by the more uncharitable light of day, none but a very determined amateur of the "amusing" could feel that its ugly glass-paintings, huge, garish, badly proportioned rooms and gigantic dragon-chandeliers had very much to recommend them. Nor was the decadence of English taste confined to the Pavilion (an edifice as obese and unwieldy as the owner himself), Pugin's cast-iron conservatory at Carlton House or to the neo-Gothic mansions planned by Wyatt. We find a trace of the same decadence in details of furnishings; for it was during the Regency that curtains and hangings began to imitate those of the Near East, heavily fringed, made of heavy rich materials, red velvet trimmed with gold being especially popular. Rich . . . the word is evocative of the Romantic Age. "Un mobilier riche" was the dream of every Romantic poet and novelist—Balzac, who wore out his health preparing a Romantic background worthy of one of his own novels; even Baudelaire, whose early dandyism soon exhausted his small inherited fortune. The decline of taste and the spread of Romanticism went hand in hand; and in the rooms of many a young Romantic, with their Renaissance *bahuts*, curtained alcoves, inlaid tables, Turkish weapons and pipes, and exotic plants,[1] Byron's features glimmered down from a lofty pedestal. To write a study of Byronism would be to survey the entire field of Romantic poetry, music, painting. As far afield as Russia and as late as the close of the nineteenth century, Byron's spirit continued to range abroad. It haunts the pictures of Delacroix, the music—and the life—of Berlioz, the verses of Hugo, Lamartine and Alfred de Musset, the stories and the poems of Lermontov.[2] It inspired fashions, affectations, a manner of thinking, feeling, suffering that, although it was not altogether new, since Chateaubriand had launched *René* into the world some ten years before the publication of *Childe Harold*, had never before been carried to such a point of personal drama.

We have all heard how, when the news of Byron's death reached England, Tennyson, then a boy, ran out of his parents' parsonage and took refuge in a quarry, where he scratched on a sandstone cliff the words "Byron is dead"—a statement so tremendous and so appalling that he could scarcely believe it. And for a whole generation—Tennyson growing up to be the laureate who would attempt to cast a veil of romance over an English sovereign and her German consort; the Brontë children who incorporated Lord Byron, prototype of the fascinating and wicked Mr. Rochester, in the

[1]An illuminating account of a late Romantic interior is included in *Confessions of a Young Man*. "The drawing-room was in cardinal red, hung from the middle of the ceiling and looped up to give the appearance of a tent. . . . There were Turkish couches and lamps. . . . The bedrooms were made unconventional with cushioned seats and rich canopies, and in picturesque corners there were censers, great church candlesticks, and palms. . . ." George Moore bought himself a python and a Persian cat; while his friend Henry Marshall "used to sleep beneath a tree of gardenias in full bloom."

[2]On Pushkin, however, his influence is said to have been negligible; for Pushkin was not only the greater poet, but possessed something of the same "demonic" personal energy.

novels that afterwards gave birth to *Wuthering Heights* and *Jane Eyre*
—Byron's importance was conterminous with that of poetry. For
them, he was the greatest poet of modern times. In the eyes of
enthusiastic French admirers, Byron was less a human being,
however remarkable, than a portent, the personification of natural
forces:

> *Toi, dont le monde encore ignore le vrai nom,*
> *Esprit mystérieux, Mortel, Ange, ou Démon,*
> *Qui que tu sois, Byron, bon ou fatal génie,*
> *J'aime de tes conceits la sauvage harmonie.*

To the revolutionary French youth of the Romantic 'thirties, he
represented the very essence of their own struggle.

It was his virtue to release the energy of others. We may assert
that his influence was maleficent because (as Goethe observed) he
understood himself but dimly, and exercised his power in a wayward, half-unconscious and largely irresponsible fashion. Yet his
influence was salutary because, although Romanticism—and its
bastard offspring, romantic nationalism—destroyed much that was
of value and precipitated many disasters, both in the political and
in the literary sphere, it opened a new universe to adventurous
intellects. Henceforward the artificial hegemony—a kind of Haps-
burg Empire—imposed on the diverse and warring factions that
go to make up the human soul, could never be re-established. The
classicist treats Man as indivisible; he invokes Reason to produce a
semblance of quietude and harmony where none exists; while a
Romantic prefers chaos to fictitious calm. Thus the Romantic poet
who demanded liberty for the oppressed races of Europe—whether
they were Italians, Greeks, Poles or Magyars—demanded, too, that
his passions and emotions should be freed from the despotic
government of reason and good sense. Rousseau, by the pitiless
dissection of his mixed and miserable nature, had already demon-
strated that any human being, if he examines his past life beneath
the microscope, will find that the noble and the ignoble, the disinterested and the petty, are confused there beyond all possibility
of separation, that "good" or "bad" is rarely a valid term; and
Rousseau, though Byron professed to ignore the relationship,
together with Chateaubriand was a direct ancestor of Childe
Harold.

The Years of Fame

Byron was a man divided against himself; Childe Harold, a type of the individual whose conflicting impulses hurry him from place to place, from mood to mood, but who finds in the conflict itself a gloomy interest:

> Yet oft-times in his maddest mirthful mood
> Strange pangs would flash along Childe Harold's brow,
> As if the memory of some deadly feud
> Or disappointed passion lurk'd below:
> But this none knew, nor haply cared to know:
> For his was not that open artless soul
> That feels relief by bidding sorrow flow,
> Nor sought he friend to counsel or condole,
> Whate'er this grief mote be, which he could not control.

To-day, handled and worn by a thousand imitators, *Childe Harold's* affectations seem a little foolish; yet they echoed a profound uneasiness in the life of his time. For *Childe Harold* foreshadows the spirit of a new age, that would gaze and wonder at the extent of its own complexity.

Chapter 10

WITH a slight sense of bewilderment, one turns from a consideration of Byron to his literary or demonic rôle—Byron the sinner, Byron the wanderer, Byron the misanthrope—to the human being revealed by his letters and his journals. It is as though a faint sardonic smile were magically to play over the sullen and imperious features of Thorwaldsen's scowling bust; as though beneath the mask of the defiant and histrionic personage presented by Phillips's grandiose portraits—those portraits that impressed Hobhouse as most unlike —we should catch a glimpse of his genial and amusing friend! But *Childe Harold* was not all affectation, and the letters, though they possess the charm of brilliant spontaneity, were not entirely unstudied. Very often the same sallies and tricks of phrase were repeated for the benefit of several readers; and, as early as November 1812, he had observed to Lady Melbourne that a certain initial might be expected to puzzle future generations "when our correspondence bursts forth in the 20th century."

No, his letters were not completely unpremeditated; yet, while his character had a darker, more devious and, incidentally, a more heroic side, it is in his letters that we follow Byron from day to day. His quotidian self was cynical and speculative. "I wonder [he had scribbled in his diary] how the deuce anybody could make such a world. . . ." He could not be sure that he was happiest when alone; but this he did know—that he was never long "in the society even of *her* I love . . . without a yearning for the company of my lamp and utterly confused and tumbled-over library. Even in the day I send away my carriage oftener than I use or abuse it." It was now four days—he was writing on April 10th—since he had stirred from the shelter of his Albany rooms; but every morning he had a sparring bout with Jackson. Otherwise, fortified by biscuits and draughts of soda-water, he had read, written and idled through his solitary hours.

Yet his dull moments alternated with bursts of gaiety. At the end of March, just before he moved into his new apartments, he had dined *tête-à-tête* with Scrope Davies at the Cocoa Tree and, between six and midnight, had helped to drink one bottle of champagne and half a dozen of claret, returning home none the worse for his potations. Scrope, however, was left behind "tipsy and pious . . . on his knees praying to I know not what purpose or pagod." We hear of another occasion, too, when, in company with three friends, he sat up at the same club from six o'clock until four or five the next morning. Until two o'clock, they had consumed claret and champagne, had then supped and finished off the night with "a kind of regency punch," concocted of brandy, madeira and green tea, no real water being admitted to dilute the effect.

Lent provided the excuse of an access of *gourmandise*. A collar of brawn, eaten after "an enormous dinner," brought on severe indigestion; but the poet's appetite soon recovered; and it became "a subject of jocular resentment" (we learn from Moore) that once, when Lady Rancliffe invited him to dine after the play, the promised dinner should have dwindled to a mere supper, and that he had been regaled with a "damned anchovy sandwich." Heavy meals were accompanied by late hours, the year 1814 being one of balls, parties and public solemnities and celebrations beyond number. On April 20th, Louis XVIII, returning to his throne, had made a triumphal entry into London. The Regent had gone to welcome him as far as Stanmore; and from that town, where Louis, gouty, infirm and obese, was lifted bodily out of his carriage to greet the Prince, who, dressed in the uniform of a field-marshal, stood waiting at the door of a local inn, they had driven through vast crowds of cheering citizens. It was dusk before the royal carriages, escorted by Horse Guards, trumpeters splendid in gold lace, a hundred gentlemen on horseback, outriders, and "all the pomp and rabblement of royalty," drew up at Grillon's Hotel, Albemarle Street. "The people unanimously huzzaed;" ladies flourished their handkerchiefs; and the mountainous monarch, clutching the Prince Regent's arm, allowed himself to be conducted to the principal parlour. "Much overcome with fatigue," he accepted a chair. On his left was the Duke of York, on his right the Prince Regent and the Duchesse d'Angoulême; the Prince de Condé and the Duc de Bourbon sat facing him; and his suite and ambassadors and dignitaries packed the room.

In Albany Byron had listened to the roar of the crowd; but as a good Jacobin and the author of "a very beautiful *Ode to Napoleon Buonaparte*" (composed, during his fit of seclusion, on April 10th) he did not condescend to add to the triumph of "Louis the Gouty." Nor was he greatly impressed by the arrival of the Allied sovereigns, the King of Prussia and the Emperor of Russia, who reached London, accompanied by a large and distinguished *entourage*, on June 6th and remained until June 27th. "They have dined and supped [he told Moore] and shown their flat faces in all thoroughfares, and several saloons. Their uniforms are very becoming, but rather short in the skirts. . . ." London, meanwhile, was turned upside down. Every street had its mob. No tradesman, complained a middle-class Londoner, could get anything done. In the mornings it was impossible to buy new bread. Sometimes there was no milk, "as the cows are all frightened out of the Green Park by the constant huzzas, and many people cannot get their clothes washed, as the washerwomen work for Princes and Kings." Day and night a huge concourse of sightseers was gathered in front of the Pulteney Hotel in Piccadilly, which enclosed the autocrat of Russia, and Clarence House, St. James's, where the King of Prussia and his attendants had their lodging. Blücher and Platoff, Hetman of the Cossacks, were heroes of the rascality; "Blücher and Platoff was the cry, and the populace appeared ready to eat them up."

The excitement of the *grand monde* was equal to the enthusiasm of the proletariat. A great party was given by Lady Castlereagh, at which Blücher, who came straight from a banquet at Carlton House, had some difficulty in getting upstairs. At Lady Cholmondeley's, the Emperor, in a plain coat and kerseymere breeches, waltzed with Lady Jersey, "lovely as ever" and particularly pleased by these attentions since they displeased the Prince Regent, who refused to recognise her now that she championed the cause of the Princess. On June 11th the visiting royalties attended the opera to hear

Grassini; and, from Lady Tavistock's box, Hobhouse looked across at a box full of potentates, the King of Prussia, plump and hearty, the Emperor, whiskerless but magnificent, and the Prince himself, "a sad contrast to the healthy-looking monarchs between whom he sat," more than a little nervous in the neighbourhood of his unwanted wife. When she entered, "not very opportunely," the royal party, a phalanx of red and gold uniforms broken only by "the blue king of Prussia," rose to their feet and bowed over the auditorium in the general direction of their host's consort. There was some applause; but Hobhouse felt that it was half-hearted. For the time being, in the dazzling display of stars and ribbons, bitter domestic quarrels were laid to rest, and Whig and Tory forgot their differences in the pleasures of waltzing. 1814, which saw the restoration of legitimate monarchy, was as wild and feverish as that period of wonders 1812.

Byron soon succumbed to its heady influence. Did Moore recollect, he inquired, writing from Italy during 1822, "in the year of revelry 1814, the pleasantest parties and balls all over London"? Did he remember warbling duets with Lady **, "and my flirtation with Lady **, and all the other fooleries of the time? while ** was sighing, and Lady ** ogling him with her clear hazel eyes. But *eight* years have passed. . . ." It was now "amidst balls and fooleries, and after coming home from masquerades and routs, in the summer of the sovereigns," that he dashed off *Lara*, and, on June 12th, that he composed one of his most celebrated short poems. Lady Sitwell, the renowned bluestocking, had sent him a card for a party at her house in Seymour Road. Thither he went with Wedderburn Webster, and there for the first time met the wife of a second cousin, the beautiful Mrs. Wilmot, who was in mourning and wore a dark dress sewn with spangles. "When we returned to his rooms in the Albany," Webster explains, "he said little, but desired Fletcher to give him a *tumbler* of *Brandy*," which he drained to Mrs. Wilmot's health, then retired to bed and was (Webster learned afterwards) "in a sad state all night." Next morning, however, he wrote the verses that begin with a line so magical that, by comparison, the rest of the poem appears to dwindle away into insignificance:
She walks in Beauty like the Night . . .
A month earlier, at his special request, he had sent Moore a song:

I speak not, I trace not, I breathe not thy name,
There is grief in the sound, there is guilt in the fame:
But the tear which now burns on my cheek may impart
The deep thoughts that dwell in that silence of heart.

Too brief for our passion, too long for our peace,
Were those hours—can their joy or their bitterness cease?
We repent, we abjure, we will break from our chain,—
We will part, we will fly to—unite it again!

—"an experiment which has cost me something more than trouble."
There seems no doubt that the obsession to which he refers was
the passionate feeling that still bound him to "the Other A."

At present his preoccupations were more conventional; and,
during 1814, two young women had revived the ideas of marriage
and domestic respectability that were never far from his mind.
There was Lady Adelaide Forbes, daughter of Lord Granard,
towards whom he had already felt "seriously inclined" in 1813,
and whose features reminded him of the Apollo Belvedere; and
there was Lady Charlotte Leveson-Gower, daughter of Lord
Stafford, who, people assured him, was not pretty, but who had
"an air of *soul*" and the "shyness of the antelope." With Lady
Adelaide, he informed Lady Melbourne, he had never got beyond
the limits of polite conversation; and not a syllable of love had
passed between them, "but a good deal of heraldry, and mutual
hatred of music; the merits of Mr. Kean, and the excellence of
white soup and plovers' eggs for a light supper." With Lady
Charlotte, on the other hand, an acquaintance of Mrs. Leigh's, he
had had a brief and embarrassed, but somewhat emotional, meeting,
during which her confused reference to Mrs. Leigh—"a friend of
mine—a great friend of yours . . ." "Perhaps you mean a relation?"
"Oh yes, a relation"—set him off (he told Augusta) into "one of
our *glows* and stammers." For, although brazen enough when
occasion demanded, even now, Byron admitted, he was very often
shy.

Augusta encouraged and abetted him; and, during the summer of
1814, the chief enemy of Byron's peace of mind was Lady Caroline,
in whom, after a period of comparative quiescence, the spirits of
frenzy and mischief were again aroused. So closely did she beset his

door, he grumbled to Lady Melbourne, in a letter written on June 26th, that he was "already almost a prisoner." Lady Melbourne had talked of "keeping her out." It was impossible! "She comes at all times, at any time, and the moment the door is opened in she walks. I can't throw her out of the window. . . ." She was "a foolish, wicked woman." She had "no shame, no feeling," no single estimable quality. "If there is one human being whom I do utterly *detest* and *abhor* it is she. . . . She has crossed me everywhere, she has watched and worried and grieved and been a curse to me and mine."

Such was the discarded mistress who still hoped to badger him into accepting her as the companion of his life. But "I would lose a thousand souls rather than be bound to C."; and, if the worse came to the worst, he would fly from England and brave the censure of the world by taking Augusta[1] with him. Meanwhile it was difficult to repel her attacks. In she darted, inquisitive, reproachful, passionate; and one day, returning home, he found that she had effected an entrance and across the title-page of a copy of *Vathek*, which happened to be lying on his table, had scrawled the pathetic apostrophe: "Remember me!" "Yes," observed Byron, "I had cause to remember her;" and, "in the irritability of the moment," he sat down and wrote the eight furious and vindictive lines that, when Lady Caroline read them after Byron's death, are said to have done much to aggravate the condition of semi-insanity in which she passed her later years:

> *Remember thee! remember thee!*
> *Till Lethe quench life's burning stream,*
> *Remorse and shame shall cling to thee,*
> *And haunt thee like a feverish dream!*
>
> *Remember thee! Aye, doubt it not,*
> *Thy husband too shall think of thee:*
> *By neither shalt thou be forgot,*
> *Thou false to him, thou fiend to me!*

But there was another and a more momentous incident. Writing

[1]In the original letter the name of the person with whom he threatened to leave England has been carefully crossed out. The inference I have drawn seems permissible.

to Medwin in November 1824, Lady Caroline admits her passion, admits the scene at Lady Heathcote's ball and the Brocket *auto-da-fé*, admits that, after burning Byron in effigy, she had visited his rooms disguised as a carman, and therewith proceeds to give an account of their "last" meeting.[1] It occurred, she announces, at Albany. Byron appears to have been more than usually compassionate. He embraced her; and, as he pressed his lips on hers, " 'Poor Caro,' he murmured, 'if everyone hates me, you, I see, will never change— No, not with ill usage,' and I said, 'yes, I *am* changed, & shall come near you no more'—For then he showed me letters, & told me things I cannot repeat, & all my attachment went. This was our last parting scene—well I remember it. It had an effect upon me not to be conceived—3 years I had *worshipped* him."

Were it less typical of Byron, this story might perhaps be rejected as a figment of Lady Caroline's already disordered imagination. But the anecdote is curiously characteristic—just as characteristic in its own manner as the story (quoted by Lord Lovelace) of how, during the spring of 1814, he had given away the daughter of his attorney, John Hanson, at her marriage to the weak-minded Earl of Portsmouth,[2] and, while he led her up the church, had whispered an inquiry as to whether she recollected the circumstances in which he had seduced her several years before. Both anecdotes are disagreeable; both are unsupported by solid evidence; and yet in both of them we catch a glimpse of the Byron—afterwards to become painfully familiar—who experimented, coldly and cruelly, with human emotions. Was it in this mood that he confessed himself to Lady Caroline, that he "showed her letters, and told her things" so terrible—or, as her mother would have said, so "diabolick" —that all her affection vanished at a blow?

Yet his indiscretion may have had a practical motive. Possibly it interested him to put Lady Caroline's loudly expressed devotion to the supreme proof of entrusting her with a secret that has puzzled and disturbed two generations of critics and commentators; but it is also possible that, by divulging the real passion of his life and breathing the "dear, sacred name" that, even in his letters to Lady

---

[1] It was not their last meeting, as she goes on to explain in her next paragraph.

[2] This marriage, which did the Hansons and, incidentally, Byron little credit, was bitterly opposed by the Portsmouth family and ended in an acrimonious lawsuit.

Melbourne, is usually concealed behind an initial, a cross or the significant pseudonym "Corbeau Noir," he may have hoped that he could rid himself of her importunities. Whatever the motive, his confidences—and they were always ill-considered—can seldom have been worse placed. To Medwin in 1824 and to Byron during the troubled April of 1816, Lady Caroline denied—and denied with the utmost indignation—that she had originated, or had helped to spread, the rumours that were the cause of his public fall; but hints and head-shaking are as effective as direct statement. Lady Caroline had a strong sense of the melodramatic; and it is extremely difficult to believe that she held her tongue.

It would be interesting to know whether she was a repository of the tremendous secret at the time of the celebrated Watier's Masquerade, organised on July 1st by the members of Watier's Club[1] at Burlington House in honour of the Duke of Wellington's return. Certainly her efforts to gain Byron's attention had not then been relaxed. John Cam assumed an Albanian garb, Byron a monastic habit; and, as he sat in a retired part of the room "discussing points of Platonism" with another young woman, she passed "so frequently and remarkably" in front of his chair, masked and dominoed but making a great display of the "green *pantaloons*" which emphasised her unusually pretty legs, that he spoke to her in order to avoid a fracas. Dawn had begun to appear through the windows of Burlington House. Earlier in the evening, we learn from John Cam, Lady Caroline had asserted herself by playing "the most extraordinary tricks—made Skeffington pull off his red guard's coat—walked up into the private rooms." And Byron, shocked by the unfeminine bravado with which she exhibited her pantaloon-sheathed calves, "scolded her like a grandfather upon these very uncalled for, and unnecessary gesticulations."

It had been a strange, adventurous, disorderly evening, with the Duke of Wellington "in great good humour," the Duke of Devonshire presenting tickets for a raffle, and Colonel Armstrong, aide-de-camp to the Duke of York, disguised as "an old, stiff, maiden-lady of high rank in the reign of Queen Anne." There he sat,

---

[1]To this club, one of the most fashionable of the period, Byron had just been elected. He belonged, during his residence in England, to no less than ten clubs of various kinds, including the Alfred, the Cocoa Tree, Watier's and the Pugilistic.

flanked by two young rakes of fashion, dressed as his attendants, fanning himself and cracking outrageous pleasantries. Supper "in the temporary room, in which 1,700 people sat at ease," Hobhouse pronounced "the most magnificent thing of the kind ever seen." His Albanian costume was "much admired;" and he was more than a little vexed when a mask—"'twas one of the Miss Kinnairds"— approached him with the facetious interrogation: "Is that your electioneering dress?" Byron, in his monastic robes, "looked very well." Did he not look beautiful, marvelled a young lady, whose interest John Cam would have preferred to direct towards his own more resplendent Eastern trappings. But Miss Rawdon was not the only woman whose admiration was kindled at the sight of his splendid forehead, dark curling hair and the unearthly pallor—the "moonlight paleness"—of his skin. An unknown admirer lurked in the background. Harriette Wilson, one of the most celebrated and exclusive courtesans of her day, had been gazing—or so she told Byron many years later—at his "*very* beautiful countenance" and, while she gazed, imagining "a new sensation produced by the warm pressure of your lips to mine . . . wild and eager as your poetry."

"Jupiter [she concluded ambiguously] was all powerful in a cloud & *ladies* have been known to admire a *Horse*, but there is a *quieter, better*, more voluptuous feeling for a *woman*, and *you can't give it her*." She shook hands with him and suffered her own hands and feet—both very graceful—to be admired in return. So much we know from a collection of letters,[1] written to Byron in varying tones of passion, commiseration and moral reproof, that has recently come to light among his archives. She had accosted him; he had responded—as casually, no doubt, as he had replied to a host of other admirers who took advantage of the opportunities of the masquerade. But, when the time came to write her recollections, Harriette enlarged on this chance meeting until it assumed the importance of a heart-felt colloquy. Byron had been busily occupied from midnight to dawn; yet Harriette claims to have found him all alone, lost in meditation, posed amid a *décor* exactly suited to the musings of a romantic poet. For the room contained, "in a

[1]These letters were printed for the first time in the *Cornhill*, April 1935, with a commentary and introduction by the present writer. They have since been reprinted in *To Lord Byron*: Paston & Quennell. 1939.

profusion almost incredible," every kind of exotic plant and shrub. It was illuminated "by large ground glass, French globe-lamps, suspended from the ceiling at equal distances. The rich draperies were of pale green satin and white silver muslin. The ottomans, which were uniformly placed, were covered with satin to correspond with the drapery, and fringed with silver."

Harriette, who had been "mixing carelessly in the motley throng" and had received perfervid protestations from several gallant masks, one of whom had kissed her with such ardour that she was nearly suffocated—she loved a masquerade, she said, "because a female can never enjoy the same liberty anywhere else"—did not make her way to this charming retreat for some long time. When she entered, she caught sight of a solitary figure. "He was habited in a dark brown flowing robe, which was confined round the waist by a leathern belt, and fell in ample folds to the ground. His head was uncovered, and presented a fine model for the painter's art. He was unmasked . . . His age might be eight and twenty, or less; his complexion clear olive[1]; his forehead high; his mouth, as I afterwards discovered, was beautifully formed, for at this moment the brightness of the eyes and their deep expression fixed the whole of my attention. 'Surely that man's thoughts are occupied with intense interest on something he sees, which is beyond our common sight or conception,' said I, encouraging the mysterious turn of ideas, which had obtained the mastery over my imagination; 'and I will speak to him.' I approached slowly, and on the points of my feet . . ."

When she addressed him, "he started violently and reddened;" then answered, "rather peevishly," that he would advise her to look elsewhere, for he was "a very stupid masquerade companion." He rose; but Harriette seized "one of his beautiful little hands." "Listen to me," she implored dramatically. . . . It is unfortunate that, in the conversation she professes to report, Harriette should have been guilty of several egregious blunders. Thus, Byron discusses Lady Caroline's novel *Glenarvon*, which was not published until May 1816; and her letters make it quite clear that the friendship said to have flowered from this meeting—a platonic friendship

[1]"Are you as dark as at the Masquerade, or were you painted?"—Harriette Wilson to Byron at Ravenna.

spiced with much religious argument—was invented to soothe her wounded *amour propre*. Byron had had the bad taste to reject her homage. During his residence in Albany, Harriette, who, as she confesses, "had long been, sentimentally, in love with Lord Byron," wrote him a letter, begging to be allowed to make his acquaintance:

As nobody is to be found to introduce your Lordship, have you any objection to introduce yourself to a very impertinent young woman, who feels anxious to be allowed the honour of speaking to you?—I feel I am doing a very cool thing, but it was never my way to think of *forms* much. At the same time, I shall be miserable if I have disgusted by my want of ceremony the very person I am most disposed to admire. . . . If you think it is to make anything like *love* to you, don't come; but if you think you would like to see me (and I tell you I am melancholy and not worth it) write me word when you will call that I may be alone. If not, pray don't tell anybody that I wrote to you. I rely upon this; though I can scarcely flatter myself that Lord Byron will be at the trouble of making friends with   HARRIETTE WILSON

Byron, who had never been, in the ordinary sense of the word, a *coureur de femmes*, did not reply to this overture for three days; and when Harriet wrote, expostulating, she elicited a polite but guarded reply, in which he assured her that, although he was "not unacquainted" with her beauty and talents, he himself was not a person she would like "either as a lover or as a friend." Harriette was completely undeterred; she wrote again, closing her letter with a seal that represented a Cupid and bore as its motto the single word HUSH:

Thank you for your condescension. I did not mean that I could not love you, but merely that I would not make myself *de trop*; neither am I schoolgirl enough, at six and twenty, to imagine every man will turn out to be as delightful as his writings— *very* much the contrary. But I know you are clever and unhappy, and I am perfectly sure that I could love you with all my heart and soul. . . . If you would permit me, time would convince you that, whatever your faults and defects may be, *one* honest heart would love you; and, if at last you could be brought to feel comforted one moment at the reflection of being so dear

to me, I should think I had not lived in vain. . . . I have
neither talent nor beauty; a warm affectionate heart is my *only*
merit; and, though you are a stranger to me, I can never cease
to regret that *you* are not happy, and still more that you can
think it *happy* not to wish to be beloved. God bless you. May
I not hope once to kiss you before I die?

But Childe Harold's patience was quickly exhausted. He wrote,
coldly and stiffly, trusting that "this most brilliant acquaintance"
might now be permitted to end. Harriette retaliated by describing
his letter as "an *affected, prosing, stupid scrawl;*" she regretted, she
said, "that Childe Harold should have a fault in his whole composition, except *profligacy* which I should like . . ." and swept
from the stage with all the acrimony of injured pride.

Since they include no mention of the Masquerade, it seems
probable that these letters were written and received before July 1st.
Soon afterwards Byron paid a short visit to Six Mile Bottom,
returning on the 7th by way of Cambridge, where he dined with
Hobhouse and Scrope Davies, and setting out again on the 20th
of the month. Some three weeks were spent quietly at Hastings.
His companions were Augusta, Hodgson and Captain George
Byron, his cousin and heir presumptive. But, even at the seaside,
he did not remain unmolested for very long. Mary Chaworth, in
whose imagination the legend of Childe Harold continued to
ferment, had pursued him to London, and, having failed to surprise
him at Albany, followed him to Hastings, where she took rooms
in the same hotel. But she was too late; her quarry had eluded her.
He had been "swimming and eating turbot, and smuggling neat
brandies and silk handkerchiefs," listening to Hodgson as he
rhapsodised about the perfections of his future wife, "and walking
on cliffs, and tumbling down hills and making the most of the
dolce far niente. . . ." His nerves, however, were still troublesome;
and we hear that one day, becoming enraged with a large bottle of
ink, he seized and hurled it out of the window, so that it struck and
grievously bespattered a statue of Euterpe in the public garden.

The spectacle of Hodgson's felicity had done nothing to convince
him of the blessedness of the married state; but Augusta, who had
her own reasons for wishing to see him wed, supplied arguments of
a more effective kind. Jealousy seems to have had little place in

that childish and unreflecting nature; and "she wished me much to marry [he told Lady Melbourne] because it was the only chance of redemption for *two* persons," and she felt confident "if I did not that I should only step from one scrape into another, particularly if I went abroad." Was it at Hastings that he finally gave way? The candidate she sponsored was Lady Charlotte; whereas Byron, though he liked this timorous and graceful young woman well enough, was inclined towards the Princess of Parallelograms, with whom he had been carrying on a sentimental correspondence since the autumn of the previous year. Their friendship, it was true, had had many lapses; but, as often as Byron's attention had flagged, Miss Milbanke had been at some pains to revive his interest; and, after his return from Newstead in February, he had received a long and involved epistle, in which she discussed Conrad, the piratical hero of *The Corsair* (whom she compared to the satanic hero of *Paradise Lost*), and advised Byron to read Locke's defence of Christianity. She inquired anxiously whether he intended to leave England. Elsewhere she admitted that the hopeless love, hinted at in her opening letter, had been very largely fictitious; while, in the letter that followed, *à propos* the rumour that Byron had proposed and had been rejected a second time, she added a suggestion that a second proposal might be more favourably entertained. . . . "A letter from *Bella* [Byron noted in his Diary]. I shall be in love with her again if I don't take care." Then, on April 13th, she had invited him to visit Seaham. Byron's response was courteous and a trifle evasive; but to Lady Melbourne he delivered himself in a different style.

"If she imagines [he observed acidly] that I . . . delight in canvassing the creed of St. Athanasius, or prattling of rhyme, I think she will be mistaken." Perhaps Miss Milbanke understood that she had gone too far; and hostilities were suspended till the month of June, when she wrote begging him to let her know how he was, for she had been "rendered uneasy" by his long silence. "Prim and pretty as usual," recorded Childe Harold. At the end of June he answered her appeal; and on this occasion he recurred to her suggestion that he should visit her parents' house. His complaisance made Annabella "very happy;" and she confessed that every time she had met him in London last year, she had been

"vexed by the idea of having been repulsively cold towards you."
Meanwhile Byron had gone down to Hastings; but, although during
August their correspondence adopted a slightly warmer tone, it
became even more ambiguous, and Byron reported to Lady Melbourne that he feared Annabella had "been bewildering herself
sadly." Yet such tactics were not without effect. In the labyrinth
of Miss Milbanke's epistolary flirtation, Byron himself was beginning
to lose his way; and on the 10th of August she brought him to the
point. "I did—do—and always shall love you." It was a challenge,
both to Annabella and to his own destiny.

She replied with a mixture of innocence and guile. Amid fine
phrases and pious circumlocutions, Miss Milbanke expressed a
doubt as to whether Lord Byron were capable of making her happy;
and Byron's answer was both petulant and a shade relieved. "Very
well," he concluded crossly, "—now we can talk of something else."
Emboldened by his rejoinder, which she professed to interpret in
the literal sense, Annabella wrote, begging him to recommend
certain volumes of modern history. The declaration of undying
love had been composed while he was at Hastings; but, about the
middle of August, Byron and Mrs. Leigh travelled up to Newstead,
and it was at Newstead that he complied with her request. This was
on August 25th. . . . There comes a moment in the drama of
human affairs when, having passed the rapids, the stream rushes
smooth, swift and almost noiseless towards the shelf that hides the
falls. Then human actions assume an unnatural celerity. At
Hastings Byron had still no thoughts of marriage. Augusta, he
knew, was negotiating in his interest with Lady Charlotte; but these
manœuvrings did not cause him great concern. At Newstead,
however, Augusta's negotiations reached a decisive stage; she had
warned him against trying for Miss Milbanke—she reminded him
that he "hated an *esprit* in petticoats"—and Byron, pliable as always,
appeared to agree. With his consent, she drew up a definite proposal, which was duly forwarded to Lady Charlotte Leveson-
Gower.

Byron awaited her reply without anxiety. His attitude to the
whole affair was one of good-natured cynicism; and, when an
agitated refusal arrived at Newstead, he consoled Augusta, adding
(he explained to Lady Melbourne) "that I would try the next myself,

as she did not seem to be in luck." "The next," of course, was Annabella—the Princess of Parallelograms, the superior girl, whom Augusta might respect, but whom she did not at all approve of as a wife for her dear, tempestuous, exacting and unsettled B. Nevertheless, he was determined to take his chance. There was no gainsaying him; down he sat and, when the epistle was finished, he passed it to Augusta. She read it through, serious and perturbed. But her expression softened. "Well," she remarked, "really this is a very pretty letter; it is a pity it should not go—I never read a prettier one." "Then it *shall* go," Byron exclaimed; and thus it came about that two days after his letter of the 7th, in which he mentioned Porson and Epicurus and continued his list of historical authorities, he approached her with a second offer of his heart and hand. Odd that Augusta should have thought his letter "pretty"! The tone is cautious and stilted; Byron appears to write less in the hope that he will be accepted than in the determination to leave no possibility unexplored. Beginning with an apology, the letter hurries forward to an abrupt question: ". . . Are the 'objections' to which you alluded insuperable? or is there any line or change of conduct which could possibly remove them? I am well aware that all such changes are more easy in theory than practice; but at the same time there are few things I would not attempt to obtain your good opinion. At all events I would willingly know the worst. Still I neither wish you to promise or pledge yourself to anything; but merely to learn a *possibility* which would not leave you the less a free agent."

Byron himself did not anticipate that his proposal would be accepted. It was dispatched on the 9th of September; and on the 13th he wrote to Hobhouse, suggesting that they should join forces and cross the Channel. Money, at the time, was unusually plentiful. Claughton had forfeited his deposit of £25,000; Byron had £4,000 at the bank; he had finally broken his rule of refusing to pocket the profits of his pen, and *Lara* had brought £700; while "the Newstead Michaelmas will give me from a thousand to 15—if not 1800 more." His coach, saddles and bedding were all in order. Would not Hobhouse snap the few links that held them both to London, and set out for Italy—for the warm countries of the Mediterranean, for the lotus-lands that beckoned from the Near East? There was a possibility (he averred), a very remote possibility, that such a plan might become infeasible; but it was as unlikely as that Joanna Southcott would succeed in convincing mankind that she was the mother of a future Messiah. Little did Byron suspect the relief and exhilaration with which Miss Milbanke had received his second offer of marriage. She wrote immediately: ". . . I am and have long been pledged to myself to make your happiness the first object in life. *If I can* make you happy, I have no other consideration. I will *trust* to you for all I should look up to—all I can love. . . . This is a moment of joy which I had too much despaired of ever experiencing." And lest her letter should miscarry, she wrote two versions— apparently they were not duplicates, as Hobhouse pretends—which she posted, one to Newstead and one to Albany.

In what spirit did Byron read this passionate avowal? Again one notices the extraordinarily dramatic quality that he managed to infuse into all the decisive passages of his personal life. He was at Newstead, that melancholy and dilapidated building, already the witness of so many momentous and poignant scenes—Newstead, theatre of the cruelties, extravagances and follies perpetrated by his dim ancestral prototype, the Wicked Lord; Newstead, where he had quarrelled with Lord Grey de Ruthyn; where his mother had died; where Lady Frances had confessed her love but had not fallen; where he had been snowbound a memorable week with Mrs. Leigh. Here the doom that pursued the Byrons was omnipresent—in the naked skyline, stripped of its oak trees by the Wicked Lord; in every stone of the Abbey; underfoot, in the very soil on which he trod. And now, as he awaited a reply from Annabella, a gardener came to him with a ring that he had dug up in a flower-bed. It was his mother's wedding ring, lost many years before; and Byron decided that, if her reply were favourable, with this very ring he would himself be married. . . . He was at dinner when Miss Milbanke's acceptance arrived. Save for Augusta and the apothecary who had charge of his health, he was alone. Byron broke the seal and read the letter, then handed it across the table to Mrs. Leigh. "It never rains but it pours," he observed wryly, looking so pale that she thought he was about to faint.

Augusta's response was more ebullient. Feather-headed, foolish, optimistic, now that this marriage had been settled on, Augusta had made up her mind that it was to be a great success. "It is the best and prettiest I ever read!" she cried rapturously, as she returned the letter. Henceforward (she must have imagined) life—so difficult and beset with dangers during the last twelve months—would be as simple as her own simple and easy-going temperament demanded. There were periods during her later life when, having been forced into a career of subterfuge and deception, Mrs. Leigh may have seemed feline, treacherous and sly; but by disposition she was ill suited to the rôle of *intrigante*. She loved Byron; and there is no doubt that—both on his behalf and on her own—she was genuinely anxious that her brother should reach the haven of a successful marriage. Intuitively, she understood him; but, intellectually, the problems of his character were far beyond her grasp. She had allowed herself to be entangled in the Byronic web; but, though an impulsive and affectionate creature, "the good Goose" was also a woman of the world; and the worldly disaster that Byron had courted was horribly clear. Marriage offered an excellent solution; and Augusta gave the project all her support.

Byron seconded her enthusiasm as best he could. He wrote to Hobhouse, announcing his engagement—his note reached John Cam "a post or two after" the letter inviting him to leave England —and he wrote to Annabella, declaring that her acceptance had given him a new life: ". . . It was unexpected—I need not say welcome—but *that* is a poor word to express my present feelings— and yet equal to any other—for express them adequately I cannot. I have ever regarded you as one of the first of human beings. . . . I know your worth—and revere your virtues as I love yourself and if every proof in my power of my full sense of what is due to you will contribute to *your* happiness—I shall have secured my own.— It *is* in your power to render me happy— you have made me so already." He admitted that he had been on the point of leaving the country, "without hope, without fear—almost without feeling," and that his proposal had been a last, a desperate, throw; but his attachment (he assured her) had never waned. As he wrote, he may have believed what he was writing; and in private he made plans for immediate reform.

Chapter 11

DURING the earlier episodes of his career, the study of Byron's life resolves itself into a study of detail. From month to month, sometimes from day to day, we follow him through the labyrinth of adventure and intrigue, noting always amid a crowd of different actors the fixity that distinguishes the central personage. Inconstant, mobile, never at peace—and yet how constant are the impressions that a study of that curiously unchangeable character must leave behind! As the narrative proceeds, the tragic implications of the story become more and more obvious. Byron's personality is the force that sets the lesser personalities in motion; but, "unnerved" by past events, resigned to a fate he cannot control, he himself accepts the part of mere spectator. Let the women marry him if they thought it best! Augusta wished it; Lady Melbourne had assured him that marriage would be his salvation; and so confident was he of his adaptability that he felt sure that "*ma tante*" must be right. ". . . I could love anything on earth [he had announced] that appeared to wish it." The word "love," it was true, admitted of many diverse interpretations. "You won't believe me," he had written to Lady Melbourne on April 30th, ". . . but I really believe that I have more true regard and affection for yourself than for any other existence. As for my A., my feelings towards her are a mixture of good and diabolical. I hardly know one passion which has not some share in them. . . ." Both women had determined that he must marry; and, once he had proposed and had been accepted, and the initial shock of acceptance had died away, he enjoyed a delightful sense of duty done. Augusta noticed that, immediately after the engagement, his temper and spirits were exceptionally good.

Heaven, he said, had been kinder to him than he deserved.

To Lady Melbourne he wrote, hoping that she would give him her benediction and assuring her that he meant "to reform most thoroughly, and become 'a good man and true,' in all the various senses of these respective and respectable appellations." "Seriously," he concluded, "I will endeavour to make your niece happy . . ." It was a match of her making, he reminded her; his own attitude towards the marriage was the "very reverse" of lukewarm. Augusta (who had written to her future sister-in-law) was enchanted; but then, Augusta—though Lady Melbourne, of course, would "never believe that either of us can have any right feelings"—was "the least selfish person in the world. . . . Her only error has been my fault entirely, and for this I can plead no excuse, except passion, which is none." Unfortunately the mood of elation could not last. There was much to arrange; and Hanson, who was in trouble with the family of his son-in-law, the lunatic Earl of Portsmouth, proved extremely dilatory. The Milbankes had invited him to Seaham; Lady Melbourne was anxious that he should go; but Byron persisted that, until the lawyers should have met and settled the financial side of this alliance, this was out of the question. ". . . I am going, am I not? What would mine aunt have?" By the 17th he was "horribly low-spirited;" and, to Hobhouse, writing on the same day, he confessed that "the character of wooer in this regular way does not sit easy upon me. I wish I could wake some morning, and find myself fairly married."

There was no marrying, he was afraid, without bustle; and "I do hate . . . all fuss, and bustle, and ceremony so much." He had returned to London and, what with Hanson's dilatoriness and his own natural aversion from taking a decisive step, it was not till the end of October that he was again on the road. *En route* he halted at Six Mile Bottom; he was "proceeding very slowly" towards Seaham, he reported to Lady Melbourne when he had reached Newark; but as Lord Wentworth, Annabella's uncle, who was particularly desirous of meeting his heiress's betrothed, had already left, he considered it "very foolish dragging me out of town before my lawyer had arrived." He would not stay above a week, if he could help it; as Newstead was close, he was not sure that he would go at all. "Poor Mrs. Chaworth" had lost her wits. Altogether, "I am in very ill humour."

He reached Seaham on the evening of November 2nd. Annabella was in her room; she was reading; and, when she heard the wheels of his carriage, she blew out the candles and, "prudent and reflecting" as ever, deliberated within herself what she should do. She decided that she would go downstairs and meet him. He was in the drawing-room. There he stood beside the chimney-piece; he did not come forward as she approached, but took her extended hand and kissed it, and for a moment or two neither of them could summon a phrase. "It is a long time since we met," he murmured presently; then Annabella excused herself and hurried away.

She had pretended that she wished to call her parents. Annabella had been born fifteen years after the Milbankes' marriage and had grown up in the atmosphere of exclusive and concentrated affection by which the only children of middle-aged parents are often surrounded. Lady Milbanke had been "a dasher in her day." In 1814 she was a cheerful, managing person, who wore a wig and kept a firm hold upon her improvident but good-natured husband, that "honest, red-faced spirit," the epitome of eighteenth-century country gentleman and minor member of parliament, who had been nicknamed, by his more aristocratic sister Lady Melbourne, "old twaddle Ralph." Both parents were determined that the fascinating and formidable young man whom their daughter had chosen should see them at their best. The evening passed in general conversation; Byron talked of Kean—a favourite subject—and, as he talked, Annabella observed the air—it may well have been a symptom of extreme ennui—with which he manipulated the links of his large watch chain.

When they parted, Byron inquired at what time Annabella usually came down in the morning. About ten, he was informed. Punctually at ten, after a night of suspense and anticipation, she made her appearance; but at noon there was still no sign of the London dandy, who was apt (as we have already learned) to spend three hours dawdling through his toilet; and his betrothed took a solitary walk along the beach. . . . Byron remained at Seaham a whole fortnight; and during this period Lady Melbourne received several bulletins. He liked Sir Ralph, though his anecdotes were a little tedious; but for Lady Milbanke he felt a decided, though inexplicable, antipathy. Annabella herself was "the most *silent* woman I ever encountered," and her silences embarrassed him: "I like them to talk because then they *think* less." He had been studying her, he said; "but I fear she won't govern me; and if she don't it will not do at all." His next letter was somewhat more optimistic. "Annabella and I," he remarked, "go on extremely well." She was, as Lady Melbourne knew, "a perfectly good person;" but he had ascertained that "not only her feelings and affections, but her *passions*" were stronger than they either of them had supposed. Byron's first two letters are dated the 4th and the 6th of November; and his last, dated the 13th, shows an abrupt, ominous and disconcerting change of tone. He had doubts, he began, if the marriage would take place. Annabella's character was very far from being what they had imagined. She was "overrun with fine feelings, scruples about herself and her disposition," and, "to crown all," retired to bed with some mysterious malady once every three days. Moreover, she had recently made him a scene, "not altogether out of C.'s style," which was "too long and too trifling to transcribe" but which had done him no good.

Of this scene, as it happens, we have another and quite different account, furnished by Annabella in later life. His behaviour had not been ingratiating; upset by his moody and unaccountable manner when they were alone, Annabella, with characteristic firmness, offered to release him from the engagement; at which Byron "fainted entirely away." Then she was *sure* he must love her, she told her confidante, "speaking with great effort;" and, although Byron's conduct was often "peculiar," there were times when he was as winning and gentle as she could have desired. Of his sister, he talked tenderly and at length; but, while he explained that Augusta treated him as if he were a child and that Annabella reminded him of Mrs. Leigh "when you are playful," he added that no one else would ever possess so much of his love as the Other A.; and Annabella felt a pang of jealous grief. Nor was she reassured by his insinuation that, had she but married him two years ago, she would have spared him an experience that "I can never get over."

Byron left Seaham on November 16th. His sojourn had been longer than he had expected; and Annabella, who found the conflict of passion and common sense too much for her nerves, would appear to have suggested that it should be curtailed. From her point of view, his visit, so eagerly anticipated, so often and so unaccountably postponed, had been full of doubt, anguish and perplexity; but these emotions she did not divulge to her mother and father. They, at all events, had been captivated by their future son-in-law; around them he had woven that insidious and almost feminine charm which was one of his greatest gifts, listening, confabulating, laughing at jokes, until even the family solicitor had succumbed to his magnetism. As soon as he was gone, Annabella felt ashamed of the doubts that had possessed her while she was seeing him every day, and wrote to apologise for the anxiety that her troubled "visage" had sometimes caused; "when you return my troubles will be ended . . ." Posting back towards Augusta, by way of Newstead, Byron dispatched an affectionate but flippant reply.

He continued to write with the utmost regularity. Before his visit, he had been a faithful correspondent; but, though his letters were seldom short and usually contained one or two expressions of warm regard, as love-letters they are never very convincing. The mention of love seems to occur as an epistolary afterthought. Byron may have believed that he was in love; but his passion certainly did not overflow on to the paper of its own accord; whereas Annabella's, though pompous and consequential, have a nervous and vibrant quality that speaks for itself. In bulk, their correspondence makes tiresome reading. Still, read it must be, if we are to understand the characters of the young man and young woman who proposed, with the sanction of church and law, to spend the rest of their lives beneath the same roof. The outlines of Byron's character have now appeared; that of Annabella is indistinct; and, from the letters that she wrote before the 20th of September, we gain—somewhat too exclusively—the impression of a high-minded and priggish girl who had been "Clarissa Harlowed into an awkward kind of correctness." But she was by no means the insipid personage we may have supposed her. Annabella had strong feelings, a strong will and a strong determination to do good according to her lights. Were virtue a matter of determination, Miss Milbanke would have been a heroine, a martyr or a saint. She had been taught that she must think first, and must never act until she had reflected upon the possible consequences of her action as deeply and conscientiously as her nature allowed; and thus it came about that, being conscientious and naturally reflective, her response to life was often lacking in spontaneity.

There were many who said that her heart was cold. They had misjudged her. Her emotions were vivid; now and then they became positively violent; but even more imperious was the willpower that ordered, modified and held them in check. Yes, Annabella was a *good* woman. During her entire existence, we may doubt if she committed herself to a single gesture that was deliberately, purposefully and self-consciously wicked. It is unfortunate that goodness should not always depend upon good intentions. The effects of spiritual pride are extremely insidious; and, if there was one sin that Annabella must plead guilty to, that sin was pride. Her weakness was a blighting self-sufficiency; she had studied a large variety of subjects and, although she was a stern critic of her smallest shortcomings, her opinion of her own judgment was unusually high. Holmes's miniature (which bears a marked resemblance to a daguerreotype portrait of Annabella as an elderly woman) reveals a face agreeable rather than pretty, and uncommonly decided when we remember that it belonged to an unmarried girl who, at the time she sat for her likeness, was only twenty years old. The miniaturist had insisted that she should loosen her hair; but this touch of romanticism hardly accords with her straight, firmly drawn eyebrows, with her sharp but well-modelled nose, with her thin lips and the hint of obstinacy about her jawbone. The face is not unpleasant but oddly masterful. She loved Byron; she was prepared to devote her life to making him happy; but her love was an exacting passion of the brain and nerves. Annabella was inclined to love through her sense of duty; and dutifulness was not a trait that Byron valued.

He liked women whose love was sensual and spontaneous, who laid no claims, made no demands. Augusta, for example. . . . He had hastened back to Six Mile Bottom, and thence reiterated Mrs. Leigh's sisterly messages and her regret that, as she was still nursing Medora, she had not been able to accept the Milbankes' invitation. From Newmarket he went to Cambridge, "to vote for a friend who is a candidate for a medical professorship." There he met Hobhouse,

Hodgson and Annabella's first cousin, George Lamb; and, as he entered the crowded Senate House, "the young men [wrote Hodgson] burst out into the most rapturous applause." A few days later he had returned to Albany; no date had been fixed for the approaching marriage; but at Seaham there were preparations, a cake was baked and Sir Ralph set to work on an epithalamium—the Milbankes had a huge store of domestic pleasantries—which he intended to read aloud when the happy moment came.

In London Byron was contending against Hanson's slackness. He had drunk too much; the parrot had bitten his fingers. Claughton had renewed his offer to purchase Newstead, on the same terms as before; but in the end this proposal fell to the ground. The details of the marriage settlement were drawn up—£60,000 to be settled by her husband on Annabella, who, as her dowry, was to receive £20,000 from Sir Ralph. Annabella's jointure was £1,000 a year; and, according to the settlement, her husband agreed to allow her £300 as pin-money. Byron, in fact, expected to gain a mere £700; but it was understood that Lord Wentworth, an old and infirm man, had made Annabella his heiress and that, when he died, she would inherit a comfortable fortune. Byron's debts were an immediate source of anxiety. He had some scruples about marrying while Newstead was still unsold; and in the middle of December he wrote to Miss Milbanke, suggesting, very tentatively, that, as Claughton had again failed him, it might be advisable to postpone marriage until his prospects brightened. ". . . 'To marry or not' that's the question—or will you wait?" But she would neither wait nor hearken to his excuses; she would marry him, she declared, rich or poor. When did he intend to go through the ceremony? It was no easy matter to nail him down to a definite reply.

He hedged; he temporised; he dawdled. A special licence must be procured from the Archbishop of Canterbury. He had written for it, and hoped to set off, he announced—this was on December 18th—"on Saturday next;" but it was "proper to add" that he might be subpœnaed to give evidence in "Lord Portsmouth's lunatic business," the lawsuit between the Hanson and Portsmouth families, which hinged on a question as to whether Lord Portsmouth, when he married, had been of sound mind. The lawsuit, however, did not delay him. At Seaham the Milbankes had been growing restive;

but the promise of "next Saturday" cheered their spirits. "Dearest —you and happiness will come together," wrote their daughter, with the emotion of recovered serenity.

Hobhouse had been chosen as best man. The two friends left London on the 24th; but Byron was in no hurry; and, at Chesterford, they parted, Hobhouse bound for Cambridge, Byron for Six Mile Bottom, where he had elected to spend Christmas Day. It had been arranged that they should meet again on the 26th; but Byron did not appear until the afternoon. "Never was lover less in haste . . ." recorded John Cam, and, a little later: "The bridegroom more and more *less* impatient . . ." On the evening of the 30th they reached Seaham; and by this time Lady Milbanke was so much agitated that she had retired to her room. Annabella intercepted Byron in the passage, "threw her arms round his neck and burst into tears. She did this *not* before us . . ." Hobhouse explains; he himself was in the library and, as he waited there, expectant and embarrassed, the door opened and Miss Milbanke crossed the threshold. She approached and, "with great frankness," took his hand. "Rather dowdy-looking," Hobhouse observed. Annabella, though she had excellent feet and ankles, wore "a long and high dress . . . The lower part of her face is bad, the upper, expressive, but not handsome . . ." She seemed to improve when he studied her closely; quiet, sensible and modest, she spoke seldom and inspired an interest that it would have been easy enough (Hobhouse considered) to mistake for love. While they were talking, Sir Ralph "tottered in." Gradually the family party began to assemble—the host prosy "but by no means devoid of humour," the hostess "pettish and tiresome," Mr. Hoar, Sir Ralph's confidential agent, and an illegitimate son of Lord Wentworth, the Reverend Thomas Noel, the clergyman who was to perform the marriage ceremony.

Hobhouse had stammered out some vague excuses. Their "want of expedition" was hard to explain; but Byron was completely unabashed and, while he charmed the parson "by his kindness and open manners," Hobhouse continued to watch Miss Milbanke—of his friend, he noted, "she seemed dotingly fond"— as she gazed with delight on "his bold and animated face." Her adoration, nevertheless, was "regulated . . . with the most entire decorum. Byron appears to love her personally, when in her company . . ." Sir Ralph related a series of anecdotes; altogether the evening passed off more pleasantly than one might have expected. Next day, the 31st, dawned fine and brilliant; and Hobhouse went for a walk along the beach. After dinner the party amused themselves with a mock marriage, in which John Cam enacted the rôle of bride.

The New Year was rung in, and they shook hands. The first day of 1815, overshadowed by the impending marriage, was somewhat less successful; dinner was "not quite so jolly" as the day before, "but fair considering;" and, late that night, Byron sounded a despondent note. "Well, Hobhouse," he said pensively, "this is our last night; to-morrow I shall be Annabella's." *Absit omen*, commented Hobhouse in his journal. He, at least, recognised the strength of affection that united Byron to friends of his own sex; and he may have doubted if a young and inexperienced girl—though Hobhouse had changed his opinion of her appearance and decided that "the young lady is most attractive"—would succeed where more experienced women had failed. But it was impossible to turn back at the eleventh hour. Morning came; Hobhouse, in full dress, with white gloves, went downstairs and found Byron, already up and prepared, Sir Ralph and Thomas Noel robed in his canonicals. "Her Ladyship could not make tea, her hand shook." At half-past ten, Byron and Hobhouse withdrew, and, after a short interval, ascended to the drawing-room. Byron was wearing kid gloves, a white embroidered waistcoat and frilled shirt;[1] Noel and another clergyman were in attendance, and, when the whole party had taken their places, Miss Milbanke entered the room, followed by her governess and her mother's companion, "the respectable Mrs. Clermont." "She was dressed in a muslin gown trimmed with lace at the bottom, with a white muslin curricle jacket, very plain indeed . . ." Cushions had been arranged, and the couple knelt; Noel officiated, while the second clergyman read the responses.

Looking steadfastly at Byron, Miss Milbanke remained "as firm as a rock" throughout the entire ceremony; her voice was clear and decided; but Byron "hitched at first" as he began: "I,

[1]Gloves, waistcoat and shirt are now preserved in the collection of Sir John Murray at 50 Albemarle Street.

George Gordon . . ." and when he came to the words: "With all my worldly goods I thee endow," he glanced up at Hobhouse with a half smile. At eleven o'clock they were pronounced man and wife. A year later, in *The Dream*, Byron gave a poetic account of the emotions that had traversed his mind that memorable day:

A change came o'er the spirit of my dream.
The Wanderer was return'd—I saw him stand
Before an Altar—with a gentle bride;
Her face was fair, but was not that which made
The Starlight of his Boyhood . . .
And he stood calm and quiet, and he spoke
The fitting vows, but heard not his own words,
And all things reel'd around him; he could see
Not that which was, nor that which should have been—
But the old mansion, and the accustom'd hall,
And the remember'd chambers, and the place,
The day, the hour, the sunshine and the shade,
All things pertaining to that place and hour,
And her who was his destiny—came back
And thrust themselves between him and the light:
What business had they there at such a time?

His narrative is dramatic but disingenuous. There was no giving it up, the romantic legend, so well suited to the purposes of sentimental biography, that a disappointed passion for Mary Chaworth had warped the entire course of his early life—"poor Mrs. Chaworth," of whose marriage he had spoken to Hobhouse in a tone that was anything but reverential, whom he had avoided meeting, and who lingered on as a half-demented invalid!

Yes, it seems improbable that thoughts of Mary Chaworth—of "her who was his destiny"—loomed very large in Byron's imagination as he knelt there, upon one of the two hard cushions that had been laid out in the Seaham drawing-room, and heard Noel pronounce the words that sealed his fate. His memoirs would appear to have repeated the story told by *The Dream*. "In that Memoir [wrote Tom Moore, drawing from what he recollected of the destroyed manuscript] he described himself as waking, on the morning of his marriage, with the most melancholy reflections, on seeing his wedding-suit spread out before him. In the same mood, he wandered about the grounds alone, till he was summoned for the ceremony. . . . He knelt down, he repeated the words after the Clergyman; but a mist was before his eyes—his thoughts were elsewhere; and he was but awakened by the congratulations of the bystanders, to find that he was—married."

He wished (he had declared, two months earlier) that he could wake up some morning and find himself married; and now—if we are to accept the story quoted from his memoirs—his wish had come literally true. After a period of merciful anæsthesia, he had woken up to the discovery that he was a married man. Hobhouse embraced him "with unfeigned delight." His mother-in-law kissed him; she was "much affected," as was Annabella's governess, Mrs. Clermont. The register was signed; and Annabella, her eyes full of tears when she looked at her father and mother, hastily left the room. "Byron was calm and as usual." Hobhouse's wedding present was a complete collection of Byron's Poems bound in yellow morocco; and, a little before noon, he handed Lady Byron downstairs and into the carriage where this appropriate gift had already been stowed away. He wished her many years of married happiness. "If I am not happy," replied Annabella, in resolute tones, "it will be my own fault."

Of his "dearest friend," he "took a melancholy leave." Through the carriage window, Byron had grasped his hand and, even when the carriage had begun to move, seemed unwilling to let it go. Did Hobhouse understand the implications of his tenacity—of that desperate clinging, not only to the world of masculine companionship in which he had always been most at his ease, but to youth itself and to the very spirit of youthful freedom? But, whatever Hobhouse's response, it was interrupted. Reluctantly, Byron released his hold; accompanied by the bangings of a *feu de joie* and the clashing and tinkling of the little bells of Seaham Church, the carriage lumbered off and was lost to sight. Had she not behaved well, demanded Lady Milbanke, "as if she had been the mother of Iphigenia."

From this point, Annabella is our chief authority. Lady Byron may have been an unsympathetic, but it is clear that she was an extremely truthful—indeed, an almost mathematically meticulous—young woman; and a study of her later life leaves us no grounds for imagining that she suffered from "delusions" of the kind that were imputed to her by her husband's defenders after Mrs. Beecher Stowe's indiscreet and ill-timed revelations in the year 1869. The events of that day and of the next few weeks were ineffaceable. Moreover, the actions and utterances that she reports are so Byronic that it is difficult to believe that Annabella, who, with all her intelligence, was completely devoid of imagination, could have invented them to blacken her husband's name. She had set out determined that she would make him happy. She did not minimise the task that she had undertaken; but, through their engagement, she had harboured a pathetic belief that, once they were wedded— once the marriage ceremony had delivered him to her care—their troubles would gradually grow lighter. Good sense and good feeling *must* prevail! But the carriage that bore her away from Seaham—from a doting mother and father, from the tiny sheltered universe in which she had been brought up—was hurrying her to a very different spiritual clime, towards a region beyond the frontiers of her understanding. Here good sense and good intentions were ineffective; the single quality that might have assisted her she had never possessed.

Her nature was curiously inelastic; and it was just that inelasticity —that touch of stubborn self-will—which was calculated to madden her irascible bridegroom; whereas the *bonté* of more experienced but less intellectual women comforted and charmed him. A long journey lay before the married couple; Halnaby Hall, Sir Ralph's Yorkshire estate, was their destination; and Lady Byron, wrapped in a slate-coloured satin pelisse (which Hobhouse mis-remembered as being trimmed with bands of white fur), sat back, tensely prepared to do her duty. From his corner, Byron did not speak; "a wild sort of singing" presently escaped him; but it was not until they reached the outskirts of Durham and heard the bells greeting them from the church towers—Sir Ralph had represented the city in parliament—that Byron condescended to a first remark. "Ringing for our happiness, I suppose?" he observed, in a voice of bitter sarcasm.

"It *must* come to a separation!" he declared, a little later. She should have accepted his original offer of marriage; for in the meantime something had happened of which the effects could never

be repaired. It was her fault. . . . He would be even with her. . . .
She would find that she had married a devil. . . . His attitude was
violent, almost frenzied. But soon his mood changed; he laughed
when he noticed that she seemed hurt, bade her pay no attention to
what he said, and concluded by expressing "every feeling of
tenderness." And so the miserable comedy went on. He might
comfort her; but soon the pressure of his own secret emotions
was too much for him, and he mused—aloud—as to how long he
would be able to sustain the part he had been playing and insinuated
that he and her aunt were fellow conspirators. Annabella, the
spoiled child, was now in his power; "and [he promised gloomily]
I shall make you feel it."

Thus they drove south through a snowy afternoon, Annabella
puzzled and distraught, Byron continuing—with phrases so
characteristic that, even on authority much worse than Annabella's,
it would be difficult to dismiss them as invented or garbled—to
pull down the fabric of happiness she had carefully reared. But
room must be found for another anecdote, derived from Joanna
Baillie, who repeated the story to Benjamin Haydon: "She said
[writes the painter] that Byron had told her that, on the very
morning he and Miss Milbanke were married and were driving
home through the grounds, Byron said to her: 'What could induce
you to marry me?' 'Good heavens!' said Lady Byron, 'because I
loved you.' 'No,' said he, 'you have a spice of Mother Eve; you
married me because your friends wished you not to do so. You
refused me twice and I will be revenged.'" In this anecdote the
accent has slightly changed. No doubt, during the drive to Halnaby,
Byron indulged in a kind of sadistic teasing and in outbursts of
rhetorical desperation, sharpened by the conflict that was being
waged within himself; but one conjectures that he did not intend
she should take him seriously: it was mere melodrama, with a real
tragedy behind the scenes. Yet, making the utmost allowance for
his braggadocio, he must have understood—and perhaps relished—
the desperate pain that he inflicted.

They reached Halnaby, and the butler was on the steps. Byron
(he informed Harriet Martineau in later years) did not hand his
wife out of the carriage, but walked away; while Lady Byron dismounted "with a face and attitude of despair." She entered the

house "with a countenance and frame agonised and listless." So young and so lonely did she seem, that her father's servant longed to offer her his arm. According to friends who were privileged to read his memoirs, Byron claimed there that he had consummated his marriage on a sofa before going in to dine. After dinner, remembered Lady Byron, the bridegroom explained that he hated sleeping in the same bed with any woman, but she might share his bed if she chose, and added that, provided she was young, one woman was as satisfying as another. They spent their wedding night in a large bed with red damask curtains. The light of the fire, and of a solitary taper, glimmered through—for Byron was always fearful of the darkness; and, in that wavering ruddy illumination, she heard him wake up with the cry, furious and anguished: "Good God, I am surely in Hell!"

That cry set the tone of the whole honeymoon. Elsewhere Byron is reported to have said that he had "a great mind to believe in Christianity for the mere pleasure of fancying I may be damned;" and to this remark we must append the footnote that, if Byron did not believe in Christianity, he certainly believed in the doctrine of sin and damnation, and that, lacking a belief in some definite and predetermined system of pains and penalties, he was obliged to provide the torments of his own inferno. But this was an aspect of his character that very few of his intimates were allowed to see. Next morning he met Annabella with "words of blighting irony." It was too late now, he said; what had been done could not be undone. Yet that very day he sat down to compose a letter to Lady Melbourne in his usual affectionate and flippant vein, and painted a pretty picture of domestic bliss. As he wrote, Bell was lying "fast asleep on a corner of the sopha." They might have been married, to judge from appearances, full fifty years. The ceremony had gone off "vastly well;" though "Lady M. was a little hysterical, and fine-feeling; and the kneeling was rather tedious, and the cushions hard." However, they were now man and wife, and shut up together at Halnaby "according to approved custom."

His confidante, presumably, was somewhat relieved. Yet she had misgivings. It was Lady Melbourne's unshakable conviction that, far from being the simpleton she pretended, Mrs. Leigh was "very wicked and very clever;" and, at the end of January, she wrote to remind him that, "although you have no *Corbeau Noir*, actually *noir*, you may have one flying about, with *many* black feathers in her plumage." Little did Lady Melbourne suspect that, on the morning after his marriage, the *"cher Neveu"* had received a letter from Augusta, which opened with the phrase: "Dearest, first, and best of human beings," and referred to the emotions she had experienced at the hour of the ceremony: "As the sea trembles when the earth quakes . . ." This letter had stirred him to "a kind of fierce and exulting transport;" and he had read the first words to Annabella, inquiring triumphantly: "What do you think of them?"

Hints and innuendoes fell all around her—his uncontrolled fury when, happening to read Dryden's *Don Sebastian*, she questioned him about the subject, and manifold allusions of the same tendency. He repeated his assertion that, between his first and second proposal, something had happened that he could never get over. He was a villain to have married her—he could convince her of it in three words;[1] yet, if she had married him two years ago, she might have saved him. "I only want a woman to laugh," he announced, "and don't care what she is besides. I can make Augusta laugh at anything. No one makes me happy but Augusta." Annabella, it was true, could not make him laugh; yet, during those early days, she showed an unexpected skill in calming his more obviously distempered moods. She had grasped the fact that his lameness was responsible for much of his eccentricity, and persuaded him to talk of it without reserve. Under her influence, he displayed his childish side, was grateful for small services—"You are a good kind Pip— a good-natured Pip—the best wife in the world"—or spoke of himself in the third person. "B's a fool," he would murmur, "—Yes, he *is* a fool" and, disconsolately, "poor B—*poor* B."

There were moments of playfulness, as when he nicknamed her "Pippin"—a reference to the roundness of her face—to which she retorted, rather inexplicably, with the pet-name "Duck"; of tenderness, almost reverential, as when, after a particularly atrocious scene, he exclaimed: "If anything could make me believe in Heaven, it is the expression of your countenance at this moment"; of passive

---

[1]Byron seems to have hinted, on various occasions, that he was already married; and there is some evidence that, at an earlier period, he may have gone through an irregular ceremony, which he believed might possibly be binding.

grief, as when, in Walter Scott's latest poem, he pointed out to her, "with a miserable smile," lines that seemed to describe just such a bridegroom as himself. Often pity was uppermost in her emotions. Surely, she felt, the stories that he told her—those horrible and half-incomprehensible reminiscences of past sin, of his affair with Lady Oxford and of how he had attempted to seduce her thirteen-year-old daughter Lady Charlotte—must proceed from a mind radically disordered. She noticed his terror of approaching age; the misery that he suffered when, among his thick chestnut curls, he discovered a single grey hair; his fear of the dark, and—even more perplexing—his dread, vouched for by other witnesses, of some mysterious foe bent on his destruction.

Did he not travel fully armed? In the library itself, where they read together, and Byron wrote and Annabella copied the *Hebrew Melodies*, his weapons lay handy on the table. Sometimes, at night, when Annabella, bewildered and broken, had retired to her room, he would pace hour after hour, girt with dagger and pistol, up and down the deserted gallery of the old house. Once he reached her bed, woebegone to the verge of collapse. "Seeking to allay his misery," she moved her head so that it rested beneath his shoulder. "You should have a softer pillow than my heart," he said; and she replied: "I wonder which will break first, yours or mine."

They were "the only words of despair he ever heard me utter." Still Annabella clung to her belief that good intentions, patience, magnanimity, must prevail against the sickness, moral or intellectual, that had warped and disfigured her husband's mind. Yet, knowing Byron as we do, it is impossible to dismiss the idea that the frenzy of those catastrophic weeks may have been, to some extent, factitious. The remorse was deep and genuine; but it was deliberately enlarged on. The conflict existed; but, though Annabella's virtues were calculated to inflame the passions of remorse, pride and resentment they were intended to subdue, one suspects that he was not unmindful of his legendary prototype, and that his thoughts may have strayed back to the Wicked Lord. He, too, had been proud, lonely and unhappy; he, too, had alienated and misused his wife.

The three wretched weeks passed at Halnaby drew to a close. At best, Byron's behaviour had been odd, violent, inconsiderate —the attitude of a *poseur* who seemed determined to play Petruchio and the Prince of Denmark as the same part; at worst, savagely and intentionally cruel. Admitted that few honeymoons run entirely smooth; that the wife was as limited and literal-minded as the husband was prone to paradox and wild hyperbole; yet the sentences she records ring disturbingly true. Byron alone could have conceived and acted such a rôle; Byron alone, amid an extravagant display of his worst qualities, could have remained so lovable, so strangely attractive, that Annabella determined that no hint of her misery should be allowed to pass her lips. For three weeks the demon had been at large. Then again it subsided. From Halnaby, the Byrons returned to Seaham; and here, apparently a devoted couple, they remained as guests of the Milbankes until March 9th.

To Annabella, Byron was kinder than usual; and, soon after they arrived, on February 5th, an accident occurred that shook him profoundly. He had a habit of writing late in his dressing-room; annoyed by the heat of a large fire, banked high with the produce of Sir Ralph's collieries, he drenched it with water—and was almost suffocated by the fumes that it produced. Half asphyxiated, he had the presence of mind to stagger into the bedroom. Describing this adventure for Lady Melbourne's benefit, Byron passes it off lightly, remarking, however, that "if Bell had not in the nick of time . . . sluiced me with Eau de Cologne" and similar restoratives, "you might now have been repairing your latest suit of black to look like new for your loving nephew." Annabella herself relates the sequel; when he recovered consciousness, he imagined that he was dying and "broke forth into the wildest ravings of despair, saying that he knew that he was going to Hell, but that he would defy his Maker to the last, with other expressions of a revengeful nature. . . ." Presently his fears quieted and he became gentle. "I have tried everything—I will try virtue, I think," he said. "Perhaps I shall go to Heaven, holding by the hem of your garment."

For a time his behaviour was uncommonly mild. But even more dolorous than the desperation he had evinced at Halnaby was the resignation with which he adapted himself to life at Seaham. He did his best to support the part of dutiful son-in-law. There were long, long domestic evenings to be got through; and Byron scribbled *bouts-rimés*, played at draughts with Mamma, and on one occasion, when the whole family acted charades, so far forgot himself as to appear in his dressing-gown turned inside out and Lady Milbanke's long-haired wig—snatched from her head for the purpose; while Annabella assumed "his travelling-cap and long cloak, with whiskers and mustachios." "Only think of B. playing drafts!" wrote Augusta, in one of her faintly feline epistles, which she addressed to Annabella, but punctuated with allusions that were intended, no doubt, to catch Byron's private eye: "He has now so many occupations . . . but I am vain enough to think he does not forget Guss."

Certainly her brother had not forgotten her; and on February 2nd, he wrote to Lady Melbourne, remarking that he supposed "your 'C—— noir' is X; but if X were a raven, or a griffin," he must still continue to take omens from her flight. A few days later "ma tante" reopened the theme. In one respect, she confessed, her thoughts were "as black, and as hideous as any Phantasm of a distempered brain can imagine;" but, barring the passionate aspect of the situation, she knew of nobody "more fitted for your *Corbeau blanc*, from cleverness, good humour, and a thousand agreeable qualities"—quite apart from a sympathy with, and knowledge of, his character that rendered the Other A. "more able to manage and advise."

Her nephew seemed "altogether mighty comfortable." . . . Comfortable he may have been; but, at the same time, he was bored to distraction. Life at Seaham—then a little fishing-village, perched on a dreary and weather-beaten coast—went by in a monotonous round of local affairs. News there was none, save talk of ship-wrecks and county meetings. After dinner, left alone with honest, red-faced Sir Ralph, Byron listened to the monologue that his father-in-law mistook for conversation, until he could bear it no longer and abruptly absconded. He wished (he complained to Lady Melbourne, who had also suffered from her brother's provincial garrulity) that Sir Ralph "would not speak his speech at the Durham meeting above once a week after its first delivery." It was in the exasperation produced by one of these sessions, when he had risen from the table and abandoned Sir Ralph still rehearsing his periods, "over various decanters, which can neither interrupt him nor fall asleep,—as might have been the case with some of his audience," that he wrote to Tom Moore, for the third time since his marriage. At the end of the letter, he was summoned to tea. "Damn tea," he ejaculated. "I wish it was Kinnaird's brandy. . . ." From the cliffs of Seaham he had witnessed a sudden tempest, "in all the glories of surf and foam;" and this vision (he told Moore) had rekindled a yearning for the Grecian islands "and the interesting white squalls and short seas of Archipelago memory."

The tone of his letters grew progressivly more dejected. Would not Moore (he inquired on February 10th) consider accompanying him to Italy? "If I take my wife, you can take yours; and if I leave mine, you may do the same." Ten days later he learned of the death of an early friend—the Duke of Dorset, who had been killed by a fall out hunting. "We were at school together, and there I was passionately attached to him. Since, we have never met. . . . But there was a time in my life when this event would have broken my heart." The first days of March found him, as before, in "a state of sameness and stagnation." Moore's companionship, Kinnaird's brandy, the white seas and blue skies of the Aegean—all seemed as far away as if they had never existed. Childe Harold was domesticated with a vengeance; and he was so stupefied (he informed Moore) eating, playing dull card games, yawning, trying to extract some interest from the daily papers and old copies of the *Annual Register*, gathering shells and watching the growth of stunted gooseberry bushes in the garden, that he had neither the leisure nor the intelligence to write at length.

On March 18th the Byrons were "in the agonies of packing and parting; and . . . by this time to-morrow [he prophesied grimly] I shall be stuck in the chariot with my chin upon a band-box." They were bound for Augusta's house at Six Mile Bottom. Byron had at first proposed that Annabella should not accompany him, but she had insisted; while Augusta herself had raised objections, pretending in her vague and flustered fashion that she had no room. During the early stages of the journey Byron was in an exceedingly evil humour. "Take care of Annabella," Lady Milbanke had exhorted him, as she saw the carriage off; to which Byron had rejoined irritably: "What on earth does your mother mean by telling me to take care of you? I suppose you can take care of yourself!"

Yet it was during this journey—late at night, when they had

reached Wandsford—that Byron spoke the kindest words Annabella "could ever have wished to hear." "You married me to make
me happy, didn't you?" he asked. "Well, then, you do make me
happy." A burst of "passionate affection" was followed by hints at
"some impending, inevitable misery" that she could not escape.
They arrived; and from the earliest moment of their stay Byron's
behaviour changed. "The blackness of his countenance" was
unmistakable; and that evening he inflicted a brutal wound. "Now
I have *her*," he said savagely, "you will find I can do without *you*—
in all ways."

Thereupon the nightmare began again. If at Halnaby Annabella's existence had been purgatorial—haunted by wild and hideous
imaginings, by guesses more painful than certain knowledge—
after Seaham she plunged into the abyss. Both Annabella and
Augusta were Byron's victims; and not the least misery of those
tormented weeks was the spectacle of Byron's daily wretchedness.
For the sufferings he inflicted sprang from his own. Through them
he punished himself; in the humiliations to which he subjected the
two women he committed the final and most excruciating assault
against his own moral nature. His sense of delinquency was
overpowering; and, as the passion of remorse increased, so did it
demand fresh material. Annabella and Augusta should suffer
equally. Augusta had thwarted him; it was Annabella's misfortune
that she should stand in his way. They were confederates; and,
since they clung together for sympathy, he had decided that his
wife and his sister must be torn apart. No innuendo, no half-
confidence was spared. . . . Towards the end of the last century
Six Mile Bottom was pulled down and entirely remodelled; and yet
as one glances at a yellowed photograph—the old house, its low,
irregular façade, its big Georgian sash windows and the large tree
that still dominates the lawn—one expects, almost, some reminder
of its previous inhabitants. Outwardly, a commonplace house
enough; yet it was here that Annabella, dismissed to her room—
"We don't want *you*, my charmer"—awaited his "terrible step"
upon the stairs and heard him, as he undressed, swearing at Fletcher
"with a degree of rage that seemed to threaten his life."

Here Annabella was the witness of morning scenes. Byron
would greet his sister with allusions that "sometimes made Augusta

ready to sink;" and Mrs. Leigh "seemed fearful of every word he uttered, and fearful of checking him." Thus, Byron had presented her with one of "two golden brooches, containing his hair and hers, with three crosses on them;" and he amused himself by drawing attention to these ornaments and reminding Augusta of the signs by which they had communicated while they were snowbound at Newstead. "Well, Guss [he would remark], I am a reformed man, ain't I?" Only in the presence of Medora did his attitude soften; "the tenderness of his expression" was "quite lovely;" but when Annabella said that she would like to have him painted looking at the little girl, she was surprised and alarmed by his display of feeling. "You know," he observed, on a later occasion, "that is my child," and set out to support his assertion by explaining how long Colonel Leigh had been away from home at the time Medora was conceived.

Amid these storms, Augusta was Annabella's sole comfort. She appeared "to have no other view but that of mitigating his cruelty . . ." Even more hurtful than Byron's cruelty was a return of the indifferent, sardonic kindness that he had already displayed during the "treaclemoon" at Halnaby Hall. There were nights when he seemed to regard her with physical aversion—when, in her sleep, she moved towards him, and he awoke her with the words, delivered in tones of "raging detestation": "Don't touch me!"—and there were times when she "heard the freezing sound of heartless professions—more intolerable than his uncontrolled abhorrence."

Augusta did not seek to prolong their stay. On March 28th they bade farewell and started south for London, where John Cam, commissioned by his friend, had taken the Duchess of Devonshire's house, No. 13 Piccadilly Terrace,[1] at the rent of £700 a year. During the next ten days Byron was gentler and more affectionate than his wife had ever seen him. Given happier circumstances, *marriage à la mode*—for such Byron had determined that his married life should be—might even now have settled down into the ordinary channels. On Annabella's side, there were devotion and forbearance; on Byron's—outrageous and uncontrollable as he became in moments of extreme emotional stress—the good humour of a man

---

[1]Remains of this house, which had once formed part of a larger hous: belonging to "Old Q.", still exists behind the modern façade of No. 139 Piccadilly.

who hated scenes. Superficially, at least, he was not ill-natured; and among the servants who welcomed them to Piccadilly Terrace was Mrs. Mule, the gaunt and witch-like housemaid who had attended him during his residence at Albany, whom his friends had implored him to discharge, but whom he had kept on because (as he said) "the poor old devil was so kind to him."

Yet good nature, gratitude, real tenderness were not proof against the foes that assailed Byron's peace of mind both from within and from without. Encouraged by the rumour that he had married an heiress—when, in fact, his marriage had entailed little financial gain—his numerous creditors combined to embarrass and annoy him. Before long there was an execution in the house. Annabella, accustomed to the vicissitudes of her impecunious father, was prepared to face these troubles with philosophy; but Byron was infuriated and ashamed. Nor was this execution a solitary mischance. In the next nine months it was succeeded by ten others.

Financial misery dogged him at every step. To escape from his vexations—and from the moral torments that had pursued him during his honeymoon—he took refuge in late hours and heavy drinking, and thus became involved in a vicious circle of excitement and depression that served to aggravate the gloom it was intended to cure. He was feverishly busy that he might lack the leisure to think; and an opportunity of spending much of his time abroad presented itself in the shape of the Drury Lane Committee, to which he had been elected, along with Lord Essex, George Lamb, Douglas Kinnaird and Peter Moore. Soon he was deep in the concerns of the theatre. The life distracted him; he enjoyed the intrigues of the Green Room, the hectic, dusty world behind the stage, the pretty actresses who squabbled over his favour with as much *empressement* as ladies of fortune and fashion at a time when he was still a novelty and had not yet submitted his neck to the married yoke. All through the year 1815 the amateur committee-men struggled against the intricacies of casting and rehearsing, the difficulty of finding suitable plays and the apparent impossibility of persuading a large company of actors and actresses to work together on harmonious and sensible lines. Byron took his share of the dramatic drudgery. ". . . The scenes I had to go through!

[he noted in his *Detached Thoughts*]—the authors, and the authoresses, and the milliners, and the wild Irishmen—the people from Brighton, from Blackwall, from Chatham, from Cheltenham, from Dublin, from Dundee . . . to all of whom it was proper to give a civil answer. . . ." Here, for example, was "Miss Emma Somebody, with a play entitled *The Bandit of Bohemia*, or some such title or production;" and here a Mr. O'Higgins, a Celt of savage aspect, "then resident in Richmond, with an Irish tragedy, in which the unities could not fail to be observed, for the protagonist was chained by the leg to a pillar during the chief part of the performance."

Once, at least, there was "a devil of a row" among the dancers. Miss Smith—whom Byron "used to protect . . . because she was like Lady Jane Harley in the face"—had "been wronged about a hornpipe." She appealed to her champion; the committee itself had interfered; but Byrne, "the damned ballet-master," obstinately refused to give way. At the meetings of the committee, all was confusion. "There was Peter Moore who contradicted Kinnaird, and Kinnaird who contradicted everybody . . . our two managers, Rae and Dibdin; and our secretary, Ward! and yet we were all very zealous and in earnest to do good and so forth." Thus, one gentleman put forward the revolutionary proposal that the theatre should be lighted with gas; another set himself the arduous task of persuading Kean "not to get drunk; the consequence of which is, that he has never been sober since." The work was hard; but it was "really very good fun." And, though besieged by authoresses and bothered by ballet-masters, the poet was still considerably more at his ease than in the dun-ridden purlieus of Piccadilly Terrace, where Annabella—and presently Augusta—watched his movements and discussed his reformation.

The Byrons had arrived at Piccadilly Terrace at the end of March; and only a week later Mrs. Leigh—apparently at her sister-in-law's request—came up to join them from the country. In the whole situation—perhaps in the whole history of Byron's life—nothing is more extraordinary than Annabella's attitude towards the woman whom she had learned to regard as a dangerous, though an involuntary, rival. It is on this attitude that Lady Byron's detractors are inclined to found a large part of their case.

Is it credible, they demand, that, if Annabella had had real cause to suspect Byron and Augusta of an incestuous relationship, she would have written to Mrs. Leigh in the warmest terms and encouraged her to visit the London house? The fact remains that, even after Lady Byron, at her lawyer's instance, had recorded her suspicions, together with her reasons for continuing to receive Mrs. Leigh, her behaviour was as affectionate—or almost as affectionate—as in the past. Certainly such behaviour is very strange; but then, so was the situation—so were the three passionate and ill-starred personalities whom it involved. Lady Byron (her biographer has pointed out) was always prone to romantic attachments for other women; and Augusta had a great deal of the Byronic charm. At her own house, Augusta's kindness had been unforgettable. She had stood alone between Annabella and Byron's fury.

It was Annabella's "unalterable belief" (she announced in 1817) that Augusta had never meant to do her harm; she was "always so devotedly kind to me;" while Augusta—a very important consideration—had the knack of calming Byron's darker moods. Loving Byron as she did, Annabella could hardly escape the attraction of a woman who had known him during his obscure and unhappy childhood, and with whom his tragic destiny was so closely connected. Yet life at Piccadilly Terrace was by no means smooth. Of Annabella's temperament, her mother had once declared that it was "like *Proof-Spirits*—not fit for common use;" and again she steadied herself for a tremendous trial. "It was hopeless to keep them apart—it was not hopeless, in my opinion, to keep them innocent. I felt myself the guardian of these two beings *indeed* 'on the brink of a precipice.' " Her magnanimity, however, had a dangerous side. There were moments when Annabella, distracted "by the continual excitement of horrible ideas," was tempted to plunge a dagger in her friend's heart, and looked around her, prepared to grasp a deadly weapon. ". . . I was almost mad—and to prevent myself indulging the passion of revenge, I was obliged to substitute another—that of romantic forgiveness."

Byron had met Mrs. Leigh, when she arrived at Piccadilly Terrace, "with lowering looks of disgust and hatred." There was a milder repetition of the scenes at Six Mile Bottom. Both women suffered from his moods; and both agreed that the late hours and convivial committee-meetings, which accompanied his business at the theatre, had a disastrous effect upon his health and nerves. Not until the end of June did Augusta leave London; and in the meantime, during the first weeks of April, Annabella was called away to Kirkby Mallory, where her uncle lay dying. Lord Wentworth expired on the 17th. It had been anticipated that his fortune would go directly to Annabella; but it now appeared that Lady Milbanke (who was to reassume her maiden name of Noel) would enjoy the income of his estate as long as she lived. No hope of salvation from that quarter! While she was still at Six Mile Bottom, Annabella had thought that she might be pregnant; and during April she learned definitely that she was carrying a child. "Dearest . . . I won't have you worried . . . Pray, come home," wrote Byron with unaccustomed tenderness, to her uncle's house in Leicestershire. Annabella obeyed his urgent plea; and although, before she left Piccadilly, Augusta had been shocked by his behaviour, once she had gone he grew vastly more amenable. They "shared a sort of conventional language of nonsense," which relieved his fear of sentiment and high-flown speeches.

He would give play to his imagination, deliver himself of the deepest reflections, "then shrink away from them into frolic and levity. The transitions had all the grace of genius. . . . They were [added Annabella, with the melodramatic pomp of diction she sometimes affected] as the foam that might float on the waters of bitterness." To her parents, the bitterness of her married life was still undisclosed. Augusta was her sole confidante, her only support; and even Augusta did not yet perceive that Annabella had seen the situation in its true colours. Allied to extreme youth, such constancy of purpose, such an almost inhuman strength of will, though admirable, is a little horrifying. In one respect, it stood her in good stead. Yet, whereas Augusta's pliancy and vagueness could charm Byron even in his grimmest moods, his wife's strength of character merely exasperated him. Did he distinguish a vein of hardness beneath the surface—a self-will that clashed cruelly against his own?

Chapter 12

TOWARDS the end of August Byron set out, unaccompanied, for Six Mile Bottom. During the last few days he had been "perfectly ferocious;" but, as he left, "half earnestly, half jestingly," he begged Annabella to excuse him. From Epping he posted a friendly note. "Dearest Pip—" he began, and went on to complain that "the learned Fletcher with his wonted accuracy" had omitted to include in his medicine-chest "*two phials* labelled 'drops';" which Annabella would please send to him "at Goose's per coach." Lady Byron's letter, headed "Darling Duck," was no less conjugal. In his absence the house had been devoted to a tornado of scrubbing and sweeping; and Mrs. Mule—the witch-like Mrs. Mule—who, during her employer's residence, flew "like a sylph on tiptoe," now woke Annabella early in the morning by thundering up and down stairs "like a troop of dragoons at full gallop."

Byron replied with a picture of Augusta's household. The children looked "shockingly—quite green—& Goose being as red as ever, you have no idea what a piece of patchwork might be made of the family faces." A mouse-trap, left by Augusta in his bedroom, had nearly cost him a toe. "Goose is taking a quill from her wing to scribble to you—so—yours always most conjugally . . ." Such were the Byrons' letters at their more tranquil moments—such the nonsense-language in which they took refuge from the ennui, irritation and anxiety that overclouded Byron's darker days. Amid the storms there were brief intervals of calm. Then Byron's good nature would rise to the surface; and Annabella would be found— as she was reminded during the controversy of 1816—on her husband's knee, with her arms around his neck.

Outwardly there was little evidence of dissension. It is true that

Byron's closest friends suspected that the marriage was not going well. Moore had heard talk of flying abroad; while to Hobhouse, almost as soon as he reached London, Byron spoke warningly of the married state. Don't marry! he advised; though he concluded by saying that Annabella was the best woman in the world. Acquaintances received a different impression. Throughout the year 1815 Byron paid frequent visits to John Murray's parlour at 50 Albemarle Street; and, in April, his publisher told James Hogg that Lord Byron had "just come to town" and was "in every respect . . . very greatly improved."

It was on April 7th, under Murray's auspices, that Byron and Walter Scott met and talked for the first time; and Murray's son, who was present at the interview, retained a vivid recollection of "the two greatest poets of the age"—both lame and both carrying sticks—as they stumped down the staircase side by side. Byron's appearance was hard to forget; "a rather short man, with a handsome countenance, remarkable for the fine blue veins which ran over his pale, marble temples," he wore many rings, a brooch on the front of his open-necked shirt, and "a black dress-coat . . . with grey, and sometimes nankeen trousers." The friendship was sealed by an exchange of gifts. Byron presented Scott with a silver urn brought back from Greece, and accepted an engraved Turkish dagger. For Scott had exactly those qualities that, among his fellow writers, Byron found most reassuring. Elsewhere "the noble poet" was less at his ease; and, although during 1815 he was to renew his acquaintance with Leigh Hunt and to correspond at some length with the unhappy Coleridge (whom he encouraged to produce a tragedy for Drury Lane), neither contact developed into genuine intimacy.

His real friends were chosen from a different set—from a set, incidentally, of which Lady Byron did not at all approve. His female associates were bad enough. With some reason, she distrusted her aunt Melbourne, smooth, clever, irreligious old woman who had heard so many stories of Byron's youth, abetted the conquest of so many mistresses; with whom he had gossiped—perhaps laughed—about Annabella. At Melbourne House, on one occasion, when she had been obliged to visit Lady Caroline—now restored to comparative sanity and respectability—she had come face to face with Mrs. Chaworth-Musters; and "such a wicked-looking cat I never saw. Somebody else"—this somebody, of course, being Lady Caroline—"looked quite virtuous" by comparison.

Melbourne House was not for Annabella; nor did she find the society of Holland House, and the agnostic atmosphere of Lady Holland's drawing-room, very much to her fastidious moral taste. Lady Holland, after all, was a divorced woman. She had attended one of the Hollands' brilliant dinner parties, "which amused me [she told her parents, who were accustomed to receiving Annabella's strictures on London morals and modes] for as long a time as I can possibly *laugh* at the Varnish of Vice. Lady H . . . wears a sort of *amabilité* in my presence, which is as little consistent with her general habits as with her Nature. She evidently does not know what to make of me, and handles me as fearfully as if I were a Hedgehog. . . ." To these intimacies, Annabella might object; but her sternest condemnation was reserved for the masculine friends among whom Byron spent his afternoons and nights. Hobhouse himself came to be voted a bad influence. Who could tell what depths of scepticism and misogyny lay concealed behind that saturnine mask, the high solemn forehead, the hollow jowl and heavy hooked nose? And then, foxy-faced, hard-bitten Douglas Kinnaird! the instigator of gatherings at which Byron drank brandy to excess and returned home, haggard and furious, in the glimmer of dawn.

It was a party of this kind that Byron described in an appreciative and high-spirited letter to Tom Moore. Sheridan represented the old order. Kinnaird was there and Sir Gilbert Heathcote, Colman, Harry Harris of Covent Garden, "and others, of note and notoriety. Like other parties . . . it was first silent, then talky, then argumentative, then disputatious, then unintelligible, then altogethery, then inarticulate, then drunk. When we had reached the last step of this glorious ladder, it was difficult to get down again without stumbling." At the end of the evening, Kinnaird and Byron— himself very far from sober—were obliged to help Sheridan "down a damned corkscrew staircase . . . to which no legs, however crooked, could possibly accommodate themselves. We deposited him safely at home, where his man, evidently used to the business, waited to receive him in the hall."

Parliamentary schemes had been long in abeyance. The House of Lords disgusted him; while of European politics Byron, like other English liberals, preferred not to think. During June, a young American tourist, George Ticknor, arrived at Piccadilly Terrace with an introduction from Gifford. Byron, who appreciated youth and felt a particular interest in the reports that had reached him of his fame beyond the Atlantic, was extremely affable. "Instead of having a thin and rather sharp and anxious face [noted Ticknor] as he has in his pictures, it is round, open and smiling; his eyes are light, and not black; his air easy and careless . . . the tones of his voice low and conciliating. . . ." Ticknor's earliest visit lasted an hour and a half. The conversation wandered over many subjects —America, *English Bards*, Walter Scott, whom Byron referred to as "undoubtedly the first man of his time;" and, when Ticknor was about to go, a stranger, Sir James Bland Burgess, came hurrying into the room. "My lord, my lord," he exclaimed breathlessly, "a great battle has been fought in the Low Countries, and Bonaparte is entirely defeated." "But is it true?" demanded Byron. "Is it true?" "Yes, my lord, it is certainly true; an aide-de-camp arrived in town last night; he has been in Downing Street. . . . He says he thinks Bonaparte is in full retreat towards Paris." "I am damned sorry for it," Byron replied. "I didn't know [he added, after a pause] but I might live to see Lord Castlereagh's head on a pole. But I suppose I shan't, now."

Before he left, Ticknor caught sight of Annabella. "Lord Byron's manner to her was affectionate; he followed her to the door, and shook hands with her, as if he were not to see her for a month." "The prevalent expression of her countenance is that of ingenuousness." On the whole, decided Ticknor, she was not pretty; but, when he called again, he found her alone; and, "for the quarter of an hour during which I was with her, she talked upon a considerable variety of subjects—America, of which she seemed to know considerable; of France, and Greece, with something of her husband's visit there—and spoke of all with a justness and a light good-humour that would have struck me even in one of whom I had heard nothing." On the occasion of Ticknor's third visit, when he spent the greater part of the morning in Byron's company, he was again struck by the show of affection and solicitude with which Byron escorted his wife to her carriage. Soon after Ticknor's arrival, Mrs. Siddons—whom Byron had attempted to engage for Drury Lane—was announced in an adjoining room. "Her portraits are very faithful as to her general air and outline, but no art can express or imitate the dignity of her manner or the intelligent illumination of her face." Her conversation was "rather stately" but, "though accompanied by considerable gesture, not really overacted . . . She formed a singular figure by Lady Byron, who sat by her side all grace and delicacy, and this showed Mrs. Siddons' masculine powers in the stronger light of comparison and contrast."

Ticknor's description of the poet as round-faced and smiling may be compared with the account of his own appearance that Byron gave Moore in a letter written on July 7th. Since his marriage (he complains) he has lost much of his paleness "and— *horresco referens* (for I hate even *moderate* fat)—that happy slenderness, to which when I first knew you, I had attained. . . ." But fatness with Byron was not always an indication of peace of spirit. For the second time, Newstead had been up to auction at Garroway's Coffee House and, for the second time, the reserve price had not been reached. His emotion on hearing the news of Waterloo soon gave way to a disgusted acquiescence in the old system; he was "sick at heart of politics and slaughters; and the luck which Providence is pleased to lavish upon Lord Castlereagh is only a proof of the little value the gods set upon prosperity, when they permit such ——s as he and that drunken corporal, old Blücher, to bully their betters." By the poet's acquaintances, Ticknor had been assured that he was indeed a reformed man, and that the imaginary characters of his verse were "the personification of feelings and passions that have formerly been active" and were now set aside; but, although their optimistic belief may have had some foundation during June, July and the early part of August, October and November were less propitious. From Six Mile Bottom, he had returned home "most kind" to Annabella but bitterly offended with Mrs. Leigh—so offended that he would only refer to her by her surname; and during September Drury Lane reopened its doors. Once again he had determined to "make life an amusement;" but now his amusements had a colouring of desperation.

He grew day by day more nervous, abrupt and odd. He had

always been prone to violent and impulsive gestures; and when Annabella remarked, thinking to amuse him, that the parrot had bitten her foot, he seized the bird and cage and hurled them out of the window. "Am I in your way?" inquired Annabella, on another occasion, as she entered his study. "Damnably," he replied —this last being one of the few instances of rudeness that he afterwards admitted. He suffered, too, from a recurrence of his midnight terrors, fancied that he heard mysterious footsteps, and "lay afraid to stir," allowing Annabella, then within three or four months of her confinement, to investigate them alone. Anxious letters passed between Piccadilly and Six Mile Bottom—letters that make it quite clear that the singularities of Byron's conduct at this period were not merely a figment of Annabella's imagination. Mrs. Leigh herself was much perturbed. Was her brother mad? For her own reasons—partly, no doubt, because this hypothesis helped to explain the damaging innuendoes of which Byron was prodigal as often as all three were together under the same roof—Augusta appears to have encouraged the belief that he was. "His misfortune [wrote Annabella to Augusta] is an habitual *passion for Excitement*' which is always found in ardent temperaments, where the pursuits are not in some degree organised." It was "the Ennui of a monotonous existence" that drove people of this type to the most dangerous paths. "The love of tormenting" arose chiefly from this source; and "Drinking, gaming &c. are all of the same origin." How far it depended on mind or body was difficult to decide; but "I am inclined to think that a vitiated stomach, particularly if arising from habits of excess, is the chief cause of the sensation of Ennui."

The following night, a bailiff—"a sad brute"—took up his quarters in the house. Byron's library, which included the fine collection of Romaic volumes he had lately shown to Ticknor, was itself threatened; and Annabella reported to Augusta that she had suffered, and was still suffering, from "B's distraction, which is of the *very worst* kind." He had rushed out of the house, telling his wife that he would "at once abandon himself to every sort of desperation, speaks to me only to upbraid me with having married him when he wished not, and says he is therefore acquitted of all principle towards me, and I must consider myself *only* to be answerable for the vicious courses to which his despair will drive him. The going out of the house & the drinking are the most fatal." Yesterday, he had been "really quite frantic . . . and it seemed impossible to tell if his feelings towards you or me were the most completely reversed; for as I have told you, he loves or hates us together. . . ."

His creative impulse found vent in writing *The Siege of Corinth* and *Parasina*, while his "passion for Excitement" he satisfied at Drury Lane. Annabella made no secret of disliking the whole business; and she cannot have approved if she knew that, in a pantomime representation of the famous Watier's Masquerade (given by "us youth" the year before), Byron and Kinnaird, mingling with a crowd of theatrical supers, had actually appeared behind the footlights. He had many opportunities of desultory love-making; and a curious little episode of amorous spite and professional jealousy is revealed by two letters from Miss Boyce, a young actress with whom Rogers remembered having once found the poet closeted in a dark corner of his private box:

My Lord,

I fear I shall have cause to lament to the last hour of my existence your conduct to me, since it *has not been uniform*. In the first instance, you paid so much attention to me in the Theatre. At a time I was *respected and loved by all* you caused me to be the talk of all the people there. When everyone believed you had a particular liking for me, you without reason scarcely spoke to me; and now, my Lord, I am the jest of the *dirt* and refuse of the theatre . . . The impudent Miss Cookes dare to make a boast that you would not leave talking to them to notice me. Allow me to say, my Lord, you ought on Saturday night to have *come to me* from them and spoke to me and not notice me in the *distant manner you did*. It was a duty I consider you owe me. When you recollect *all circumstances* I am sure you will think as I do. . . . I have been an ass, a fool. Oh would I could go back the last six months. I am almost broken hearted. I have hoped a *vast deal from you* because I knew you were unhappy, but *I had a thing said to me on Saturday* night that makes me resolve to say all I have to say and make a change in one or two things. You have not

behaved towards me as I deserved, my Lord, as you *professed*
to *feel towards me*. . . . I cannot, *will not*, bear this state of
misery. Let me know what your feelings *really* are towards *me*
and your *intentions* . . .
. . . God Bless you. I *would, could love you*, but you will not
let me, I fear. . . .

The second letter, scribbled in pencil, is dated 1816; but both letters
refer to the events of the autumn and winter of 1815, when Byron's
theatrical interests were at their height:

My Lord,
It is *very evident* from the rudeness of your answer and manner
last night when I asked you how you were, and indeed from
the whole of your behaviour lately, that my attention to you is
very *offensive*. I will never *in future*, my Lord, so offend. . . .
I *have waited* frequently, *which was the case last night*, to say how do
you do, but in future I shall spare myself the mortification.
. . . Good God, what could Dibdin think? No matter; you
intended to wound the *feelings of one* who never thought or behaved
otherwise than honestly to you, and, if 'twill give you any
satisfaction to know you *did wound* me in my tenderest part, rest
satisfied, for you *did indeed* . . .

At home Byron spoke freely of his escapades. Mrs. Leigh
returned to Piccadilly Terrace on November 15th; and, stimulated
by her proximity, he often referred to his connections with "women
of the theatre"—boastings, he told his wife, "as much to vex
Augusta as you." So alarming did his behaviour now become that
Augusta persuaded his cousin and heir, George Byron, to pay them
a visit. It was in these circumstances that Annabella completed her
progress towards maternity. Some weeks before the accouchrement
was due, her mother's companion, Mrs. Clermont, arrived from the
country; while Lady Noel had written a long and affectionate letter
stating that she "*highly approved*" of her engaging Mr. Le Mann—who,
she believed, was very clever—in preference to any of the more
fashionable, but less dependable, male midwives of the period.
Her child was born on Sunday, December 10th; and, as Annabella
gave birth to a daughter in the room above, Byron staged a dramatic
scene in his study below. He had disturbed her (alleged his wife)
by hurling soda-water bottles against the ceiling. Byron and his

supporters denied the charge; and John Cam, after gravely reviewing the evidence, decided that Byron's conduct had been blameless, and that the hubbub of which Annabella saw fit to complain had been caused, not by the flinging of bottles, but by her husband's customary method of opening them—which was to smash off their necks with the help of a poker.

Either procedure argues a certain degree of inconsiderateness. "The child *was* born dead, wasn't it?" he is said to have demanded, as soon as he was admitted to Annabella's room. Byron indignantly denied the story; and it remains one of those anecdotes equally difficult to accept or to reject; for, though incredible, they have a distinctly Byronic ring. The child was christened Augusta Ada— the last a name that had been in the family since the days of King John. It was "very flourishing and fat," and "squalled and sucked;" but paternity made little difference to Byron's plans, and he continued to talk of breaking up his household, and taking bachelor rooms or going abroad, unaccompanied, at the very earliest opportunity. Bailiffs were still in and out of the house; and on January 6th Byron sent Annabella a brief and formal note, in which he suggested that, once she was fit to move, she should leave London and seek shelter with her mother. Byron's account and Annabella's disagree. Byron declared that, although Annabella had been offended by his note at the time, a reconciliation had quickly followed; whereas Annabella maintained the exact opposite. "When shall we three meet again?" he inquired ironically, bidding his wife and child good-bye.

Annabella, with child, maid and nursemaid, set out for Kirkby Mallory on January 15th. Byron did not leave his room to see them go; their separation was conceived as a temporary expedient; yet, as she passed his door that morning, Annabella felt a sudden longing to throw herself down across the threshold, where his big Newfoundland dog—the successor of Boatswain—used to lie, "and wait at all hazards." But it was only a moment; she controlled herself and entered the carriage. If she had any forebodings, they were rapidly subdued; and from Woburn she posted a letter in her usual vein:

Dearest B.—The Child is quite well, and the best of Travellers. I hope you are *good*, and remember my medical prayers and injunctions. Don't give yourself up to the abominal trade of versifying—nor to brandy—not to anything or anybody that is not *Lawful & Right* . . .

Ada's love to you with mine.

PIP

When they reached Kirkby Mallory, they were driven up to the kitchen entrance by mistake; and, no sooner were they installed, than she wrote announcing her arrival and giving a description of the amenities of the house, which included, among its other comforts, a new water-closet:

Dearest Duck—We got here quite well last night, and were ushered into the kitchen instead of the drawing-room, by a mistake that might have been agreeable enough to hungry people. Of this and other incidents Dad wants to write you a jocose account, & both he and Mam long to have the family party completed. Such . . .! and such a *sitting*-room or *sulking*-room all to yourself. If I were not always looking about for B., I should be a great deal better already for country air. . . . Love to the good Goose, & everybody's love to you both from hence.

Ever thy most loving

PIPPIN - - - PIP - - - IP

Byron did not reply in person. It had been understood that Augusta, who had remained at Piccadilly Terrace after Annabella's departure, should write in his stead; and on January 16th Annabella informed Mrs. Leigh that she had "made the most explicit statement" to her parents and that nothing could exceed "their tender anxiety to do everything for the sufferer." They would invite him to make an indefinite stay at Kirkby; he was to be treated as an invalid. Naturally, wrote Annabella, her mother was "deeply affected;" but she was none the less "quite composed;" and Annabella hoped that her "dearest Sis" would exert all her ingenuity towards keeping Byron in a calm and rational state of mind. He had lately become addicted to laudanum-drinking; and Lady Noel had suggested that, rather than take the bottle away, Mrs. Leigh should dilute its contents "with three-quarters of water, which won't make any observable difference . . ." Could she not persuade him to take his pills? So far the anxious consultation between wife and sister had pursued its accustomed and futile course. But then an event occurred that changed, not only the entire situation, but the whole tendency of Annabella's thoughts and desires. Before leaving London, she had consulted several doctors, and had requested her own doctor to see Byron and report on his health—a commission that Le Mann promptly executed. A letter, received after two days' respite, assured her that, though irascible and violent, Byron was in full possession of his senses.

Mad or bad?—it was a question on which she had often brooded. Mad, she had almost convinced herself, backed up in this belief by the vague assertions or insinuations of Mrs. Leigh. She had never quite believed the stories that he told her. There were hints and confidences at which every instinct had revolted, and from which she had taken refuge in the idea that they were the imaginings of a disorderde brain. While she was sick, she could still hope to effect his amendment; he was still an object for that romantic magnanimity which it is so difficult to dissociate from spiritual pride. Now, at last, she understood that her hopes were doomed. She could never change him. His aberrations proceeded from downright wickedness, and his wickedness from a desire—a positive determination—to do wrong. Henceforward duty pointed another course. She must flee the contagion—for her child's sake, leave the sinner to the ruinous multiplication of vices and follies. She loved him; but duty, not pleasure, must be her aim. . . . And in this mood she approached her mother and father. Her revelations were as appalling as they were unexpected; they sent her mother hot-foot to London for legal advice.

Yet, even now, while Lady Noel was in London, meeting Mrs. Leigh to inveigh against her "unmanly" son-in-law, conferring with Dr. Lushington—a grave ecclesiastical lawyer, who listened to her complaints and shook his head, but pronounced that a reconciliation might still be effected—Annabella at Kirkby Mallory passed through a crisis of agonised indecision that she never forgot. Well might Mrs. Fletcher, her maid (who afterwards signed an affidavit to the effect that Lady Byron had been persuaded to leave her husband contrary to her wishes), write of her as distracted and hysterical, rolling on the floor in an ecstasy of grief. In her saner moments, she galloped recklessly across country "like Lady

C. L., and felt something like good spirits [she told Augusta] whilst I was in danger of fracturing my sconce." A previous letter had summed up her ponderings since she had received Mr. Le Mann's decision. "Disease or not—[she declared] all my recollections and reflections tend to convince me that the irritability is inseparably connected with me in a greater degree than with any other object, that my presence has been uniformly oppressive to him from the hour we married. . . . The causes I won't pretend to determine, the effects have been too constant and are too fixed; and had we continued together he *would* have gone mad. It would be the same again: Le Mann don't know all, or he would think so.

". . . I have done nothing [she continued pathetically] except on the strictest principle of Duty, yet I feel as if I were going to receive sentence from the Judge with his black cap on. . . . O that I were in London, if in the coal hole." With that last cry, that last despairing admission that the loss of dignity, the loss of honour, the contravention of every moral code, might be preferable to the loss of her painful happiness, the old Annabella begins to disappear. Up till now, she had played a romantic part. Romantic love—the romantic desire to accomplish the reformation of a "very good, very bad man"—latterly, the passion of romantic forgiveness, were superseded by a determination to do right. No longer would she listen to the promptings of impulse. For a moment it had seemed that she might give way—defy her mother and father, and rejoin her husband—seek the pagan household at Piccadilly Terrace; then Conscience reaffirmed its implacable veto. "Feelings must not now be indulged;" her magnanimity must discover a different outlet.

The inner hardness of her temperament slowly emerged. Beneath the surface, it had always been perceptible; but now it was to develop into a moral inflexibility that nothing could shake. While she wavered, her parents had supported her; but, after January 28th, when Lady Noel, primed with legal advice and over-flowing with motherly indignation, returned to Kirkby Mallory from London, there is no evidence that they acted against her will. As soon as Lady Noel arrived, Sir Ralph wrote to Byron, proposing an amicable separation. Mrs. Leigh, however, intercepted and sent back his letter; whereat Sir Ralph immediately drove to

London. His next letter, written on February 2nd, was delivered by hand. In stiff and forbidding sentences, it announced that Lady Byron's parents could not feel justified in permitting her return, and that Sir Ralph must ask Lord Byron to appoint a legal representative to discuss the terms of separation.

On Byron, the effect of this letter was overwhelming. He had fully intended to visit Kirkby; and Augusta and Annabella had surmised that his plan was to join his wife and beget another child —this time, he hoped, it would be a boy—before he broke up his household and went abroad. He might desert Annabella; but it had not occurred to him, even as a remote possibility, that the Princess of Parallelograms could herself take the initiative. Never had the childish and irresponsible side of Byron's temperament— his knack of forgetting, at least temporarily, everything that it was not in his interest to remember—been more in evidence than during the next few weeks. Thus, he was hurt, indignant, puzzled and shocked by turns. He agreed, of course, that he was moody and ill to live with; but the circumstances of the last year had been such as to vex and harass him almost to the point of madness. As for Augusta—why, that was an old story; Annabella (he told her long afterwards) had nothing to complain of; "—on the contrary—you are not aware of the obligations under which you have been to her.—Her life & mine—and yours & mine—were two things perfectly distinct from each other—when one ceased the other began . . ."

He knew that he was ill-suited to the married state; but then his emotionalism had a way of reconciling the most contradictory ideas. There was the reality of marriage; and there was the dream. There were the long months of irritation, gloom and embarrassment; and there was the vision of marriage—of quiet, well-being and domestic harmony—that had so often floated before him as the goal he sought. The fact that reality had proved unpalatable did not lessen his grief when the poetic vision crumbled and dissolved; and to regret were added the pangs of wounded pride. "I have the consciousness [he admitted during a *tête-à-tête* with Lady Blessington] that had I possessed sufficient command over my own wayward humour, I might have rendered myself so dear and necessary to Lady Byron, that she would not, could not, have left me. It is certainly not very gratifying to my vanity to have been *planté* after so short a union."

Annabella had cast him from his pedestal. Only a short time before Sir Ralph's letter arrived, Byron had spent the evening with George Byron and Augusta. At first he was good-tempered; but, as the evening wore on, he "grew *fractious*," declared that he had no intention of going to Kirkby Mallory if he could help it, and "from that moment [wrote Augusta to Annabella] talked all sorts of strange things—fell on me as usual—abused my spouse, my children—in short all as you know, and have heard before." Of Annabella, he spoke "quite coolly and of his intention of going into a lodging by himself . . . One of the things he said was . . . that he considered himself 'the greatest man existing.' " "Except Bonaparte," suggested George Byron, the honest naval officer, trying to laugh off his cousin's rodomontade. "God," retorted Byron, "I don't know that I do except even him."

While he was in this frame of mind, the shock caused by Sir Ralph's letter must have been particularly acute. Accustomed to the chief part in his own tragedy, he had not expected so commonplace a *dénouement*, or that the last act would be thus travestied and abridged. Demon he might be; but his feelings were human and sensitive. He had been betrayed, traduced; Childe Harold was the victim of a conspiracy engineered by a mother-in-law, whom he disliked, and her vulgar companion, the one-time governess, whom he despised. When Hobhouse called at Piccadilly Terrace on February 5th, he found his friend "exceedingly depressed, more so than in an intimacy of eleven years he had ever seen. Lord B. at first seemed unwilling to mention the cause of his dejection; but at last, with tears in his eyes, and in an agitation that scarcely allowed him to speak, mentioned the proposition he had received from Sir Ralph Noel. He attributed the determination of his wife, if determination she had taken, to the influence of Lady Noel, and of Mrs. Clermont. . . . He solemnly protested that Lady Byron and himself had parted friends. . . . He as solemnly declared that he could not *guess* at the immediate cause of this resolution."

John Cam, though he had noted in his private journal as early as November 25th that "in that quarter"—Piccadilly Terrace— "things do not go well," could hardly believe his ears. As soon as he received Sir Ralph's letter (Hobhouse now learned) Byron had written a firm but temperate answer, stating that he was at a loss to imagine why a separation should be proposed, and, at the same time, had directed Mrs. Leigh "to write to Lady Byron in terms of inquiry relative to her share in this extraordinary proceeding . . ." He himself wrote a conciliatory epistle. To her husband, Annabella had not replied; but to Mrs. Leigh she wrote a cold and succinct assurance that her parents were acting with her full knowledge and consent; while, as for her motives—"I will only recall to Lord Byron's mind his avowed and insurmountable aversion to the married state, and the desire and determination he has expressed ever since the commencement to free himself from that bondage as finding it quite insupportable. . . ."

Once again Mrs. Leigh withheld a letter. Thus, when he saw Hobhouse, Byron had as yet received no word from Kirkby Mallory; and John Cam begged permission to write to Annabella himself. For his own part, Byron composed a second appeal: "Dearest Bell—No answer from you yet—perhaps it is as well— but do you recollect that all is at stake—the present—the future & even the colouring of the past. The whole of my errors—or what harsher name you choose to give them—you know; but I loved you, & will not part from you without your *own* most express & *expressed* refusal to return to or receive me . . ."

At Hobhouse's instigation, this letter was posted, not directly to Annabella, but under cover to Mrs. Fletcher, her maid; and on February 7th it evoked a crushing reply: "If I had not written to Mrs. Leigh what I deemed a sufficient answer to the contents of your first letter, I should not have deferred the still more painful task of addressing yourself." She was surprised (Annabella added) at the manner in which his letter had been delivered, "since my correspondence as well as my determination is free." He knew what she had suffered, and would have sacrificed to avoid this extremity; but, after seriously and dispassionately reviewing the misery that she had experienced almost without interval from the day of her marriage, she had finally determined on the measure of a separation. It was unhappily her husband's disposition (she concluded, with an insight that must have wounded him more deeply than many pages of moral reproof) "to consider what you *have* as worthless—what you have lost as invaluable. But remember that you declared yourself most miserable when I was yours."

Hobhouse, meanwhile, not satisfied with his first hurried note, dispatched a second, of great length and almost parliamentary dignity, which, beginning as an appeal, ended up as something dangerously like a lecture. Francis Hodgson, too, rushed out in his "dear friend's" defence. He had known Byron—"thoroughly," as he believed—"for many trying years;" and, "after a long and most confidential conversation," he was convinced that "the deep and rooted feeling of his heart is regret and sorrow for the occurrences that have so deeply wounded you, and the most unmixed admiration of your conduct in all its particulars. . . ." He wished to state, nevertheless, "that Lord B., after her general acknowledgment of having frequently been very wrong, and from various causes in a painful state of irritation, yet declares himself ignorant of the specific things which have given the principal offence, and that he wishes to hear them, that he may, if extenuation or atonement be possible, endeavour to make some reply. . . ."

Neither pleas nor remonstrances were of the least avail. Coldly and politely, Annabella turned aside every attempt at friendly intervention; and, coldly and curtly, she answered her husband's letters. By the 8th he had descended to indignant pathos. Had she *never* been happy with him, he demanded. ". . . Have no marks of affection, of the warmest and most reciprocal attachment, passed between us? or did in fact hardly a day go down without some such on one side and generally on both?" He had not denied the distracted state of his mind; but she knew its causes; "& were these deviations from calmness never followed by acknowledgment & repentance? Were not your letters kind?" Had he not confessed all his faults and follies, "& assured you that some had not—& would not be repeated. . . . You say 'It is my disposition to deem what *I have* worthless' . . . Did I ever so express myself to you—or of you—to others? You have changed within these twenty days, or you would not have thus poisoned your own better feelings—and trampled upon mine."

To letters in this strain, Annabella merely replied by deprecating what she called "the language of feeling," which she herself had decided, "*if possible*," not to indulge when writing to him. She admitted that she had written affectionately after leaving Piccadilly Terrace; but "it can be fully and clearly proved that I left your house under the persuasion of your having a complaint of so dangerous a nature that any agitation might bring on a fatal crisis. . . . My absence, if it had not been rendered necessary by other causes, was *medically* recommended on that ground, as removing an object of irritation. I should have acted inconsistently with my unchanged affection for you . . . by urging my wrongs at that moment."

On February 22nd, strong in the belief that she was carrying out a painful duty as best she could, Annabella left Kirkby Mallory and came up to London, where she took rooms with her father at Mivart's Hotel. That same day she called on Dr. Lushington. She saw him alone; and it was on this occasion that she poured out the full and unexpurgated story of all that she had suffered, heard and suspected during the last twelve months. To her parents—another proof of Annabella's extraordinary firmness of mind—the whole story of their son-in-law's iniquity had not yet been divulged; and Lushington, though he had once favoured a reconciliation, now declared that it was quite impossible; that, if such a step were to be contemplated, he himself "could not, either professionally or otherwise, take any part towards effecting it."

It only remained to bring the husband to his senses. But while letters, tender or indignant, flew to and fro, while friends confabulated and lawyers bustled, while Augusta—still at Piccadilly—watched her brother, fearing that he might, as he had so often threatened, seize pistol or laudanum bottle and end his existence, rumour ran round London from door to door. Lady Melbourne had heard a whisper on February 5th, and wrote to her dear nephew in great perturbation, begging him to deny the reports that he and Annabella had separated. From Augusta and George Byron, Hobhouse had gathered anecdotes of Byron's conduct—of "very great tyranny, menaces, furies, neglects and even real injuries"— that shook his simple faith[1]; and, when he visited Lady Melbourne, he was disconcerted by the imperative manner in which she recommended that the letters she had written Byron should be committed

[1] This disturbing conversation took place on February 12th. Soon afterwards Hobhouse went so far as to accuse Byron of having misled him, and "got him to own much of what I had been told in the morning." See an interesting biography of Hobhouse, *My Friend H.*, by Michael Joyce. Murray, 1948.

to the flames. The stories current in the drawing-rooms of London during 1813 and 1814 were again abroad; and Annabella, with a return of generosity, wrote to Mrs. George Villiers, one of Mrs. Leigh's closest friends, asserting that *"not one* of the many reports now current have been sanctioned or encouraged by me, my family, or my friends. . . ."

It will be noticed that, although Annabella denied that she and her friends were responsible for the reports "reflecting on Mrs. Leigh's character," she did not pause to discuss their authenticity; and on March 4th, wishing to do all that she could to mitigate the discomforts of Mrs. Leigh's position, but, at the same time, reluctant to abandon an advantage that might stand her in good stead were Byron to carry out his threat of removing his child and handing her over to Augusta's guardianship, she allowed a document to be drawn up, in which she set forth her suspicions—they did not, she admitted, amount to proof—and explained her reasons for continuing to receive Mrs. Leigh on friendly terms. . . . So much scandal-mongering was excited by the disaster of Byron's marriage —so many angry voices have since been raised, so many controversial volumes written in support of this or the other thesis—that it is difficult to examine the situation from a simple, straightforward and non-controversial view. One fact, at least, emerges clearly. Annabella did not leave her husband because she had discovered, or suspected, an incestuous relationship with Mrs. Leigh. She believed—and apparently her faith was justified—that Augusta had refused Byron's advances as soon as he became a married man; hence his rage and misery at Six Mile Bottom. She believed, too, that a wife was not entitled to make offences that her husband might have committed while he was still unmarried an excuse for leaving him—even offences "deepest in the catalogue of human law" —and that nothing counted save "the will to go on sinning."

The impression that Annabella left Byron primarily because she had learned of the secret of his relationship with Mrs. Leigh arose in part from contemporary rumour, in part from Lady Byron's extremely ill-judged confidences to Mrs. Beecher Stowe, and the inaccurate and indiscreet fashion in which Mrs. Beecher Stowe elected to make use of them. Annabella's suspicions at the time of the separation were almost a year old; and the separation drama can only be understood if, to historical research, we add a sympathetic appreciation of the three human characters whom it involved. It was a drama in which the full potentialities of those characters—both for good and for ill—were called into play. Firstly, we have the Immoralist, Byron himself, wavering between levity and tragedy, the man haunted by a sense of fate, whose destiny moulded him against his will. At any other period, Byron's energy—his greatest gift to literature—might have found an outlet in war, princely dissipation, state-craft or the impassioned advocacy of some particularly exacting religious creed. Coming as he did at a time when the prospects just opened by revolution had been suddenly and brutally closed by the forces of reaction, he was obliged to exercise his talents in the personal field. He wanted power; and the reality of power was denied him. He wanted faith; but contemporary Protestantism could not provide the ascetic strain that lurked deep in his nature with the encouragement it needed. He wanted love; and it is conceivable that had he been born, during the fifth or fourth century before Christ, at Athens or at Sparta, his amatory existence might have developed on happier and more harmonious lines. He revered friendship; but friendship and love are seldom allies. He distrusted sensuality, and satisfied both his sensationalism and the puritanism that he never quite outgrew by exploiting women and maltreating them at the same moment.

His worst sins—if sins they can be called—were committed against himself, as an expiation of offences that a more casual wrong-doer might have enjoyed and promptly forgotten. He was obsessed by what he afterwards described as "the nightmare of my own delinquencies;" and in previous chapters I have attempted to explain how this nightmare—once a fantasy, with very little real basis—gradually accumulated substance and tragic import. In everything he did there was a contradiction, his vices, as not uncommonly happens, being the reverse side of his qualities. Self-indulgence made him kind; but his kindness often led him into situations from which there was no escaping save by downright brutality. He was lovable because he was sensitive to human emotion; but his very sensitiveness produced an irascibility that inflicted untold suffering. He had a respect for goodness; but the knowledge that his own nature included many dark, intractable, even satanic, impulses, drove him to over-emphasise his smallest defects, to exhibit his private punishment on a public stage. Good or bad, he must fly to a dramatic extreme; "for [as he subsequently observed] I was always violent."

It was unfortunate that in Mrs. Leigh, the woman he knew and loved best—the human being most closely connected to him by ties both of blood and of affection—he had discovered the exact complement of his own nature. For Augusta had much prudery, but very little sense of sin. There was something fascinating in her passivity, her utter receptiveness; and Byron contrived that she should bear his imprint, that she, too, should share the Byronic doom. But, of all this, Augusta herself, fashionable, affectionate and foolish, had only the vaguest inklings. She hoped—she hoped persistently—for the best. She played for time, concocted fibs and subterfuges, soothed Byron, befriended Annabella, hovered dizzily on the verge of a confession—"Ah, you don't know [Annabella remembered her sighing] *what* a fool I have been about him," and again: "He can never respect *me*"—and scurried, head down, through the gathering tempest. A good heart, surely, and no principles; but her good-heartedness raised her high in her brother's esteem.

And then, Annabella, the "extraordinary" Annabella. . . . There had been a time when Byron thought that he loved her because she was extraordinary—a young woman of wonderful talents and unfeminine virtues—and there was a time when he hated her for the same reason. The Moralist became an embodied reproach. Now and then (he told Hobhouse, during the first flurry of the separation proceedings) he had been "much annoyed, on lifting up his head, to observe his wife gazing at him with a mixture of pity and anxiety." The solicitude he had once invited soon exasperated him. He misunderstood the meaning of that tender, troubled and furtive glance which followed him about the room; while Annabella, for her part, misunderstood his vehemence, his trick of rhetorical exaggeration, what Hobhouse considered his vein of playful paradox and "singular love of the marvellous in morals." She had borne her lot steadfastly a whole year. She had displayed great heroism; but, like her husband's, Annabella's

virtues were not unconnected with her vices; and, if she was patient
and long-suffering, she was also stern. She had been prompt to
embrace a perilous happiness; that happiness, as promptly and
decisively, was cast aside.

The consciousness of rectitude is fraught with danger. Believing
that she was in the right, Annabella became every day more and
more possessed by the conviction that her opponents must be
shamefully and irremediably in the wrong. To no purpose did
Byron plead his debts, the state of his liver, his inability to control
his tongue. Her decision was "irrevocable," she had informed
Hobhouse, in reply to his pompous and well-meant letter. "I have
consistently fulfilled my duty," she told her husband on February 11th.
". . . It was too dear to be resigned till it became hopeless. Now
my resolution cannot be changed." But the errant husband would
not accept his dismissal. After a fortnight, "passed in suspense, in
humiliation, in obloquy, exposed to the most black and blighting
calumnies of every kind," he still declared that, "bad or good, mad
or rational," he loved her and would continue to do so, "to the
dregs of my memory and existence." Byron's friends at this period,
according to Hobhouse, were seriously concerned lest the poet
should attempt to end his life; but when Augusta met Annabella
in London and reported that, unless she returned, it was probable that her husband would commit suicide, "her Ladyship
reflected, '*she could not help it, she must do her duty.*'"

Consistent, perhaps, but a little chilling! Yet events proved
Annabella right; for, though Byron dashed himself again and again
upon the rock of Annabella's resolution, though he refused food,
canvassed his friends as to whether they had heard him speak
harshly or disrespectfully of Lady Byron—to which they returned
a unanimous negative—he did not seek to conclude his misery by
violent means. He admitted that he had often behaved unkindly.
Writing to Moore, he repeated the story of his embarrassments of
the last few months—embarrassments "which have frequently
driven me to excess"—and added that something might also be
attributed "to the strange and desultory habits which, becoming
my own master at an early age, and scrambling about, over and
through the world, may have induced. I still, however, think that,
if I had a fair chance . . . I might have gone on fairly."

He admitted a single act of infidelity, committed while Annabella was pregnant; but the real causes of the separation, he protested, he was quite unable to divine. Nor did his advisers, when they applied to Sir Ralph Noel and Dr. Lushington, evoke any satisfactory response. Mystery shrouded the whole business; and, in this atmosphere of mystery, suspicion and malicious invention shot up on all sides. Byron himself suspected a machiavellian conspiracy between Lady Noel and her confidante and "spy" Mrs. Clermont; and the world at large was pleased to think the worst, alleging now that Mrs. Leigh was at the bottom of the whole business, now that Byron had been guilty of an unnatural attempt.[1] Both of these charges—though denied by Annabella—received wide circulation. We know of the document that Annabella had signed in Dr. Lushington's chambers; but that was a weapon only to be employed in the last resort; and it seems probable that, if the Noel family had been obliged to fight the issue, the "brutality" and "indecency" of Byron's behaviour, coupled with the admitted act of misconduct, would have supplied them with sufficiently damaging grounds.

Through February and the early days of March, each party dared the other to come out into the open; but neither showed any particular anxiety to execute its threats. At the beginning of March, Lord Holland assumed the rôle of intermediary; but his intervention was no more successful than that of Hobhouse or Francis Hodgson a few weeks earlier. Byron made a forlorn effort to meet his wife. ". . . Indeed [writes Hobhouse] at one time he had actually ordered his carriage to take him to Mivart's Hotel at six o'clock, so entirely was he convinced that an interview would give him a very good chance of arranging the whole affair. . . ." At the last moment, however, he wrote instead; and Annabella, shortly and firmly, declined his proposal; since it would subject her feeling to "a still more distressing trial." The expedition to Mivart's Hotel was countermanded; and every hope of a reconciliation disappeared.

On March 16th, Augusta, at the instance of her friends, left Piccadilly Terrace for the rooms in St. James's Palace, to which she was entitled as Bedchamber Woman to the Queen; and, a day later,

[1]See Michael Joyce, op. cit.

Byron agreed in writing that a deed of separation should be prepared. Its terms were still a matter of dispute; and in the meantime, while the lawyers haggled over the details of the separation, the hero of the tragedy had been caught up into one of those small, pathetic, poignant and yet ridiculous dramas that, at almost every stage, formed the background of his adult life. Even now there were women to write him letters! Out of the unknown descended a young woman who signed herself "E. Trefusis" and, beginning with the customary parade of reluctance and desperation, ended with the customary proposal. Her feet, she explained, were on the edge of a precipice . . . She placed her happiness in the poet's hands . . : "If a woman, whose reputation has yet remained unstained . . . should throw herself upon your mercy, if with a beating heart she should confess the love she has borne you many years"—what would Lord Byron do? "Could you betray her, or would you be silent as the grave?"

The answer to these ingenuous queries was more simple than "E. Trefusis" had anticipated. Lord Byron did nothing. He did not reply; and, adopting a new signature—the initials "G.C.B."—his correspondent wrote again, requesting him to state "whether seven o'clock this Evening will be convenient to him to receive a lady to communicate with him on business of peculiar importance." Wearily, Byron responded that he was "not aware of any 'importance' which could be attached by any person to an interview with him, and more particularly by one with whom it did not appear that he had the honour of being acquainted;" but that he would be at home at the hour she mentioned. And it was thus that he encountered a personality singular and determined enough to make him relax—at least for a short time—the attitude of polite indifference behind which he had at first taken shelter. A handsome, dark-haired young woman, her good looks only marred by a nose of a somewhat too prominent and irregular conformation, "E. Trefusis" and "G.C.B." now revealed her identity as Clara Mary Jane Clairmont—Jane to her friends—daughter of the philosopher William Godwin's second wife. Her career had already been adventurous. For, when, in July 1814, her step-sister, Mary Godwin, had eloped at a very early age with the son of an obscure baronet, Clara had accompanied the lovers abroad, had wandered with them on foot across France and had returned to England in the character of romantic rebel. Was it a spirit of sisterly emulation that induced her to open a clandestine correspondence with the most celebrated and notorious poet of the time? Mary had her Shelley; but Lord Byron was a capture calculated to put that shrill, dishevelled, wild-eyed young gentleman completely into the shade. Having once met Byron, Miss Clairmont called at Piccadilly Terrace again and again. Very often his servants made his excuses; but she was not to be deterred; and Byron learned the whole story of Mary, of Shelley—against whom he seems to have delivered a serious warning—of Shelley's projects, poems and quarrel with his father; while, for her own part, she gave him a full account of her opinions on a variety of subjects, including feminism and free love.

She solicited his interest at Drury Lane, but, when he offered an introduction to Douglas Kinnaird, announced that she had written part of a novel and had decided that literature was her real vocation. Soon it was clear that nothing would satisfy her but to become his mistress. "I was young and vain and poor [wrote Claire Clairmont, as an old woman]. He was famous beyond all precedent—so famous that people and especially young people hardly considered him as a man at all. . . . His beauty was as haunting as his fame." Her eighth letter contained a suggestion that even Byron, with his painful and extensive experience of determined women, must have found a little bold. They were to go out of London one evening "by some stage or mail about the distance of ten or twelve miles. There we shall be free and unknown; we can return early the following morning." Byron, his sensuality at length aroused, retaliated by proposing they should meet at a house in Dover Street; and it was here, presumably, that Miss Clairmont achieved her object. But if she wished to instal herself as *maîtresse en titre*—and by this time she had heard that he was going abroad—her hopes were soon disappointed. Byron scolded her, called her "a little fiend," lectured her about the opinions she had adopted from Shelley, and, patiently and repeatedly, begged to be left alone. "Now pray go . . . Now will you go?" he used to cajole her, when his unwanted mistress had settled down in obstinate siege.

One day she brought Mary to the house. Her step-sister did not know of their relationship; but it was some consolation to be able to show off the author of *Childe Harold* in the rôle of confidant and familiar friend. And Mary was delighted. "She perpetually exclaims: 'How mild he is! How gentle! How different from what I expected.' " The appearance of the two girls—Mary fair and thin, Clara dark and animated—must have been in strange contrast to the usual atmosphere of Piccadilly Terrace, distracted by lawyers and advisers, and just then menaced by the eleventh execution in the history of Byron's married life. The whole world seemed to be collapsing about his ears. The dreams of Napoleonic grandeur had evaporated; and it is curious to read an unpublished note, dated March 25th, in which "J. Tournier" offers to sell Byron "the Coronation robes of Buonaparte," of which the poet had apparently asked for the first refusal. London itself was proving unkind— London, of which he wrote so pensively to James Hogg, at the beginning of March, that it was "a damned place to be sure, but the only one in the world (at least in the English world) for fun." He had hated it. He had loved it. He would never forget it. Now he was to remember its brilliance and bustle—

The line of lights, too, up to Charing Cross . . .

the noise of its traffic, the extent of its rapidly spreading suburbs, its shop-windows and the spectacle of its fast mail-coaches as they arrived and departed at a spanking trot; and now it would come back to him in the tinkle of a waltz, played on a barrel-organ under his window, one sultry, dead-quiet Italian day—a waltz (he wrote) that he had heard ten thousand times in London ballrooms between 1812 and 1815.

The waltz had ushered in his triumph; and now the same measure played him off the stage. For a month the scandal had been growing in magnitude. From a whisper it had swelled to a hubbub of gossip; and from the drawing-rooms and clubs, where it found a ready audience among those who remembered the rumours of 1812 and 1813, it had burst with redoubled volume into the streets. The public had found a war-cry after its own heart. At a time when every public man was exposed, as a matter of ordinary politics, to the most venomous personal criticism that the malice ingenious adversaries could devise, when the champions of freedom exulted in the prospect of seeing their opponents' pallid heads carried round London on the tops of pike-shafts, Byron,

Whig and reputed atheist, could expect no quarter. At last the Tory press had its revenge. Fame so extensive carries within itself the seeds of future detestation; and, though Byron had delighted his countrymen, the envy he had aroused was of the kind that is never far removed from hatred. He had puzzled England: and the English are not a race who enjoy the sensation of being puzzled for very long. Journalists, great ladies, the mob—less knowing than their betters —who were convinced that an actress, Mrs. Mardyn, was the culprit and threatened to create an uproar if she appeared at Drury Lane, all turned against the poet with self-righteous fury; and a moment came, towards the end of March, when he hesitated to pay any further visits to the theatre, under the apprehension that he might be hissed. Not that Lady Byron escaped criticism. After all (observed the Duchess of Devonshire, whose son, Augustus Foster, Annabella had once refused, and who was soon to have the mortification of seeing Byron leave Piccadilly Terrace with his rent unpaid) "she *would* marry a poet and *reform* a rake;" but Byron must be "mad or a Caligula" if some of the stories were founded on fact; ". . . he has at length proved himself the true *Childe Harold.*"

Since the birth of his daughter—indeed, ever since his marriage —Byron's expeditions into the great world had been comparatively rare; and the reality of his social disgrace was not brought home to him until April 8th, when Lady Jersey, who, together with a fellow dragoness of Almack's, Madame de Lieven, had rallied to his support, gave a large party to which Byron and Augusta were both invited. It was Lady Jersey's courageous purpose to rehabilitate them. But all the authority of Almack's could not avert the disaster of that tremendous and tragic evening—a social catastrophe that it would require the eloquence of a Proust to depict with the force and vividness it demands. A chill crept through the gathering as the couple approached. Mrs. George Lamb—primed, one imagines, by her sister-in-law, Lady Caroline, now more than ever full of significant hints as to the confidences she had received when she visited Byron at Albany in 1814—ostentatiously cut Mrs. Leigh; while Byron's entry was the signal for "Countesses and ladies of fashion" to leave the room "in crowds." Only one woman, besides his hostess, consented to speak to him. As he stood leaning against a chimneypiece, lonely and defiant, and heard the petticoats of outraged fashion go sweeping past, "a little red-haired, bright-eyed coquette"—Miss Mercer Elphinstone—"came flirting up . . . and with a look that was exquisitely insolent, said, 'You had better have married me. I would have managed you better.' "[1]

He was alone now, as he had been alone when he was obscure. How curiously fate had completed the pattern, conjuring always the inevitable out of the unexpected, and circumscribing within a period of less than five years the movement from isolation to isolation that seems, in the last resort, to be the course pursued by every human life! With what patience Byron himself had aided his destiny, urging it on, and yet stepping back, horrified and distraught, when it reached the climax towards which some deep and half-hidden strain in his nature had persistently impelled him! At times he revolted against the admission; and then Annabella became the focus of his shame and rage—his moral Clytemnæstra, the "infernal fiend" who had traduced and betrayed him, robbed him of his daughter and driven him, homeless and disconsolate, from his native land. For there was no doubt that Annabella had gained the victory. It was a Pyrrhic victory; it had cost love and happiness; it would cost her her youth; while the effects of that victory were to deprive her of the little elasticity and spontaneity she had ever enjoyed. . . . After a wrangle that had lasted since the middle of March, and revolved mostly round the readjustment of the marriage settlement and the future partition of the Wentworth estates, the terms of the separation were at length arranged, and the deed was presented for Byron's signature. Byron signed it on Sunday, April 21st; Annabella at her hotel the following day.

During those last distracted weeks, he had had much to do. On March 17th he wrote the lines entitled *Fare Thee Well*, a somewhat maudlin apostrophe to the faultless but unforgiving wife; and on March 29th, in a spirit of raging recrimination, he sat down to compose *A Sketch* of Mrs. Clermont, whom he suspected—apparently quite without reason—of having plotted against him with his detestable mother-in-law:

---

[1]From another version of this story, and from the fact that he wrote gratefully to Miss Mercer Elphinstone and sent her one of his old school prizes, it is clear that Byron himself did not interpret her remark as deliberately offensive.

Born in the garret, in the kitchen bred,
Promoted thence to deck her mistress' head;
Next—for some gracious service unexpress'd
And from its wages only to be guess'd—
Raised from the toilette to the table—where
Her wondering betters wait behind her chair.
With eye unmoved, and forehead unabash'd,
She dines from off the plate she lately wash'd.
Quick with the tale, and ready with the lie,
The genial confidante, and general spy,
Who could, ye Gods! her next employment guess—
An only infant's earliest governess! . . .

Both poems were printed for private circulation only; but
Byron must have guessed that they would soon find their way into
the hands of a larger public; and, John Scott (a journalist who
hated Byron because the poet had failed to notice him when they
dined together with Leigh Hunt) having procured a copy from
Brougham, the farewell verses appeared in the *Champion*, a Sunday
newspaper, on April 14th. The impression they produced was
decidedly mixed. "*Je n'aurais pu m'y tenir un instant*," cried the
enraptured Madame de Staël, comparing her own facile sensibility
with the altogether Anglo-Saxon coldness displayed by Lady Byron.
"Wretched doggerel, disgusting in sentiment, and in execution contemptible," pronounced Wordsworth. "I protest [observed Curran,
a man whose wit and intelligence Byron had always valued]—I
protest I do not understand this kind of whimpering; here is a man
who first weeps over his wife, and then wipes his eyes with the
public."

Such was the diversity of opinion in literary circles. But
journalists and caricaturists were not slow to make the most of
their opportunity; and in the print-sellers' windows coloured sheets
soon appeared, showing the poet in a number of dramatic and
entirely fictitious situations. Thus, one print depicts Byron leaving
Piccadilly Terrace, with Mrs. Mardyn's arm around his neck,
spouting as he goes the notorious farewell lines, while Mrs. Clermont—a grim and witch-like figure—and Lady Byron, carrying the
child, retire indignantly through the opposite door; and another,
etched by Cruikshank, reveals him as a plump and smiling reprobate,

embarking at Dover, in a boat that, besides its feminine cargo, contains the skull goblet, and a store of bottles, labelled conspicuously: *Old Hock*.

Almost a month after writing his poetic farewell, on Easter Sunday, April 14th, Byron bade good-bye to Mrs. Leigh, who had quitted her apartments in St. James's Palace and was returning to her husband and children at Six Mile Bottom. Exactly what passed between them on this occasion we shall never know. But there were bitter tears, protestations of remorse and love; and that same day Byron wrote to Annabella:

"More last words—not many—and such as you will attend to; answer I do not expect, nor does it import; but you will at least hear me—I have just parted from Augusta, almost the last being whom you have left me to part with.

"Wherever I may go—and I am going far—you and I can never meet in this world, nor in the next. Let this content or atone. —If any accident occurs to me, be kind to Augusta; if she is then also nothing—to her children."

Now the drama was concluded, and it was time to go. The 23rd had been fixed for Byron's departure; and, during the 22nd, a few remaining friends called to wish him God speed. Rogers appeared; Kinnaird, with a cake and two bottles of champagne; Hanson, the lawyer, who reported that he had just seen Lady Byron, who looked well but "torn *here*," putting his hand to his heart; while Nathan, the Jewish composer, who had set *Hebrew Melodies* to music, supplied a touch of Oriental romanticism in the form of a gift of Passover bread.

On the morning of the 23rd, Hobhouse, who had been staying at Piccadilly Terrace for the last three weeks, hurried downstairs at six o'clock; but, though bailiffs were expected to descend at any moment, Byron was not ready till half-past nine. His entourage consisted of three servants—Berger, a Swiss, Fletcher and Robert Rushton—as well as John William Polidori, a pretentious and incompetent young man whom he had appointed his private physician. Scrope Davies and Hobhouse both accompanied him. There was a crowd around the door to watch them go. Hobhouse set out first with Polidori in Scrope Davies's chaise; and Byron and

Davies followed in the poet's "new Napoleonic carriage," built for him by Baxter the coachmaker at a cost of some £500.

Their escape was lucky; for ten minutes later bailiffs entered the house, seized everything that he had left behind—even his servants' belongings, the birds and a tame squirrel—and announced that, if it had been possible, they would have seized the carriage too. The cavalcade reached Dover at eight o'clock. On the 24th the wind was strong and contrary; but Hobhouse, fearing that the bailiffs might pursue them to Dover, arranged for his carriage to be put on to the boat out of harm's way. After dinner the friends walked up to view the cemetery where Charles Churchill lies buried. An old sexton showed them round the place. They saw a rough green hummock and a small headstone engraved with a quotation from the poet's own verses: "Life to the last enjoyed, here Churchill lies"; and Byron lay down and measured his length there, then handed the old man five shillings to have the grave returfed:

I stood beside the grave of him who blazed
The comet of a season, and I saw
The humblest of all sepulchres, and gazed
With not the less of sorrow and of awe
On that neglected turf and quiet stone,
With name no clearer than the names unknown,
Which lay unread around it; and I ask'd
The gardener of that ground, why it might be
That for this plant strangers his memory task'd,
Through the thick deaths of half a century?
And thus he answer'd—"Well I do not know
Why frequent travellers turn to pilgrims so;
He died before my day of sextonship,
And I had not the digging of his grave." . . .

Next day the whole inn was thronged with sightseers. Faces, wondering, inquisitive and hostile, lined every passage; and it was said that certain ladies of fashion had disguised themselves as chambermaids, merely to catch a glimpse of the poet when he left his room. But Byron, dilatory as always, did not appear. The wind had changed; Scrope Davies and Hobhouse went on board; the captain declared that he could not wait; yet Byron refused to hurry his dressing. At last, "after some bustle" and much agitated running to and fro, he emerged and, taking Hobhouse's arm, limped down towards the jetty. Every eye followed him—a small, compact figure, dignified, disdainful, his chestnut curls, which escaped from beneath the peak of his ornate travelling-cap, already lightly touched with threads of grey. The excitement of departure kept him in spirits; but he "looked affected" when the hawsers had been loosened and the packet began to glide out towards the waters of the open Channel. Hobhouse ran to the end of the wooden pier; "and as the vessel tossed by us through a rough sea and a contrary wind, I saw him again; the dear fellow pulled off his cap and waved it to me. I gazed until I could not distinguish him any longer. God bless him for a gallant spirit and a kind one."

Byron in Italy

Chapter 13

THE OTHERS had gone below; only Dr. Polidori remained on deck.
A young man, handsome, romantic, conceited, he had recently
registered a double triumph: Lord Byron, the greatest poet of the
age, had appointed him his personal travelling physician, and Mr.
John Murray, Lord Byron's publisher, had promised him a sum of
five hundred guineas if he would render an exact account of their
foreign journey. This evening, then, he preferred to remain on the
deck of the packet boat. It was April 26th, 1816. His employer at the
last moment had limped aboard; Hobhouse, the poet's closest friend,
had hurried down the jetty waving and smiling, to which Byron had
replied with gesticulations of his gold-trimmed travelling cap; the
"barren-looking" cliffs had slipped away till Dover Castle in the
distance showed small and miserable; now everything and everybody
"wore an aspect of grief." Other passengers retired to the cabin:
John Polidori, alone and exalted, looked out over the phosphorescent
swirl of the waters, peered into the star-lit obscurity of the sky above.
No sound reached him but "the sullen rushing of the vessel" and the
hoarse cries of a sailor heaving the lead. There was no illumination
except a crepuscular dimness; but "a beautiful streak" followed the
lead through the waves. Next morning the boat arrived in Ostend
harbour, and Lord Byron disembarked with his attendants and
carriage.

Having passed through the customs, they withdrew to an inn. And
here Byron, for whom foreign travel had a psychological significance
that his travelling companions could not long ignore, suddenly
revealed himself in an unfamiliar aspect. "As soon as he reached his
room [recorded Dr. Polidori] Lord Byron fell like a thunderbolt

upon the chambermaid." [1] In his own room the doctor was disturbed
by a smell of fresh paint and by the fact that the tea provided was of
a scented variety; and he was not sorry when he awoke to set out
through the town. There booksellers' windows disconcerted him by
displaying volumes of "the most obscene nature"; he saw "little girls
of all ages" wearing remarkable head-dresses, "women with wooden
shoes" and "men of low rank basking in the sun." He dashed into a
café where the waiters were very civil, and thence into a shop where
no one spoke French. He tried German, but "half a dozen women
burst out laughing," and was eventually obliged to buy two books
he did not want "because I let a quarto fall upon a fine girl's head
while looking at her eyes."

That afternoon, the cavalcade, which included Byron, Polidori,
Fletcher, Byron's querulous English valet, Bob Rushton, his north-
country sparring partner, and Berger, a Swiss, set off in the direction
of Ghent and Antwerp. Byron and Polidori enjoyed the comforts of
the enormous travelling carriage ("copied from the celebrated one
of Napoleon taken at Genappe") which Byron had commissioned
before leaving England and which among its other amenities contained "a *lit de repos* . . . a plate chest, and every apparatus for dining."
Through Bruges with its "long roof-fretted streets" they rumbled,
and so on to Ghent, where the gates were shut against them and
only bribery enabled them to enter the town. The landscape of the
Low Countries proved displeasing. At its best, Polidori decided, it
was "tiresomely beautiful." The tile-roofed, white-washed cottages
looked very neat; but fine trim avenues led to ugly churches, and the
prospect seemed "as unchangeable as the Flemish face. . . . All even-
ness, no genius, much stupidity." They yawned and dozed, and were
vastly relieved to arrive at Antwerp. Dutifully they paid a visit to the
Cathedral, which still showed signs of its spoliation by French
republican soldiery who had destroyed or removed as much of the
fabric as they could lay their hands on, leaving five feet of piled-up
rubbish to encumber the floor. At Rubens's canvases they gazed with
interest but little edification. Polidori tried his hardest to be properly
appreciative; but the poet, who knew nothing of the plastic arts, soon

---

[1] This sentence was cut out of Polidori's manuscript by a female descendant, but
restored from recollection by her nephew, W. M. Rossetti, Polidori's editor, who was
confident that he remembered "the precise diction of it."

admitted his discontent with Rubens's models, their high colouring, heavy shoulders and deeply dimpled flesh. It might "all be very fine"; but he was bored and satiated. Vandyke he preferred "a hundred times over . . ."

From Brussels they took horse to the field of Waterloo; and here at last was a scene that Byron found stimulating. His own career had often been likened to Napoleon's—and not by hyperbolical admirers alone; for he, too, in his stormier and more arrogant moments saw and admitted a parallelism between their destinies. He had been "damned sorry" when he had heard the news of Napoleon's fall. Now himself fallen, defeated, in exile, he rode slowly with Polidori across that pastoral upland where the peasants were whistling as they worked in the fields, and only patched plaster on farmhouse walls showed the effects of artillery fire. The farm of Hougoumont, however, was still in ruins. Fifteen hundred Englishmen had been slaughtered just beyond its garden. Here the Scots Greys had parted their ranks to allow a masked battery to pour its broadsides into the waves of furiously advancing cuirassiers. There, through a gap in the garden hedge, the French had charged again after dreadful losses. "A little farther on [noted Polidori] we were shown the spot where Colonel Howard, my friend's cousin, was buried before being carried to England." For Byron the memory of this young man had a double interest, since Howard was the son of his guardian, Lord Carlisle, whose neglect had done so much to embitter his boyhood, and to whom he had consecrated one of the most savage couplets of his early satire. In the poem he was already preparing he would make amends. . . . Meanwhile, peasant boys with glittering handfuls of buttons ran beside their stirrups. There were French cockades on sale, swords, eagles and helmets, breast-plates scarred by bullets, dinted and seamed by lance or sabre. Always a great collector of tokens and trophies, Byron made some purchases to send back to England. Then they turned their horses' heads and galloped homewards, helter-skelter over the springy turf of the battlefield, Byron chanting the refrain of a wild Turkish song.

Leaving Brussels, the travellers moved on to the Rhineland. Through Cologne they went. Then Bonn rose before them, crowned with pinnacles. Meadows and steep vineyards climbed up towards castellated crags; the Rhine rushed at their feet "with its massy swells"; rain-black hills lowered in the far distance. From some peasant girls whom they met upon the high road Byron accepted a bunch of violets which he immediately sent back to his sister in England, accompanied by a long lyrical address. Unlike the stanzas he had composed at Waterloo, the verses were not shown to Polidori (no doubt because the feelings they expressed were too painful for immediate publication), though a fair copy was afterwards inserted in *Childe Harold*. . . . Finally, they crossed the frontier into Swiss territory. For more than half a century this small rocky corner of monarchical Europe had been the refuge and the playground of revolutionary thought. To an entire generation it was the "home of freedom"; and from the sepulchral pyramid that marked the battle-field of Morat, where the Swiss burghers had defeated Charles the Bold, Byron pulled out some mouldering fragments—enough bones to have made "a quarter of a hero." On May 25th they reached the shores of the Lake of Geneva and dismounted in the suburb of Sécheron at the Hotel d'Angleterre. Among other details jotted down in the hotel register, Byron described himself as aged an hundred years.

It was a typical stroke of Byronic bravado: but, as in so many Byronic outbursts of the same kind, there was an element of sincerity and a pang of deep feeling beneath the surface. Life (he had always considered) was not a matter of years: only in the sufferings of heart and head could the passage of human existence really be measured: and, judging by these standards, he had exceeded his appointed span. Nor was this idea of particularly recent growth. From a much earlier period, the feeling that he had "anticipated life" (which seems to have originated in some mysterious childhood experience, now and then vaguely alluded to in his notebooks and journals) had pursued him through a bewildering series of adult conquests. It was as if the capital of emotion had already been squandered: he had been overdrawn on life before life began. Henceforward he would live as it were in retrospect.

He was twenty-eight. And yet his hair was already greying. Not without a kind of desperate satisfaction he considered the astonishing completeness of his personal destiny which had transported him in a moment to the heights of fame, then plunged him back with almost as little notice to the depths of disaster. That disaster, it was true, he had perhaps exaggerated. The injury to his pride had been extremely severe; the appalling scene at Lady Jersey's party, where half fashionable London had assembled to cut him and he had stood lonely and defiant amid a collapsing world, was the kind of episode that it is hard to live down; both his love and his self-love had been cruelly mangled; but he had still friends, prodigious celebrity, freedom, health and an unbroken spirit. Hobhouse at least, the prosy devoted friend to whom Byron showed always his most amenable side,[1] and who took a resolutely common-sense view of the "dear fellow's" vagaries, declared afterwards that there "was not the slightest necessity even in appearance for his going abroad," and that his fears of being hissed in public were entirely unfounded. But then, Hobhouse was more affectionate than perspicacious; and though it might have been possible for Byron to stand his ground and dare the disapproval of the London *beau monde*, putting such a plan into operation would at the time have been by no means easy. His financial affairs were still in a state of chaos; and having suffered eleven executions during the course of his married life, sacrificed his library and lost his furniture—the birds and the tame squirrel had also been seized by the bailiffs—he had escaped from Piccadilly Terrace with only minutes to spare. And, as it happened, he had long intended to go abroad again. During his wife's pregnancy he had discussed the project with Tom Moore; for, though his affections were rooted in London and Newstead, the memories of that early tour through the Near East—of his sensuous bohemian life at Athens and the azure calms and white squalls of the Ægean Sea—month after month had beguiled and teased him as he laboured beneath an increasing burden of domestic miseries. Besides, some instinct ordered him to complete the circle—to round off the course of his fate by a dramatic gesture, leaving England just as he had left it when he was an ingenuous nineteen, but with prospects and preoccupations that were very different. It was not that he hoped or expected to escape from his memories: they were more actual and far more vivid than the landscapes around him.

---

[1] "I do not write to you in good spirits, and I cannot pretend to be so. . . . I only request you will say nothing of this to Hobhouse, as I wish to wear as quiet an appearance with him as possible." *Byron to Mrs. Leigh*, September 14th, 1816.

Byron in Italy

Like a sleep-walker, then, he strayed through Europe, reached Sécheron, dismounted at the Hotel d'Angleterre and renewed the daily business of half-hearted sight-seeing. At the hotel he had been preceded by another English party. Byron had suspected he might possibly find it there; but no encounter appears to have taken place till May 27th, when, as he alighted from the boat in which he had been rowed over to Diodati (where he thought of taking a property beside the lake) he was confronted by a young Englishman and his two companions. At Piccadilly Terrace, several months earlier, he had occasionally been at home, but more often had been obliged to deny his door, to a dark-haired, enthusiastic girl named Mary Jane Clairmont—personally she preferred the Christian name of Claire or Clara—the step-daughter of William Godwin. She had proved talkative, passionate, an uncommon nuisance—anxious not only that he should make her his mistress (which Byron after much pestering had eventually consented to do) but that he should become the confidant of all her aspirations and perplexities. It seemed that her step-sister Mary had had a runaway love-affair; and this sister one day had been brought to the house—a blonde, slender, intellectual girl with aquiline features—and had gone home again much impressed by the poet's "gentleness." The two girls, Jane Clairmont and Mary Wollstonecraft Godwin, now greeted him as he stepped ashore. Accompanying them was Mary's lover, Percy Shelley, the rebellious son (as Byron had already heard) of a respectable member of parliament, but himself a Godwinian atheist and an apostle of free love.

Byron knew him already by reputation. Indeed, among other brief and teasing lectures delivered to Miss Clairmont at Piccadilly Terrace, interspersed with impatient pleas that she would not bother him, he had produced a serious warning against the principles of this quasi-brother-in-law. The reformer's notoriety was as nothing beside his own; but Shelley's pranks at Eton and expulsion from Oxford had created in their small way sufficient stir, and his seduction of Godwin's daughter had completed the scandal. Like many professional libertines, Byron had a deep regard for the domestic proprieties; and Shelley's particular brand of social theorising—all green tea and fine feelings and high-flown radicalism—was of a kind that he found most distasteful. Yet Shelley, met face to face, had an extraordinary charm; and it is just that quality of fascination—difficult to analyse after the lapse of a century, yet experienced very strongly by those around him—which makes him so elusive and so remote a figure. Even his physical likeness is vague. The legend that grew up round Byron entailed distortion but solidified in a recognisable and definite outline; Shelley's legend has developed as a kind of luminous blur. All his literary portraits (to borrow a photographic image) would seem for some reason to have been over-exposed, so that a misty halo of "halation" obscures the features. Of actual portraits, the best known is the least revealing. Amelia Curran was an untalented amateur; and no human being who had read and thought and suffered could have worn quite the expression of that pantomime Ariel, with its large intense feminine eyes and sexless mouth. Mary Shelley's pencil portrait drawn from recollection, which follows the general attitude of Miss Curran's daub, returns the same baffling reply to a modern questioner.

Shelley's appearance at Sécheron is not easy to visualise. Byron's portraits, both literary and pictorial, are so detailed and so persuasive in their verisimilitude that hardly an aspect of his physiognomy remains unfocused. Small, pale and compactly built—he was an aspiring, slightly self-conscious five foot eight—Byron had fine abundant reddish hair, darkened by the lavish use of macassar oil, which curled on the brow and around the temples, a straight classical line of nose and forehead (the tip of the nose a little too solid when observed in full-face), a sulky sensuous mouth and a heavy chin. It was about the mouth that his emotions often revealed themselves. When he was bored, discontented or ill at ease, the upper lip (as Annabella Milbanke had once noticed) would wrinkle upwards into an expression of "impatient disgust." His lips fell "singularly at the corners"; and even when he smiled he seemed contemptuous—at least, while he played his Byronic role at a London party; for in smaller companies he could be boisterous and almost schoolboyish, fond of laughter and wine and convivial hubbub. Among strangers he was supercilious because suspicious, on guard against some affront to his feelings and dignity, and, so long as the suspicion lasted, affected and haughty—a mood that might again dissolve into jocular friendship. His lameness was perceptible but not disfiguring—it gave to his walk a curious gliding or slithering movement. Of his beringed hands—white and woman-sized—he was exceedingly proud.

Admiration, affection, passion—he might evoke them all; but at a first encounter distrust was apt to predominate, since he himself evidently distrusted the world about him. Shelley's approach was one of enthusiasm, if not of confidence. His very gait was somehow enthusiastic; for his was a big-jointed but shambling body, with fragile rounded shoulders and hollowed chest, the head thrust forward with questing eagerness. Whereas Byron strained on tiptoe to achieve his full height, Shelley's stooping and unselfconscious carriage caused him to appear much shorter than, in fact, he was. There was something headlong about him, wild, precipitate, a mixture of clumsiness and delicacy, of speed and violence, that made his ascent of any staircase a series of tumbles. His voice was shrill, feminine, extremely discordant, his fine skin roughened by neglect and exposure, his thick brown hair long and always untidy. Eyes very large and very bright, a skull unusually small in circumference, a small sensitive mouth with a pouting underlip, a long nose that seemed to appeal for assistance and sympathy, completed a face that, not strictly handsome, was oddly captivating. If Byron's face was a mask composed from within, which betrayed feeling involuntarily or dramatised it for the especial benefit of some chosen observer, Shelley's was a transparency that revealed his inner life and the various characteristics that governed his intellect—his gullibility, his swift enthusiasm, his erratic ardour. His peculiar temperament had bestowed upon him an air of agelessness. Chronologically or personally, he refused to be classified.

Of his social origins, however, the traces were clearly marked. Byron was quick to notice—and noticed with gratitude—that Shelley retained the manners of the patrician class and was "as perfect a gentleman as ever crossed a drawing-room." Shelley's opinions might be perverse and his behaviour eccentric—his clothes might be rumpled and stained and tattered—but he had inherited a grace and a *savoir vivre* that Byron appreciated—envied perhaps, for his own manners were shy and awkward: he had been brought up by a dram-drinking mother in provincial obscurity. Not that Shelley would have paid homage to any social law. Indeed, there was nothing that he considered more despicable than the *beau monde*

Byron in Italy

"with its vulgar and noisy *éclat*"—the world from which Byron had so lately fallen and to which he looked back afterwards with such a longing gaze—but the effects of breeding and association were still apparent.[1] Glad already to meet a fellow reprobate, another exile cast out by English society, Byron was doubly glad to meet him on the footing of a man of the world. True, the situation was not altogether simple. Claire expected that he should take her seriously as *maîtresse en titre*, the companion of his soul, as Mary was of Shelley's; and he neither loved her nor had just now any appetite for romantic philandering. Could she not understand that he had succumbed through boredom, that his sensuality was diffuse and uncontrollable —easily aroused, quickly satisfied—and that there was no necessary link between desire and affection: that all the love he possessed was disposed of elsewhere? Still, something must be done about this assiduous concubine: it was not like him to be unkind, when kindness was easy, even though temporary kindness might have permanent consequences. Very soon he would slip back into a passing love-affair. Meanwhile, he had decided to settle at Diodati, where John Milton had once stayed on his travels through Switzerland.

Whether Shelley and Mary had yet learned of the connection between Claire and Byron is not apparent from the records they have left behind. Mary was dominated by her lover's theories; Shelley was enthusiastic rather than commonsensical; and, if they knew of it, they made no objection and raised no protest. There was no cloud over the charm of their lakeside meeting. Across the gloomy gulf of so many years, the words that they exchanged have failed to reach us —only the inflection of their very different voices: Byron's low and musical, Shelley's a high-pitched recurrent scream. Their attitude was cordial if a trifle guarded:

> Yet still between his Darkness and his Brightness
> There passed a mutual glance of great politeness

and the pact was sealed by a common interest in literature and a common preoccupation with the cause of freedom. On the evening of their first meeting Shelley was invited to dine; and Polidori, who

---

[1] Hobhouse, however, thought otherwise. And in his presentation copy of *Moore's Life*, against a passage in which Moore suggests that Shelley was "an aristocrat by birth and . . . also in manners and appearance," he retorts: "Not the least, unless to be lean and feeble be aristocratical."

during the earlier part of the day had been out alone in a boat nursing a fit of temper, had his first glimpse of the author of *Queen Mab*— "bashful, shy, consumptive; [he noted] . . . separated from his wife; keeps the two daughters of Godwin, who practise his theories; one L.B.'s." Next morning Shelley returned the invitation, and Polidori was presented to the poet's mistress. All dined together on May 29th and, the following day, met for breakfast after rising late. Shelley talked at length of his early sufferings; and Polidori heard that he had "gone through much misery," that his father had attempted to confine him in a madhouse and that, under the impression he was a dying man, he had "married a girl for the mere sake of letting her have the jointure that would accrue to her," but had then recovered and "found he could not agree." In fact, Shelley was not and had never been consumptive; nor was there much foundation for the statement that he had married Harriet because he believed that his case was desperate and only decided to leave her when he recovered his health. The truth was somewhat cruder and less romantic; but Shelley, though in many respects remarkably shrewd, was on the whole of an exceedingly gullible temperament and just as often deluded by himself as deceived by others.

Soon the breakfasts and dinners became a habit. Mary, always anxious to improve her mind, construed Italian verse with Polidori; and the five of them were rowed on the lake till the sun had gone down. Claire, who had a pretty voice, would be asked to sing; and diurnal reality dissolved into crepuscular sentiment; or they listened in silence to the drip of the oar-blades, breathed the "living fragrance" of lakeside meadows, which drifted out with the stridulation of summer insects, while mysterious sounds murmured in the woods above:

> *There seems a floating whisper on the hill,*
> *But that is fancy . . .*

Once, when a sudden squall ruffled the waters and the boatmen were struggling against a north-east wind, Byron, to whom a hint of danger was always exhilarating, proposed that he should render an Albanian song. ". . . Be sentimental," he shouted, "and give me all your attention." But "it was a strange, wild howl that he gave forth," afterwards laughing at his companions' disappointment; they had expected a dulcet Eastern melody in the manner of Southey or of

Byron in Italy

Tom Moore. Now and then they landed to stroll by the water's edge, and Byron, on these occasions, was inclined to lag behind—he hated walking because it drew attention to his lameness—and "lazily trailed" his sword-stick. Through the dank chill of an Alpine evening they would row back to Sécheron, and there finish the day with tea and politics and verse and ghost stories.

At the end of May, Shelley, Mary and their household, which numbered, besides Claire, their child and its nursemaid, moved from the hotel to a small property five or six minutes' walk from the Villa Diodati, known as Campagne Chapuis or Campagne Mont Alègre. Byron transported his more cumbrous retinue to Diodati some fortnight later; and on June 23rd, leaving the women and Polidori—the latter most fortunately had sprained his ankle—Byron and Shelley set sail in the boat they shared, having determined to circumnavigate the Lake of Geneva. It was an expedition through the literary past they had both inherited; for on the 25th, coasting along the southern shore, they ran before a fresh gale to the village of Meillerie and entered the poetic landscape of *La Nouvelle Héloïse*. Byron had had the forethought to bring the novel with him; Mrs. Byron had once discovered a resemblance to Rousseau in her equally difficult and exacting son; and, though Byron had often disclaimed the parallel, he was deeply moved by the misfortunes of Julie and Saint-Preux and stirred, in spite of himself, by his earliest glimpses of Clarens and Chillon beneath the chestnut woods and black pine forests and glistening snow-peaks. After dining at Meillerie they re-embarked; but a storm had risen, the waves on the lake had grown more turbulent, sheets of foam danced in front of them and streamed behind them; their vessel, half-swamped, was on the point of sinking; and Byron began hurriedly to strip his coat off. He was a good swimmer. Shelley, who had never learned to swim, though he was passionately devoted to rowing and sailing, followed his example, but then folded his arms and otherwise declined to budge. Fear (he explained subsequently) had been a subordinate feeling. In its place, he experienced a "mixture of sensations" which would have been less painful had he not been alarmed and humiliated by a conviction that Byron might risk his life by attempting to save him. "Positively refusing" any offer of help, he sat down (according to another account) upon a locker, stubbornly grasped the rings at either end and announced that he proposed to sink "without a struggle." Shelley's attraction to, and courtship of death must be analysed elsewhere; for the moment his gesture remained indefinite. In a few minutes the boat had been got under control; the sail—released by a frightened boatman—had been recaptured; and they were driven back, shaken but stimulated, to the port of St. Gingoux.

Next day they sailed out as far as the source of the Rhône. The weather had broken among the mountains; the "live thunder" leapt and reverberated from crag to crag; and the big rain thrashed down on to the water's surface which, after dark, seethed with a phosphorescent glow. For two rainy dismal days, they were storm-bound at Ouchy; but they visited, nevertheless, the Castle of Chillon (where Bonnivard's dungeon proved immensely impressive), paid a passing tribute to the shade of Voltaire:

> *The one was fire and fickleness, a child*
> *Most mutable in wishes, but in mind*
> *A wit as various—gay, grave, sage or wild—*
> *Historian, bard, philosopher, combined;*
> *He multiplied himself among mankind,*
> *The Proteus of their talents: but his own*
> *Breathed most in ridicule—which, as the wind,*
> *Blew where it listed, laying all things prone—*
> *Now to o'erthrow a fool, and now to shake a throne.*

and ventured into the deserted garden of Gibbon's house, where Byron plucked rose- and acacia-leaves to send home to Murray. A melancholy place, dishevelled and derelict: yet it was on this terrace and in this summerhouse (now fallen into ruins) that the third member of the mighty Genevan trinity had

> *. . . Shaped his weapon with an edge severe,*
> *Sapping a solemn creed with solemn sneer*

—piling up antithesis against weighty antithesis, elaborating an endless series of splendid paragraphs, dignified yet full of the movement and drama of history, each sentence concisely turned yet expressive and fluent; till an evening came when the gigantic work was at length concluded, and Gibbon, uplifted by an immense relief, but suffering at the same time a feeling of enormous loneliness, walked out along the moonlit paths of his garden:

Byron in Italy

After laying down my pen, I took several turns in a *berceau*, or covered walk of acacias, which commands a prospect of the country, the lake, and the mountains. The air was temperate, the sky was serene, the silver orb of the moon was reflected from the waters, and all nature was silent. I will not dissemble the first emotions of joy on the recovery of my freedom, and, perhaps, the establishment of my fame. But my pride was soon humbled, and a sober melancholy was spread over my mind, by the idea that I had taken an everlasting leave of an old and agreeable companion, and that whatsoever might be the future date of my *History*, the life of the historian must be short and precarious.

It was here, too, that—fascinated by the beauty of Lady Elizabeth Foster, whom Byron knew as an antiquarian Duchess—the writer had slumped on to his knees and proposed marriage, only to discover, the proposal refused, that his corpulence made it quite impossible to rise to his feet again. Shelley had little use for the graces of Gibbon—his cool Augustan mastery of the English language, in which sense dictated the choice of every epithet, and yet sober common sense assumed the quality of inspiration: he preferred the romantic vagaries of Julie and St. Preux. During the early morning, while Byron still lay in bed, he would be scrambling uphill among rocks and meadows, gathering such flowers as he had never seen in England and "hunting the waterfalls" which dropped in ravelled threads from the cliffs above. Finally, "after two days of pleasant sailing," on Saturday the 30th of June they returned to Mont Alègre.

Polidori greeted them with the announcement that he had fallen in love. Neither of the poets was impressed or interested; for so over-stimulating had been the effect of Byron's society that the doctor's behaviour had grown more impossible with every passing week, and both his employer and his new friends were now heartily sick of him. He had proved touchy, bumptious, arrogant, over-reaching; and the fact that he was not unaware of his own deficiencies, and sadly noted in his journal the confusion they caused, made it no easier for him to reform his conduct. So entirely out of his depth, he could not help but flounder, exploding into impertinent remarks that he at once regretted, then retiring to meditate in solitude on his woes and grievances. Absurdity dogged him from morning to midnight.

Even his sprained ankle had had a ridiculous history; for the accident had occurred when Byron had suggested that he ought to jump down from the low balcony on which they were both standing and give his arm to Mary Godwin who was walking up the hill. Polidori executed a precipitate jump, but tripped and stumbled. Byron helped to carry him indoors, had prescribed cold water for the swollen joint and had limped up to his bedroom to fetch a pillow. "Well, I did not believe you had so much feeling," was Polidori's only response to this unusual kindness.

There had been other scenes as unnecessary and as disagreeable—for instance, when Polidori out on the lake, by clumsy mismanagement of the oar he was handling, had struck Byron a sharp blow across the knee-cap. Byron had winced with pain and had turned away, then observed that he wished Polidori would be more careful, for the misadventure had hurt him a great deal. "I am glad of it," ejaculated the doctor. "I am glad to see you can suffer pain." "Let me advise you, Polidori," retorted Byron in "a calm suppressed tone," but with not unnatural emphasis, "when you, another time, hurt any one, not to express your satisfaction. People don't like to be told that those who give them pain are glad of it; and they cannot always command their anger. It was with some difficulty that I refrained from throwing you into the water and, but for Mrs. Shelley's presence, I should probably have done some such rash thing." This, according to Moore, was said "without ill temper"; but the snubs and checks that he occasionally administered did not prevent the young man becoming violently jealous of Shelley and, at one moment, actually challenging him to fight a duel. Shelley, as a convinced pacifist, had laughed and refused; but Byron, half laughing and half angry, had felt obliged to remind Polidori that, although his friend might have scruples about duelling, he himself had none (as he had already proved) and would be willing at any time to act as Shelley's substitute!

Yet it is difficult not to sympathise with Polidori's feelings—tormented by desires and ambitions he could never satisfy, baffled by the dazzling superiority of Byron's talents. Sometimes he revolted against his spiritual servitude. What could Byron do, he had inquired furiously, that was beyond his power? "Why, since you force me to say," answered Byron, "I think there are three things . . .";

and when Polidori demanded that he should name them: "I can swim across that river—I can snuff out that candle with a pistol-shot at a distance of twenty paces—and I have written a poem of which fourteen thousand copies were sold in one day."[1] No wonder that, after a particularly humiliating squabble, Polidori had rushed up into his room, selected a phial of poison from his medicine chest and was only hesitating over the composition of a farewell letter when Byron tapped on the door and entered with extended hand. Poor Polidori had burst out crying; and he admitted afterwards that nothing could have exceeded Lord Byron's kindness "in soothing his mind and restoring him to composure." But dark thoughts of suicide still hung about him, and he moved fretfully and unhappily through their daily routine, clinging yet cantankerous, aggressive yet diffident. When he submitted a tragedy he had begun to the assembled circle and Byron volunteered to read it aloud—halting, now and then, to praise it "most vehemently," but usually winding up his praises with the somewhat tepid declaration: "I assure you, when I was in the Drury Lane Committee, much worse things were offered to us"—while Polidori's eyes wandered anxiously from face to face, always on the look-out for an incipient smile, he failed to achieve the triumph his conceit demanded and sank into even profounder depths of nervous misery. It is characteristic of such a condition that one should long to please—that the heart should be overflowing with affection and good-will—but that the means of pleasing should grow more impracticable as the desire increases.

His fate might be ignominious: it was by no means tedious. Shelley's irresponsible and hectic fervour, and the half-imaginary tale of his early sufferings, Byron's dark moods and teasing wit, Mary's exalted devotion to Shelley and Claire's much more interested yearning for Byron, were all mirrored on the troubled surface of the young man's mind. Names and images crowded his imagination; and the journal which he had started in such an ambitious style—it represented literary fame and five hundred guineas—little by little grew more brief and more fragmentary. How could he hope to do justice to such remarkable subject-matter? For instance, in mid-June, just before Byron and Shelley had set out on their expedition round

[1] Byron was referring to the success of *The Corsair*, published in 1814.

the lake, the whole party had sat down to exchange ghost stories, prompted by the translation of a German book they had all been reading.[1] It is a significant, and perhaps a disturbing, fact that, to counterbalance their dissimilarity on the moral plane, the two poets (from whom nineteenth-century literature was to derive so many of its poetic standards) were both of them profoundly superstitious, and suffered violent accesses of persecution mania which ebbed and flowed with the waxing and waning of their inward crises. In Shelley's case the crises were accompanied by hallucinations; his mysterious persecutors were visibly present and, at least once, he had attempted to retaliate with the help of firearms. That, at any rate, seems the most plausible explanation of the strange midnight episode at Tremadoc which preceded his headlong flight to Dublin. Peacock, a sensible and trustworthy witness, had noted these ebullitions of Shelley's fancy and had come to the conclusion that the perils he complained of were largely baseless. As to Byron, it is on record that, even for the purpose of a short journey from London to the suburbs, he made a point of travelling heavily armed; that he had a dagger often or always about him; that his weapons were placed within reach when he retired to bed, and that he was the victim of inexplicable midnight terrors. Laudanum and brandy may have aggravated his nervous plight; but Shelley led, comparatively speaking, a blameless existence,[2] and his spiritual maladies had a deeper and less objective origin—in some fundamental disequilibrium of the poet's psyche. Though at times he was apt to prove himself uncommonly sensible, his grasp of reality was often precarious; and the long conversations that he enjoyed with Byron on such subjects as the first principle of life, the possibility of re-animating a dead body, galvanism and other exciting and alarming topics, scattered sparks on his combustible imagination till it blazed up into a nerve-storm of unusual violence. Polidori was the startled witness of these curious happenings, and in his diary made a brief note of the scene and its background.

[1] This work, which was entitled *Fantasmagoriana, ou Recueil d'Histoires d'Apparitions, de Spectres, Revenants, etc.*, fell into their hands while they were kept indoors by bad weather.

[2] There is some reason for believing, however, that Shelley, like so many other nineteenth-century writers, at least during his Italian period may have been a laudanum addict.

Byron in Italy

Twelve o'clock was the hour, on June 18th. The evening had been spent in ghostly gossip, and at midnight Byron helped further to obscure the atmosphere by repeating certain lines from Coleridge's *Christabel*:

> *Beneath the lamp the lady bowed,*
> *And slowly rolled her eyes around;*
> *Then drawing in her breath aloud,*
> *Like one that shuddered, she unbound*
> *The cincture from beneath her breast:*
> *Her silken robe, and inner vest*
> *Dropt to her feet, and full in view*
> *Behold! Her bosom and half her side—*
> *A sight to dream of . . .*

He was interrupted by a piercing shriek from Shelley. Grasping his ruffled head between desperate hands, the poet staggered to his feet, caught up a candlestick and flitted through the door into darkness beyond. Followed and pacified with a douche of cold water and a whiff of ether, he presently explained that he had been gazing at Mary when he remembered a story he had been told of a woman who "had eyes instead of nipples, which taking hold of his mind horrified him . . ."

Byron did not confine himself to the relation of ghost stories. He also talked, vaguely but expansively, of his early life, divagated on his adventures in Eastern countries and described how, when he was living in Constantinople, he had had an unfaithful concubine sewn up in a sack and tossed into the Bosphorus. Again "Thirza" (he said) was a girl whom he had seduced and by whom he had had two children. When he refused to marry her, she had committed suicide; and Byron added that he had "fretted very much . . . but nothing, not even that, would have made him marry her because she was of mean birth." Though Shelley hastened to assure his companions it was "all untrue"[1] and derived merely from "a childish love of astonishing people and creating a sensation," he was himself a little shocked by Childe Harold's heterodoxy and, on July 17th, gravely reported to Peacock that Lord Byron was "an exceedingly interesting person," but "a slave to the vilest and most vulgar

[1] Byron had remained in Constantinople for a little more than two months—from May 14th to mid-July, 1810.

267

prejudices, and as mad as the winds." He might not approve, but to withhold his admiration he found impossible. The force of Byron's genius seemed to overwhelm him, till he had begun to lose faith in the existence of his own abilities. But so generous was his nature that he felt no bitterness. To him, as to the other members of the circle, Byron was an object of absorbing interest, changeable, fascinating, pettish, intolerant: very masculine in his attitude towards the opposite sex (whom he professed to regard sometimes as vassals and playthings), yet feminine, too, in his susceptibility and his need for affection. One moment he would be rendering an Albanian ballad (by his friends he was at this time nicknamed "Albé") and the next trying the effect of some perverse opinion, with illustrations and embellishments deliberately designed to appal. Bad enough that he should have been responsible for murder and suicide—these offences had a fine colouring of romantic frenzy; but he had refused to marry his mistress because her birth was humble!

So, indeed, were the origins of his present favourite. But even though marriage had not been out of the question, Claire could scarcely have expected that Byron should make her his wife, since she laughed at the conventional ties imposed by society. Nor did she hope that he would remain exactly constant. Here again her views were advanced and altruistic; and already, before Byron arrived at Sécheron, she had informed him that, were he to fall in love with Mary (who, she admitted, was "very handsome and very amiable") and were "blest in his attachment" (as no doubt he would be) he need have no fear that he would find her jealous or obstructive. Quite the contrary—"I will redouble my attentions to please her . . ." What she did expect was that she should be allowed the conviction that she was enacting a distinguished rôle. But this small mercy her lover persistently declined to grant. He neither pretended to a degree of passion he did not experience nor troubled to disguise the acute boredom from which he often suffered. "*Poor thing,*" he would call her in his "most gentle tone": but "*little fool*" or "*little fiend*" when she pursued and badgered him.

He was lazy; he "hated bother"; he distrusted sentiment. Besides, the shattering events of the last year had been such as to disable him for effusive feeling; they had left his heart bruised to numbness, his emotions exhausted. Who was Claire that she should imagine she could bring them to life again? Tact was not a quality she had ever boasted. He abhorred women who ran after him—as women were apt to do; yet no sooner had he arrived at the Hotel d'Angleterre than his mistress was pestering him with impatient notes, demanding to know how he could be "so very unkind," and adding that he could no longer allege, as once in London, that he was "overwhelmed with business" and had not a moment free. "I have been in this weary hotel this fortnight" (she lamented); but Byron was in no hurry for a private reunion. Would he not go "straight up to the top of the house . . . at half past seven and I will infallibly be on the landing place and show you the room. Pray do not ask any of the servants to conduct you for they might take you to Shelley's room which would be very awkward." Thanks more to Shelley's charm than to her own attractions, she soon succeeded in re-establishing her place as bedfellow; but the relationship was hardly flattering or satisfactory. He endured her importunate attentions: he did not welcome them. And, when she had hurried up from Chapuis to Diodati, as likely as not she would find Polidori continuing to hold the floor. Could not Byron (protested Claire) get rid of the doctor? He might be deputed to compile a dictionary "or visit his lady love." But the poet remained strangely impervious to either hints or pleas. He was difficult of access; his doctor, omnipresent. Byron's apathy grew more pronounced, and his interest fainter.

Yet as a literary copyist Claire was useful. The poems that he was finishing needed transcription; and from time to time she walked up from the vineyards below to make a fair draft of his scrawled and disordered manuscripts. Once Byron had checked her with an abrupt inquiry. Did she not think (he had demanded) that he was "a terrible person"? No (Claire replied loyally) she would not believe it. He had then unlocked a cabinet and had spread a number of his sister's letters upon a table. He had opened some and had invited her to read them. But, although "the beginning was ordinary enough—common news of their friends, her health," these passages were followed by "long spaces written in cyphers which he said only he and she had the key of—and unintelligible to all other people." They had started to collect the letters and put them aside, when Byron had suddenly announced that there was one letter missing and had

accused Claire of having stolen it: "He was extremely agitated."
Claire, however, protested that she had done nothing of the sort and
begged that Byron would look through the papers again, which he
did until he had found the missing document and immediately
apologised for having suspected her. "I mentioned the cyphers to
Mary and Shelley but the latter said they most likely were used to
convey news of his illegitimate children—I supposed so too and
thought no more of Mrs. Leigh. . . ."

Though his relationship with its inmates remained his chief
diversion, Campagne Chapuis was not the only house that Byron
visited. For example, he was often to be found at Coppet, where an
old London acquaintance, Germaine de Staël, was passing the last
months of her exhilarating and troubled career. Her daughter,
Albertine, whom she had tried unsuccessfully to market in England
—"a beautiful, dirty-skinned woman [Polidori noted]; pleasant, soft-
eyed speaker; dances well, waltzes"—was now married off to the duc
de Broglie. And with her daughter and her son-in-law and M. de
Rocca, her own youthful and exceedingly good-looking second
husband, Madame de Staël continued to preside over crowded
gatherings, packed with Genevan dignitaries and fashionable foreign
tourists. Her energy and her love of life were still undaunted. Hers
was the volubility that only Death can quiet. Death, indeed, was
preparing his supreme extinguisher; but meanwhile, squat, courageous, indefatigable, she poured forth the same overpowering flood
of talk that had deafened and delighted her English audiences.
Towards Byron her attitude was both admiring and critical. With the
hardihood that is the concomitant of a certain insensitiveness, she
even lectured him on his behaviour to Lady Byron;[1] and Byron
listened patiently and nodded obediently. Madame de Staël (he
knew) was a generous and good-hearted woman; and for the spoiled
celebrity who had sat through dinner parties with half-closed eyes,
whom she had once declared to be a demon in human shape, she
now revealed an almost maternal kindness. No doubt she was not
displeased that at least one of his visits should have been distinguished
by a scene in the romantic manner. He had been invited, as he
thought, to a family party; but, when he entered, he saw that the

[1] With Madame de Staël's encouragement he made an abortive attempt at reconciliation.

room was crowded with strangers, who had come to stare at him (he complained bitterly) "as at some outlandish beast." Mrs. Hervey, aged sixty-five, a sister of Beckford, had swooned away with the wild emotions induced by seeing him!

Later she rallied sufficiently to return for a closer view. But Byron, though he appreciated Madame de Staël, was never quite at his ease in the Coppet circle—it expected far too much in speech and sentiment. True (as he told Augusta) the hostess had been "particularly kind and friendly . . . and (I hear) fought battles without number in my very indifferent cause." He was amused to have her impressions of *Glenarvon*, Caroline Lamb's pathetic and preposterous story—concerning which she reported "marvellous and grievous things"—and glad to observe the duchesse de Broglie's happiness—"nothing (he remarked pensively) is more pleasing than to see the development of the domestic affections in a very young woman"; yet he was not sorry to descend to less exalted spheres. English acquaintances suited him better. During the early part of August there arrived in Switzerland, on his way home from the huge plantations he had inherited in Jamaica, Mathew Gregory Lewis, a slight, wispy, boyish-looking man, with large, bulging, curiously flattened eyeballs which projected from his cranium like the eyes of an insect. Strange that this unimpressive and often tedious person should have produced one of the most shocking best-sellers of the age in which he lived! Byron's susceptibilities were easily ruffled; and, after "reading the worst parts of *The Monk*" in 1813, he had remarked that they "might have been written by Tiberius at Caprea . . . the *philtered* ideas of a jaded voluptuary . . . all the sour cream of cantharides," and that it was inconceivable that Lewis should have composed such a work before he was twenty-one. In private life, the author was prosy and sentimental. But, "damned bore" though he might be, Byron was fond of him and, after presenting Lewis to Shelley on August 14th, he joined him in a short pilgrimage to the house of Voltaire. On the 18th there was another meeting at Diodati and the company plunged deep into a discussion of spiritualism. Neither Byron nor Lewis would admit that he believed in ghosts; but Shelley, who since boyhood had been the familiar of phantoms, adopted a point of view that was more irrational and more poetic. He did not agree that it was impossible to believe in ghosts without believing in God—personally he was both a spiritualist and a convinced agnostic; and he did not think "that all the persons who profess to discredit these visitations, really discredit them; or, if they do in the daylight, are not admonished, by the approaches of loneliness and midnight, to think more respectfully of the world of shadows." Under the influence of his revolutionary acquaintances the rich slave-owner decided that he should change his will; and according to a codicil dated August 20th, 1816, and witnessed by Byron, Shelley and Polidori, he laid down that the inheritor of his Jamaican estates must pass at least three months every three years upon the property, that not a single negro should be sold or disposed of, and no "comforts or indulgences" abrogated that he had himself decreed.

Byron at the time was expecting Hobhouse and Scrope Davies; and it was perhaps as well that the appearance of John Cam should have been preceded by the departure of the Shelley *ménage*; for though Hobhouse might not have disapproved of the association on the grounds of morality—he was above all things, he liked to assure himself, a hard-headed man of the world—he had as much Tory prejudice as could be squared with Whiggish principles. He would have appreciated neither the ghost stories nor the irreligion, and might have displayed little patience with Shelley's theory that mankind, being at bottom naturally good, at any moment by a common exertion of will-power could restore to earth the reign of peace and happiness. But Shelley during August had received a summons from his lawyers calling him back to London; and, in the last week of that month, he set out with his household, travelling to Paris by way of Dijon and pausing to visit Versailles and Fontainebleau which inspired him to appropriate reflections on "the hollow show of monarchy," as he explored the vast solitudes of park and palace. Among the responsibilities that he took to England—together with a load of Byron's manuscripts, which he had been commissioned to deliver to John Murray—was one at least that the friend he left behind might have more suitably shouldered: the immediate problem of Claire Clairmont and the child whom she was carrying.

Just when she had discovered that she was pregnant we cannot exactly tell—nor in what manner the news was conveyed to Shelley.

Byron in Italy

There was some explanation, however, between Shelley and Byron; and Shelley, by whom the difficulties of persons he liked or loved were as a matter of course taken over to increase his own, immediately volunteered to escort Claire homewards, and to harbour and protect her until she had borne her child. Naturally, it was an arrangement that suited Byron. There could be no question of allowing Claire to become a fixture; and, since he had never welcomed her assiduities and demonstrably had done nothing to raise her hopes, he considered that he was under no obligation to respect her feelings. Besides, she had involved him in yet another scrape. It was bad enough to be pursued by English tourists, to be obliged to edge past their carriages on some mountain road and see the green veils lifted and the eyebrows raised. It was intolerable to learn that with the help of spy-glasses they had scanned the façade of the Villa Diodati and had mistaken some tablecloths hanging from a balustrade for "robes and flounces"—an indication of the populous seraglio within its walls! He learned, moreover, that news had gone back to England that he and that notorious atheist, young Mr. Shelley, had established a satanic "league of incest" and were living with two sisters "in promiscuous intercourse"; and, when he received a flurried letter from Mrs. Leigh, who had several motives for alarm at the rumours circulating, he despatched a succinct account of his latest love affair:

... As to all these "mistresses" (he protested on September 8th), Lord help me—I have had but one. Now don't scold; but what could I do?—a foolish girl, in spite of all I could say or do, would come after me, or rather went before—for I found her here—and I have had all the plague possible to persuade her to go back again.... Now, dearest, I do most truly tell thee, that I could not help this, that I did all I could to prevent it ... I was not in love ...; but I could not exactly play the stoic with a woman, who had scrambled eight hundred miles to unphilosophise me. Besides, I had been regaled with so many "two courses and a *desert*" (Alas!) of aversion, that I was fain to take a little love (if pressed particularly) ...

The sequel he reserved for a second missive:

I forgot to tell you that the demoiselle who returned to England from Geneva went there to produce a new baby B....

Thereupon he turned to the society of the new arrivals. After the stimulating yet exhausting companionship of Shelley, Hobhouse's solidity and Davies's cynicism came over him like a breath of his carefree London past—a whiff of fog and steaming "Regency punch" and midnight candle-grease. He was determined they should not find him changed or saddened; and Hobhouse, always anxious to discount his friend's extravagances, was able to send a reassuring report to England. ". . . Your excellent relative [he told Augusta] is living with the strictest attention to decorum . . ." The tablecloths, he could promise, had *not* been petticoats; and "in sober sadness I can give you very good accounts from this place, both as to morals and other material points. A considerable change has taken place in his health; no brandy, no very late hours, no quarts of magnesia, nor deluges of soda water. Neither passion nor perverseness . . . ; he seems as happy as he ought to be; by this of course you will see that I mean, as happy as it is consistent for a man of honour and common feeling to be after the occurrence of a calamity involving a charge, whether just or unjust, against his honour and his feeling."

Davies was in a hurry to get back to England; but he had time enough to make an expedition with Byron, Hobhouse and the doctor from Diodati to Chamouni, during which Byron, opening the visitor's book at Montavert and finding Shelley's name followed by the self-description *atheist*,[1] thought it worth his while to remove the entry. Davies's departure coincided with the doctor's dismissal. The experiment of engaging him had been a failure from start to finish; but again Byron was not regardless of the young man's *amour propre*; and he had "determined upon our parting (wrote Polidori)—not upon any quarrel, but on account of our not suiting. Gave me £70 . . ." In a letter to Murray several months later, Byron's references to his attendant were fair and charitable. The doctor, he explained, understood his profession well and had no want of general ability. "His faults are the faults of a pardonable vanity and youth. His remaining with me was out of the question. I have enough to do to manage my own scrapes; and, as precepts without example are not the most gracious homilies, I thought it better to give him his *congé*: but I know no great harm of him, and some good." Subsequently, however, addressing the same correspondent, Byron's

[1] The inscription ran: Εἰμι φιλάνθρωπος δημωκρίτικος τ᾽ ἄθεος τε

animadversions upon poor dear "Pollydolly" were a trifle more splenetic. In retrospect he wondered that he had been able to endure him; for "I never was much more disgusted with any human production than with the eternal nonsense and *tracasseries* and emptiness and ill-humour and vanity of that young person: but he has some talent, and is a man of honour, and has dispositions of amendment in which he has been aided by a little subsequent experience, and may turn out well."

Polidori took his leave on September 16th; and, as soon as they were free of him, Byron and Hobhouse set out on an extended tour. For thirteen long stormy exciting days, often drenched to the skin, in danger of tumbling down precipices, among "Glaciers, Clouds, and Summits of eternal snow," they wound their way through the pinnacles of the Bernese Alps. It was such scenery as stirred Byron to the depths of his consciousness. The vacancy and inhumanity of mountain landscape, untrodden by man and untainted by the reminder of human virtues and vices, afforded his towering egoism the scope it needed. Yet only in intensity—not in attitude—are Byron's descriptions of the scenes he passed through to be distinguished from the eloquent and romantic letters that Gray and Walpole had sent home almost eighty years earlier. "Not a precipice, not a torrent, not a cliff" but was pregnant with ideas of "religion and poetry," wrote Gray in anticipation of *The Prelude*; while Walpole, the less philosophic of the two companions, who was apt to regard the Alps as a prodigious picture gallery hung with masterpieces in the style of Salvator Rosa, fell into ecstasies over the "silver speed" of waterfalls, mountain-sides "obscured with pines or lost in clouds," desolate ruined hermitages and tottering foot-bridges. The Romantic point of view had certainly preceded the Romantic movement; and the essence of Byron's genius was not a manner of feeling so much as the sheer energy with which he felt and suffered—his incomparable aptitude for self-projection, combined with a degree of self-absorption no less extraordinary.

Beneath an air of apparent calm he was living at the time in a state of almost continual nervous tension; and very unlike Hobhouse's reassuring report to Mrs. Leigh is Byron's own account of the condition of his mind and heart during the summer and autumn months of 1816. Incessantly he turned over thoughts of his late disaster. Now he raged furiously against his wife, the authoress (he sometimes persuaded himself) of all his miseries. Now remorse tortured him and he felt that he had accomplished the total ruin—impelled who could say by what ancestral curse?—of the human being he had loved most tenderly and most unselfishly.[1] Now he came face to face with appalling conviction that he could neither justify nor repent of the harm he had done, and stared down as from a cliff's edge into the moral void.[2] He was alarmed, yet fascinated, by the conflict within. Even by the exercise of rigorous self-control —a quality he had seldom troubled to display—it seemed a nearly hopeless task to keep hold of his sanity; and there were moments when he felt that his grasp was weakening. He had been "half mad," he declared later of this period, "between metaphysics, mountains, lakes, love unextinguishable, thoughts unutterable, and the nightmare of my own delinquencies. I should, many a good day, have blown my brains out, but for the recollection that it would have given pleasure to my mother-in-law . . ." Yet, as once before, the interest of self-observation—and to some extent, perhaps, the charms of self-dramatisation—proved stronger than the impulse that counselled suicide; and, like Manfred, he started back from the lip of the precipice. The tempest that had been gathering at Diodati, and had had its origins in the now far-off days at Piccadilly Terrace, exhausted its vehemence among the crags of the Jura. He returned to the lakeside refreshed and reconciled.

[1] *She was like me in lineaments; her eyes,*
Her hair, her features, all, to the very tone
Even of her voice, they said were like to mine;
But soften'd all, and temper'd into beauty:
She had the same lone thoughts and wanderings . . .
Pity, and smiles, and tears—which I had not;
And tenderness—but that I had for her;
Humility—and that I never had.
Her faults were mine—her virtues were her own—
I loved her, and destroy'd her!

[2] *There is a power upon me which withholds,*
And makes it my fatality to live,—
If it be life to wear within myself
This barrenness of spirit . . .
                              For I have ceased
To justify my deeds unto myself—
The last infirmity of evil.

Byron in Italy

With him he brought the journal he had kept from day to day—a strange document, fragmentary, unselfconscious, in which every image reflects the mood of the writer and every flash of poetry has a certain colouring of desperation. His sense of beauty was instinct with a sense of terror—reflected even by the cold glassy surface of a lonely mountain lake, "in the very nipple of the bosom of the Mountain." The clouds which boiled up from the valleys below, "curling up perpendicular precipices," were "like the foam of the Ocean of Hell, during a Springtide . . . white, and sulphury, and immeasurably deep . . ." A torrent, as it leapt from a rock, suggested "the tail of a white horse streaming in the wind, such as it might be conceived would be that of the 'pale horse' on which Death is mounted in the Apocalypse . . . Neither mist nor water . . . its immense height . . . gives it a wave, a curve, a spreading here, a condensation there, wonderful and indescribable." A glacier was compared to "a frozen hurricane"; and, the same day, when they passed "whole woods of withered pines, all withered; trunks stripped and barkless, branches lifeless . . . their appearance reminded me of me and my family." During the greater part of the expedition, Byron rode a mare he had recently purchased—"young and as quiet as any thing of her sex can be—very good-tempered, and perpetually neighing when she wants anything, which is every five minutes . . . a very tame pretty childish quadruped"; but the steeper slopes he sometimes ascended on foot, struggling along gallantly in his companion's footsteps, till the sweat rained from his forehead on to a patch of snow, "making the same dints as in a sieve." Regularly an avalanche roared down the mountain-side; and, when the reverberation of its passage had died away, his ear would catch the piping of a shepherd—"very different from Arcadia (where I saw the pastors with a long Musquet instead of a Crook, and pistols in their Girdles). Our Swiss Shepherd's pipe was sweet, and his tune agreeable." On September 25th, the party arrived at Thun and the more interesting stages of the tour were finished. On the 29th Byron completed his journal with a postscript addressed to Augusta Leigh by whom, for reasons that will afterwards become clear, it was received with somewhat mixed and painful feelings: ". . . In all this [he wrote] the recollections of bitterness have preyed upon me here; and neither the music of the shepherd, the crashing of the avalanche, nor the torrent, the mountain, the glacier, the forest, nor the cloud, have for one moment lightened the weight upon my heart, nor enabled me to lose my own wretched identity . . . I am past reproaches; and there is a time for all things. . . . *To* you, dearest Augusta, I send, and *for* you I have kept this record. . . . Love me as you are beloved by me."

Chapter 14

THAT AUTUMN, in a symbolic as well as in a geographical sense, Byron turned his back upon the mountains. From lake-shores and pine forests and radiant snow-peaks—and the ardours of thought and the extremes of suffering with which in his imagination they had become associated—he dropped down to a warmer and more prosaic level. On October 6th, accompanied by Hobhouse, he left Diodati, crossed the Simplon and emerged among the vines and poplar trees of the Lombard plain. A dull but easy journey brought them to Milan, the rich, busy, music-loving metropolis that Henri Beyle (now tired of a military life and somewhat satiated with Napoleonic grandeurs) was to describe as the gayest and pleasantest in the whole of Italy. Nowhere else (considered that supremely romantic realist) could the Italian way of living and the many genial qualities that flourished in the Italian soul be observed more commodiously or to greater advantage. Here the Italian system of sentiment was carried to perfection. Less priest-ridden than the aristocracy of the Papal States, not so vitiated by sunshine as the inhabitants of Naples on whom weighed the rule of a Bourbon despot, less frivolous and less depraved than the Venetians, the Milanese were friendly, vivacious, passionate, devoted to music and eloquence and the arts of love, the latter being cultivated with a peculiar thoroughness and dignified with an almost religious ceremony. Thus violent jealousy might be permitted to the lover, but was ridiculous and unbecoming when displayed by the husband whom decency enjoined to respect the lover's rights. Here reigned a kind of ordered promiscuity which, in Beyle's opinion, gave scope to some of the finest qualities of the heart and the intelligence. Better still, since Italian society disdained concealment and deep passion for its own sake was condoned and recognised, Milan from the point of view of an itinerant novelist suggested the convexity of a crystal beehive, swarming with strange stories and dramatic anecdotes.

The central chamber of the hive was the splendid opera house; and to the Scala Byron resorted soon after his arrival. He noted the cliques, the air of intrigue, the constant whisper and ceaseless coming and going between gilded boxes; and he was a little taken aback when in a conspicuous part of the house a mother and son were pointed out to him and pronounced by his informant to be "of the Theban dynasty . . . The narrator (one of the first men in Milan) seemed to be not sufficiently scandalised by the taste or the tie." At Milan, moreover, who should reappear but Dr. Polidori! Evidently much re-relieved to have escaped from Byron's shadow, the doctor was cutting a dash in Italian society (where his swart good looks and his glib tongue were important assets), and, but for his gift of making the wrong move, might have continued to do so. Alas, his fatal genius pursued him even to the opera house. Byron had received him with particular kindness and had gone to the trouble of correcting an English essay which he intended to publish in *The Pamphleteer*. The bad impression he had made at Diodati was almost forgotten; until one night, in a party at the Scala, Polidori, Hobhouse and a young Italian acquaintance happened to descend into the pit to watch the ballet, while Byron remained talking in a box above. Lombardy, at the time, was an Austrian vassal state; and between Polidori and the dancers on the stage there arose the tall figure of an Austrian officer, wearing his greatcoat and a grenadier's shako. Polidori, by tradition at least, was an Italian patriot; and, touching the intruder upon the arm, he requested firmly that he would be so kind as to remove his head-covering. "You would like me to?" said the Austrian. "Yes, I should like you to!" replied Polidori in imperative tones. His antagonist, who, as it most unfortunately turned out, was the officer on guard at the theatre that evening, proposed that Polidori should accompany him; to which Polidori, delighted at the prospect of a duel, immediately consented—only to be shoved and hustled through the guard-room door. Declamations followed, protests, floods of "Billingsgate German," and much consternation along corridors and among the boxes. Head over heels in a "philosophical argument on the principle of utility," Beyle (who had met Byron some days earlier)[1] saw the poet Silvio Pellico run up "in breathless haste to apprise Lord Byron that his friend and physician Polidori had been arrested." A large company, including a number of Italian *literati*, loyally accompanied them to the nearby guard-room, where Polidori was discovered "beside himself with passion . . . his face red as a burning coal," still declaiming violently against the wrong he had suffered. "Byron, though he too was in a violent rage, was on the contrary pale as ashes. His patrician blood boiled as he reflected on the slight consideration in which he was held." There ensued a wild uproar of conflicting voices: the Austrian summoned his men who began to seize their weapons: then the poet Monti stood forth and allayed the tumult or, at any rate, produced the formula that rendered it manageable. Some ten or fifteen Italians, two Englishmen and various Austrians had all been engaged in fierce dispute at uncomfortably close quarters. "*Sortiami tutti,*" he exclaimed. "*Restino solamente i titolati!* Let us all leave. Let only the noblemen stay!" He was obeyed; and, while the commoners filed from the room, the noblemen inscribed their names and titles, which were handed to the wearer of the obstructive shako, who excused the affront and released Polidori from confinement. But that same evening he received an order signed by the Austrian governor to quit Milan within the space of twenty-four hours.

Shedding tears of humiliation, "foaming with rage," and swearing that he would "one day return and bestow manual castigation on the Governor," but helpless against authority's offended might, Polidori left the city early next morning. Byron, though the *contretemps* involving a former member of his household had brought him into some discredit with the Austrian secret police, already suspicious of his alleged republican views, remained to explore Milan a few days longer, before setting out again in the direction of Verona and Venice. If not contented or acquiescent, he was at least composed; but the autumn rains had given him a touch of rheumatism and—a further reminder of approaching middle age—he suffered from attacks of faintness and giddiness (which made him

[1] "J'ai diné avec un joli et charmant jeune homme, figure de dix-huit ans, quoiqu'il en ait 28, profil d'un ange, l'air le plus doux. C'est l'original de Lovelace, ou plutôt mille fois mieux que le bavard Lovelace. . . . C'est le plus grand poète vivant, Lord Byron." Stendhal, Corresp., 20-x-1816.

fear that, like Swift, he might "die at the top" first); while grey strands were multiplying among his chestnut curls. On the credit side, his teeth were in excellent order, firm and white and sound as during his hey-day; but sometimes he fancied they were "*looseish*," and the old horror of any physical blemish returned to plague him, with the old superstitious dread of age and deformity. "Would you not think" (he wrote to Augusta on October 28th) "I was sixty instead of not quite nine and twenty."

Yet there could be no doubt that he had benefited by his stay at Milan. Old and loyal friends had reappeared in the persons of Lord and Lady Jersey; new acquaintances had emerged from the Italian literary world—among others, the before-mentioned Vincenzo Monti, renowned author of *La Basvigliana* (in which he had reviled the French), *Mascheroniana* (welcoming the advent of Napoleon) and subsequently of various mythological poems, written to celebrate the return of the Austrian armies. The variability of the sentiments that inspired them was only equalled by the grace and eloquence of the verses themselves; and when, at a dinner party given by the Marquis de Brême, Monti was prevailed on to recite the whole opening canto of *Mascheroniana*, Henri Beyle, still hovering in the background, noticed how Byron's usual *hauteur*—"that kind of haughty look which a man often puts on when he has to get rid of an inopportune question . . . which rather took away from the beauty of his magnificent countenance"—suddenly dissolved into "an expression of happiness. . . . Never shall I forget the sublime expression of his countenance: it was the peaceful look of power united with genius."

Beyle's deep interest in Byron was scarcely reciprocated. But then, Beyle in 1816 was not yet Stendhal—merely an argumentative and inquisitive Frenchman, sharp-eyed, square-faced, bewhiskered, stocky, who had good stories to tell of Napoleon and the campaign in Russia. To these topics he owed the conversations he held with Byron. Both were enthusiasts for the imperial legend; and, after some preliminary misunderstanding caused by Beyle's belief that any Englishman must detest the Emperor, they settled down to a long and impassioned colloquy. But if the young Englishman's capacity for enthusiasm did him credit, and the emotion that he displayed when he listened to poetry and music, his vanity (Beyle considered) was strange and shocking. He was disconcerted by Byron's frequent references to his patrician birth, by his perverse parade of aristocratic prejudices and by his desire to be regarded as a dandy and a man of fashion. Brummell no less than Napoleon was the poet's hero; and so self-conscious was he on the subject of his own attractions, and so constantly preoccupied with the effect they made, that there were moments when he seemed oddly impervious to the appeal of the opposite sex. Positively he had declined an introduction to "several young, noble, and lovely females," one of whom at least had been eager to meet him; and, though he had gazed in the theatre, he had retired in the ballroom, preferring masculine discussions of verse and philosophy, whether from "pride, timidity, or a remnant of dandyism" it would have been hard to say. Beyle, too, with many other of Byron's acquaintances, was disconcerted by the manifestations of a mysterious sense of guilt (which he hazarded might have to do with some death connived at—the assassination perhaps of an unfaithful Grecian slave). But, whatever the origins of his trouble, the result was ominous: "it must be admitted, that during nearly a third of the time we passed in the poet's society, he appeared to us like one labouring under an access of folly," which often approximated to downright madness.

In fact, the crisis was drawing to a slow conclusion. Some reminiscent pangs, however, were still experienced; and one day, as he explored the Ambrosian Library, he was intensely moved by being shown the love-letters that had passed between Lucrezia Borgia and Cardinal Bembo, and a long smooth golden curl from Lucrezia's head. For the sheer satisfaction of seeing them and turning them over he revisited the Library again and again—"to the scandal of the librarian who wanted to enlighten me with sundry valuable MSS., classical, philosophical, and pious." When permission to copy the letters was refused him, he contented himself with getting by heart certain passages;, and, since it was impossible to remove the hair, he took surreptitious possession of a single shining thread. Nothing in Milan had given him an equal pleasure—the hair of the dead woman "so long—and fair and beautiful," and her letters and verses "so pretty and so loving it makes one wretched not to have been born sooner to have at least seen her. And pray what do you think is one of her *signatures* (he concluded; for he was writing to Augusta)—why this + a cross . . . Is not this amusing?" Mrs. Leigh, he knew, would understand the reference: a cross was among the private symbols they had themselves employed. Whether she would find it amusing was somewhat more doubtful.

The charm of Milan had been exhausted by the end of October. During the first week of the following month, he was again on the road, skirted the Lago di Garda, which the travellers were able to admire "in all its vexation, foaming like a little Sea, as Virgil has described it," and paused for a brief visit to Verona where the amphitheatre impressed him as "wonderful—beats even Greece." Though (he admitted) but an indifferent and half-hearted virtuoso, he appreciated the Gothic burial place of the Scaliger family and made an expedition to the so-called "Tomb of Juliet," a plain open stone coffin "with withered leaves in it, in a wild and desolate conventual garden, once a cemetery, now ruined to the very graves," bringing away "a few pieces of the granite, to give to my daughter and my nieces." These sights seen and relics gathered, he continued his eastward journey—the East had for Byron a special significance—reaching Venice on the eleventh of November.

There are cities that mark a definite stage in life's development. For no reason that the mind can immediately follow—sometimes through the force of beauty, now and then through the power of their impressive ugliness—they absorb and localise the workings of the imagination; until the outlines of their roof-tops, the colour and configuration of their walls, the changing yet recurrent pattern of odours and street-noises, and most of all perhaps the quality of the light that clothes them, damp and concealing or sharp and crystal-clear, become associated with the mood and emotions of a particular period. Such on Byron was the effect produced by Venice. Weary of travel and sick of sight-seeing, he left the mainland, was ferried out from Mestre across the torpid lagoon and opened his eyes, pleased and bewildered, to a new experience. Monuments, for their own sake, had ceased to interest him. Even in Greece, when he was younger and far more impressionable, he had shocked Hobhouse as they gazed up at the ruined Parthenon by observing glumly that it was "very like the Mansion House"; and since that time he had had an overdose of churches and picture-galleries.

No character, in the ordinary sense, could have been less "Victorian"; yet it is remarkable in how many of his tastes and prejudices

Byron in Italy

Byron anticipated the limitations of the coming age. There was his deep, though thwarted, respect for the domestic proprieties; there was also that strain of aesthetic philistinism which made him completely insensitive to the appeal of the visual arts. In the long brilliant letters he sent back from the Continent, references to works of art are almost entirely lacking, and such references as do occur are flat and perfunctory. He might be interested by the human charm of an epitaph, moved by the memorial of some historic drama: for mere buildings, paintings, statues he had little affection. Not once, during the years he was to spend in Venice, is there any descriptive mention in his letters of its most conspicuous glories. The great murmuring grotto of St. Mark's, where every surface gleams with a smooth subaqueous lustre and the rolling pavement imitates the wave-worn floor of a submarine cavern: Verrochio's presentation of Colleoni, with its *"vista superba"* and "piercing and terrible" eyes: the vast devotional fantasies of Tintoretto: huge sunny rooms frescoed by Tiepolo and Veronese—if not unregarded, they remained uncelebrated. They did not touch his sensibility and added nothing to the colouring of his imagination. Very different was the view of the city that so quickly captivated him—more mundane yet, in its own way, perhaps more permanent; since its foundations had been laid by Shakespeare and Otway and, behind the fascinating spectacle of its modern inhabitants, moved the tragic Jew, pitiful, proud and cringing, the jealous Moor, Pierre and Jaffier and Belvidera, and the cloaked conspirators meeting on the bridge at midnight. Nor was there a dearth of activity in the immediate foreground. Venice was half-way to Greece and Turkey; and though Eastern merchants had long ceased to perambulate the Piazza San Marco, and only a red-capped Greek sailor, lounging here and there, recalled the proximity of the cities of the Levant, Venice had still a hybrid atmosphere neither of East nor West, just as itself it was neither of earth nor water, but seemed to hover like a mirage in some mysterious middle-space where sky met water, and water marble, and buildings and the reflections below them could scarcely be separated, so bright and clean was the inverted imagery of dome and palace-front.

Towards the watery element both Byron and Shelley felt a profound attraction. Shelley, though no swimmer and a clumsy sailor, was seldom happier or more carefree than by sea or stream: even a rivulet or a small pool would inspire and soothe him. Maternal yet destructive, uncontrollable by human will or human reason, the sea is an image of death and eternity: the earth, of the human mind and its finite conquests. The origins of Byron's feeling were partly matter of fact; and, if he loved the sea and delighted in Venice, it was because he found water a friendly medium which gratified his liking for speed and his desire for power. On land he moved awkwardly and was aware of his handicap; but, when he swam, his deformity was not perceptible. The limbs that baulked at a dance-floor could traverse the Hellespont; he was daring and self-confident, strong and envied. Here in Venice he could minimise the effort of walking—on to the Piazza San Marco he rarely ventured—but slip indolent, cool, reflective down endless waterways.

Besides, Venice gave him the privacy he had always wanted. No longer the city of feverish and intricate dissipation where every illicit love had its secret bolt-hole, and noble Venetians, in obscure apartments near the great piazza approached by passages of which even a gondolier could not discover the issue, led nocturnal lives unsuspected by the world and their families, it preserved something of that same atmosphere of adventurous licence which many years earlier had enchanted Beckford. But the gaiety had almost vanished, though the intrigue remained. A traveller who explored the Piazza in 1816 would hardly have admired its "thoughtless giddy transport" or noted, at the hour when lamps were lit, that "anything like restraint seemed perfectly out of the question . . . However solemn a magistrate may appear in the day [Beckford had written in 1780] he lays up wig and robe and gravity to sleep together, runs intriguing about his gondola, takes the reigning sultana under his arm, and so rambles half over the town, which grows gayer and gayer as the day declines." Nor from his balcony as dawn was breaking could a tourist have looked down on to the Grand Canal full of barges laden to the water's edge with peaches, grapes and melons, and observed, stepping delicately from boat to boat, last night's pleasure-seekers, distinguished by their masks and *tricornes*, in search of fruit to cool their palates before they retired to their morning's rest.

Since 1797, the city's decay had been very rapid. Yet even that crucial period of the Republic's agony (when the Great Council, distraught but ineffective, voted for complete submission to General

Bonaparte, then threatening them from beyond the lagoon with his troops and warships, and the last Doge, the hundred and twentieth to bear the title, discarded his robes and doffed his cap of office) had merely accentuated the decline of Venetian fortunes. Venice had outlived its utility, if not its dignity. By the fall of Constantinople, the closing of the caravan road from Asia and the development of modern ports on the western seaboard, the commercial life of the Republic had been slowly strangled: till there remained only the shadow of power without financial substance. Yet the city had derived added splendour from its increasing decrepitude; and, as their ultimate means of livelihood grew more precarious, so Venetians had made fresh advances in the arts of living, cultivating the happiness of the moment and the beauty of the present day. But now Venetian arts had followed Venetian liberty. Transferred by its conquerors to the Austrian Empire, Venice had sunk to the status of an obscure provincial town, doubly sad and doubly silent because its streets were water-paved. The slimy canal flood sucked and gurgled on deserted palace-steps: huge scutcheons hung mouldering over empty doorways.

The golden horses of St. Mark's, it is true, had returned to the piazza. Having been mounted on the triumphal arches of Nero and Trajan, led in captivity from Rome to Byzantium, and from Byzantium by the Doge Dandolo to Venice, they had travelled from the Piazza San Marco to the Place du Carrousel (with other spoils of the generalissimo's Italian conquests) and journeyed back again as Napoleon's gift to an Austrian Emperor.[1] But another symbol of Venetian sovereignty had gone for good. In January 1798, "to the surprise and distress" of the Venetian populace, the *Bucentaur*,[2] the long painted and gilded two-decker used every year in the ceremonious espousals of the Republic to the Adriatic Sea, had been stripped and despoiled by their foreign masters. "All the gilt work" had been torn off and burnt in a heap on the island of San Giorgio Maggiore, and the hull degraded to various menial purposes, sometimes employed as a coastguard battery ship, sometimes moored out

---

[1] They had been replaced in their original position a year before Byron's arrival by the Emperor Francis.

[2] This last *Bucentaur* had been built at the Venetian Arsenal in 1722 from the designs of the naval architect, Michele Conti. It was finally broken up by the authorities in 1824.

in the lagoon as a vulgar prison-hulk. In 1816 it still survived, but rotting and derelict: once the *panache* of the Republic's pride, now the emblem of its decadence and humiliation.

To Byron, however, these signs of decay were by no means displeasing. He had expected much of the city; it had "always been," he told Moore, "(next to the East) the greenest island of my imagination. It has not disappointed me; though its evident decay would, perhaps, have that effect upon others. But I have been familiar with ruins too long to dislike desolation." Venice (he wrote a little later to John Murray) was one of those places that, before he saw them, he felt he already knew. He appreciated the silence of Venetian canals and the "gloomy gaiety" of quietly passing gondolas. His ear was agreeably touched by the Venetian *patois*—"very naïve, and soft and peculiar, though not at all classical"—and he had immediately set to work to acquire its usages. Women of the upper class, he remarked, were not well-featured—that was an observation he had made elsewhere throughout the Continent—but among the people he saw many faces that impressed and charmed him: black braids and dark eyes beneath painted eyelids, impudent appraising glances and jetty eyebrows.

Naturally, he lost no time in beginning a love-affair—this was a method of settling down he had always favoured. It reassured him to be loved and to believe that he loved in turn: but the need was psychological rather than strictly physical, for, though Byron's appetites were impetuous and even greedy, like many other philanderers, who make love their business, he exploited his gift of attracting women at least as often as he employed it to gain him pleasure. Were the sexual impulse always governed by sexual motives, human relationships would present a somewhat easier study. In fact, the emotions that we find it convenient to describe as "desire" or "love" usually split up under analysis into several component passions, many of them apparently divorced from sexual feeling. Social vanity, for example, may play an exceedingly important part; and men or women who have established their own attraction tend to utilise it as a weapon against society—either as an aggressive weapon to subdue their fellows (now and then by humiliating and torturing a weaker partner) or as a means of upholding their pride and defending their self-esteem. Conversely, love may be a method of self-punishment; but here again the issues involved are far from simple; and the lover (as at times had happened to Byron) may find punishment in an acute consciousness of the harm he is doing, or may create a situation in which he is bound to suffer injury, in which betrayal must succeed to confidence as night to day. Unhappy lovers are frequently lovers who seek unhappiness, suffering being the intoxicant they distil from pleasure. The physical satisfaction that the downright "sensualist" considers he aims at may be subordinate to a dozen mysterious motives, besides which the influence of desire is slight and transitory.

No theory, however comprehensive, no type, however detailed and well-established, will quite cover any single human being. Infinitely monotonous yet immensely various, nature produces a thousand patterns—the vast majority obedient to an established formula—yet each signed with some minute distinctive oddity. Characteristic merges into characteristic; the peculiarities of a single given type—psychological, glandular, social, literary—are curiously interwoven with the traits of another; and it is one of the most interesting features of Byron's mind and life that very few aspects of his personality (which is not to be confused with the personal legend he himself created) do not rest on some dramatic contradiction. To a combination of tremendous natural gifts and an intellect, comparatively speaking, light and shallow, we owe the absorbing spectacle his career affords us. His native intelligence was quick and strong; but at no period could he have been described as an "intellectual"; and, though his flashes of intuition were extremely vivid, whether applied to his own life or the lives of others, he failed to co-ordinate them in any general system. His grasp of ideas was often lax; his character, for good or bad, was not of the heroic mould, being disfigured by evasions and spiritual self-deception. Yet through the self-deception ran an astonishing vein of honesty. If there were times when the pretences he dealt in suggested deliberate humbug, there were also times when his openness amounted to shamelessness, and he stepped forth smiling and unabashed, without guile or subterfuge. He believed in the reality of his emotions as long as he felt them deeply: he did not hesitate to discard them as the occasion prompted.

Thus, in Venice, there occurred a complete overhaul of his feelings and point of view. Because his mood had been desperate and almost demented, he saw no reason why he should continue to "sup on horrors" once his nature had begun to incline him to more cheerful prospects. Soon after reaching Venice, he was violently agitated by reminders of England, when a report reached him that Lady Byron considered going abroad and proposed taking with her his infant daughter, Augusta Ada. Such a move, considering the condition of the Continent, would be selfish and dangerous; and he immediately wrote off several angry letters of protest, finally eliciting from his father-in-law and wife a formal declaration, delivered through his lawyer, that "there never has existed nor does there exist the remotest intention of removing Miss Byron out of the kingdom."[1] Otherwise, he had determined that he would exist in the present. Having touched the rock bottom of gloom and agony, his spirits bounded up again towards the surface, and burst out into the sunshine of an ordinary sensual life. To his surprise, he had discovered that he could still enjoy himself. The transformation was remarkably expeditious; for he did not arrive in Venice till the eleventh of November and by the sixteenth he was already writing to Tom Moore with the information that he had recently fallen in love, "next to falling into the canal . . . the best or the worst thing I could do." Kinnaird received the same news a fortnight later, and an explanation in the letter-writer's most characteristic style—detached in tone yet with a hint of defiant jauntiness. He had intended (he wrote) to "give up gallivanting" when he said good-bye to England "where I had been tolerably sickened of that and everything else." But, in spite of his resolutions, the old habit had somehow returned and, at the moment of writing, he could not pretend that he was sorry: ". . . I know not how it is, my health growing better, and my spirits not worse, the '*besoin d'aimer*' came back upon my heart . . . and, after all, there is nothing like it." His new mistress was "a very pretty woman," so much so that even Hobhouse thought her attractive, and—yet another advantage—she was securely married. As to the steps by which they had arrived at their present footing, he was a

---

[1] Byron's letter of protest, to his lawyer John Hanson, is dated Venice, Nov. 11th, 1816. The final reply, signed by Anne Isabella Byron and Ralph Noel, was written on January 30th of the following year. He learned at the same time that his daughter had been made a ward in Chancery.

little vague—when he said that he had fallen in love he told no more than the literal truth: his amatory career had been all along a series of spills and stumbles. "Nevertheless . . . we do exceedingly well together."

Indeed, his choice was neither romantic nor ambitious. The "*besoin d'aimer*" had returned—that was the important thing; and very fortunately the wife of his Venetian landlord, a draper who kept a house and shop in the Frezzeria (at the sign of *Il Corno*—a name that had been changed by his apprentices to *Il Corno Inglese*) gave him any encouragement he may have felt he needed. Marianna Segati was twenty-two years old. Described by a later traveller as "a demon of avarice and libidinousness, who intrigued with every resident in the house, and every guest who visited it," she had "large, black, oriental eyes, with that peculiar expression in them . . . which many of the Turkish women give themselves by tingeing the eyelid . . ." Her temperament proved to be all that her eyes predicted. As to her features—they were "regular, and rather aquiline—mouth small—skin clear and soft, with a kind of hectic colour—forehead remarkably good"; while her hair was "of the curl and colour of Lady Jersey's." Besides, she was fond of singing and had a pretty figure. But her greatest merit (he added, when narrating the episode to John Murray) "is finding out mine—there is nothing so amiable as discernment." Plainly, Marianna was prepared to save him trouble: no assistant could have been better suited to his scheme of forgetting the past and weaning away his fancy from remorseful retrospect. "I am sick of sorrow [he was to write to Mrs. Leigh a few weeks later] and must even content myself as well as I can: so here goes—I won't be woeful again if I can help it."

His friends were soon made aware of this salutary determination. Though Byron had often resented the publicity to which he was exposed, and loved Venice because it promised him a chance of concealment, he had by no means resigned himself to being completely forgotten. His sister, his acquaintances in London and even his publisher were frequently entertained with glimpses of his new liaison; for, apart from his natural communicativeness and his taste for letter-writing, their amusement or disapproval would give the episode the relief it needed. Yet we cannot dismiss Byron as an amatory *poseur*. At least honest enough to have no thought of concealing his vanity, he was also ingenuous enough to expose his vanity in its very simplest form. And there was something of defiance, too, beneath the apparent bravado. Conscious of—perhaps one might add, in secret sympathy with—that excellent and self-righteous section of the British public which professed to regard him as an irreclaimable sinner, he paid a tribute to conventional standards by boldly flouting them. Finally, a brilliant narrator and a born spectator, gifted with an appreciation of drama and a sense of comedy, he had been fascinated always by the odd spectacle his life afforded.

He was amused and cheered by these new diversions: he was not obsessed. And because the pleasures of the head must be brought in to supplement those of the heart and senses—his mind (he had discovered) "wanted something craggy to break upon"—he undertook the study of the Armenian language. It was the kind of pursuit that its apparent futility makes yet more profitable. Moreover it imposed routine, created a habit and, like other persons of an irritable and nervous humour, he found almost any habit soothing and re-assuring. Every day, then, he would have himself conveyed to the Armenian Convent on the island of St. Lazzaro where it had been established since the closing decades of the seventeenth century. Within the convent walls he often remained from morning till evening—in the library which looked out across the burnished lagoon, in the closed garden with its cool paths under the tunnelled vine arbours, or in the rooms which the monks had allotted to him for his private use. As a means of repaying the tuition that he received, he undertook the publication of the Librarian's Armenian-English grammar, contributing a thousand francs for five hundred copies; and by the latter part of December he had made some progress, mastered thirty out of thirty-eight Armenian characters and begun to spell his way with Father Pasquale through the Armenian psalms. There his studies faltered, till they were gradually discontinued. Meanwhile, the company of simple and pious celibates—the Superior "a fine old fellow, with the beard of a meteor," and Father Pasquale who assured him that "the terrestrial Paradise was to be found in *Armenia*"—was a pleasant prelude to the amusements that began when night descended. "Studious in the day . . . dissolute in the evening," his existence did not admit of much variety; but he was calm and composed now as he had not been for many months and years. It amazed him, when he considered it—the extent of his composure. No doubt it would not last; yet "if I could but remain as I now am [he wrote to Kinnaird on November 27th], I should not merely be happy, but *contented*, which in my mind is the strangest, and the most difficult attainment of the two—for any one who will hazard enough may have moments of happiness." His present way of life was rational and yet voluptuous. Not only had he books and "a decent establishment," "a fine country" and the language that he preferred; but thrown in with them was "a handsome woman," who did not bore him, who had neither prudery nor principles, was neither chaste nor calculating. ". . . I do not tire of a woman *personally* (he explained to his publisher) but because they are generally bores in their disposition . . ." Marianna was unusually attractive and seemed uncommonly sensible; and, if he grew tired of the intrigues of the Frezzeria, he could always remove himself to some Venetian *salon*—to the drawing-rooms of the Countess Albrizzi or the Countess Benzoni, where he was received with the consideration due to his rank and fame. Venice lacked nothing—not even respectable company. Madame Albrizzi had been called the Madame de Staël of Italy (though "a very poor copy indeed," wrote John Cam Hobhouse) and her salon was an indifferent replica of the Coppet gatherings. Here verses were exchanged and literary characters, composed by the hostess, were sometimes read aloud. Men stood; the women sat in a decorous semi-circle; while glasses of punch—Byron had something to say about its flavour—and trays of ices were handed round among the party, and conversation remained elegant and mild and low-pitched, with "none of that snip-snap . . . which makes half the talk of Paris and London." To Madame Benzoni's house—she was the Albrizzi's greatest rival—Byron was attracted a little later; and he continued to visit her when Madame Albrizzi had begun to annoy him. "Thoroughly profligate," but "very pleasant and easy" (as Moore observed on being presented to her in 1819), she was to become the indulgent censor of Byron's escapades and extended her patronage to one at least of his Venetian favourites.

For the moment he stood in no need either of advice or of reprobation. At the end of November he had reported himself extremely happy; and during mid-December he was able to confirm his previous bulletin, adding that "the last month has been one of the pleasantest, and withal the *quietest*, in my recollection." Hobhouse had left for Rome; but Byron lingered, still charmed by Marianna, delighting in Venice, and given up to his daily round of pleasures and studies. When spring came, he planned vaguely that he would return to England—it was not that he intended ever again to make a home there; but he wished to support the reform party in the House of Lords and was anxious to pay visits to his barber and dentist, Mr. Blake and the incomparable Mr. White. Besides, during January came news of the "complete success" of his latest publications. Disposed of through the agency of Shelley (who in this as in other transactions of a similar kind revealed himself unexpectedly brisk and business-like) for a down payment of no less than two thousand guineas, the Third Canto of *Childe Harold* had been published on the 18th of November, and followed on December 5th by *The Prisoner of Chillon and Other Poems*. Murray wrote to describe how at a booksellers' banquet he had taken orders for seven thousand copies of each volume; and his communication, accompanied by a letter from Mrs. Leigh, reached Byron in Venice on the 2nd of January. It was the anniversary, he remembered, of his "accursed marriage."

To most correspondents Byron's replies were full and punctual. But there was one whom, through indolence or impatience, he did not trouble to gratify; since letter-writing was a kind of thinking aloud and he seldom thought of her. Claire Clairmont continued to remind him of her life and feelings—in neither of which could she flatter herself that he retained the smallest interest—and her methods of approach, though impulsive and tender, were not judicious. Particularly ill-chosen were her attempts at light-hearted *badinage*. Jokes about Byron's fondness for *petits pois* and his regrettable tendency to sit up drinking were accompanied by an unfortunate reference to Augusta: "Don't look cross at this letter [she had warned] because, perhaps by the same post, you expected one from Mrs. Leigh, and have not got it. That is not my fault, dearest." Elsewhere she abandoned the attempt at flippancy and addressed her "dearest Albé," her "dearest dear" in a more pathetic strain, begging for the favour of "a little letter to say how you are, how all you love are, and above all if you will say you sometimes think of me without anger . . ."

Both appeals proved equally ineffective; and Claire's disappointment was so obvious and painful that Shelley, writing on November 20th, begged that, even though he did not wish to write to Claire directly, Byron's letter to himself should include some friendly message. He had shown her a previous letter, "which I should have withheld had I been aware of the wretched state into which it would have thrown her. I need not say that I do not doubt that you were as little aware of such an effect. But the smallest omission, or the most unpremeditated word often affects a person in a delicate state of health and spirits."

Early in the spring, Byron learned that he was again a father. At the Shelleys' lodgings in Bath, on January 12th, 1817, Claire was delivered of a "beautiful girl . . . a creature [wrote Shelley] of the most exquisite symmetry," who was named first "Alba," but afterwards "Clara Allegra," and who was said to have betrayed, even at her birth, "a vigour and a sensibility very unusual." The same letter brought the news of the death of Shelley's wife. Bewildered and aggrieved, at odds with her family, Harriet had written a farewell note on November 9th, addressed to her sister Eliza Westbrook (whose advice she reproached herself bitterly for having neglected), then slipped off through Kensington to the autumnal Serpentine. A month later her body was recovered. The circumstances of her last days remain mysterious; but at the time of her suicide she was believed to have been pregnant, while Shelley added (in his account of the affair to Mary) that, having been driven by her sister from her father's house, "this poor woman . . . descended the steps of prostitution until she lived with a groom of the name of Smith, who deserting her, she killed herself." There could be no question, he continued with mounting passion, that "the beastly viper her sister . . . has secured to herself the fortune of the old man . . . by the murder of this poor creature." Proof of Shelley's allegations is entirely lacking.[1] Indeed, through the course of the whole episode (which for a time, according to Leigh Hunt, "tore his being to

---

[1] We have only Shelley's word for the suggestion that Harriet latterly became a prostitute; and, oddly enough, three days after this letter to Mary, Shelley wrote to Eliza Westbrook, assuring her that he gave "no faith to any of the imputations generally cast on your conduct or that of Mr. Westbrook. . . . I cannot help thinking that you might have acted more judiciously, but I do not doubt you intended well." See *Shelley's Lost Letters to Harriet*, ed. Leslie Hotson.

pieces") his character appears at its least trustworthy and most irrational, in very definite contrast to the aspect it assumed at other periods. All his indignation is reserved for the accursed Westbrooks —for the "libidinous and vindictive" Eliza and her decrepit parent —who, in an attempt to secure command of his children, Charles and Ianthe, had dragged him (he told Byron) "before the tribunals of tyranny and superstition," or in other words, had instituted a Chancery lawsuit. There are a few words of sorrow for the unlucky Harriet. But no sense of responsibility is revealed in his attitude— nothing of the humanity that neither questions nor criticises, and accepts the inevitable interdependence of right and wrong.

It was in this vein that he wrote of Harriet's death to Byron; and since Shelley's character and that of his fellow poet are often compared—almost invariably to the latter's moral detriment—the ghost of Harriet must be pursued a little further. Her death (Shelley informed Byron) had communicated a shock that he did not know how he had survived, but he admitted that he had not expected it would move him deeply and that it "followed in the train of a far severer anguish"—the death of plain lonely Fanny Imlay (Mary Wollstonecraft's child by Gilbert Imlay, Mary Shelley's half-sister and Godwin's step-daughter) who left home to commit suicide that same lugubrious autumn. Shelley had always been fond of her and regretted her loss bitterly. It tortured him to think that perhaps he had failed her; but that he had failed Harriet—though in a very different degree and more complex fashion—was an idea that would seem never to have troubled his consciousness. No, Harriet had failed *him*: and that was the root of the matter—not by infidelity which he might or might not have tolerated—but by proving unable to outgrow her sister's influence or develop spiritually and intellectually as he had himself prescribed. "A noble animal," docile, affectionate, feminine, she could not "feel poetry and understand philosophy." And in the letters which he wrote her after his elopement with Mary (which had been preceded by a period of sentimental dalliance with those two egregious blue-stockings, Cornelia Turner and her mother Mrs. Boinville) he refers again and again to the limitations of her spiritual outlook. Regarding his own qualities, the tone is complacent. "It is no reproach to me [he declared] that you have never filled my heart with an all-sufficing passion." And later: "Since I first beheld you almost, my chief study has been to overwhelm you with benefits . . . And it would be generous, nay even just to consider with kindness that woman whom my judgment and my heart have selected as the noblest and most excellent of human beings." In this mood he had put forward a sublime suggestion that Harriet should join himself and Mary, and form the platonic apex of a triangular *ménage*. Measured by the yardstick of Shelleyan dogma, the project satisfied every requirement of magnanimous feeling. That Harriet should have thought otherwise was strange and troublesome. It confirmed him in his contempt for her mind and principles.

In the "shock," then, that he experienced on hearing of Harriet's death, there was less of human pity than of moral indignation. Byron's reply to his letter has not been preserved; nor is there reason to suppose that he wrote to Claire, though he was pleased enough by the acquisition of a second daughter. Carnival had begun at the end of January, with "fiddling, masquing, singing" in Ridotto and opera house, and Byron had plunged headlong into a vortex of gaiety. The weeks that followed were feverish and highly enjoyable. Venice seemed to wake up to its ancient animation; every gondola was bound on some illicit errand; in every masquerade there was a promise of adventure; and the *tempo* of the carnival increased as the days went by. In the midst of these diversions and dissipations, he was made the hero of an upsetting but amusing scene. A gondolier brought him a note requesting an assignation. He gave an appointment at his rooms in the Frezzeria, during the evening while his mistress and her husband were out of the house. Ten o'clock arrived; "and in walked a well-looking and (for an Italian) *bionda* girl of about nineteen, who informed me that she was married to the brother of my *amorosa*, and wished to have some conversation with me." Byron agreed, and the talk was progressing favourably, when the door was again burst open, this time to reveal "Marianna Segati, *in propriâ personâ*" who, "after making a most polite curtsey to her sister-in-law and to me, without a single word seizes her said sister-in-law by the hair, and bestows upon her some sixteen slaps, which would have made your ear ache only to hear their echo. I need not describe the screaming which ensued." As Moore knew—for it was to him that Byron related the story, though a brief sketch of it was also given to Douglas Kinnaird—the poet had a long experience of feminine scene-making. No one who had survived the attentions of Lady Caroline Lamb and had weathered the tremendous rumpus at Lady Heathcote's party, where Lady Caroline had attempted to stab herself with a pair of scissors and had succeeded in cutting her hand with a broken custard-glass, could be much dismayed by the evolutions of a Marianna. As soon as the slapped visitor had rushed from the room, he grappled with and forcibly detained Signora Segati until, "after several vain attempts to get away," she "fairly went into fits in my arms; and, in spite of reasoning, *eau de Cologne*, vinegar, half a pint of water," continued in that condition past the stroke of midnight.

It was as if Congreve had composed a farce in collaboration with Goldoni! For this was not all. An hour later "in comes—who? Why, Signor Segati . . . and finds me with his wife fainting upon the sofa, and all the apparatus of confusion, dishevelled hair, hats, handkerchiefs, salts, smelling-bottles—and the lady as pale as ashes, without sense or motion." Moore, however (he added), had no cause for alarm. Jealousy was not the order of the day in Venice; and next morning some plausible explanation was produced, and hysterical wife and ruffled husband were quietly reconciled: "how they settled it, I know not, but settle it they did." One thing, nevertheless, was fairly evident: Marianna was not the quiet and tactful young woman he had expected. The amusements of the Carnival had begun to wear him down, and "three or four up-all-nights" in quick succession lowered his vitality and shook his nerves. "The mumming closed [he explained to Moore] with a masked ball at the Fenice." Now Lent was here with its abstinence and sacred music; and suddenly, as the third paragraph of an indifferent letter, he introduced his finest and most famous lyric, the only memorable short poem he would ever achieve, in which every period is like a sigh of weariness, and the muse of poetry (who is also the muse of memory) distils a mysterious charm from the immense lassitude of flesh and spirit:

> *So, we'll go no more a-roving*
> *So late into the night,*
> *Though the heart be still as loving,*
> *And the moon be still as bright.*

Byron in Italy

For the sword outwears its sheath,
And the soul wears out the breast,
And the heart must pause to breathe,
And Love itself have rest.

Though the night was made for loving,
And the day returns too soon,
Yet we'll go no more a-roving
By the light of the moon.

These lines were sent to Moore on February 28th, and some days later he was confined to his bed. Luckily, his complaint proved not to be "the low, vulgar typhus, which is at present decimating Venice . . . but a sharp gentlemanly fever that went away in a few days." At the end of March, he was once more "very well, with a monstrous appetite" and much amused to learn of a current story (reported to him by Hobhouse who was still in Rome) that he had latterly eloped to Naples with a Milanese opera-singer. Yet his illness, though now passed, had sounded a serious warning. He wanted a holiday from Venice: perhaps, too, he needed a rest from Marianna Segati. During March he continued to play with the idea that he might return to England; but in mid-April he posted a letter to Hobhouse announcing that it was his "indelible purpose" to join him very shortly. In less than a week the promise had been honoured. Once more his cumbrous equipage took the road, passing through Ferrara, Padua, Bologna, Florence and drawing up in Rome on April 29th. The impressions of that journey constituted the material of the Fourth and last Canto of *Childe Harold*; and it is by a re-reading of the poem that they can best be studied. Arqua recalled the shade of Petrarch. In Ferrara, with its "wide and grass-grown streets," he remembered the Estes and visited Tasso's prison-cell. His stay in Florence was irradiated by the Venus de Medici, whom privately he considered built for admiration rather than for love, but to whom in his public character he paid a glowing and effective tribute. Rome itself inspired other and far deeper emotions. The whole city opened in a vast perspective of decay and splendour which delighted him "beyond everything, since Athens and Constantinople." His days were spent on horseback either riding around the city, to the Colosseum, a lunar skeleton patched with shaggy forest growths, to the Palatine, a jungle-ruin half man-made and half natural, or out towards the Alban hills over the Campagna, where the broken aqueducts stepped away across the landscape and Soracte, along the tawny horizon, swept upwards in a gentle curve—a long delicate fluid line like an arrested ocean-swell.

Hobhouse accompanied him on many of his expeditions; and, when he needed to rest his mind from sight-seeing and the "strong and confused" impressions it engendered, he had the society of some friendly English tourists—the Jerseys again and the Whig magnifico, Lord Lansdowne. Otherwise English visitors to the city were few; but such of his unknown countrymen as he did encounter were by no means well disposed. It was at this time that an English matron, coming face to face with him among her offspring on the roof of St. Peter's, ordered the young ladies to avert their eyes: so deadly was the fascination of the most casual glance he threw! During this same visit, at the request of Hobhouse, he sat for his portrait-head to the celebrated sculptor Thorwaldsen, who was amused to notice that, as soon as Byron had settled down into a chair, he "at once began to put on a quite different expression from that usual to him." "Will you not sit still?" said Thorwaldsen; "You need not assume that look." That was his expression, Byron answered. "Indeed?" said the artist and proceeded to represent him as he wished—a sulky Apollo round whose mouth and nose hovers a shade of petulance, and between whose eyebrows runs a vertical impatient cleft, but whose luxuriant hair is beautifully ringleted and carefully ordered. The bust pleased his friends and annoyed the poet. It was most unlike, he protested —but not on the obvious grounds that he looked arrogant and ill-natured. His real expression, he wished to point out, was "more unhappy."

For a man who professed to be wretched he was at least extremely active. Not content with the usual round of sights in and around the city, and with seeing "the Pope alive, and a cardinal dead—both of whom looked very well indeed," he took a fancy to attend a Roman execution. It was not the first time that he had witnessed such a spectacle; for in 1812 he had sat up all night with two old school friends, Baillie and John Madocks, to see the crazy assassin Bellingham "launched into eternity" among the grim and squalid appurtenances of an English public hanging, the sanded drop, the huge

ferocious drunken crowd roaring and tossing in dark waves beneath
the scaffold, and the yells of execration that greeted the appearance
of the hangman. By comparison, the guillotine seemed a merciful
instrument, and the whole ceremony dignified and almost hieratic—
"the *masqued* priests; the half-naked executioners; the bandaged
criminals; the black Christ and his banner; the scaffold; the soldiery;
the slow procession, and the quick rattle and heavy fall of the axe;
the splash of the blood, and the ghastliness of the exposed heads . . ."
Here was nothing of the "dog-like agony" he had watched in Bellingham; but, although two of the criminals "behaved calmly enough,"
the first to suffer "died with great terror and reluctance, which was
very horrible . . . and the priest was obliged to drown his exclama-
tions by still louder exhortations." Then the knife thudded smoothly
down and the scene was over. Byron had a place close to the scaffold;
and, being an amateur of strange sights and violent sensations—one,
moreover, who was engrossed by the idea of death—he had come as
to the theatre equipped with an opera glass. Now his hand shook so
that he could scarcely hold it; and the experience left him, he discovered, "quite hot and thirsty"; but the second and third deaths
had little effect on him (though he admitted that he would have saved
the men had it been within his power) "which shows how dreadfully
soon things grow indifferent": an observation that alone was perhaps
worth making.

Rome detained Byron from May 5th to May 28th; but before his
time was he up had begun to long for Marianna. He returned, however, only briefly to his Venetian rooms; and, while Venice sweltered
and stank with the approach of the dog-days, he established his
household and received his mistress in a *villeggiatura* that he had taken
beside the Brenta where rich Venetians for many centuries had found
a summer refuge and had built the villas that Palladio planned on
correct Vitruvian principles, and Veronese and Tiepolo had been
proud to decorate. *La Mira* was a pleasant house, if a trifle dusty.
There Marianna joined him, released by unknown means from
Signor Segati's superintendence, and thither Hobhouse followed at
the conclusion of July. He found his friend well and in excellent
spirits. Monk Lewis was staying at *La Mira* when Hobhouse
arrived and remained in residence during the next few weeks,
annoying John Cam by his contradictiousness and pettish egotistical

susceptibility. But listening to Lewis's anecdotes was not their sole diversion; and on August 5th Hobhouse recorded in his Journal (from which any reference to Marianna has been carefully excised) that he had "passed the evening, strolling about on horseback with Byron and making assignations." These evening rides became part of their summer regimen; and, as they jogged home, the moon would rise clear and honey-pale in one quarter of the heavens while the snow-peaks of the distant Alps were flushed with sunset, and day "died like a dolphin" above the shadowy river-banks.

It was on such a ride, during the summer of 1817, that the horsemen encountered a group of peasants among whom (wrote Byron) "we remarked two girls as the prettiest we had seen for some time." Byron was already a public personage and, the countryside being just then miserably impoverished, he had contributed to the relief of his peasant neighbours, generosity (he said) making "a great figure at very little cost in Venetian livres . . ." One of the girls recognised and hailed him, asking why, since he helped others, he did not help them too. "*Cara* [he replied, turning in his saddle], *tu sei troppo bella e giovane per aver' bisogno del' soccorso mio.*" She answered that, if he saw her hut and the food she ate, he would not think so. "All this passed half-jestingly"; but a few evenings later they met again; the conversation was renewed, an appointment given and accepted; and, though the smaller of the two girls took fright at Hobhouse—not so much at John Cam himself, as because it transpired she was not yet married; "for here no woman will do anything under adultery"— Byron's choice, after "some bother," proved more easily manageable. He had offered to help her without conditions, supposing, that is to say, she were in genuine want. She explained, however, that on her own account she would not have hesitated—she was married, she observed, "and all married women did it: but that her husband (a baker) was somewhat ferocious." During the course of subsequent meetings her fears were dissipated. Margarita Cogni, otherwise known as the Fornarina, a fierce product of Venetian slums and backways, assumed a dominant position in Byron's household.

For two years that position was jealously guarded; and with her appearance beside the Brenta—a tall black-haired, black-eyed young woman, wearing the *fazziolo* or white Venetian veil which women of the poorer classes still affected—begins a new stage in the history of Byron's moral evolution. Marianna Segati was not swept aside, but she was daunted and crushed by Margarita's wild effrontery; for, when she and her friends ventured to accost the rival and advise her threateningly to refrain from meddling, the other had thrown back her *fazziolo* and retorted in an explosion of Venetian dialect. Marianna was not Byron's wife, she had cried; nor was she herself. "*You* are his *Donna*, and *I* am his *Donna*; *your* husband is a cuckold, and *mine* is another. For the rest, what *right* have you to reproach me? If he prefers what is mine to what is yours, is it my fault? . . . Do not think to speak to me without a reply because you happen to be richer than I am." Having thus signalised her victory, she went on her way. Nor did Marianna from that time dispute her ascendancy, but appeared content to take the smaller share of Byron's favours. Byron did not entirely neglect the Antelope—it was to that graceful beast he had compared his first Venetian favourite—and for the time being she remained his "regular *Amica*," recognised as such by the easy Venetian code; but the wilder mistress attracted him far more profoundly, with her greedy passion, her outrageous *naïveté* and strident humour. To "the strength of an Amazon" she added the disposition of Medea—"a fine animal" but, as it turned out, "quite untamable."

For the student of Byron's career she has not only a scandalous, but also a symbolic, interest; since, although Byron dismissed her lightly as a splendid animal—a "gentle tigress" who displayed a snarling contempt for her surly baker husband, trampled on her rivals and terrorised her lover's lazy and dishonest servants—her fascination was psychological as well as sexual, and the need she satisfied as much of the imagination as of the body. In every artist's nature, more or less acutely developed, there exists the impulse that has been conveniently, if perhaps not very accurately, entitled *la nostalgie de la boue*. With the love of order coexists a feeling for disorder; with the desire for clarity, propriety and delicate distinctions —lacking which a work of art cannot emerge from chaos—goes a taste for the kind of experience that is gross but lively. So rarefied is the atmosphere in which art is born that the artist, when he transfers his attention from art to life, often chooses to breathe a steamy and relaxing climate, the air of the brothel, the crowded restaurant, the smoke-fogged drinking party. "*Oh mes amis, que j'ai besoin de m'encanailler un peu!*" Rachel is said to have exclaimed—true, it was between the frigid walls of Victorian Windsor—after a particularly distinguished and moving performance; and many lesser artists have echoed the same impatient cry. Thus Byron's growing attraction towards debauchery went far deeper than—though, of course, it comprehended—mere time-wasting and superficial self-indulgence: one might almost suggest, indeed, that it had a moral basis. Hitherto he had often struggled against the drift of his nature; now he would resign himself to its control and await the outcome.

What had he to lose—and what to gain? Very little, he told himself with that inborn fatalism which did not preclude ordinary human cheerfulness or deter him from a strenuous pursuit of the pleasures of living. Thank heavens, he was in robust health and had vigorous appetites. *Manfred*, his fantastic dramatic poem, sent back to Murray during the spring just before he embarked on his journey to Rome, had helped to exorcise some of his gloomier preoccupations; and the idea of a return to England grew more and more shadowy. By the 9th of August (when it was shown to Lewis) he had completed the Fourth Canto of *Childe Harold* and had finally bidden good-bye to the character in whom so much of his earlier self, both the genuine and the factitious, had originally been embodied. It was a significant farewell, accompanied by a bold outpouring of rhetorical defiance:

> *But I have lived, and have not lived in vain:*
> *My mind may lose its force, my blood its fire,*
> *And my frame perish even in conquering pain;*
> *But there is that within me which shall tire*
> *Torture and Time, and breathe when I expire . . .*

Elsewhere the tone of the Canto is more impersonal than that of any of its predecessors. The "gloomy wanderer" of Cantos One and Two is almost lost to sight among the elaborate set-pieces through which the poem moves—the Dying Gladiator, the Pantheon, the Tomb of Cecilia Metella; he makes his final bow a little languidly and the stage is vacant. For Byron had outgrown *Childe Harold*: or rather he had absorbed him—had lived up to and had then exceeded his imaginary self-portrait. That autumn he began to play with the idea of novel-writing; and the adventures of Don Julian—otherwise Don Juan—was the theme he chose.

Chapter 15

England—Lady Byron and Augusta Leigh—The Palazzo Mocenigo—Bohemianism—
Margarita Cogni—Death of Lady Melbourne—Shelley in Venice—"Spooney and Young
Spooney"—A Dandy in Decline.

ON THE WHOLE it had been a pleasant year, and it ended pleasantly.
There was a short journey with Hobhouse to Arqua and Padua,
followed by a lively meeting with Douglas Kinnaird and his brother
at Venice. Byron then returned to his *villeggiatura*, and John Cam
presently rejoined him, finding his friend "well, and merry and
happy, more charming every day." Till mid-November they remained together in the country—"a strange life; [noted Hobhouse]
very tranquil and comfortable." Finally, on the 13th, they were ready
to leave; and, while Byron resumed his residence in the Frezzeria,
Hobhouse established himself in lodgings opposite. His stay lasted
through the autumn and winter of 1817. Byron made a habit of rising
late; but during the afternoon they were often rowed out to the Lido,
the bleak melancholy island beyond the lagoon, occupied only by
market gardens and a Jewish cemetery,[1] where Byron had hired a
stable in which he kept his horses. Here on the tawny beach, beside
the pallid sluggish waters of the Adriatic, they could ride from St.
Andrea towards Malmocco, "a spanking gallop" of several miles'
length over resilient sand. Ferried home again across the lagoon as it
flamed with the setting sun, they would prepare to attend the
Countess Benzoni or visit the playhouse or dine with Richard
Belgrave Hoppner, the English consul. Byron was talkative, calm,
good-humoured; and, when Hobhouse left him, it was with reluctance but without anxiety.

Before he said good-bye, they had seen in the New Year. 1818,
so far as Byron was concerned, began with the happiest and most

---

[1] A Venise, à l'affreux Lido,
Où vient sur l'herbe d'un tombeau
Mourir la pâle Adriatique . . .

prosperous auguries, since he had recently heard from his lawyer of the sale of Newstead[1]—a sacrifice he regretted but to which he had long resigned himself—and was therefore richer by nearly ninety-five thousand pounds. At last he could hope to pay off his creditors, and he had written Hanson a precise and careful letter explaining just how he wished him to arrange a settlement. Other assets, it is true, were still unrealised; but, even so, he was rich enough, if he stayed in Italy, to maintain an establishment suited to his tastes and interests. Besides, the desire to see England again had gradually withered away. He liked his personal independence and the freedom from moral supervision; the ties that bound him to his own race had slowly weakened. The single human being who might have induced him to travel northwards—whose summons he would have obeyed at any cost, as he had repeatedly told her—was of all his correspondents the least encouraging.

At this point, both in time and in space, a digression is needed. From 1818 we must revert to 1816, and from Byron magnificently established at the Palazzo Mocenigo—the great gloomy palazzo overlooking the mid-curve of the Grand Canal which he had taken for himself and his dependants early in the New Year—we turn back to a set of small rooms in St. James's Palace and to various hired houses and furnished lodgings, restless resting places of the two women he had most deeply injured. England he might forget, but not his wife and sister—not Annabella because he felt subconsciously that she had proved too strong for him, with her cool, obstinate, undeviating sense of duty: not Augusta because she knew so much of his best and worst side, because he loved her as he was firmly convinced he would never love again, and because, after all, she was a part of himself. There had been a period when he still hoped that they might be reunited. Let Augusta give him a sign and he would recross the Channel! Or could not he prevail on her to join him in Switzerland, bringing with her a bevy of his nieces and nephews? To these proposals the replies he elicited were oddly evasive. He coaxed: he reminded: she continued to escape him. More and more ambiguous became her answers: more and more nervously did she

---

[1] The abbey was sold to a Harrow acquaintance, Colonel Wildman, who proceeded to remodel a large part of the fabric in the very worst traditions of nineteenth-century Gothic.

shrink away into that language which was so peculiarly her own, made up of hints and mysteries and second-hand pietism—Augusta's "damned crinkum-crankum" was her brother's name for it. Now it seemed that Augusta's heart was hardening, though the process of hardening was a trifle fragmentary and between the lines he caught an occasional glimpse of her despair and passion. But there could be no doubt that she was undergoing a metamorphosis—that a new influence had begun to work upon her simple nature. The authoress of such a transformation was, of course, his wife!

In these suspicions Byron had been perfectly justified. Some weeks before the actual separation, Mrs. Leigh, at the instance of her friends, had left her brother's house in Piccadilly Terrace (where she had been doing her best to calm and comfort him) and had retired to her private apartments in St. James's Palace. There, occupying the strange double position of fashionable attendant to an elderly and extremely strait-laced Queen and heroine of a shattering private scandal, she had watched and waited and hoped desperately to ward off disaster. She knew of the reports that were being propagated. She understood that, if she were to preserve a vestige of moral reputation and save her struggling household from utter catastrophe, Lady Byron's friendship must be retained. Among her champions was Mrs. Villiers; and, though described by her contemporaries as broad-minded, sympathetic and intelligent, Thérèse Villiers was not a woman it would have been easy to like. Perhaps she was betrayed by her sense of drama. After all, it was no slight pleasure and privilege, while the rest of London was buzzing with speculation, and Holland House dinner parties were saying this, and Melbourne House satellites were declaring that, and Lady Caroline Lamb was running in furious circles, giving currency to the wildest and most shocking rumours, to be made a confidante of the whole disastrous story. For Mrs. Villiers had remonstrated with Lady Byron; and Annabella, delicately but very definitely, had explained that there were reasons—grave and conclusive reasons—why, fond as she might be of poor Augusta, she could not afford her unqualified support and assistance. Mrs. Villiers was immensely perturbed but intensely interested. If the story were true—and Lady Byron's veracity was so obvious as to be almost alarming—then it was high time to adopt a different standpoint. Not that she was anxious to condemn Augusta! But, although Augusta was the victim of her brother's wickedness, to some extent she must be considered his accomplice and, as accomplice, she should be obliged to expiate the wrong she had done. Henceforward Mrs. Villiers was pledged, not only to advise and encourage Lady Byron, but to promote the moral redemption of Lady Byron's sister-in-law; and, as the situation grew more interesting, her fervour increased.

Lady Byron, to her credit, was a reluctant persecutor. In the past, Mrs. Leigh had earned her gratitude; she was always acutely sensitive to the Byronic charm; and during that dreadful visit to Six Mile Bottom, the gloomiest episode of her wretched marriage-journey, and the more protracted anguish of life in London, they had been drawn together by a thousand bonds of fear and suffering. But now at all costs she must learn to throw off sentiment. Doyle and Horton and the solemn Dr. Lushington—the advisers who had been at her side in the separation drama—kept up their warnings against Mrs. Leigh and urged that she should take precautions for any emergency, if possible by extracting a confession of guilt. Lady Byron's response was characteristically deliberate. She was unwilling to be swayed by personal motives; but it hurt her—perhaps it also piqued her—that Augusta, between fits of violent depression when she made muddled miserable references to the state of her soul ("I don't know what *you* may all be, but I am sure *I'm* not prepared for the next world . . ." she had wailed suddenly at a dinner party of Mrs. Villiers's), should still sometimes affect an attitude of "conscious innocence!"

Lady Byron's feelings had yet another side. Mixed with prudence, a tinge of natural irritation and a touch of the vengefulness that usually accompanies offended virtue—even in a temperament so carefully self-controlled, so minutely self-appraised as that of Annabella—was one of the strongest and most irrational of human emotions, the passionate instinctive jealousy of love rejected. Yes, she was jealous of Augusta and would always remain so. Typical of jealousy in its extreme forms is the belief that, when certainty has been arrived at, as soon as the worst is known and the depths of humiliation have been explored, the intensity of the pain felt may begin to diminish. Thus the suggestions of her counsellors (who now included Mrs. Villiers) she was prepared to meet half-way. For the sake of her own peace she must be *sure*—while now she had merely suspicions not amounting to proof; she must exchange intuitive for positive and definite knowledge: she must hear the tale of Byron's guilt from the guilty partner. Did she hope that full knowledge would bring her understanding—that she would know, at last, why trying so hard she had failed so dismally?

Augusta was rounded up like a beast for the sacrifice, Lady Byron adopting the rôle of calm high-priestess, grave and determined in the performance of duty, Mrs. Villiers an officious but collected ministrant. Augusta was just then recovering from one of her numerous *accouchements*; and, as soon as her physical health was on the mend, the two ladies set about her moral well-being. During May, Annabella was still hesitant as to the propriety and practical advisability of consummating the sacrifice then and there. The fever of passion (she considered) had not yet subsided—"it is perhaps the crisis. . . . From all I learn of her present temper, no result but that of precipitate desperation can be expected." Mrs. Leigh might fly the country to join Byron; and there was one point on which the poet's wife and Doyle and Lushington were in entire, though not explicit, disagreement. For their part, Annabella's advisors would have welcomed Mrs. Leigh's flight; by completing the ruin of her reputation, it would effectually have cleared Lady Byron's name of the charges of her heartlessness and "implacability" that then, and at a later time, were brought against her. But Annabella's feelings were somewhat more complicated. She had decided that it was her duty to "save" Augusta; "My great object, [she wrote to Mrs. Villiers on May 16th, 1816] next to the Security of my Child, is . . . the restoration of her mind to that state which is religiously desirable." She had also decided, impelled by motives that were all her own—motives with which no one else could be expected to sympathise, and to which she herself may not have possessed the real and secret clue—that brother and sister must never be permitted to resume their intercourse. What part had instinctive jealousy in this determination? At any rate, the influence of jealousy was carefully sublimated; and her apparent motives were such as she could take a pride in, such as her friends and supporters were bound to approve. She must assume control of the weak and erring victim and guide her back through expiation into the paths of virtue, using obligations to chain her and threats to compel. To assist her redemption, she must slay her pride and destroy the last struggling hopes of unlawful happiness.

After due reflection and much consultation with Mrs. Villiers, Annabella opened her campaign on June 3rd. The letter she composed was wily and diplomatic, meaning and yet deliberately noncommittal, minatory yet couched in a tone of affectionate platitude. Before her confinement "dearest Augusta" was not to be agitated; but, having learned to her satisfaction that Mrs. Leigh was now recovered, Annabella could no longer conceal the existence of "reasons," unspecified in so many words but vaguely alluded to, which "imposed the duty" of "*limiting*" their future friendship. Augusta was alarmed and puzzled by this communication, replying in her usual effusive and flurried manner that, although not "*wholly surprised* at its contents," she was pained and disconcerted by its general terms; for "if I were on my death bed I could affirm as I *now* do that I have uniformly considered you and consulted your happiness before and above everything in this world." Annabella, on reflection, was far from satisfied; and, discussing the reply with Mrs. Villiers, she admitted that it contained "no offensive or irritating expression towards me" but observed that it showed a lack of true contrition: "her assertions are not exactly *to the point*—though it is evident she perfectly understands me." However, it was "perhaps the best letter she *could* have written"; and one must face the fact that Augusta was not as other women—at least, not as women like herself and her friend: her moral principles at the best of times were loose and hazy: "she did not appear to think these transgressions *of consequence*." She had meant well, and believed that to mean well was the essence of virtue—a delusion that Annabella must at once eradicate.

It is unnecessary for the purposes of the present narrative to describe in any great detail the various epistolary turns by which Mrs. Leigh was cornered, the different means—some of them very subtle—that were employed to inject her with a sense of her former guilt, or the state of humiliation and tremulous self-abasement to which she was gradually but mercilessly conducted. But from one asseveration she would not budge. Intentionally she had never harmed her brother's wife—a statement in which Byron himself afterwards concurred. "Dearest A—— [she wrote] *I have not wronged you. I have not abused your generosity . . .*"; and elsewhere, alluding to her stay in Piccadilly Terrace, she declared that had she at the time "entertained the *slightest* suspicion of any '*doubts*' of yours—I never could or would have entered your house . . ." On an additional point—a point extremely important to Lady Byron's feelings—the testimony of her letters could not be shaken. She acknowledged (according to the report furnished by Annabella to Mrs. Villiers) her moral culpability before Byron's marriage—"as much as she could do on paper"—but stoutly maintained "her *innocence* since . . . Finally, she entreats me in the most humble and affecting manner to point out in pity to her anything by which she may 'atone for the past.' "

The old flighty Augusta was not yet extinguished. ". . . You know I am of a sanguine disposition," she had remarked rather pathetically to Annabella; and, when she came up to London for the Regent's Fête which she was obliged to attend in her official capacity, at her first meeting with Mrs. Villiers—a meeting her friend had "dreaded beyond measure"—the "whole conversation turned on *Gauzes and Sattins*," and she looked "quite stout and well . . . and perfectly cool and easy, having apparently nothing on her mind . . ." It was during this visit to the metropolis that Augusta and Annabella met face to face. Their interview had been carefully prearranged; its results were all that Lady Byron had anticipated. Exactly what passed we shall never know—what degrees of suffering were endured, what refinements of torture and self-torture were then applied, what reproaches were uttered, what tears were shed. But questions painfully asked were as painfully answered. Mrs. Leigh broke down and told her story, still clinging, however, to her previous assertion that she had not "wronged" Annabella since the Byrons' marriage, and that she "had never felt any suspicion of my suspicions except at the time in the summer of 1815 when I evidently wished she would leave us." She had often told Byron, Augusta declared, that he "said such things before me as would have led any *other* woman to suspect"; but he had always been able to convince her that her fears were unfounded; and Augusta seemed to have acted upon the principle—indeed, it was almost the only principle that had governed her conduct—"that what could be concealed from me was no injury."

Questioned as to whether Byron had displayed remorse, Augusta replied that she had observed no signs of it, except once—"the night before they parted . . ." But in a literary form he had acknowledged his responsibility; and Augusta admitted that the notorious verses:

I speak not, I trace not, I breathe not thy name . . .

written in 1814, had been addressed to her. Surely there was now little more that the culprit could add? But the appetite of jealous passion is not easily satisfied; and, though Annabella, during the course of her visit, renewed her questioning of Mrs. Leigh on several occasions, the unhappy intensity of her private feelings did not decrease. One confession, she decided, was not sufficient. Mrs. Villiers must also extort her old friend's secret, but she must do so without letting it become apparent that her preliminary information was derived from Lady Byron and must pretend that it *"originated with Lord B."* (who had assured Augusta that he had never betrayed her confidence) and reached Mrs. Villiers *"through an authority she could not doubt."* Mrs. Leigh submitted, though somewhat reluctantly. During the earlier stages of the long-drawn sacrifice, she had kept her spirits up, considering the situation, remarkably well; and there exists a brief note scribbled to Annabella on the morrow of one of their momentous interviews, wherein she professes herself, in her customary goose-ish vein, "so sorry for your bad night—and for your *idea* of my *uncomfortableness*—which is however quite a *fancy of your own*—but I dare say I *looked* something or other which made you fancy."

There must have been moments when the two devotees began to despair of their task. Could Augusta never be brought to a proper comprehension of her appalling moral plight? Would she still (like a naughty child after a parental talking-to, which, because it has wept and accepted its reprimand, looks forward confidently to complete forgiveness) continue to appeal cool and easy and carefree? But even Augusta's buoyancy was at length exhausted. The ordeal of a second confessional interview, accompanied by the information that Byron had blabbed (as, in fact, he had done, though not in the manner suggested) brought down her spirits to a more appropriate level; and it was in deep dejection that she returned to Newmarket and her husband and family. Her friends could congratulate themselves that their work was accomplished. Augusta (reported Annabella) had been reduced to "the humblest sense of her own situation." She had been horror-struck by what she had learned of her brother's treachery;

and "all this [commented Mrs. Villiers] will help to alienate her feelings from him." Lady Byron she described as her Guardian Angel; and to that angelic mentor she now submitted Byron's letters —they were *"absolute love letters,"* Annabella noted—and begged for advice as to "how she can stop them," or how she could best reply to their entreaties and arguments. In finding herself the censor of this correspondence—an eavesdropper on her husband's passionate out-pourings—-Lady Byron tasted the final bitterness of her Pyrrhic victory.

Youth, spontaneity, peace of mind—she had renounced them all. A young woman of strong passions and lively feelings, who had known the passing savour if not the full enjoyment of normal happiness, she now fell back on the conviction that she was "doing her duty" and on the stern and lonely consolations of spiritual self-love. She was proud; she was intractable; her choice was deliberate. Yet, as time went by, she was to observe with increasing perplexity, and with a growing sense of the corruption and ingratitude of her fellow human beings, that her noblest intentions were seldom operative, and that the closest attachments she formed were the most disastrous. Her capacity for gaining affection had somehow evap-orated. Capable of deep devotion towards those she loved, she was incapable of that real and lasting tenderness which adapts itself to the vagaries of human conduct and, because it is uncritical and makes no moral demands, is rarely disillusioned. A person of more sensitive spiritual fibre, however stern and conventional her moral prejudices, might have recoiled from assuming so exclusive an authority— backed up by subtle methods of intimidation—over a woman to whom she had at one time been deeply indebted, and who was now, as they both of them recognised, altogether at her mercy. Even though she had considered it essential by every religious standard, she might have felt that the "alienation" of Mrs. Leigh's feelings and the substitution of distrust for attachment between brother and sister (whose love had been innocent and confiding as well as passionate) were duties of an exceedingly painful and perhaps a degrading kind. She was unhappy on her own account, gloomy and feverish, moving restlessly from place to place with her child and nursemaid, writing long detailed reflective letters to Mrs. Villiers; but throughout she kept her head clear and her intentions definite. Her pity remained the prisoner of her sense of duty. That sense of duty was not unconnected with her self-esteem.

Soon her counsels and her commands were practically indistinguishable. Already during July, before their meetings, when (as she explained to Mrs. Villiers) she was leading on Augusta step by step "to promise that she will never resume a confidential intercourse by letter—or any personal intercourse," she had given precise directions as to how Mrs. Leigh should regulate such correspondence as she could not avoid. She must seek to *rectify*, "instead of *soothing* or *indulging*," and above all she must beware of those private signs, those innuendoes, jokes and personal references, with which Byron's messages were often sprinkled. Let her, therefore, eschew "all phrases or *marks*, which recall wrong ideas to his mind . . . and let me also warn you [Annabella continued] against the levity and nonsense which he likes for the worst reason, because it prevents him from reflecting seriously . . ." Yet Augusta must not, of course, suppose that her Guardian Angel was anxious to dictate any line of conduct; and it was part of the subtlety of Lady Byron's method that she insisted again and again on Augusta's freedom. At the same time, Mrs. Leigh should remember her family—"both as respects the world's opinion of yourself and still more from the injury young minds must receive in the society of one so unprincipled"; and she need not be offended if her well-wisher added that "I think his mind too *powerful* for you—I could not feel secure that he would not bewilder you on any subject . . ." Augusta, therefore, must always be on her guard against, and in justice to herself must never encourage, "his criminal *desires*, I think I may add *designs*." Otherwise, she must remember that she was a free agent; "for anxious as I feel to support and comfort you in the recovered path of virtue, I could not hope to do so by an attempt to impose my own opinions. On the contrary, I would, as far as possible, remove every obstacle to independence of conduct on your part." Augusta accepted her friends' "honour system": indeed, she had little choice. The alternative was too black and terrifying to be confronted lightly.

Her character began to change; and the change was disastrous. A shy, startled, diffident, uncertain being, under the pressure of persecution and her well-wishers' vigilance, Augusta grew at first wary, then deceitful and latterly developed a strain of self-protective humbug. Thus she recollected and exploited her early religious training. Presently she was in correspondence with Francis Hodgson, one of those dim prosaic figures whom Byron befriended because, though admiring and companionable, they were not competitive. Hodgson had recently taken orders, and therefore might be of very great assistance in Mrs. Leigh's moral rehabilitation with which—at least from the practical standpoint—she was much concerned. To him she wrote at rambling length of her brother's weaknesses. She was sure, she told Hodgson, without stating her evidence, that he had recollections fatal to his peace of mind, which would have prevented his ever being happy with a woman as spotless as Lady Byron. Nothing could remedy this tragic cause save the consolations to be derived from religious faith "which alas! dear Mr. H. our beloved B. is I fear destitute of . . ."

Something of the same note eventually crept into her correspondence with the exile. Mrs. Leigh's letters to Byron have not been preserved; but from his frequent and often agitated rejoinders—seen and duly commented on by Lady Byron—it is clear that they were neither unambiguous nor satisfactory. Augusta had accepted her fate and had learned her lesson. One promise, it is true, she still refused to give: if "dearest B." returned from the Continent, she could not engage that she would decline to see him. For the rest, she bowed meekly before her guardian's wishes and appeared, little by little, to be withdrawing from the Byronic influence. Yet there was a touch of hypocrisy beneath Augusta's flightiness. In the interests of her personal safety and her family's welfare, she advertised her deep contrition and implicit obedience—while to Hodgson she adopted an attitude of superior virtue, loftily concerned with Childe Harold's sins; but the devices and desires of a rebellious heart were not completely neglected. It is obvious that she continued to write to Byron in an encouraging strain; there is no evidence that she attempted to improve or check him, though the letters she continued to receive were often passionate; but she wrote vaguely, mysteriously, with a hint of troubled reserve, which exasperated Byron because he could not analyse it. He replied impatiently, sometimes bitterly; he pleaded and joked with her. But time passed and their separation grew more and more definite.

A sense of his isolation was slowly gaining on him. In Byron's nature his relations with Mrs. Leigh had brought out not only the worst of his temperament—those anarchic and self-destructive impulses that made it necessary for him to torture himself and torture others—but also his kindest, steadiest and most generous traits. Mrs. Leigh had been tormented because she was a part of himself—she, too, had inherited the blood of the Byrons, and for that reason must share in the Byronic doom: but she had been loved as ideally one might love a sister, with a tenderness into which desire had scarcely entered and from which passion might eventually have died away. To a man or woman who has brought out the best in us we are always grateful; a person we have deeply injured it is hard to forget; and Mrs. Leigh had both claims on Byron's memory—she was his chief victim and his closest intimate at one and the same moment. Her love had satisfied him as he had never before been satisfied. On the small packet that enclosed a lock of Augusta's silky dark brown hair and included also a few lines in her handwriting:

> *Partager tous vos sentimens*
> *ne voir que par vos yeux*
> *n'agir que par vos conseils, ne*
> *vivre que pour vous, voila mes*
> *voeux, mes projets, & le seul*
> *destin qui peut me rendre*
> *heureuse*

had he not inscribed a single sentence: "La Chevelure of the *one* whom I most *loved*," adding the cross that had a special significance in their relationship? He did not know that every letter he wrote to Augusta, after her final subjugation in the summer of 1816, was passed on to Annabella to be read and criticised.

Lady Byron's feelings as she opened them are not easy to conjure up; but it may well have been with a certain masochistic eagerness that she turned over these scrawled impatient letters from Switzerland, from Milan and then from Venice, in which her husband wrote freely and passionately as he had never written to her, consoling Augusta, soothing and reassuring . . . No, Augusta was not to be alarmed by the prevalent rumours. Who, among their friends, would take seriously the false and wicked inventions of Lady Caroline Lamb—Augusta did not know that she had been one of Byron's confidantes—a crazy strumpet and "seventy times convicted liar"? "Do not be uneasy [he pleaded]—and do not 'hate yourself'. If you hate either let it be *me*—but do not—it would kill me; we are the last persons in the world—who ought or could cease to love one another." This was from Diodati at the end of August. During September 1816 he received intelligence that Lady Byron had been "very kind," and begged leave to take the news with a touch of scepticism. "And so—Lady B. has been 'kind to you' [he wrote] . . . 'very kind'—umph—it is as well she should be kind to some of us, and I am glad she has the heart and the discernment to be still *your* friend." Here and there, he gave indications of normal jealousy, and when he heard from Hobhouse that Lord Frederick Bentinck was often to be found at his sister's house, he wrote to demand why "that fool" was a regular visitor: did Augusta suppose that his intentions were amorous? To Lady Byron his references were rarely charitable; and unmindful of the agonies he had himself inflicted, he dwelt angrily upon the sufferings he had been made to endure. The separation (he declared illogically) had broken his heart; "I feel as if an Elephant had trodden on it"; and, though it was "a relief—a partial relief to talk of her sometimes to you," he requested that Augusta would not mention her name. Of Lady Byron's conduct she might judge for herself; "but do not altogether forget that she has destroyed your brother. Whatever my faults might or may have been—*She*— was not the person marked out by providence to be their avenger . . . I do not think a human being could endure more mental torture than that woman has directly or indirectly inflicted upon me—within the present year."

Meanwhile, she was to reflect upon his invitation. The country was beautiful, travelling easy; he would "return from any distance at any time" to see her. The obstacle, he supposed, was his fatuous brother-in-law, "that very helpless gentleman your Cousin," horsy, improvident, perpetually embarrassed, for whom she wrote letters, solicited loans and warded off creditors. No doubt "the usual self-love of an elderly person would interfere between you and any scheme of recreation or relaxation, for however short a period"; and he raged miserably against the limitations of the married state which had torn them apart and now held them asunder:

What a fool was I to marry—and *you* not very wise, my dear— we might have lived so single and so happy—as old maids and bachelors; I shall never find any one like you—nor you (vain as it may seem) like me. We are just formed to pass our lives together, and therefore—we—at least—I—am by a crowd of circumstances removed from the only being who could ever have loved me, or whom I can unmixedly feel attached to.

Alas, Mrs. Leigh was neither an honest nor an eloquent letter-writer. In her new position she wrote to Byron less and less frequently; and by the mid-autumn he considered that he had cause to remonstrate. A whole month had gone by without a single letter: he mentioned this, he said, "not from any wish to plague you—but because my unfortunate circumstances perhaps make me feel more keenly anything which looks like neglect . . ." And when letters did arrive, they were not illuminating, full of "mysteries and alarms" and ambiguities, coupled with a suggestion that hurt him deeply. "You surely do not mean to say [he protested on October 28th, 1816] that if I come to England in Spring . . . you and I shall not meet. If so I will never return to it . . ."

Simultaneously, his descriptions of his wife's behaviour grew more extravagant. It is doubtful if at any time he had really loved her —indeed it was to escape from passion that he had embarked on matrimony; but he had esteemed and admired the quiet, serious, unsmiling girl who had pursued him with such a bizarre devotion throughout their months of courtship, who had been so determined to marry the poet and reform the libertine. Conveniently for himself he could usually forget what he did not choose to remember; and his outbursts and nerve-storms during the year of marriage, when he had worried her with mysterious references to his sins and secrets, or left her alone while he sought the comfort of Kinnaird's brandy parties, or talked of suicide or of separation as soon as the child was born, were not permitted to influence his judgment when he discussed her attitude. It was her coolness, her inflexibility, he could not tolerate. That she should have resisted all his entreaties and his supplications, decided on the line of duty and calmly held to it, reduced him to transports of helpless fury in which he invoked the judgment of heaven or threatened lawsuits or prophesied that he would live to witness her utter downfall. She was his "moral Clytemnaestra," and "infernal fiend" . . . At Diodati a reconciliation had still seemed possible; but from Venice, on March 5th, 1817, having heard of the Chancery proceedings with regard to his daughter, he wrote to inform his wife that the hope had been given up. "No one [he concluded] was ever even the involuntary cause of great evils to others, without a requital. I have paid and am paying for mine—so will you."

In Augusta the confidence he had placed was not yet broken. She at least was no "cold-blooded animal," no unbending moralist; but, while his wife's nature was all self-restraint and unflinching rectitude, his sister's was so unfocused as to be quite amorphous—she was a moral opportunist who took any shape that the occasion demanded. She annoyed him; she disappointed him; she seemed to elude him. Yet he looked forward with eagerness to her infrequent letters—only to be puzzled and exasperated when the letters came. If only the "good Goose" were a little less muddle-headed—not quite so flustered by anxieties she declined to particularise, obsessed by sorrows he was often unable to make head or tail of! Thus, acknowledging a bundle of letters received at Venice, he remarked crossly that they were "full of woes, as usual, megrims and mysteries," and added that his sympathy must be held in abeyance since "for the life of me I can't make out whether your disorder is a broken heart or the earache—or whether it is *you* that have been ill or the children— or what your melancholy and mysterious apprehensions tend to . . . whether to Caroline Lamb's novels—Mrs. Clermont's evidence— Lady Byron's magnanimity—or any other piece of imposture." But love her he did and must, and could never cease to do—"always . . . better than any earthly existence." Time was smothering, but it had not yet extinguished the passion he felt. Though she might recede, he continued to follow; and the summing-up would not be composed till 1819. He had never ceased to feel (he then wrote) "that perfect and boundless attachment which bounds and binds me to you," and rendered him utterly incapable of *real* love for any other human being.

My own XXXX (he exclaimed in the same letter), we may have been very wrong, but I repent of nothing except that cursed marriage, and your refusing to continue to love me as you had loved me. I can neither forget nor *quite forgive* you for that precious piece of reformation; but I can never be other than I have been, and whenever I love anything it is because it reminds me of you . . . It is heartbreaking to think of our long Separation, and I am sure more than punishment enough for all our sins. Dante is more humane in his "Hell," for he places his unfortunate lovers (Francesca of Rimini and Paolo whose case fell a good deal short of *ours*, though sufficiently naughty) in company and, though they suffer, it is at least together. If ever I return to England it will be to see you . . . Circumstances may have ruffled my manner, and hardened my spirit. You may have me seen harsh and exasperated with all things around me, grieved and tortured with *your new resolution*, and the soon after persecution of that infamous fiend . . . ; but remember that, even then, *you* were the sole object that cost me a tear. And *what tears!* Do you remember our parting . . . ? They say absence destroys weak passions, and confirms strong ones. Alas! *mine* for you is the union of all passions and of all affections, has strengthened itself but will destroy me.

Such statements may be emotionally accurate at the time of writing; but the element of truth that they contain is strictly relative; and Byron at this period—indeed much earlier—had thoroughly accustomed himself to separation from Mrs. Leigh. She was a symbol of lost love, of frustrated tenderness. Thanks to his own capacity for living in the moment, and Augusta's incapacity for continuous feeling, she had ceased to be a practical consideration.

> *All suffering doth destroy, or is destroy'd*
> *Even by the sufferer . . .*

—That was a lesson already learned when he composed the last Canto of *Childe Harold*. He had not been destroyed, but the pain had destroyed itself; and, as it did so, he had discovered the virtues of acquiescence, the satisfaction of existing for the present day yet maintaining a separate unflawed identity in the midst of turmoil. Lounging, remembering, making love—yet squeezing the utmost from each spell of creative energy—he had hit on a mode of life that occupied the imagination and engaged the senses.

It is customary to deplore Byron's existence at the Palazzo Mocenigo. Many of the details of his two years' tenancy are still obscure; what we can gather of his intimate life between 1817 and 1819, among his horde of quarrelsome servants and grasping mistresses, suggests a bohemianism verging on extreme disorder; but his critical faculty was undimmed, his genius active. Dissipation is to some men stimulating, to others stupefying; and Byron, though his physical stamina was decidedly limited and he was no debauchee of the heroic eighteenth-century mould—a Casanova, a Maurice de Saxe or even a Sheridan—would appear to have belonged to the former category. Compromises he did not disdain, but half-measures, at least in his amusements, he had always detested; and, whereas his first Venetian years had been cheerfully dissolute, the second became a race against advancing middle age—on January 22nd had he not celebrated his thirtieth birthday?—a headlong career in the pursuit of extreme sensation. Again the Carnival had descended and caught him up. Soon he was "in the *estrum* and agonies of a new intrigue" with (he explained to his publisher) he could not tell exactly "whom or what, except that she is insatiate of love, and won't take money, and has light hair and blue eyes . . . and that I met her at the Masque, and that when her mask is off, I am as wise as ever." He was determined, he added, to make what he could of the remainder of his youth. He would work its mine (he told Moore) "to the last vein . . . And then—goodnight." He could feel that he had enjoyed and lived.

Here, as at so many stages of Byron's history, the affectation and the sincerity are hard to disentangle, since the apparent pose was founded on a real emotion. This year, when the Carnival had come to an end, there was no slackening in the whirligig of Byron's pleasures. His establishment was well-suited to the life he led. Presided over somewhat inefficiently by his English valet, "the learned Fletcher," who hated foreign countries and had already been dragged to Athens and Constantinople and whose frequent escapades bore a certain resemblance to those of his master, it included "about fourteen servants," mostly Italian footmen, besides a floating population of Venetian parasites. Unnamed and unnumbered, his concubines came and went —usually women of the poorer class, loud and quarrelsome, yet gifted with a power of expression that often delighted him. Thus, such a one—a rival of Margarita Cogni—announced that there was war to the death between them—a *Guerra di Candia!* And was it not odd (he asked) "that the lower order of Venetians should still allude proverbially to that famous contest,[1] so glorious and so fatal to the Republic." Other turns of phrase also amused and struck him. How

[1] Candia fell to Turkey in 1669, after a siege that had lasted twenty-five years.

characteristic of these tall violent-tempered doxies that they should speak, not of their hearts, like a love-lorn Englishwoman, but of their *viscere* or entrails! Visceral, indeed, was his own response to their caresses. Yet there was an intellectual charm, too, in these curious contacts and in the sudden glimpses they brought of manners and characters—some flash of eloquence from the lips of a Venetian prostitute, some movement, expressive of passion and pride and dignity, in which the splendour of the fallen Republic seemed to have risen again.

Of the English labouring classes he had known little or nothing, though he had been a familiar of the flash world of boxers and fencers, and had taken a paternal interest in the affairs of his Newstead household. But in Venice he surrounded himself with men and women drawn from the very lowest levels of the Italian populace— harlots and pimps and gondoliers and their dependants and families. During the same century, another Englishman—one of very different aspect and moral outlook—was to devote his genius to the declining city and make a temporary home there. But when Ruskin walked the Piazza before the great basilica, he averted his eyes with shuddering revulsion from the spectacle of the Venetian proletariat—from the knots of men who, in the porch of San Marco, among the columns of jasper, porphyry, serpentine, beneath the delicate interlacements of Byzantine capitals, lay "all day long . . . basking in the sun like lizards"; while "unregarded children—every heavy glance of their young eyes full of desperation and stony depravity, and their throats hoarse with cursing—gamble, and fight, and snarl, and sleep, hour after hour, clashing their bruised centesimi upon the marble ledges of the church porch." It is not unreasonable to imagine that, in these savage *congeries*, were the sons and grandsons of men who had once known Byron, who had run clandestine errands for him in Venetian by-ways or had enjoyed his hospitality in the servants' quarters of the Palazzo Mocenigo. More philosophic and less intellectual than the Victorian aesthete, Byron discovered that he had much to learn from the Venetian underworld.

Energy he worshipped; and it was certainly abundant here. The Fornarina, who, though not for some time a regular inmate, strode in and out of his apartments just as it suited her, was the personification of force and greed and animal violence, mixed with animal devotion to her chosen bed-fellow. Regarding his other favourites, when they were out of her sight, she remained indifferent. He might have a hundred, she declared; but to her she knew that he must always return; and such was her physical hold that for many months the boast was justified. Moreover, she made him laugh—an exceedingly important point. ". . . In her *fazziolo* . . . she looked beautiful; but alas! she longed for a hat and feathers"; and in spite of anything that Byron could say or do, in spite of his burning her hats as soon as she had bought them, she insisted on attempting to play the lady. "Then she would have her gowns with a *tail* . . . nothing would serve her but '*l'abito colla*' . . . and as her cursed pronunciation of the word made me laugh, there was an end of all controversy, and she dragged this diabolical train after her everywhere."

Naturally, there were outrageous scenes, as when on the last night of the Carnival, she had snatched the mask from the face of the distinguished and high-born Madame Contarini who happened at the moment to have accepted Byron's arm.[1] He could daunt her, he found, if he was really angry; but more often he would dissolve into good-natured laughter because her slang and impudence and buffooneries were so disarming. At her most passionate she was invested with a kind of splendour; and among other impressions of the wonderful virago, recalled at a later period, was the picture of La Fornarina, one stormy night, awaiting him on the steps of the Palazzo Mocenigo. He had been overtaken as he returned from the Lido by a heavy squall; "the Gondola put in peril—hats blown away, boats filling, oar lost, tumbling sea, thunder, rain in torrents, night coming, and wind increasing. On our return, after a tight struggle, I found her on the open steps . . . with her great black eyes flashing through her tears, and the long dark hair, which was streaming, drenched with rain, over her brows and breast . . . The wind blowing her hair and dress about her tall thin figure, and the lightning flashing round her, with the waves rolling at her feet, made her look like Medea alighted from her chariot, or the Sibyl of the tempest . . . On

[1] ". . . I omitted to tell you her answer when I reproached her for snatching Madame Contarini's mask. . . . I represented to her that she was a lady of high birth, '*una dama*,' etc. She answered, '*Se Ella è dama, mi (io) son Veneziana*'—'If she is a lady, I am a Venetian.' This would have been fine a hundred years ago . . . but, alas! Venice, and her people, and her nobles, are alike returning fast to the Ocean." *Byron to John Murray,* August 9th, 1819.

seeing me safe, she did not wait to greet me . . . but calling out to me
—*Ah! can' della Madonna, xe esto il tempo per andar' al'Lido* (ah! Dog of
the Virgin, is this a time to go to the Lido?), ran into the house, and
solaced herself with scolding the boatmen . . . I was told by the
servants that she had only been prevented from coming in a boat to
look after me, by the refusal of all the Gondoliers of the Canal to
put out into the harbour . . . and that then she sate down on the steps
in all the thickest of the Squall, and would neither be removed nor
comforted. Her joy at seeing me again was moderately mixed with
ferocity, and gave me the idea of a tigress over her recovered Cubs."

To those qualities she added a smattering of the more domestic
virtues; and when, following a quarrel with the baker her husband
(whom she stigmatised as that *becco ettico* or consumptive cuckold),
she finally established herself at the Palazzo Mocenigo in the rôle of
housekeeper or *donna di governo*, "the expences were reduced to less
than half, and everybody did their duty better . . ." even the English
valet whom she had terrified into complete submission. Byron
appreciated a chance of economising. Almost for the first time his
expenditure did not exceed his income; the rent of his palace on the
Grand Canal, which he had taken fully furnished from its Venetian
owner, amounted only to two hundred pounds a year; and, although
he had spent five thousand since his arrival in Venice, at least two-
thirds of that amount had been devoted to women. But with security
developed a recognition of the value of money. The writer who had
once declined to accept his royalties (which he preferred should
become the perquisite of his old friend Dallas) had now a very
different attitude towards literary money-making, drove a hard
bargain with his London publisher and was peremptory in his
demands for a punctual settlement. Independence had begun to
bring out a vein of stubbornness; and the egotism of a man who had
always been lazy was now complicated by the habits that are bred of
solitude, the self-sufficiency of an egotist who has been much alone.
His freedom of action and peace of spirit he was determined to
safeguard. Claire had continued to write to him after the birth of
Allegra; and her pleas, which he continued to leave unanswered—
he could not forgive her initial shamelessness: there was still a trace
of the Scottish puritan in Byron's temperament—were often accompanied by letters from Shelley. Something must be done about

Allegra's future. But, whereas Byron's intentions were generous, his plans were vague. On one point, however, he was extremely definite; and, when his comfort seemed in danger, he was often brutal. He would not permit Claire Clairmont to enter his life again.

If she liked to give up the child, he would gladly adopt her. "I shall acknowledge and breed her myself," he had written to Kinnaird, "giving her the name of Biron (to distinguish her from little Legitimacy) . . ." But there could be no place for Claire in any arrangement he made; and Shelley, assuming that curiously diplomatic style which he employed when it became imperative to write to Byron, needed all his tact to prepare the way for a working compromise. Claire, he admitted, was exacting and tiresome—he had himself suffered from her moodiness and fits of temper; but if Byron sought to violate a mother's claims, "the opinion of the world might indeed be fixed on you, with such blame as your friends could not justify . . . wholly unlike those ridiculous and unfounded tales which . . . make your friends so many in England, at the expense of those who fabricated them." At last, after some bickering and, on the part of Claire, much misery and anxious hesitation, it was decided that the child should be handed over to her father. The Shelleys were now legally man and wife, for they had been married with Godwin's blessing on December 13th, 1816; and during March 1818, accompanied by Claire and Allegra and their own two children, they left England, reaching Milan on the 4th of April. Hence Allegra, under the charge of a Swiss nursemaid, Elise Foggi, was despatched on the 28th to join her father's household at the Palazzo Mocenigo. Byron admired the little girl's beauty and liked her spirit. Though anxious that she should be provided for in a proper manner, he was scarcely qualified to superintend her upbringing which devolved on her nurse and the Italian servants, with occasional help from Margarita Cogni, who was inclined to spoil her and upset her stomach by gifts of sweetmeats. But Mrs. Hoppner, the wife of the British consul, like Elise "a Swissesse," pronounced by Shelley to be "mild and beautiful, and unprejudiced in the best sense of the word," was there to keep an eye on the child's development and safeguard her against the more mischievous effects of her Italian background.

Wild stories of Byron's life in Italy had already been circulated. Much might be forgiven to an Englishman who was young and rich;

but even in Venice he was considered a somewhat extravagant personage; and he himself had never been reluctant to improve a scandal. Otherwise what need to keep John Murray posted in the details of his love affairs and escapades? He knew that his letters would be handed around in Murray's parlour; and that literary gatherings at decorous Albermarle Street, in a setting of mahogany and damask and Turkey carpet, beneath the solemn classic busts that adorned the bookcase, would be stirred and enlivened by his account of some passing passion—the Carnival acquaintance, "a little Bacchante," whom he had made an appointment to meet that evening at her milliner's, or the peasant girl he had picked up on his daily ride. In scandal as in everything else he liked effrontery. But, although his reputation, which by that time was beyond repair, suffered perhaps very little further damage, and though the faculties of mind and imagination did not deteriorate, there were presently hints that his nerves were rattled and his health disordered. Solitude was beginning to make him touchy and petulant. True, he enjoyed the society of his social inferiors, but he missed his equals; and it infuriated him that his London friends, absorbed in their world of pleasure and politics— Kinnaird getting rid of his mistress, John Cam angling for election to Parliament—should be inattentive to his requests and unpunctual in the replies they sent to his letters. Might they not have guessed that he was sometimes lonely? The commissions he gave them were seldom executed; and, when he wrote for magnesia, hair-oil, tooth powder, the wrong articles were often procured, or the books and medicaments he required were delayed in transit. Hobhouse, Kinnaird, Murray had all annoyed him. His lawyer, John Hanson, nicknamed "Spooney," had had the impertinence to suggest that he should leave Venice, and meet him half-way beside the Lake of Geneva, merely to sign papers connected with the sale of Newstead. He would do nothing of the kind, he wrote to Hobhouse. Hanson must pack his bags and set out for Venice. He was unwell, he announced in April, and he could not move. The origins of his indisposition he did not specify.

It depressed him, moreover, to learn of the death of Lady Melbourne.[1] The time had gone by when he "could feel for the dead," and such events left only "a numbness worse than pain," comparable

[1] Lady Melbourne died at Melbourne House, Whitehall, on April 6th, 1818.

in terms of the body to the effect of a violent blow on the elbow; but he remembered and regretted her as "the best, and kindest, and ablest female I ever knew—old or young." She had been his "greatest *friend*," he remarked elsewhere, "of the feminine gender:— when I say 'friend' I mean *not* mistress, for that's the antipode." There is reason to suspect that it was merely the difference of ages— the fact that, at the time of their first intimacy, Lady Melbourne was sixty-two and her admirer not yet twenty-five—that saved a delightful friendship from collapsing into a conventional love-affair. Had "dear Lady M." been a few years younger, what a fool she might have made of him, he once reflected. Luckily, although young in spirit and fresh in mind: she had been past the time of life when a "scrape" was feasible; and their association had had some of the charms of love, yet lacked its difficulties. The voice with which she spoke to him had the authority of an earlier period, an epoch that, although it accepted passion and cherished romantic vagaries, still subordinated both passion and romanticism to the dictates of common sense, and was rational and reflecting first and impulsive afterwards. She had no use for the extravagances and tantrums of Lady Caroline Lamb. Not that—even to her own favourite second son—she would have expected any wife to be entirely faithful: what had disgusted her was the romantic parade of unbridled feeling, the perverse enjoyment of emotion for emotion's sake. Byron shared her prejudices and admired her worldly wisdom. In theory, at all events, he was the least romantic—indeed, the least Byronic—of human beings; and, had it been his way to live more by reflection and less by instinct, with Lady Melbourne's help, theory and practice might perhaps have been reconciled. As it was, though he had learned much from Lady Melbourne, had sought her advice during his miserable affair with her daughter-in-law and made her the *confidante* of his perplexities over Lady Frances Webster, "the white rose" whose virginal innocence had been so nearly sullied, "*ma tante*" was herself indebted to him for many strange discoveries—that there were situations in which common sense might be unable to shed its light, dark corners of the human spirit she had not yet penetrated, depths of moral indecorum beyond her guessing. In the end, it was Lady Melbourne who had been shocked and flustered, and she had weakly encouraged him to pay his court to her brother's daughter: *marriage-à-la-mode* would calm and steady him. The collapse of her *protégé*'s marriage, and tremendous hubbub that had centred around the separation, had quite jolted Lady Melbourne out of the remains of her *savoir vivre*; and from that point she had declined any further part in the Byronic drama.

For Byron her death meant the disappearance of yet another tie between himself and England. He valued friendship as he had never valued love—there were both elements in his passionate feeling for Augusta; and the loss of Lady Melbourne helped to increase that sense of solitude—of isolation, moral, physical and intellectual—which had been growing on him since he had said good-bye to Hobhouse and had given himself up to the bohemian pleasures of the Palazzo Mocenigo. The only English acquaintance he met regularly was Richard Hoppner; for the Consul had taken the place of Hobhouse as his companion in daily rides along the Lido, and Byron occasionally attended Mrs. Hoppner's evening parties. Then Shelley wrote, announcing that he would like to see him. This was during August 1818. The rumours that Shelley had at first tactfully discounted were growing more and more persistent. They were accompanied by complaints from Allegra's nursemaid, who spoke of herself and her charge as lost in a wilderness of foreign servants, mostly Italian men servants of indifferent morals. Claire announced vehemently that she must see Allegra. It was obvious that, if she travelled to Venice unaccompanied, Byron would regard her visit as an attempt on his privacy, and Shelley therefore promised to act as escort. After an exhausting journey they arrived in a violent rainstorm; as they crouched in the damp shelter of the gondola's cabin with the rain thrashing down upon the roof and blurred lights sliding past them along dark canals, the talkative gondolier (who knew nothing of their destination) related long stories of the English nobleman who had made his home in Venice—a fantastically extravagant and eccentric personage whose luxuries and prodigalities were common knowledge. At the hotel, a waiter took up the story—evidently it was a popular one in Venice—adding further details for the edification of the English tourists. That morning, soon after breakfast, they visited the Consul. Mrs. Hoppner had immediately sent for the little girl who looked pale and appeared to have "lost a good deal of her liveliness," but, to Shelley's eyes at least, was still extremely pretty. The account that the Hoppners gave of Byron "unfortunately corresponded too justly with most of what" the travellers had already heard, "though doubtless [added Shelley] with some exaggeration. We discussed a long time the mode in which I had better proceed with him, and at length determined that Claire's being there should be concealed, as Mr. Hoppner says he often expresses his extreme horror of her arrival, and the necessity it would impose on him of instantly quitting Venice."

The same day, at three o'clock in the afternoon, followed Shelley's cautious visit to the Palazzo Mocenigo. But Byron's attitude had never been easy to forecast; and (as Shelley noted with surprise) "he was delighted to see me . . . and the anxiety he shows to satisfy us and Claire, is very unexpected." True, he was not anxious that Claire should take the child to Florence, "because the Venetians will think that he has grown tired of her and dismissed her; and he has already the reputation of caprice." Besides, very naturally, it had occurred to him that, should Claire once regain Allegra, she would be unwilling to give her up, "and there will be a second renewal of affliction and a second parting." He agreed, however, to a week's reunion, and added that, after all, he had no right over the child. "If Claire likes to take it, let her take it. I do not say what most people would in that situation, that I will refuse to provide for it, or abandon it . . . but she must surely be aware herself how very imprudent such a measure would be."

In fact, the whole conversation passed off far more mildly than Shelley had anticipated; and, though he was anxious to rejoin Claire at Mrs. Hoppner's, it was difficult (since Claire's presence was yet unknown) to refuse to accompany Byron on his afternoon's exercise. Very unwillingly, therefore, he entered the gondola and was rowed out "to a long sandy island which defends Venice from the Adriatic. When we disembarked, we found his horses waiting . . . and we rode along the sands of the sea." Their talk (Shelley told Mary) "consisted in histories of his wounded feelings, and questions of my affairs, and great professions of friendship and regard for me." The impressions of that ride and of the splendid sunset that greeted them as they returned to Venice, with the distant Alps hovering upon the northern skyline and the Euganean Hills vaguely shadowed upon the west, formed the substance of *Julian and Maddalo*. Next morning rose "rainy, cold and dim." Shelley called at the Palazzo Mocenigo before Byron had finished dressing; and, while he waited, he played with Allegra in the deserted billiard room and amused her by trundling billiard balls across the floor. Then Byron entered, again affectionate, calm and equable. Shelley's conviction of his greatness was not revised. "Count Maddalo [he was to write, in a prose foreword to the somewhat lame verses he composed that autumn] is a person of the most consummate genius, and capable, if he would direct his energies to such an end, of becoming the redeemer of his degraded country. But it is his weakness to be proud . . . His passions and his powers are incomparably greater than those of other men; and, instead of the latter having been employed in curbing the former, they have mutually lent each other strength . . . I say that Maddalo is proud, because I can find no other words to express the concentered and impatient feelings which consume him; but it is on his own hopes and affections only that he seems to trample, for in social life no human being can be more gentle, patient and unassuming . . . His serious conversation is a sort of intoxication . . . There is an inexpressible charm in his relation of his adventures in different countries."

If Byron encouraged Shelley's inclination towards hero worship, Shelley in Byron would seem to have evoked a kind of coquetry. For Byron enjoyed shocking his friend, but was delighted to please him. And, simultaneously on his best and his worst behaviour, he was now caustic, disparaging and misanthropic, now benevolent, accommodating, the creature of generous impulses. It was in the last mood that he proposed that the Shelleys and their household should take possession of a villa he had rented from the Hoppners but had himself never occupied, near Este among the Euganean Hills.[1] Shelley accepted the invitation; but no sooner had Mary arrived at Este than Clara, their second child, fell ill with dysentery and they were obliged to hurry on to Venice, where the baby died. Both parents were deeply distressed; neither of them proved ultimately inconsolable. Clara had expired on Thursday, September 24th; on

---

[1] "Allegra is well, but her mother (whom the Devil confound) came prancing the other day over the Apennines—to see her *shild*; which threw my Venetian loves (who are none of the quietest) into great combustion; and I was in a pucker till I got her to the Euganean hills, where she & the child now are. . . ." *Byron to Mrs. Leigh*, Sept. 21st.

Saturday, "an idle day," Mary went to the Lido and encountered Byron; on Sunday, after reading the Fourth Canto of *Childe Harold*, she visited "the Doge's palace, Ponte dei Sospiri, etc.," the Accademia with Mr. and Mrs. Hoppner, and the Palazzo Mocenigo in which she caught sight of the Fornarina. From Venice the Shelleys turned back to the villa at Este, a romantic place, its garden divided only by a narrow ravine from a hill which bore on its summit a ruined castle. Below them stretched the vast extent of the Lombard lowlands; ". . . there was something infinitely gratifying to the eye [wrote Mary] in the wide range of prospect commanded by our new abode;" but the restlessness that devoured Shelley was not easily dissipated and mid-October found them again in Venice with the Hoppners and Byron, preparing for an expedition to the south of Italy. By the end of October Allegra had been committed to the care of Mrs. Hoppner (who Byron had now agreed should take charge of her upbringing, since conditions of life at the Palazzo Mocenigo became every day more and more irregular) and the Shelleys flitted south towards Rome and Naples.

Meanwhile, Shelley had spent further hours in Byron's company; and Byron (one imagines) now tired of charming, had exhibited other aspects of his personality and had been more prodigal of hints and confidences than his companion cared for. The intoxication of his conversation was at length an irritant. Profound as was Shelley's reverence for Byron's poetic gift, he was disconcerted by the mood that informed *Childe Harold* and by the positive malevolence that he seemed to detect in its concluding canto. The spirit in which it was written (he remarked to Peacock) "is, if insane, the most wicked and mischievous insanity that ever was given forth. It is a kind of obstinate and self-willed folly, in which he hardens himself." He had remonstrated with the author (he added) but to very little purpose, "on the tone of mind from which such a view of things alone arises. For its real root is very different from its apparent one." The fact was that the Italian women among whom Byron spent his time were "perhaps the most contemptible of all who exist under the moon—the most ignorant, the most disgusting, the most bigoted; Countesses smell so strongly of garlic, that an ordinary Englishman cannot approach them. Well, L.B. is familiar with the lowest sort of these women, the people his gondolieri pick up in the streets." But there was worse to come—a suggestion that Byron may for a time have reverted to the habits and prepossessions of his Levantine period. Venice was a cosmopolitan, half-Eastern city; and, included in the list of his nefarious boon-companions, were "wretches [observed Shelley with chill disdain] who seem almost to have lost the gait and physiognomy of man, and who do not scruple to avow practices, which are not only not named, but I believe even conceived in England." Byron's attitude appeared to be one of splenetic lassitude. "He says he disapproves, but he endures. He is heartily and deeply discontented with himself; and contemplating in the distorted mirror of his own thoughts the nature and the habits of man, what can he behold but objects of contempt and despair?"

He did not doubt (Shelley concluded) and, indeed, for Byron's sake he ought to hope, that "his present career must end soon in some violent circumstance." Yet so remarkable are the defensive powers of human nature, and so diverse the materials on which genius feeds, that there was no dramatic or scandalous finale to Byron's existence at the Palazzo Mocenigo. It seems to have been true, nevertheless, that he was disgusted and discontented. From dissipation he had toppled over into flat satiety; and, although he was convinced that he had said good-bye to England and was out of patience with the majority of his English friends—he could not forgive Hobhouse, he wrote, "(or anybody) the atrocity of their late neglect and silence"—the present was still overshadowed by thoughts of his past life. Nervous exhaustion had begun to make him acutely sensitive. After many remonstrances and as many delays, his lawyer and his lawyer's son—"Spooney" and "Young Spooney"—arrived in Venice with the Newstead papers on November 12th. Unfortunately, they had brought only one of the three large packages entrusted by Murray to their care; and the package Hanson happened to have selected contained not a single book but "a few different-sized kaleidoscopes, tooth-brushes, tooth powder, etc., etc." Byron's indignation and disappointment were extreme. For some hours he would not be pacified. Then his gondola drew up at the steps of the hotel and, at seven o'clock in the evening, John and Charles Hanson were conducted with ceremony to their employer's presence.

As in most Venetian residences of the more pretentious kind, the ground floor of the Palazzo Mocenigo was neither furnished nor inhabited. Damp, sea-smelling, obscure, it served as a repository for Byron's carriages, stranded there with raised shafts and tarnished armorial trimmings, and as a home for the various animals he had collected. To Mütz, the Swiss mastiff (who, ferocious as he appeared, was once put to flight by a pig in the Apennines), Byron had recently added a fox and a wolf, besides an heterogeneous assemblage of "dogs, birds, monkeys . . . As his lordship passed to his gondola, he used to stop and amuse himself with watching their antics, or would feed them himself occasionally." It pleased him to live surrounded by dependent creatures: and to this trait, rather than to any genuine love of animals (though he had appreciated the companionship of several enormous and devoted dogs) may perhaps be attributed that weakness for forming menageries which added so much to the discomfort and confusion of his domestic background. Having threaded their way between coaches and animal-pens, father and son now ascended a massive marble staircase which gave access to the master's apartments on the *piano nobile*. They were ushered through a vast and empty billiard room, next through a bedchamber, finally to the threshold of an inner room where Byron welcomed them. He seemed almost painfully nervous, Charles Hanson noticed. The lawyer belonged to his youth—to Newstead and Nottingham: he had been associated with the long-drawn crisis of 1816: and Byron, suddenly confronted by his staid and prosaic figure, for some moments could not speak, while his eyes were tear-fogged. At length, with an effort, he was able to break the silence. "Well, Hanson!" he brought out, "I never thought you would have ventured so far. I rather expected you would have sent Charles."

Other details of that first visit remain unrecorded. Much legal business was gone through; on November 17th Byron signed a new codicil to his will, which Fletcher witnessed. Then, learning from the Hansons that Mr. Townsend, who had accompanied them from England as the representative of Colonel Wildman, had been at Harrow, he sent his valet with an invitation to the Hotel d'Angleterre. As soon as Townsend arrived, they moved to the billiard room; and during the two hours that the game lasted, Byron's spirits soared to the topmost level. "His questions about Harrow and the Drurys were incessant;" and as he talked he perpetually bit his finger-nails, a nervous habit to which all his life he had been addicted.

In other respects, the impression he made was singular. What the younger man had expected we do not know—what disdainful poetic apparition, compact of fashionable arrogance and literary elegance, with pure lofty brow and classic profile. If he remembered Byron distinctly, it was as young and slender. But twenty-four months of Venetian excesses and the Venetian climate had altered his physical entity as much as it had changed his moral being. Already, during the course of the previous year, he had written to inform his sister that he had "got large, ruddy, and rubustious to a degree which would please you—and shock me;" and since that time the inroads of middle age had grown more and more manifest. ". . . He looked 40. His face had become pale, bloated, and sallow." There could be no longer any doubt that he was decidedly corpulent. Whereas he had once been muscular, alert and upright, the outline of his shoulders was now heavy and stooping; and "the knuckles of his hands were lost in fat."[1] With his long, greying curls, his rings and brooches, the outmoded clothes he wore, he suggested less the eminent poet than the declining dandy—an expatriate of dubious propensities but distinguished origins, the somewhat spoiled and superannuated man of pleasure.

---

[1] "Of our poor dear B. I have received 2 letters within this last year:—the last dated Septr. This is all I can tell you *from* him, and that he wrote (*as usual to me*) on the old subject very uncomfortably, and on his present pursuits, which are what one would dread and expect; a string of low attachments. *Of* him,—I hear he looks *very well,* but *fat,* immensely large, and his hair long." *Mrs. Leigh to Hodgson,* Dec. 30th, 1818.

Chapter 16

Poetical Plans and Prejudices—*Don Juan*—Illness—Expulsion of the Fornarina—
A Mock Suicide—The Problem of the Future—Angelina—The *Cavaliere Servente*.

YET there would have been no truth in any imputation of literary decadence. However his Venetian career had affected his health and spirits, it had not dulled the edge of his creative faculty or at all hindered the execution of his poetic plans. Though during the latter part of 1818 very often he is said to have been so disturbed by the confusion of his household that he would leave the palazzo and spend the night in his gondola out on the lagoon, and though the complication of his intrigues was labyrinthine,[1] seldom had he been more busily occupied or to better purpose. Erratic hours and irregular methods had always suited him. He preferred to write when his imagination was inflamed, with the cumulative excitement of the day coursing through his system; and, since frequently he did not leave his bed till late in the afternoon and (like Brummell) passed several hours in bathing and dressing, after which he needed exercise and congenial company, he could rarely sit down to his writing table till night had descended. Then he wrote rapidly, feverishly, with few erasures. During recent months he had given much thought to the condition of poetry and, in solitude, had formed a definite scheme of his tastes and prejudices. The moderns he abhorred, though an exception was made for Crabbe and his old acquaintance, the banking poetaster, Samuel Rogers; but "I am convinced, the more I think of it [he had written to Murray] that . . . *all* of us—Scott, Southey, Wordsworth, Moore, Campbell, I—are . . . in the wrong, one as much as another; that we are upon a wrong revolutionary poetical system, or systems, not worth a damn in itself, and from which none but Rogers and Crabbe are free; and that the present and next generations will finally be of this opinion. I am the more

[1] See the last paragraph of Byron's letter of January 19th, 1819, to J. C. Hobhouse and Douglas Kinnaird: *Byron, A Self-Portrait*. Murray 1950.

confirmed in this by having lately gone over some of our classics, particularly Pope. . . . I took Moore's poems and my own and some others, and went over them side by side with Pope's, and I was really astonished . . . and mortified at the ineffable distance in point of sense, harmony, effect, and even *Imagination*, passion and *Invention*, between the little Queen Anne's man, and us of the Lower Empire. Depend upon it, it is all Horace then, and Claudian now . . . and if I had to begin again, I would model myself accordingly.

"Crabbe's the man [he continued], but he has got a coarse and impracticable subject, and Rogers, the grandfather of living Poetry, is retired upon half pay. . . ." Odd as it may strike the contemporary reader that the weak, finicking elegance of Rogers's verses and the bareness and grimness of Crabbe's rustic narrative (from which occasional beauties spring like flowers of heath or foreshore, struggling with effort through a harsh and sandy soil) should be thus admired by the more exuberant and fertile poet, there is no reason to doubt the sincerity of Byron's criticism. His own influence in modern literature he had always deprecated. If not ashamed of *Childe Harold*, he was certainly tired of him—tired of the imitation and uncomprehending adulation which the antics of that prodigious personage still aroused: and he had determined that his new poem should reflect a completely different mood—one far closer to the spirit of his Venetian holiday. Naturally, since he was above all things a creature of paradox and since, both in questions of poetry and the problems of personal life, instinct proved invariably stronger than considered judgment, the work as it took shape was by no means classical and had little in common with the concision and correctitude of the English Augustan poets. On the contrary, its scheme was loose and its detail slipshod. As before, the quality that redeemed the work was an abounding gusto.

Few poems seem to have been produced with more enjoyment than the first and second cantos of *Don Juan. Beppo*, written soon after his arrival in Venice, a dashing verse anecdote of ninety-nine stanzas, was a *ballon d'essai* for the longer poem; and, having grown accustomed to a divagatory expansive strain and abandoned his original idea of attempting a prose story, he set about the creation of a non-romantic hero. At last he would be as honest in literature as the conventions allowed him. Into the character of *Don Juan* he would pour all his own youthful experience—as much of it, at any rate, as he could convey with propriety—and the considered cynical judgment of his adult years. The tone was to be lightly astringent, mildly scathing—like youth itself, buoyant and yet bitter, carelessly cheerful and pessimistic in the same degree. It was meant (he wrote to Moore on 19th September, 1818, announcing the completion of Canto I) "to be a little quietly facetious upon everything." He doubted whether it were not "too free" for his modest public, who would tolerate libertinism only if it were sentimental. "However, I shall try the experiment anonymously; and if it don't take, it will be discontinued."

On November 12th, under the somewhat incongruous chaperonage of Lord Lauderdale, a stolid Scottish nobleman who happened to pass through Venice, the first canto of *Don Juan* was sent back to London. By way of preface, there was a "good, simple, savage" apostrophe to the Poet Laureate, Bob Southey, whom Byron had admired at Holland House—chiefly on account of his magnificent head—but for whom his feelings had now turned to violent hatred, since Southey had thrown in his lot with the government party and had circulated a malicious rumour regarding Byron's adventures in Switzerland.[1] The renegade Pantisocrat and his fellow Lake poets were soundly battered—Coleridge and his metaphysical incomprehensibilities:

> . . . *Like a hawk encumber'd with his hood,—*
> *Explaining metaphysics to the nation—*
> *I wish he would explain his Explanation*

—Wordsworth and the ponderous products of his conservative middle age:

> . . . *Wordsworth, in a rather long "Excursion"*
> *(I think the quarto holds five hundred pages)*
> *Has given a sample from the vasty version*
> *Of his new system to perplex the sages;*
> *'Tis poetry—at least by his assertion,*
> *And may appear so when the dog-star rages . . .*

[1] "I have given it to Master Southey. . . . I understand the scoundrel said, on his return from Switzerland two years ago, that 'Shelley and I were in a league of Incest,' etc., etc. He is a burning liar! . . ." *Byron to Murray*, Nov. 24th, 1818.

—Southey himself, the lick-spittle laureate of a Tory minister, who
had prostituted the language of Milton to the service of tyranny:

> *Think'st thou, could he—the blind Old Man—arise,*
> *Like Samuel from the grave, to freeze once more*
> *The blood of monarchs with his prophecies,*
> *Or be alive again—again all hoar*
> *With time and trials, and those helpless eyes,*
> *And heartless daughters—worn—and pale—and poor;*
> *Would he adore a sultan? he obey*
> *The intellectual eunuch Castlereagh?*

Equally downright was the spirit that informed his narrative poem;
and, no sooner had he introduced his Spanish hero, than in the
portrait of Don Juan's mother, Donna Inez, he began—perhaps at
first not quite intentionally—to reproduce the features of Lady
Byron, blue-stocking, mathematician, prude and moralist, the only
woman from whom he had received as much pain as he had himself
inflicted. After the complicated and agonising emotions of the last
two years, the regrets, the recriminations, the baffled fury, it was a
relief to descend to light-hearted ridicule:

> *His mother was a learned lady, famed*
> *For every branch of every science known—*
> *In every Christian language ever named,*
> *With virtues equall'd by her wit alone:*
> *She made the cleverest people quite ashamed*
> *And even the good with inward envy groan,*
> *Finding themselves so very much exceeded*
> *In their own way by all the things that she did . . .*

> *Her favourite science was the mathematical*
> *Her noblest virtue was her magnanimity;*
> *Her wit (she sometimes tried at wit) was Attic all,*
> *Her serious sayings darken'd to sublimity . . .*
> *Some women use their tongues—she look'd a lecture,*
> *Each eye a sermon, and her brow a homily,*
> *An all-in-all sufficient self-director,*
> *Like the lamented late Sir Samuel Romilly,*
> *The Law's expounder, and the State's corrector,*
> *Whose suicide was almost an anomaly—*

Byron in Italy

One sad example more, that "All is vanity,"—
(The jury brought their verdict in "Insanity.")
In short, she was a walking calculation,
Miss Edgeworth's novels stepping from their covers,
Or Mrs. Trimmer's books on education,
Or "Cœlebs' Wife" set out in quest of lovers,
Morality's prim personification,
In which not Envy's self a flaw discover;
To others' share let "female errors fall,"
For she had not even one—the worst of all.

The reference to Sir Samuel Romilly was a later addition, written in during the period of the Hansons' visit. Against that distinguished reformer and famous advocate the poet had long cherished a bitter grudge, because, having accepted a retaining fee from Byron at the time of the separation proceedings, he had subsequently acted in Lady Byron's interest.[1] During the first week of November 1818, the whole Liberal world was horrified to learn that Romilly had committed suicide by cutting his throat. It was said that the loss of his wife had unhinged his mind. The news reached Byron on November 25th. Taking his gondola, he had himself carried to the Hansons' hotel; and "How strange . . . [he remarked when he had told the story] that one man will die for the loss of his partner, while another would die if they were compelled to live together!" This remark, added Charles Hanson, was made "so pointedly that my father never again referred to the delicate subject of his domestic affairs. . . ."

Yet, that same week, Byron once more gave way to the temptation of apostrophising Annabella. His excuse was Romilly's death: his theme, the feeling of cold uncanny satisfaction with which it had inspired him. "Sir Samuel Romilly has cut his throat for the loss of his wife. It is now nearly three years since he became, in the face of his compact . . . the advocate of the measures and the Approver of the proceedings, which deprived me of mine." Little (he continued with venomous emphasis) could Romilly have supposed, "while he was poisoning my life at its sources . . . that in less than thirty-six moons . . . in the fulness of his professional career—in the greenness

[1] Romilly, however, declared that the retaining fee had been accepted by a clerk without his knowledge.

of a healthy old age—in the radiance of fame, and the complacency of self-earned riches . . . a domestic affliction would lay him in the earth, with the meanest of malefactors, in a cross-road with the stake in his body, if the verdict of insanity did not redeem his ashes from the sentence of the laws he had lived upon by interpreting or mis-interpreting, and died in violating." To complete the impression, he added a touch of outrageous rhetoric—the sort of rhodomontade that in others he found supremely ridiculous but that he himself could seldom resist when the context prompted: "it was not in vain that I invoked Nemesis in the midnight of Rome from the awfullest of her ruins"—and wound up with a curt but significant: "Fare you well."

Such was the intensity of exasperation to which thoughts of his wife's "unfeeling" and "inhuman" conduct could still occasionally arouse him! It is characteristic of Byron's two-sided temperament—and of the disingenuousness of his whole attitude towards his marriage—that in the portrait of Donna Inez already quoted he should have put forward his own case with the utmost restraint and humour, and exhibited his wife's absurdity with a quiet satirical cunning:

> *Now Donna Inez had, with all her merit,*
> *A great opinion of her own good qualities . . .*
> *But then she had a devil of a spirit,*
> *And sometimes mix'd up fancies with realities,*
> *And let few opportunities escape*
> *Of getting her liege lord into a scrape . . .*
>
> *For Inez call'd some druggists and physicians,*
> *And tried to prove her loving lord was mad,*
> *But as he had some lucid intermissions,*
> *She next decided he was only bad;*
> *Yet when they ask'd her for her depositions,*
> *No sort of explanation could be had,*
> *Save that her duty both to man and god*
> *Required this conduct—which seem'd very odd.*

Was this the aggrieved husband who had invoked Nemesis among the ruins of Rome—a conjuration also boasted of in one of his letters to Murray[1]—and who talked of the workings of Fate like a romantic Avenger, fresh from some fantastic story by Walpole or Radcliffe? In fact, though his literary gifts were at their highest pitch, his control over his private feelings had begun to weaken. Gradually he grew more moody, restless and irritable. During the day that followed his successful meeting with Mr. Townsend at the Palazzo Mocenigo, when Byron's spirits had appeared so good as to be almost boisterous, "Fletcher hinted to us [wrote Charles Hanson] that his lordship was becoming fidgetty for our departure"; and the legal party thereupon announced that they were leaving Venice, a decision "which his lordship seemed readily to acquiesce in." Now and then, he might suffer from the pangs of loneliness; he was still subject to excruciating attacks of ennui, and yawned as deeply and dismally as once in England when he had stood at his Bennet Street window and stared out at the London fog; but solitude was a condition he had come to terms with. Youth had deserted him; health threatened to follow in the steps of youth; but he had taken the measure of his own sympathies and tastes and genius.

Don Juan is the product of a completely adult mind. It is the most mature of all Byron's poems; for, notwithstanding the irregularity or redundancy of some passages, the vulgarity of others, it gives the impression of a writer who has at length achieved that balance which every writer aims at—between the style he handles and the subject he deals with, between the world on the one hand and himself on the other, between the inward and the outward view, the claims of observation and the charms of introspection. Simultaneously, he had been at work on a second manuscript—this time the narrative was in prose: but it seems possible that the two works were interdependent, and that the clarification he achieved by writing his Memoirs was of use to him when he came to compose *Don Juan*, which received, so to speak, only an essential residue. The exact nature of his autobiography will always remain mysterious. It consisted, we know, of a sketch of his existence up to the year 1816, and terminated presumably with the story of the separation; but many important circumstances—indeed, he afterwards confessed,

[1] "So Sir Samuel Romilly has cut his throat.... You see that Nemesis not yet extinct, for I had not forgot Sir S. in my imprecation, which involved many." *Byron to Murray*, Nov. 24th, 1818. See *Childe Harold*, IV., stanzas cxxxii-cxxxvii.

some of the most important—had been omitted from a regard for the
feelings or reputation of living persons; with the result (he informed
Murray) "that I have written with too much detail of that which
interested me least," and there was a danger "that my autobiographical Essay[1] would resemble the tragedy of *Hamlet* at the country
theatre, recited with the part of Hamlet left out by particular desire."
Concerning the manner of the narration, witnesses vary. According
to Lord Rancliffe, neither a trustworthy nor an unprejudiced
critic, the Memoirs were of such "a low pothouse description" as
thoroughly to have deserved the doom that overtook them in Mr.
Murray's fireplace; while the sensitive and puritanical Lord John
Russell considered that only two or three passages were in the least
improper, and that, apart from those passages, the autobiography
might well have been printed.

To-day, in the possession of his original publisher, there exists a
notebook from which more than half the pages have been removed.
Attached is a line to the effect that this notebook once contained a
transcript of a part of Lord Byron's Memoirs, burned at the same
time as the master copy. Otherwise the autobiography must be
accounted a total loss. No doubt the style adopted resembled the
prose of his letters—slightly more formal but distinguished by an
equal liveliness in the choice of epithets, as characteristic in its turns
of imagery and as sweeping in its enunciation of private prejudice.
At the end of August 1818, he had already covered "above forty-four
sheets of very large, long paper" and expected the work to extend to
fifty or sixty. His intention, he explained to Murray, was to preserve
the completed narrative among his papers, where it would serve as "a
kind of Guide-post in case of death," forestalling some lies and helping to "destroy some which have been told already." Meanwhile, the
second canto of *Don Juan* was making extremely rapid progress.
Begun on December 13th, it was finished by January 20th of the
following year. Juan, the precocious sixteen-year-old son of Donna

---

[1] "Mr. Murray is in possession of an MSS. Memoir of mine (not to be published till
I am in my grave) which, strange as it may seem, I never read over since it was written.
. . . In it I have told what, as far as I know, is the *truth—not* the *whole* truth—for if I had
done so I must have involved much private and dissipated history. . . . I do not know
whether you have seen those MSS.; but as you are curious in such things as relate to the
human mind, I should feel gratified if you had." *Byron to Isaac d'Israeli*, June 10th, 1822.

Byron in Italy

Inez, having enjoyed an illicit passage with a married woman, is shipped from Spain in the hope that he will improve his conduct. The vessel is wrecked and he is cast up on a Grecian island. Here the destiny to which he has been born once again overwhelms him; for he awakes from an exhausted swoon between the arms of Haidée, a kind of nineteenth-century Miranda in Turkish costume, and without premeditation slips into a second love affair, as innocent, animal and confiding as youth can make it. To Byron Greece and youth were almost synonymous; and, with a delicacy not found in earlier or later poems, he sets the scene and evokes the spirit of the time and place—the vast glittering emptiness of a summer sea, the enormous hush that descends at the advance of nightfall, the unperceived isolation of the embracing lovers:

> *They were alone, but not alone as they*
> *Who shut in chambers think it loneliness;*
> *The silent ocean, and the starlight bay,*
> *The twilight glow, which momently grew less,*
> *The voiceless sands, and dropping caves, that lay*
> *Around them, made them to each other press,*
> *As if there were no life beneath the sky*
> *Save theirs, and that their life could never die.*

To credit the poem with a morality or "message" would be, of course, absurd. Few works are more amoral in intention or attitude. But beneath the advocacy of feeling for feeling's sake, of sensation as an end in itself or an escape from world-despair—

> *Man, being reasonable, must get drunk;*
> *The best of life is but intoxication:*
> *Glory, the grape, love, gold, in these are sunk*
> *The hopes of all men, and of every nation;*
> *Without their sap, how branchless were the trunk*
> *Of life's strange tree, so fruitful on occasion!*

—runs a fatalism not to be confused with pagan stoicism, which owed something perhaps to the influence of Byron's Calvinist childhood. Caught in the weary cycle of emotional cause-and-effect (to which he is condemned by his "terrible gift of intimacy," the fatal domination that he exerts over the feelings of others), Don Juan must take the consequence of the emotions he rouses. Both the pleasure he gives and the pain he inflicts demand atonement. Both will recoil upon him through the ineluctable workings of fate. Retribution is implicit in every conquest of happiness:

> *Alas! they were so young, so beautiful,*
> *So lonely, loving, helpless, and the hour*
> *Was that in which the heart is always full,*
> *And, having o'er itself no further power,*
> *Prompts deeds eternity cannot annul,*
> *But pays off moments in an endless shower*
> *Of hell-fire—all prepared for people giving*
> *Pleasure or pain to one another living.*

It is the troubled background from which the point of view of the poem emerges, together with the original conception of the work itself—a modern epic poem purposely stripped of all heroic trappings —that makes *Don Juan* one of the great typical achievements of the European nineteenth century. In some respects, it anticipates the modern novel. Here (notwithstanding the author's preferences) is no attempt at symmetry or pretension to dignity. Far from wishing to attune his mind to the height of literature, the poet scales down literature to suit experience, and confers on his literary form the idiosyncrasies of his heart and temperament. An Augustan poet could address a society that shared his standards: Byron was consciously at variance with the world he spoke to; and that world, already profoundly disordered and deeply divided, still suffering from the aftermath of 1789 and from the disillusionment that had followed Napoleon's downfall, showed little cohesion either in the sphere of art or in the field of politics. Such a society invites attack by the creative writer (who suffers among his contemporaries and resents the state of critical solitude in which he is obliged to exist); and *Don Juan* is deliberately provocative from start to finish. The product of an often angry but only half-embittered man, sufficiently close to the experiences of his own youth to remember its ardours, but advanced far enough in middle age to have begun to acquire detachment, the poem was likely to puzzle the young as much as it annoyed the old. For the writer treated of youth with sympathy yet in the spirit of levity, and of age and its moral judgments with youthful cynicism.

The greatest works of literature are independent of the conditions among which they were conceived: it is as an afterthought that we inquire into the facts of their genesis. To *Don Juan*, on the other hand, our response is personal; and, as we read, we are reminded at once of the Palazzo Mocenigo and of the studious nights, following idle and self-indulgent days, when Byron, usually fortified by gin-and-water, would sit up over his manuscript till dawn had broken. He seems to *talk* in verse, with the same flashes of eloquence and explosions of wit, the same light-hearted digressions and irregular expansive flow (now rising to the level of poetry, now declining to facetiousness) that we might have expected had we been listening to his conversation, though his actual conversation according to most accounts was far less brilliant. A vast number of topics are briefly handled, from the inevitable injustice of a woman's lot to a passage of expert advice concerning the treatment of hangovers. But most characteristic of all and, indeed, most moving, since it reflects alike and gaiety and the despair of the writer's mood, is the detached stanza found scribbled on the back of Canto I:

> *I would to heaven that I were so much clay,*
> *As I am blood, bone, marrow, passion, feeling—*
> *Because at least the past were pass'd away—*
> *And for the future—(but I write this reeling,*
> *Having got drunk exceedingly to-day,*
> *So that I seem to stand upon the ceiling)*
> *I say—the future is a serious matter—*
> *And so—for God's sake—hock and soda-water!*

Byron hoped that *Don Juan* would irk his enemies; he had expected that it would be the cause of some consternation among members of his enthusiastic and gullible public; he had not imagined that it would plunge his supporters into alarm and perplexity. Yet such was the effect of its appearance at Albemarle Street. During December he was amazed to learn that Hobhouse, Kinnaird, Scrope Davies, Moore—all the friends whom John Murray had consulted—were "unanimous in advising its suppression." Many objections were alleged by these prudent men of the world—"the inexpediency of renewing his domestic troubles by sarcasms upon his wife . . . the indecency of parts . . . the attacks on religion . . . the abuse of other writers . . ." No doubt their advice was well meant; it was none the less infuriating. To Hobhouse and Kinnaird jointly he wrote back that, although the stanzas on Castlereagh might be omitted (since he was not in England to face the Minister's personal challenge) he would have no "cutting and slashing" of the body of the poem. If the composition had poetical merit, then it would stand; but he declined to give way to "all the cant of Christendom. I have been cloyed with applause, and sickened with abuse; at present I care for little but the copyright; I have imbibed a great love of money, let me have it; if Murray loses this time, he won't the next. . . . But in no case will I submit to have the poem mutilated."

At last, on Hobhouse's insistence, he decided—a decision soon afterwards revoked[1]—that *Don Juan* should be printed in an edition of fifty copies for private circulation only. The whole affair left him considerably vexed and ruffled. It was yet another proof of the slackness and cowardice of his English friends; it helped to exaggerate the condition of nervous irritability—of fidgetiness and sensitiveness, combined with spleen and lassitude—into which for the last twelve months he had been slowly sinking. This year the south wind and the Carnival arrived together. Again as during 1817 and 1818, he devoted whole nights to the pursuit of pleasure, and wrote to Murray "in a passion and a Sirocco", having stayed up till six o'clock among Carnival gaieties. By the end of January his health was causing him serious trouble. It was his stomach, he supposed, or perhaps his liver. At least, he was unable "to eat of anything with relish but a kind of Adriatic fish called *Scampi*, which happens to be the most indigestible of marine viands." Plainly the time had come when he must reform his mode of existence; to the warnings sounded by his own constitution—which threatened complete collapse or premature decrepitude—was added the headshaking of his Venetian doctors. As a preliminary measure they recommended that he should purge his household—advice that Byron accepted with uncommon mildness. There ensued a general exodus of his more outrageous favourites, and comparative quiet settled down upon the inner apartments of the Palazzo Mocenigo.

The Fornarina, however—expelled about this period, partly, no doubt, because the physical demands she made upon him grew more and more exhausting, partly because (as he told Murray) she had recently become "quite ungovernable" and other members of his

---

[1] "Tell Hobhouse that *Don Juan* must be published—the loss of the copyright would break my heart."—*Byron to Kinnaird*, Feb. 22nd, 1819.

household complained of her conduct—did not take her departure till she had put up a struggle. He had told her quietly and firmly that she must leave the palazzo—"she had acquired a sufficient provision for herself and mother, etc., in my service"—and she had gone, "threatening knives and revenge." Next day, in she stalked with her usual effrontery, "having broke open a glass door that led from the hall below to the staircase, by way of prologue." Byron was at dinner; she snatched a knife from his hand, "cutting me slightly in the thumb in the operation," but was disarmed by the valet and led down to a gondola, whence she immediately plunged head over heels into the Grand Canal. Byron, again disturbed at the dinner table, to see her carried limp and dripping up the marble stairs, superintended her resuscitation with a calm efficiency that was bred of long experience—he was no great believer in feminine suicides. His terrified servants urged him to apply for police-protection—"they had always been frightened at her, and were now paralysed . . ."; but he laughed at their apprehensions and refused their pleas. "I had her sent home quietly after her recovery, and never saw her since, except twice at the opera, at a distance amongst the audience. She made many attempts to return, but no more violent ones."

With the expulsion of the Fornarina and the reformation of life at the Palazzo Mocenigo closes a whole period of Byron's development. It had marked the decisive pause between youth and middle age, when—accompanied very often by an abrupt recrudescence of physical energy—there occurs a final precipitation of tastes and talents (crystallised at length in their adult form), and a writer looks around and begins to know himself. Not that Byron, even at this stage, had achieved self-knowledge; but he was glad now to leave his temperament the enigma he found it, and no longer harboured romantic delusions as to the enigma's import. Unluckily, such discoveries are largely negative. There remained the problem how he should dispose of the years that remained to him—whether in authorship (a calling that he still somewhat despised) or in the life of action. But what action could he nowadays contemplate—a luxurious exile, the helpless victim of his own celebrity, his every movement watched and noted by the Austrian secret police who gladly condoned his vices but would certainly not excuse any pretensions to heroic virtue? Besides, he was by temperament an exceedingly slothful person. He loved his comfort; he was becoming infected with the love of money.

During his adult life Byron had confronted many complex problems. Almost without exception, the outlet that he discovered was amatory or sentimental. In love he found a refuge from the pains of life, and in the experience of making love a shadowy substitute for some other more satisfying, more substantial experience—as to its precise nature he had never been definite. Once again he had notions of settling down. He was eminently suited, at least in his own opinion, to the domestic state and asked little enough of the women he lived with—merely that they should laugh with him and make him laugh, keep clear of him in his dark moods and respect his privacy. It was too late, he feared, for an exuberant youthful passion—

No more—no more—Oh! never more on me
The freshness of the heart can fall like dew . . .

—but there was still time, and he had still the energy, to form a new attachment in which he would stabilise the vagrant emotions of the last few years and give his heart and his senses the rest they needed. The Carnival had gone by; the agitating south wind had dropped when the spring came. Sobriety had improved his health. But recovered health (as not infrequently happens in such a case as Byron's) brought with it a hollow feeling of anti-climax.

True, the temptations of promiscuity were not altogether abandoned; and to this winter belongs the story of a young Venetian girl, "unmarried and the daughter of one of their nobles," at whose window he was espied late at night by "an infernal German," a certain Countess Vorsperg, the occupant of a neighbouring palazzo, with the result that the girl was shut up on a diet of "prayers and bread and water," while a priest and a commissary of police were despatched to Byron. He received the ambassadors civilly and gave them coffee; and afterwards, when the nights grew darker at midnight and the brother had retired to Milan and the father was laid up, it proved possible to return to Angelina's bedroom or balcony. He was dismayed, however, to learn that she was determined to marry him and "proposed to me to divorce my mathematical wife . . ." Byron replied by attempting to explain the English divorce laws, and concluded with the observation that he supposed Angelina did not wish Annabella *poisoned*! "Would you believe it? She made me *no answer*. Is not that a true and odd national trait? It spoke more than a thousand words, and yet this is a little, pretty sweet-tempered, quiet feminine being as ever you saw. . . . . I am not sure that my pretty paramour was herself fully aware of the inference to be drawn from her dead silence, but even the unconsciousness of the latent idea was striking to an observer of the Passions; and I never strike out a thought of another's or of my own without trying to trace it to its Source."

Byron's first mention of Angelina occurs in a letter to Douglas Kinnaird of March 6th, 1819, where reference to "a business about a Venetian girl," who had wanted to marry him during the previous month, shares the postscript with a description of a runaway elephant, "a prodigious fellow," which had terrorised Venice till slain by a cannon-shot. The second is dated May 18th and embellished with an exceedingly characteristic account of how, that same night, setting out to a *rendezvous*, his foot had slipped on the weedy palace-step as he entered his gondola; "and in I flounced like a Carp, and went dripping like a Triton to my Sea nymph and had to scramble up to a grated window," at which for an hour and a half he had been obliged to cling without a change of garments. The chronology of the episode is worth remarking; for, although during mid-May he was still on terms of surreptitious acquaintanceship with Angelina, at the beginning of April he had embarked on a far more serious intimacy which, in spite of himself, was to absorb him and at length subdue him, gradually robbing him of the independence he had always prized, but in return bringing the emotional security he had often hankered after. While he whispered through the bars of Angelina's casement, he was already the *cavaliere servente* of a married woman.

Chapter 17

IT WAS Byron's first experience of that peculiarly Italian institution—the triangular relationship of husband and wife and lover, founded on self-interest but trimmed with sentiment. At a social distance, such households had often amused him, and he had observed how smoothly and decorously they appeared to work—the husband, as soon as jealousy had gone the way of passion, politely resigning his functions to some acceptable lover (on the understanding that the lover was to maintain his dignity and do nothing to lower his wife's credit in their friends' esteem), the lover submitting to a voluntary servitude, carrying the fan, calling the carriage and embellishing the opera-box, in return for privileges from which the regular consort preferred to abdicate. These arrangements might last a season or endure a lifetime; and pointed out both in their own circles and the whole of the Italian world were certain couples who had established a record in adulterous constancy—the grizzled *cicisbeo* still offering his arm to the decrepit mistress, year in and year out continuing to support her salon, as permanent a part of its furniture as tables or fire-screens.

Since his arrival in Italy, Byron had been careful to keep clear of sentiment; and it is the more surprising, then, that the adventures of a very few weeks or days—an assignation proposed at an evening party, followed next day by a secret *rendezvous*—should have been sufficient to revolutionise his line of conduct. He was himself somewhat taken aback by this change of attitude. But the origins of any love affair are hard to analyse; for, besides the immediate physical or sentimental sympathy that may be assumed to spring up between two human beings (an element that in the majority of love affairs is often exaggerated) we must recognise the period of preparation that precedes acquaintanceship and the various factors that have produced a determination to fall in love. On Byron's side, the existence of preparatory factors was fairly obvious. After two years of dissipation he was sick of debauchery; mentally and physically he was a little tired; while to be out of love was a condition that had always irked him—it was as if his temperament were cut off from a drug it needed. Equally plain to distinguish were the motives of the other party. Teresa Guiccioli was between nineteen and twenty and had been married a year.[1] The third wife of a rich Romagnol landowner, she had taken over a family of grown-up step-children, and the time had come when, by all the conventions, she might demand her liberty. Nor was Guiccioli the kind of husband to dispute her wishes —fifty-eight years old, wealthy and good-natured, absorbed in local politics, a cultivated man of the world with his life behind him. He was prepared for infidelity though he would demur at scandal. Things might take their course according to the accepted usages of the Venetian moral code.

Byron was neither by birth a Venetian, nor by taste a moralist; and it remains astonishing that a naïve and sentimental Italian married woman—not very different from the married women he had known in England, no more disinterested though perhaps more downright —should have succeeded where her predecessors had so often failed. But Teresa had the strength of mind that goes with insensitiveness. And since Frances Webster, whom in some ways she slightly resembled—both were young, both ardent and both unhappily married—has been compared by Byron's biographers to an English wild-rose, with petals that have already begun to brown and curl, Teresa Guiccioli might be likened to some Mediterranean blossom whose relative permanence depends upon its leathery texture. There could be no question of the ascendancy that she soon established. Byron had first caught sight of her in the house of the Countess Albrizzi; but he was not presented till the April of 1819 at a party given by the Countess Benzoni. "This introduction [she professed to remember in after years] . . . took place contrary to our wishes, and had been permitted by us only from courtesy. For myself, more

[1] Since this book originally appeared, our knowledge of Byron's relationship with the Countess Guiccioli has been much increased by the publication of a new biographical study founded on hitherto unexplored material, *The Last Attachment* by Iris Origo. 1949.

fatigued than usual that evening on account of the late hours they keep at Venice, I went with great reluctance to this party, and purely in obedience to Count Guiccioli. Lord Byron, too, was averse from forming new acquaintances—alleging that he had entirely renounced all attachments, and was unwilling any more to expose himself to their consequences . . ." But he was unlike any man she had yet encountered. "His noble and exquisitely beautiful countenance [wrote Teresa Guiccioli], the tone of his voice, his manners, the thousand enchantments that surrounded him, rendered him so different and so superior a being to any whom I had hitherto seen, that it was impossible he should not have left the most profound impression upon me." In fact, Byron advanced a proposal which was promptly snapped up. It was no more and no less than he had done on other occasions. "From that evening [adds Teresa], during the whole of my subsequent stay at Venice, we met every day"; and when at last she deserted the city he prepared to follow. The summons reached him during the early summer months of 1819. Byron's carriages were made ready, and he set out for the mainland.

It was only to be expected that, once launched, he should begin to feel shy of the venture. Never fond of rapid movements or of abrupt decisions, from Padua, which he reached on the 2nd of June, he looked back towards the safety of Venice with slightly regretful eyes, and forward to his goal at Ravenna with a very moderate eagerness.[1] In Venice, the development of the episode had been less incalculable; but even there Teresa's imprudences had sometimes alarmed him; for, though pretty, she had exceedingly little tact, "talked aloud" when convention suggested she ought to whisper and had recently horrified a correct assemblage at the Countess Benzoni's, "by calling out to me '*mio Byron*' in an audible key, during a dead silence of pause in the other prattlers, who stared and whispered their respective *serventi*." Well, she had capitulated, as most women did; but that was not the end of the matter, since she declined to be "content with what she had done, unless it was to be turned to the advantage of the public . . ." In other words, she was "a sort of Italian Caroline Lamb," much prettier, it was true, but with "the same red-hot head, the same noble disdain of public opinion . . ." Amid the dust and glare of

[1] According to Hoppner, at a much later period, it "depended on the toss-up of a halfpenny" whether Byron followed the Guicciolis to Ravenna or returned to England.

Padua, Byron grew increasingly hesitant. Were he not a paragon of constancy, he complained to Hoppner, he might now be swimming from the beach at the Lido. Besides, there was a *before* and an *after* in every love story; and with the second stage came a diminution of the desire to move, when it meant exposing oneself to the discomforts of the Italian summer season. He would travel as far as Bologna but not a step beyond—certainly not to her home in Ravenna as she now suggested. "To go to cuckold a Papal Count . . . in his own house" seemed (as he told Hoppner) a somewhat foolhardy enterprise; there were "several other places at least as good for the purpose."

On the road to Bologna, he paused at Ferrara; and as he wandered in the Carthusian burial place outside the city, he caught sight of a pair of epitaphs that touched his imagination.

Martini Luigi
Implora pace

read one, and the other—

Lucrezia Picini
Implora eterna quiete

The modesty of the requests he found deeply moving: "the dead had had enough of life; all they wanted was rest, and this they '*implore.*'"

He hoped (he added, after transcribing the inscriptions for the benefit first of Hoppner, then of John Murray) that, were he to die, he would be buried at the Lido and "those two words, and no more" put over his tomb. Meanwhile he continued his journey towards Bologna; and it was here, some three days after his arrival, that he decided overnight to break the firm resolution he had expressed to Hoppner. Teresa he knew was ill; and her recent silence troubled him. Within a few hours he had left for Ravenna and his mistress's sick-bed.

Naturally his arrival in that obscure provincial town, amid all the pomp and circumstance of the Byronic travelling equipage—the vehicles, the carriage dogs, the numerous servants—produced the stir to which Teresa had been looking forward. Weak though she was, after a serious miscarriage, of which the effects were further complicated by a consumptive tendency, she was well enough to note that the appearance of so distinguished a foreign traveller "gave rise to a good deal of conversation. His motives for such a visit became the subject of discussion, and these he himself afterwards

involuntarily divulged; for having made some inquiries with a view
to paying me a visit, and being told that it was unlikely he would
ever see me again, as I was on the point of death, he replied, if such
were the case, he hoped that he should die also; which circumstance
being repeated, revealed the object of his journey." Teresa's husband
immediately called on Byron and begged that they might have the
pleasure of seeing him at the family palazzo; for Count Guiccioli's
sense of decorum was always faultless, and he hoped (wrote his wife)
that Lord Byron's presence "might amuse, and be of some use to me
in the state in which then I found myself . . ." Next day, Byron
accepted the invitation. "It was impossible [declared Teresa] to
describe the anxiety that he showed—the delicate attentions that he
paid me"; and, since he felt no confidence in the local doctors, he
obtained permission from the much gratified and flattered nobleman
to call in, at his own expense, the celebrated Professor Aglietti.

Such a concentration of solicitude—the anxious attentions of
husband and lover, with the sympathetic interest of the whole community—could not fail to be productive of the results desired. In a
few weeks (although Byron was still occasionally doubtful and wrote
to Hoppner that he feared "that the Guiccioli is going into a consumption. Thus it is with everything and everybody for whom I feel
anything like real attachment . . . I never even could keep alive a dog
that I liked or that liked me") the cough and the spitting of blood had
quite subsided, and "something else," he informed the Consul, "has
recommenced." The Countess bore up "most *gallantly* in every sense
of the word"; and "by the aid of a Priest, a Chambermaid, a young
Negro-boy, and a female friend" the lovers were able to renew their
meetings, though their relationship was still attended with danger
and difficulty. Byron, at least, would not have been surprised to
receive a stiletto between his shoulder blades one dark evening; but
it is possible that his view of Count Guiccioli was somewhat too
romantic; for the latter, having first invited him to visit the Countess,
continued to treat him to disarming displays of courtesy, until
Byron had to admit that he was completely baffled. *Savoir vivre* so
accomplished became at length an embarrassment. The Count (he
complained) was "a very polite personage, but I wish he would not
carry me out in his Coach and Six like Whittington and his Cat." A
pleasant contrast to these parades in the husband's carriage, under

the eyes of all the "good society" of a decaying provincial town,
were rides through the sandy avenues of the famous pine forest,
scene of Boccaccio's tale and Dryden's fable. Teresa was now sufficiently recovered to bear him company, mounted on a pony that
belonged to her husband, and arrayed in "a sky-blue tiffany riding-
habit" and a hat "like Punch's." He had ceased to regret Venice or
the life he led there. The habit of dependence, which is the habit of
fidelity, was slowly forming.

Thus, when the Guicciolis left for Bologna, Byron followed them.
The two months at Ravenna had "passed viciously and agreeably";
he had "effeminated and enervated" himself "with love and the
summer"; but the bond that held him to Teresa Guiccioli had not yet
weakened. This affair, he had already decided, was to be his *"last*
love."* But it is in Byron rather than in Byron's mistress—in the
preceding years, and the whole drift of his emotional temperament,
rather than in any immediate change effected by Teresa—that we
have to look for the explanation of his unusual constancy. Perhaps
Teresa's greatest virtue was to be largely negative. Neither hopelessly, if lovably, plastic as had been Augusta, nor wild and irresponsible as had been Caroline Lamb and many others, she gratified his
sensuality and pleased his sentimentality, but did not encroach upon
his freedonn in the more individual sphere. "A nice, pretty girl
[as Mary Shelley was to describe her at their first meeting], without
pretensions, good-hearted, and amiable," she had regular features,
statuesque but a little heavy, abundant yellow hair which she was
fond of wearing in loose tresses about her shoulders, a white skin
and gracefully modelled neck and bosom. Her expression was engaging and her smile attractive. But one defect made an immediate
impression on those who met her—her head and breast were out of
all proportion to the remainder of her body: her legs, in fact, were
far too short for the weight they carried. An enthusiast, a reader of
poetry and an easy talker, she had that bloom of intelligence which
gives a heightened quality to youth and freshness.

That Byron did not intend—or originally at least, had not intended
—to play the part of full-fledged *cavaliere servente*, or that the devotion
he professed was other than eternal, were ideas, it would seem, that
she had never harboured. What Byron knew was expected of him he
often did. Besides, in the lax mood induced by his Venetian life,

complicated by a growing sense of personal solitude, he was grateful for the readiness with which she had returned his passion, the eagerness with which she was prepared to sacrifice her husband and prospects, for the warmth and candour of her youth, the simplicity and the sincerity that she brought to a love-affair. Nor had he any excuse for defection in her husband's attitude. The Count still gave no signs of annoyance or jealousy; and, while sheer good-nature and a certain pride in his wife's accomplishments may, no doubt, have had something to do with the line he took, it soon became evident that he had a secondary motive. After many flattering attentions and drives in his coach-and-six, he tendered a request that had long been near to his heart. Like most foreigners, he under-estimated the extreme complexity of the English political and social system. Count Guiccioli was known to the police as a secret Liberal; the political game he played in the Romagna was somewhat risky; and he wished to have "British protection, in case of changes." Would not his friend, therefore, arrange, through the numerous influential connections he, of course, possessed in England, that he should be appointed honorary Consul or Vice-Consul at Ravenna? The suggestion was made during August and immediately passed on by Byron to his London publisher, who had valuable connections with the Tory party. Could not Croker do something, or Peel, or Canning? The candidate was "a man of large property—and noble, too . . . Will you get this done? It will be the greatest favour to me. If you do, I will then send his name and condition . . ."

So Byron wrote from Bologna on August 12th; for thither he had followed the Guicciolis during the previous day. The same letter contains an account of a theatre-party to see "the representation of Alfieri's *Mirra* . . ." Byron (one may infer) did not know the subject of that famous tragedy, which concerns the misadventures of a Princess of Cyprus about to be married to Pereo, the Prince of Epirus. When the play opens, Mirra is discovering a mysterious reluctance to wed the man for whom she is intended by her father. She reaches the altar, but falls into a demoniac frenzy. Pereo commits suicide; and her distraught father begs Mirra to tell him the name of the man she loves, promising that he will not oppose her wishes. Mirra then confesses that it is her father himself. The old theme! Byron had watched the unfolding of the drama with fascinated attention. It was clear (his mistress saw) that he was "deeply affected. At length there came a point at which he could no longer restrain his emotions." He had been *convulsed*, he told Murray; "I do not mean by that word a lady's hysterics, but the agony of reluctant tears, and the choking shudder, which I do not often undergo for fiction . . . The worst was, that the '*dama*,' in whose box I was, went off in the same way, I really believe more from fright than any other sympathy. . . . But she has been ill, and I have been ill, and all are languid and pathetic this morning, with great expenditure of Sal Volatile."

Some days later, the Guicciolis left for the country on a short visit; and Byron felt so disconsolate and so deserted that he sent to Venice for Allegra to relieve his tedium. By way of additional solace, he made friends with a peasant family and every day rode out to a neighbouring garden, where "I . . . walk . . . under a purple canopy of grapes, and sit by a fountain, and talk with the gardener of his toils, which seem greater than Adam's, and with his wife, and with his son's wife who is the youngest of the party, and, I think, talks best of the three." At other times, he revisited the Campo Santo. His old friend, the sexton, had "the prettiest daughter imaginable; and I amuse myself with contrasting her beautiful and innocent face of fifteen with the skulls with which he has peopled several cells . . . When I look at these, and at this girl . . . why, then, my dear Murray, I won't shock you by saying what I think. It is little matter what becomes of us 'bearded men,' but I don't like the notion of a beautiful woman's lasting less than a beautiful tree—than her own picture, her own shadow, which won't change so to the Sun as her face to the mirror. I must leave off, for my head aches consumedly: I have never been quite well since the night of the representation of Alfieri's *Mirra*, a fortnight ago."

Soon afterwards the Guicciolis returned to join him; and the Count, still complaisant or unsuspicious, presently moved on to his estates near Ravenna, leaving the Countess in her lover's charge. So far an open scandal had been avoided. Then, much to the dismay of Teresa's friends and to the stupefaction of the Austrian police spy who watched their movements, the pair left Bologna and returned to Venice, where they established themselves at Byron's house on the Brenta. Just why they should have thus affronted convention remains mysterious. Teresa (we know) had a taste for melodrama, and Byron, tired of travel and makeshift and subterfuge, no doubt hankered after the comforts of his Venetian household. Their acquaintances in Venice, including the Countess Benzoni, were greatly scandalised. Only Teresa's husband retained his *sang-froid*; and they had not been at La Mira many weeks before they received a letter from Count Guiccioli in which he requested that Byron would oblige him with a loan of a thousand pounds.[1] Some years earlier Byron had received the same request from another deluded husband; but whereas he had assisted Wedderburn Webster—an old friend, hopelessly improvident and chronically hard-up, whose matrimonial misadventures inspired him with a certain rueful generosity—he declined to come to Count Guiccioli's help, whatever the circumstances. From this snub, and from the Count's failure to obtain a consulship, dated a gradual worsening of the relations between wife and husband.

Outwardly at least, Byron did not repent of his bargain. He was prepared to shoulder the responsibility for Teresa's well-being—in his feelings towards her there was a touch of paternal tenderness; and at Bologna on the last page of a romantic novel he had written during her absence a declaration of undying love, more convincing perhaps because less declamatory than he had yet made to any woman except Mrs. Leigh. Teresa (he wrote) should she chance to find it, would not understand the language in which it was composed; "but you will recognise the handwriting of him who passionately loved you . . . My destiny rests with you." He would never leave her (he promised) unless she wished it. At the same time, inward misgivings did not cease to trouble him. In the very plenitude of love there lie the seeds of discontent; the more voluptuous the surroundings among which he passed his days, the more insistent became the prompting of that other nature, the puritan who had survived the inroads of his life at Venice, the man of action who still persisted after years of sloth. Suddenly an idea occurred to him that he might leave for the New World. In a newspaper his eye alighted upon a paragraph that spoke of a scheme of colonisation "submitted to the Government of Venezuela by a few patriotic gentlemen"; and he wrote off to Hobhouse demanding further details. What was there in his present

[1] This story, told by Moore, was denied by Teresa. We know, however, that Count Guiccioli had approached Byron for a loan earlier the same year. See Iris Origo, *op. cit.*

existence that could hold him back? Hobhouse, he announced, must not talk to him of England. The country he believed was on the brink of revolution, and revolutions he knew were "not to be made with rose-water". He had no affection for a society that had decreed his exile, "but I do not hate it enough to wish to take a part in its calamities, as on either side, harm must be done before good can accrue . . ." As to Italy—he was not yet tired of his adopted home; "but a man must be a Cicisbeo and a Singer in duets, and a connoisseur of Operas—or nothing here—I have made some progress in all these accomplishments, but I can't say that I don't feel the degradation." In South America, he believed, he might begin anew; and vaguely he envisaged a land of congenial, courageous natives— "those fellows are fresh as their world, and fierce as their earthquakes"—where he might build himself a house and establish a dynasty and turn out in the end an ordinary "decent Citizen." Anything was preferable to the life he led. "Better be an unskilful Planter, an awkward settler . . . than a flatterer of fiddlers, and fan carrier of a woman. I like women—God he knows—but the more their system here develops upon me, the worse it seems . . . I have been an intriguer, a husband, a whoremonger, and now I am a *cavaliere servente*—by the holy! it is a strange sensation."

During the course of the autumn, however, he frequently changed his mind. Hearing further reports of a Jacobin movement in England, he pictured himself, in a half serious and half facetious spirit, leading a revolutionary commission into Leicestershire and rendering an exact account of his mother-in-law's "cattle, corn and coach-horses, etc., etc., etc." The South-American project was still under consideration; and when Tom Moore, who had recently crossed the Alps for the purpose of sight-seeing, arrived on October 7th at the house by the Brenta, Byron admitted over the dinner table that he might say good-bye to Europe. Meanwhile they talked and drank and laughed immoderately. A brisk, talented, good-humoured Irishman, Moore was a friend of long standing and proved devotion. Together they could look back upon Byron's years of success, remembering, for example, 1814 and the celebrated "Summer of the Sovereigns," the exciting crowded weeks of masquerades and balls and parties given in honour of the Czar Alexander and the attendant Allied monarchs, or the Year of the Waltz by which it had been preceded—in Byron's life an even more important epoch, since it was then that he had awoken to fame and love and become the fashionable hero of the same society that had at length expelled him. Moore had been a literary supporter, a personal confidant. Byron must sneer at him sometimes and deride his snobbism, remarking that was Tom's weakness that he "always loved a lord"; but he had a deep respect both for his poetic capacities and for his domestic virtues.

Thoroughly pleasurable were the days that they passed in Venice. It was during the early afternoon that Moore alighted at La Mira; Byron, who had just risen, was still in his bath. He made haste nevertheless and soon descended; but whereas Byron noted of Moore that, although nine years his senior, he looked "quite fresh and poetical . . . this comes of marriage and being settled in the country," Moore observed of Byron that he was growing corpulent, and that corpulence had spoiled "the picturesqueness of his head." "In high spirits and full of his usual frolicksome gaiety," Byron immediately insisted that Moore should take up his quarters at Palazzo Mocenigo. Together they drove to Fusina in Moore's carriage, embarked in a gondola and were rowed to the Grand Canal. The evening was splendid; ". . . the view of Venice and the distant Alps (some of which had snow on them, reddening with the last light) was magnificent"; but his companion's conversation, Moore recorded, "though highly ludicrous and amusing, was anything but romantic . . ." Such was the devotion exacted of him by the Countess Guiccioli that Byron announced that he could not absent himself from La Mira overnight; but he remained to dine with Moore before returning and talked with his usual energy of many subjects—his own memoirs, South America and the Duke of Wellington, *Don Juan* (of which he was composing a third canto) together with "much curious conversation about his wife." Next day, Moore was introduced to Madame Albrizzi's salon; and the old lady, who proved exceedingly gay and garrulous, bade him scold Byron for the scrape he had now got into, adding, rather surprisingly: "till this, *il se conduisait si bien*"! To the heroine of the scrape Tom Moore had already been presented. At first sight she struck him as "not very pretty," though when they met again his judgment was a little more favourable. With these impressions and the manuscript of Byron's

Byron in Italy

Memoirs, which had been handed over to him to dispose of as he pleased, Moore departed for Rome and Southern Italy. A visit much less agreeable marked the month that followed. For during November who should arrive but Count Guiccioli, suddenly insistent on his matrimonial rights! Teresa must choose between himself and Byron; and, the Countess having at once elected to retain her lover, there ensued a succession of deplorable and distressing scenes, in which the Count alternately threatened and pleaded, and Byron, while his mistress enjoyed the supreme pleasures of romantic renunciation, sought to damp down the excitement with some sprinklings of common sense. The Count (Byron recorded) "actually came to *me*, crying about it . . ." Teresa's friends and relatives were in despair since "an *elopement* in Italy is the devil; worse even than with *us*, because it is *supererogation*, and shows a headlong character." With the happiness of his mistress and the honour of her family both at stake, Byron's decision could scarcely have been more difficult. On the one hand, he must sacrifice "a woman whom I loved, for life; leaving her destitute and divided from all ties in case of my death": on the other, "give up an 'amicizia' which had been my pleasure, my pride, and my passion." At twenty, of course, he would have acted differently; but at thirty "with the experience of *ten such years!*"—he reviewed the backward vista of tears and grievances and recriminations, scandals and disappointments and hopeless bitterness—he decided that he must play safe and act in the spirit of middle age. "With the greatest difficulty" he persuaded Teresa to rejoin her husband and go back to Ravenna and her home and family. For himself he did not "absolutely deny" that he might at length rejoin her. Otherwise she had declared that she would not obey him.

He had groaned now and then under the gentle servitude imposed by Teresa's passion, complaining to Hobhouse that it was not to be expected that a man should "consume his life at the side and on the bosom of a woman, and a stranger"; but once she had gone and he had begun to consider his solitude—"in a gloomy Venetian palace, never *more* alone than when alone—unhappy in the retrospect, and at least as much so in the prospect"—he felt so wretched, so cut off from any domestic comfort, that after all, he determined, he must return to England. There, at least, he would have the consolation of executing a long-cherished plan of revenge and calling out Henry Brougham, another legal villain of the drama of 1816. Perhaps he would settle down modestly and obscurely with Mrs. Leigh . . . Preparations were already far advanced, and the dreaded business of "packing and parting" had already started, when from Dr. Aglietti, the family physician, he learned that Allegra had fallen ill of the tertian fever which was then ravaging Venice. He must wait; and delay induced reflection, and accompanying reflection came indecision. By the time Allegra was recovered he had changed his plans. There was a moment, nevertheless, during the winter of 1819, at which (according to a story told by one of Teresa's confidantes) he had stood ready dressed for an immediate journey, "his gloves and cap on, and even his little cane in his hand." His luggage had been stowed away aboard the gondola; only his travelling armoury had not yet been packed. At this juncture, "My lord, by way of pretext, declares that if it should strike one o'clock before everything was in order . . . he would not go that day." The clock struck the hour, and Byron remained in Venice.

With remarkable promptitude a summons arrived from Ravenna. Since their parting Teresa's health had again deteriorated; and so terrified was her father, Count Ruggiero Gamba, that, although until now he had opposed the relationship, he obtained Count Guiccioli's leave to send for Byron. Back in Ravenna, whither he had hurried as in duty bound, Byron discovered that there was to be no escape. The husband acquiesced; the father welcomed him; and Teresa, rising as by a miracle from her bed of sickness, was proud to appear on his arm among her friends and family. To walk into a trap with eyes wide open is a course that for some temperaments possesses a certain perverse appeal; and (though Byron, writing to Hoppner *à propos* of a report that he had abducted a girl from a convent at Ferrara, had recently complained that he would "like to know *who* has been carried off—except poor dear *me*. I have been more ravished myself than anybody since the Trojan war") he now submitted with good grace to the rôle allotted him. Good-bye then to the projects he had formed in the autumn months! There was to be no more talk of South America, its volcanoes, gigantic prospects, savage freedom-loving people: no further question of a defiant return to England where he would restore his fallen credit by fighting Brougham and perhaps plunge into the turmoil of revolutionary politics. Instead, as the accepted *cavaliere servente* of an Italian married woman, neither very pretty nor intellectually distinguished, he crossed the threshold of the Marchese Cavalli's drawing-room—the Marchese was Teresa's uncle and a pillar of local "good society"—and took his place among the other *serventi* attending their mistresses, made conversation, listened to chamber music and manipulated the shawl and fan.

That it was a distinctly humdrum mode of existence he did not disguise—either from himself or from the friends with whom he corresponded; since, although the Italians visited the theatre to intrigue and gossip, they went "into company to hold their tongues." Their *conversazioni*, he commented, were "not Society at all . . . The *women* sit in a circle, and the men gather into groups, or they play at dreary *Faro* or '*Lotto Reale*,' for small sums." The obligations of *serventismo* were many and complicated: "their system has its rules, and its fitnesses, and decorums, so as to be reduced to a kind of discipline or game at hearts, which admits few deviations unless you wish to lose it." The motives of Teresa's conduct were still in-completely clear; but "it seems [he told Hoppner] as if the G. had been presumed to be *planted*, and was determined to show that she was not—*plantation*, in this hemisphere, being the greatest moral misfortune." That, however, was only guesswork; "for I know nothing about it—except that everybody are very kind to her, and not discourteous to me." Her father and all her other relatives were "quite agreeable"; even the Papal representative, the Cardinal Vice-Legate, had been exceedingly polite at the Marchese Cavalli's party; while Count Guiccioli had relapsed into his habitual quietude. Evidently Byron could not break away without creating a further scandal. He had arrived in Ravenna before the New Year and, on January 20th, wrote to Hoppner that he had as yet "not decided any-thing about remaining . . . I may stay a day, a week, a year, all my life"; the decision depended on circumstances that he could "neither see nor foresee." He had come because he had been called: he would go if he considered his departure proper. But Teresa Guiccioli had no thoughts of dismissing Byron—she was devoted to him as deeply and genuinely as her nature allowed; and on Byron himself the effects of habit were always cumulative. The snows fell and the snows melted: he had begun to enjoy his servitude. Venice, that "Sea-

Sodom," that "empty oyster-shell," was now relegated to regions of the remote past, among detested and disgraceful memories.

Yet more remote, yet more unalluring, were reminders of the English scene. On January 29th, 1820, expired George III. "Old, blind, mad, despised and dying," a ghostly shape who wandered at large through the darkened, silent rooms of Windsor, now pausing at the organ to play fragments of an oratorio by Handel, now living again the recollections of a previous century, he had long been lost to the real world of men and politics. But the closing years of his existence had been not unhappy.[1] The ingratitude of his children and the contempt of his subjects, the failure of ministers, the loss of possessions, the triumph of his foes—all had disappeared beneath the filmy curtains of madness; and there remained a dream life of imagination and of affection. In death, said the Duke of York, the least unamiable of his many ill-starred offspring, he resembled with his flowing snow-white beard a venerable rabbi. Behind him he left a kingdom torn by discontent. His eldest son, a disreputable and dis-credited figure—mistrusted alike by friends and enemies, by the Whigs he had abandoned and the Tory party whose principles he had adopted—succeeded to a throne of which he had been in fact the occupant, though with little distinction to himself or advantage to the commonwealth, since the King's reason had finally collapsed during the year 1813. For the government of Castlereagh and Liver-pool and the order it symbolised, Byron felt the detestation of every English Liberal; he had a warm though vague sympathy for the plight of the labouring classes, particularly the population of the industrial North, whose cause he had championed in his maiden speech; but the reports he heard of the reformers themselves alarmed and shocked him—a set of "low, designing, dirty levellers, who would pioneer their way to a democratical tyranny"; and he was disgusted to learn that even the fastidious Hobhouse had come to terms with "those two ruffians," Henry Hunt and William Cobbett. Thus, when he received news of the "Peterloo Massacre," at which many lives had been lost owing to a hasty and mismanaged attempt

[1] "There is something poetic in the picture of this old, blind king wandering about in his castle among shadows, talking with them; for he lived his life among the dead—playing on his organ and never losing his serenity and his illusions." *Princess Lieven to Prince Metternich*, Feb. 9th, 1820.

to disperse one of Hunt's open-air meetings, he wrote that he thought he might say that he had "neither been an illiberal man, nor an unsteady man upon politics"; but he also thought "that if the yeomanry had cut down *Hunt only*, they would have done their duty"; while, as it was, they had "committed murder, both in what they did, and what they did *not* do . . . punishing the poor starving populace instead of that pampered and dinnered blackguard," whom he had likened already to Wat Tyler or Jack Cade.

At the end of February, Thistlewood's plot to dispose of the entire English cabinet, and to follow up their mass execution by proclaiming a republic, came to light through the offices of a London police spy. What a gang of "desperate fools," exclaimed Byron, were "these Utican conspirators"! As if in London a secret could have been kept among thirty or forty persons! And, supposing they had accounted for his old friend Harrowby—"in whose house I have been five hundred times, at dinners and parties", and whose wife he remembered as one of "the Exquisites"—would the blood shed have been of any advantage to the cause of freedom? It was amusing, then—though, of course, it was also saddening—to hear that Hobhouse's association with the extremist Radicals should have led him, if not to Tyburn, at least to Newgate. For, in December, 1819, certain passages in a recent political pamphlet, of which he admitted the authorship, having been voted by the House of Commons a breach of privilege, John Cam was committed to Newgate Gaol, where he remained in nominal confinement till the following February. Byron made the occurrence an excuse for facetious rhyming; and John Cam, who had always a solemn sense of his own importance and, after his release, had been again chosen as candidate by the Liberals of Westminster,[1] was much annoyed by the levity of the doggerel verses. His "dearest Byron" would have been less lovable had he been less incalculable. Yet at such a moment one hardly expected he would side with one's persecutors!

During March arrived news of the extinction—at least so far as London was concerned—of another English boon-companion, the easy-going, irresponsible, perpetually effervescent Scrope Davies, who had at length ruined himself by gambling and had fled to Bruges. Thus poor Scrope (whom Byron recollected having deserted hope-

[1] Hobhouse was elected for Westminster on March 25th, 1820.

lessly drunk at a gambling hell where he appeared to be losing heavily, and discovered next morning fast asleep, a chamber pot brimming with bank-notes beside his bed) had followed in the footsteps of his acquaintance Brummell. At Bruges, he would be condemned to drink Dutch beer, and, no doubt, "shoot himself the first foggy morning"! With a sigh, writing from an Italian palace to Hobhouse immured in a London gaol, Byron considered his fellow exiles—"Brummell at Calais; Scrope at Bruges, Buonaparte at St. Helena, you in your new apartments and I at Ravenna, only think! so many great men! There has been nothing like it since Themistocles at Magnesia, and Marius at Carthage." But times changed, he added; "and they are luckiest who get over their first rounds at the beginning of the battle." His own seclusion might be monotonous: it was by no means painful. And, once he had accustomed himself to the initial indignities of *serventismo*, he soon settled down to the peaceful regimen of love and small talk. At due times, he visited the theatre or drove on the *Corso*. Besides, he was "drilling very hard to learn now to double a shawl," and reported that he would succeed to admiration did he not often fold it inside out or bring away two shawls instead of one, much to the confusion of the other *serventi*. By the end of March, nothing had happened to disturb his peace of mind, except that now and then Teresa had been a little jealous. Ravenna was a "dreadfully moral" city: ". . . you must not look at anybody's wife except your neighbour's."

Meanwhile, he had taken a set of rooms in the Palazzo Guiccioli. It was an arrangement that suited Byron, pleased Teresa and recommended itself to her husband's sense of pecuniary fitness. For more than a year the Palazzo Guiccioli was to be his home; and as much a part of his life as the Palazzo Mocenigo, or the dusty Palladian house beside the Brenta, became his rooms in this sombre provincial mansion in one of the obscurest and least visited of Italian cities. Venice might be dilapidated: but it had still the ocean. From Ravenna even the sea had at length retreated. In Byzantine times the wooden Venice of the Western Empire, approached and defended by a network of shallow waterways (notorious in the Roman period for their cloacal scum), it was now cut off from the seashore by miles of waste land, and lay stranded and almost forgotten among its marshes and pine forest. The capital of Honorius and Placidia, of

Valentinian and Majorian, where little Romulus Augustulus had assumed the purple and Odoacer had fallen in the Palace of the Laurel Grove to Theodoric the Ostrogoth, which Justinian had reconquered and Charlemagne pillaged, during Byron's residence Ravenna was the dull headquarters of a Papal Vice-Legate. Only the gaunt churches of S. Vitale and S. Apollinare, the Baptistery and the Tomb of Galla Placidia, lined with the triumphs of Byzantine mosaicists, blue, gold and iridescent as a tapestry of peacocks' feathers, and the mausoleum of Theodoric beyond the city, still hinted at the noisy metropolis of monks and exarchs. Byron appreciated Ravenna's historical background; but, if he visited these monuments, he did not write of them.

His chief interests and his real pleasures were alike at home. Vast, ancient, dignified and somewhat gloomy, the Palazzo Guiccioli looked out on to a deep, sunless, cobbled street, commanded by high blank walls and thick-barred windows. Its massive frontage was divided by a cavernous *porte cochère*; over the arch projected a wrought-iron balcony. Otherwise its external aspect was severely plain, pierced by large shuttered windows on the first and second floors, flush with the solid masonry of which the house was built. Such palaces are to be found in every Italian city. Seldom are the double leaves of the main door opened; but through the wicket-gate one catches a glimpse of the garden-courtyard, an external staircase and evergreen bushes flowering in pots or tubs. A number of different families may inhabit the house itself, leading separate lives and maintaining separate households, only communicating through their servants as the need arises. Byron, when he had moved into the Palazzo Guiccioli, accompanied by the menagerie that always followed him, by the lackadaisical, complaining, devoted Fletcher and Tita,[1] the gigantic gondolier he had brought from Venice, was on visiting rather than domestic terms with his host and hostess. The mornings were passed in sleep; he rode out during the afternoon; towards dusk he became the *cicisbeo*, either in the public or the private aspect.

---

[1] Giovanni Battista Falcieri, who afterwards sat for his portrait to Maclise, became a Foreign Office messenger and a protégé of Lord Beaconsfield.

Chapter 18

EVEN for our virtues we must pay a price. From the moment he took
up his quarters at the Palazzo Guiccioli, Byron gained in respectability and composure and well-being: the price that his fate exacted
of him was paid in boredom. But it was not boredom of a virulent or
particularly destructive kind—rather the acquiescent half-contented
ennui of a man who has outlived his capacity for violent feeling and
is glad to believe that the stormier emotions can no longer touch his
heart. His passion for Teresa might have lost its freshness; but he
liked the sense of security her devotion gave him; while as a man
who had suffered often from the pangs of solitude—and had never
been lonelier or more miserable than during his stay in Venice—he
enjoyed the idea that here in Ravenna he had a home and a family.
The Gambas, father and son, were gallant and well-bred. In common
with the majority of their neighbours, they were ardent patriots; and
Byron, conscious perhaps of his own imprisonment, a condition he
might not fret against but was bound to recognise, shared with them
their enthusiasm for the cause of Italian freedom. 1820 had proved a
fateful and an exciting year. Throughout Italy secret societies were
meeting and conspirators were arming. In every large city there were
groups of Liberals; the Austrian service itself sheltered Liberal
sympathisers; and the whole country, though pinned down by
foreign garrisons, bewildered and disorganised by a decade of servitude, awaited the gesture of release and redemption that would
explode its energies.

In the meantime, Metternich and the Austrian system were still
omnipotent. Directly, Vienna governed Venetia and Lombardy. By
indirect but powerful means, through Austrian princes, Metternich
controlled Tuscany, Parma and Modena. Piacenza, Ferrara, Comac-

chio were garrisoned by the Imperial troops; and Ferdinand of Naples, a brutish Bourbon, who owed the recovery of his kingdom to Austrian bayonets, had concluded a secret pact that left the Two Sicilies an Austrian appanage. Even from the Papal States Metternich's influence was not excluded; and he was confident at any future Papal election of being able to secure the choice of an Austrian candidate. But, although the effects of his system were pervasive, they were hardly uniform; and, of the three Duchies presided over by Habsburg princelings, whereas Modena endured the bigoted rule of the tyrannous Duke Francis, Parma continued to enjoy the comparatively enlightened code that had been introduced during the period of French dominion, and in Tuscany Duke Ferdinand and his minister Fossombroni had established a form of government that, described by some critics as "enervating and demoralising," was also generally acknowledged to be "mild and benevolent." Nor did the one native dynasty then in power set a good example. At Turin Victor Emmanuel of Sardinia conformed to the accepted pattern of reactionary potentate and oppressed his Liberal subjects with as much thoroughness as any Austrian Arch-Duke. For the "impure" —the subversive patriots, the poets and Liberals—were reserved "every form of intellectual and moral torment."

As confused as the situation of the peninsula were the aims of the revolutionaries. *Carbonari, Adelfi* and *Bersaglieri d'America*—all had their secrets and passwords, their lodges and ceremonies, and hatched desperate plots relieved and decorated by a touch of play-acting. Unlike the English radicals and revolutionaries whom Byron distrusted, these Italian conspirators were, with few exceptions, men of the upper and upper-middle classes. Particularly in the south, the lower classes were often reactionary; and the *Sanfedisti* of Naples (reminiscent of the "Black Hundreds" of Czarist Russia) were recruited from the slums to hunt down patriots. Liberalism went with education and a love of literature; and it was natural then that, while it partook of the literary virtues, it should also have its full share of literary shortcomings. Much time was wasted in talk, and much in sentiment. Generous emotions were accompanied by an inability to combine and organise. There were many heroes but few real leaders, and rarely a general plan. The great revolt anticipated by Liberals in 1820—for which Byron and the Gambas listened among the Romagnol marshes—was to die out crackling and sputtering like a string of firecrackers.

The exact extent of Byron's commitments is still a trifle vague. We know, nevertheless, that, incited by Teresa's father, a fine white-headed old gentleman of noble manners, and her brother, the impulsive and charming Pietro Gamba, he joined the secret society of the Carbonari and attended their clandestine meetings in the depths of the pine forest. No one, they hoped, would suspect an Englishman. Before long his rooms in the Palazzo Guiccioli were full of conspirational gear and mysterious documents, besides serving as a place of *rendezvous* for the numerous local Liberals. Not surprisingly, his landlord grew at length impatient. Count Guiccioli was apprehensive of the position he occupied; and, although he was both an indulgent husband and himself a Liberal, it did not suit him that his house should become a nest of plotters. Such, at least, seems to be the most probable explanation of the sudden change in his attitude towards Teresa's escapade. Abruptly, during the spring of 1820, while the walls of the Palazzo Guiccioli and adjacent houses were scrawled with inscriptions exalting the republic and prophesying death to popes and monarchs, and the Papal carbineers were trying in vain to unearth the culprits, Count Guiccioli announced that his patience was ended. Once again, he demanded that Teresa should give up her lover; and once again, caught in the turmoil of two furious families, Byron advised his mistress that she should obey her husband. Teresa retorted with romantic vehemence. She would stay with Guiccioli, she declared, if the Count would allow her to remain with Byron. It was hard that she should be "the only woman in Romagna who is not to have her *Amico*." Were Guiccioli to refuse her request, she would not live with him; " 'and as for the consequences, love, etc., etc., etc.'—you know how females reason on such occasions." The Count thereupon threatened to divorce his wife; but when the Gambas, who were now thoroughly incensed, proposed a separation (which involved the return of the Countess's dowry), the Count's avarice proved to carry more weight than his offended honour. The whole tangled affair was finally referred through the Papal Vice-Legate to the Pope's arbitrament; and his answer did not reach Ravenna till the twelfth of July. The Guicciolis were pronounced by Papal decree formally separated: Teresa was to leave her husband, with alimony amounting to two hundred pounds a year; but there was also a stipulation that she should retire to her father's house.

It was an admirable example of Papal tact. In obedience to the command of the Holy Father, Teresa removed to Count Gamba's villa outside the city; but Byron kept his apartments at the Palazzo Guiccioli and continued to visit Teresa by her father's leave. In essentials the situation remained unaltered. Warned to look out for an ambush in the surrounding forest—Count Guiccioli according to local rumour had already contrived or connived at two assassinations—Byron did not discontinue his evening rides, but took the precaution of increasing his usual array of weapons. Like other neurasthenics, he possessed his full share of nervous courage; and it was with an elation not by any means unpleasant that he looke forward to the prospect of a dramatic "row"—whether with Guiccioli's hired bravos or with the hirelings of the Austrian tyrant. But, week after week, then month after month, Byron's sanguine prognostications were disappointed. No thicket or pine-bole concealed an ambush: there was no attempt at a "stilletation" as he traversed the forest glades: and the only blood shed in Ravenna was that of certain local functionaries, victims of private spite or public vengeance, shot at from street corners or knifed in stabbing affairs. Nor, though the whole countryside was seething with excitement and Byron's Carbonari friends were extremely active, were there any definite signs that a general revolt might soon materialise. When it did so, he expected to give a good account of himself; but, whereas he was patient and resolute under the threat of danger, his natural irritability was not proof against minor annoyances—the supposed defalcations of his former Venetian servants and a long wrangle over the tenancy of the Palazzo Mocenigo. Worse—among the letters he received during April were two characteristic flippant but nagging effusions from that most detestable of discarded mistresses, the mother of Allegra.

From Pisa, where she was now domiciled with the Shelleys, Claire wrote, suggesting that, for the summer at any rate, which they expected to spend at the Baths of Lucca, the child should be returned to her maternal care. Otherwise she threatened to come to Venice or Ravenna—"*bada a voi* in that case. The French nurses used to still their crying charges with 'Marlborough's a-coming.' If you are not good the Fornaria [sic] will get hold of my name to frighten you into order." Only Claire could have turned so sound a cause to so little purpose, or given her pleas a tone at once so whining and so provocative. When he saw him daily, Byron was susceptible to Shelley's charm and glad to accept him in the rôle of mediator: but at a distance his attitude was far more critical, and the Shelleys' bohemianism struck as what in some aspects no doubt it was—a mixture of loose thinking and slipshod living, flavoured, despite the poet's goodness, by a touch of self-conscious intellectual superiority. Who was Claire, the girl who had thrown herself into his unwilling arms and begged for seduction as for an act of grace, that she should presume to deliver lectures on the theme of paternal duty? Had the Shelleys any qualifications to be considered successful parents? Both children born to them were already dead; for William Shelley had expired in Rome the previous summer—a catastrophe that Byron attributed, perhaps not without reason, to the effect of a vegetarian diet on youthful stomachs; and, having received the second of Claire's imploring letters, he wrote crossly to Hoppner that he would say only this: ". . . I so totally disapprove of children's treatment in their family, that I should look upon the Child as going into a hospital. . . . Have they *reared* one?" Allegra's health had hitherto been excellent and her disposition not bad. Though now and then vain and obstinate, she was also clean and cheerful; "and as, in a year or two, I shall either send her to England" (where he intended that she should live with Augusta's offspring) "or put her in a Convent for education, these defects will be remedied as far as they can in human nature. But the Child shall not quit me again to perish of starvation, and green fruit, or be taught to believe that there is no Deity."

As it happened, conditions in the Shelley household were such as to lend an added point to Byron's strictures. The horrors of a persecution part real and part imaginary,[1] the perpetual conflict between the claims of the real and ideal, which even in his relation-

---

[1] Political journalism at the time was exceptionally scurrilous, and Shelley not the only sufferer. The story he told of the attack made on him by an unknown Englishman he met in a post-office may well have been his own invention. Certainly, he could produce no witness.

ship with Mary was now becoming more and more apparent, the
miseries of hypochondria and the agonies of disordered nerves—all
had contrived to make 1818 and 1819 a period for Shelley of growing
creative strength but of increasing personal gloom. Again he was
haunted by the twin images of the sea and death; and thoughts of
extinction stole sleepily over his fevered consciousness, like the
undertone of waters rustling on a southern beach, whenever the
beauty and tragedy of actual life seemed most intolerable:

> *Yet now despair itself is mild,*
> *Even as the winds and waters are;*
> *I could lie down like a tired child,*
> *And weep away the life of care*
> *Which I have borne, and yet must bear,—*
> *Till death like sleep might steal on me,*
> *And I might feel in the warm air*
> *My cheek grow cold, and hear the sea*
> *Breathe o'er my dying brain its last monotony.*

Those lines had been written in the autumn of 1818. During the
spring that followed, wandering through the "mountainous ruins of
the Baths of Caracalla, among the flowery glades, and thickets of
odoriferous blossoming trees, which are extended in ever winding
labyrinths upon its immense platforms and dizzy arches," canopied
by the "bright blue sky of Rome," Shelley embarked on the continuation of *Prometheus Unbound*, a drama as fragmentary and fantastic, but in certain isolated passages at least as oddly beautiful, as
the wilderness of stones and flowers amid which it was composed.
In Rome died William Shelley, to be buried under the pyramid of
Caius Sestius; and the household moved disconsolately on to
Florence, where Mary gave birth to her third and last child, chris-
tened by the rites of the English Church Percy Florence, who grew
up to be a baronet, an affectionate son and husband, and a diligent
devotee of amateur theatricals.

From Florence, where Shelley in his impulsive haphazard way
engaged in a flirtation that seems to have been something more than
strictly platonic with a family connection, Sophia Stacey, they
pursued their restless course to lodgings in Pisa. Here they formed
the congenial acquaintance of a certain Lady Mountcashell, "a
singular character," described by Godwin as "a democrat and a

republican in all their sternness . . . uncommonly tall and brawny, with bad teeth, and a handsome countenance," who had eloped with a Mr. Tighe and lived with him at Pisa under the style of "Mr. and Mrs. Mason." Here, too, the Shelleys bade good-bye to the Gisbornes, thus further postponing, and being obliged finally to abandon, Shelley's airy dreams of constructing a monster steam-boat in which he had already invested much of his time and money. The entire household was meanwhile disturbed by reports of Allegra. From Venice in 1819 the not altogether good-natured Mrs. Hoppner had written that, whereas her own child was in brilliant health and spirits, "*Allegra, par contre, est devenue tranquille et sérieuse comme une petite vieille, ce qui nous peine beaucoup.*" Byron's life (she added) was "*une débauche affreuse.*" Such replies as they managed to elicit from him were curt and uncommunicative; and for six months they were without news either of the child or of its parent. Eventually they learned that he had deserted Venice and received information of his establishment at the Palazzo Guiccioli.

Naturally they supposed that his existence at Ravenna would be a repetition of the life he had led at Venice; but, in fact, beside their harassed and uneasy household, distracted by the bitter quarrels that frequently broke out between Claire and Mary, and disturbed by the electric fluctuations of Shelley's genius, Byron's way of life had now achieved an almost humdrum calm. Its pivot was the relationship, no longer very passionate but sober and semi-domestic, that he had established with Teresa; his pursuits were as regular as those of a country gentleman; literature and local politics divided his hopes and interests. Always further into the distance floated the idea of England. During the early months of 1820 Byron was half amused, half disgusted by what he read of the Queen's Trial on connected charges of adultery and high treason. A masterpiece of mismanagement from start to finish, this strange and squalid affair, which filled London with riotous indignant mobs and brought the kingdom once again to the verge of revolution, had its origins in the unscrupulous machination of Byron's old enemy, Henry Brougham, who had persuaded his client to return to England, having given an assurance to the government that she would remain abroad. Neither Brougham nor any other of her influential Whig supporters imagined that the Queen was completely innocent; they regarded her as a useful weapon with which to attack the Tories. But the commercial and lower classes were more uncritical—for them the Queen was the helpless victim of monarchic despotism: her grievances represented the woes of centuries. Castlereagh found it impossible to leave the Foreign Office; fear of his subjects confined the timorous King to Carlton House; vast processions marched with bands and placards from the City to Westminster.

Between detachment and disenchantment Byron was only remotely interested. During 1820 the letters that he wrote to England are brief by comparison with the correspondence of his earlier Italian years; and the tone that distinguishes a great many of them is harsh and irritable. Solitude has seldom a softening effect on the recluse's character. In Byron it exaggerated his natural petulance; and when Hoppner, in a letter written that autumn, repeated a scandal concerning the Shelleys that was being circulated by Allegra's former nursemaid, Elise Foggi, and her recently acquired husband, a dishonest courier whom they had once employed,[1] Byron's response was neither discriminating nor very generous. The origins of the story—for it had no doubt some basis—are no longer ascertainable. It is established, however, that during their stay in the South of Italy Claire had fallen ill and that, at the same time, Shelley had occupied himself with the welfare of an unknown *protégée*, afterwards referred to as "my poor Neapolitan." A child was somehow involved in the latter episode; and Elise now announced that Claire was Shelley's mistress; that both of them had treated Mary with the utmost brutality; that Claire had become pregnant and, in spite of her lover's attempts to procure an abortion, had given birth; at which Shelley had consigned his bastard to the Foundlings' Hospital.[2] All this was repeated to Byron by Hoppner, and by the poet immediately accepted without a word of disbelief. Claire's pleas in the last few months had been consistently exasperating; Shelley's tactful interpositions had done nothing to improve his temper. He wanted only to be left alone to the life that suited him.

[1] On discovering that the maid was pregnant by the courier, the Shelleys—rather surprisingly for people of their principles—had insisted that the pair must at once be married. Hence the dislike with which they were now regarded by Elise and her husband.

[2] It has now been discovered that, at Naples, on February 27th, 1819, Shelley registered the birth of a child, Elena Adelaide Shelley, whose parentage remains unknown, and of whom we have no further record.

Thus he was perfectly prepared to swallow Hoppner's evidence. Elise, he admitted, was an unreliable witness; "Shiloh" (or Shelley) had "talent and honour," crazily incensed though he was "against religion and morality"; "of the facts, however," he added on October 1st, "there can be little doubt; it is just like them." A story more *unlike* Shelley—at least in some of its darker details—could scarcely be conceived. But Byron was too feminine to be quite consistent, too lazy, to resist an easy cynicism. It was a simple method of dismissing Claire's pleas, of breaking Shelley's spell, of settling back again into the placid life their existence threatened; and across a letter from Claire Clairmont that he sent for Hoppner's inspection, "the moral part . . ." he scribbled, "comes with an excellent grace from the writer now living with a *man* and his *wife*—and having planted a child in the Fl—Foundling, etc."

If only patriots and oppressors would at last decide to come to blows! But, although during the previous spring and winter months the authorities had seemed thoroughly perturbed, the Cardinal had "glared pale through all his purple" and offered public prayers for the salvation of the city, while Byron and his friends had lived in momentary expectation of being called on to take up arms, the general rising, postponed till the autumn, when the autumn came was stifled unborn by the defection of Bologna, which suddenly withdrew its assistance from that patriot league. At the moment both sides displayed a partiality, that Byron could not but deplore, for "shooting around a corner"; and on the evening of December 9th at eight o'clock, just as he was donning his coat to visit Teresa, musket shots reverberated through the lane below. All the servants, he found, were clustered on the balcony, excitedly exclaiming that a man had been murdered; but only Tita would follow him as he ran downstairs. Not far from his door lay the Military Commandant of Ravenna, a brave but unpopular man, stretched on his back, pierced by five bullets. His adjutant bent over him, weeping like a child. Nearby were a surgeon who, cautiously, "said nothing of his profession," a priest "sobbing a frightened prayer," some bewildered soldiers, who attempted to prevent the Englishman passing, and "one or two of the boldest of the mob." The street was "dark as pitch, with people flying in all directions." Since none of the on-lookers would do anything but "shake and stare," Byron, brushing aside remonstrances and disregarding the soldiers, ordered that the dying man should be carried into the shelter of the Palazzo Guiccioli. There, with no word save for murmured ejaculations of *O Dio* and *O Jesu*, the Commandant expired on Fletcher's bed. Ravenna was thrown into complete confusion. The identity of the criminal was not discovered; and it remained doubtful whether the crime was the work of a private assassin or the Commandant had fallen because he was suspected of Liberal sympathies. Then, suddenly and inexplicably, the excitement subsided. Byron was considerably disappointed, if not much astonished. More and more he was driven back upon his own resources; and more and more often, during his empty nights and his indolent afternoons, when a dead summer silence filled the street outside, or winter showers pricked at the window-panes or splashed on the cobblestones, he took refuge among the pleasures and the pains of memory.

After all, the early days had been the best days. Even at the age of nineteen he was an addict of memory, obsessed by recollections of his career at school and gnawed by regrets for his vanished happiness; and at thirty-two the past, like the base of an iceberg, gigantically outmeasured the present's value. The autumn and winter of 1820 produced no change. During the first frozen week of the New Year he embarked on a journal, which he continued till he had "filled one paper-book (thinnish), and two sheets or so of another," from January 4th to February 27th, 1821. The result was a detailed survey of his thoughts and feelings. Vile weather made it almost impossible to leave the palace, for a deep snowfall had half-melted beneath the clammy south wind, and his usual ride through the pinewoods was completely out of the question. At home he stared at the fire and awaited the post-bag. It arrived late and brought six copies of Galignani's *Messenger*, "a letter from Faenza, but none from England." More neglect! "Very sulky in consequence" he sat down to devour a copious meal—with Byron a hearty appetite was often a sign of wretchedness—from which he rose, restive and thoughtful, to absorb the newspapers. He now made love, he once observed bitterly, by the stroke of the clock, and at eight he paid his regular evening visit to the Countess Guiccioli, whom he found "playing on the pianoforte," and with whom he "talked till ten, when the Count, her father, and the no less Count, her brother, came in from the theatre. Play, they said, Alfieri's *Fileppo*—well received." At eleven, or a little before, he returned to his own rooms, ruminated, wrote up his journal and retired to bed.

Such, so long as the snows lasted, was the pattern of his daily life. "Weather dripping and dense" was followed by "mist—thaw—slop —rain," and, next morning, by a further snowfall with fog and drizzle "and all the incalculable combinations of a climate where heat and cold struggle for mastery." Byron's mood was one of resigned impatience and reflective lassitude. Reading Swift, finishing a cross letter to his English publisher, who demurred at *Don Juan* and disliked his tragedies, feeding or playing with his domestic animals— the hawk, the tame crow, the monkeys, the mastiff—he dawdled his way dully but quietly through the hours of daylight. He was bored, of course, but not so bored as he had been in London; for, though it was true that all his life he had been "more or less *ennuyé*," he was "rather less so now" than ten years earlier. What was the explanation, he wondered, of this habitual spleen? It was constitutional, he supposed "—as well as the waking in low spirits, which I have invariably done for many years." Temperance and vigorous exercise brought no improvement; but tumultuous passions, if they agitated, at least enlivened him. "A dose of salts has the effect of a temporary inebriation, like light champagne, upon me. But wine and spirits make me sullen and savage to ferocity—silent, however, and retiring, and not quarrelsome, if not spoken to. Swimming also raises my spirits—but in general they are low, and get daily lower."

Still he contemplated some escape into a life of action. But an excuse failed to materialise in spite of numerous false alarms. Thus, on January 7th, after an idle day passed reading Spence's *Anecdotes*, the fourth volume of the second series of *Tales of my Landlord* and the *Lugano Gazette*, Byron was drawn aside at an evening party by Pietro Gamba, who reported he had secret information that the Papal Legate had received orders to make several arrests, and that as a precautionary measure the patriots were arming and bodies of Carbonari had been posted in the city's streets. What should be done? demanded Gamba. To which Byron replied that they must fight for it rather than be taken separately, and offered, if any of the Carbonari were in immediate danger, to harbour and defend them in the Palazzo

Guiccioli. Gamba accepted the advice, but declined to borrow his pistols; and Byron hurried home through a tempest of rain and wind.

At home, he replenished the fire and sat up to await events, turning over a score of books in search of a quotation that continued to elude him, and straining his ears for the roll of drums or the crackle of musketry. All that he heard was "the plash of the rain and the gusts of the wind at intervals"; and next day he learned that the scare was groundless; "the Government [said Gamba] had not issued orders for the arrests apprehended . . . the attack in Forli had not taken place . . . and that, as yet, they are still in apprehension only." Gamba asked "for some arms of a better sort," which Byron gave, settling meanwhile that, "in case of a row, the Liberals are to assemble *here* (with me), and that he had given the word to Vicenzo G. and others of the *Chiefs* for that purpose." Meanwhile, both Gambas, father and son, had elected to go hunting. Dismayed by this odd suspension of warlike activities, the Englishman tried on a new coat, read Bacon's *Apothegms*, wrote a letter to Murray and visited Teresa, in whose rooms he went through the usual regimen of love and small talk. Luckily, the weather had begun to change. He was soon able to ride out again over the muddy roads, occupied with reflection upon his past life and Italian liberty.

"How odd are my thoughts," he recorded on January 12th. His eyes had alighted on the words of the song from *Comus*:

> *Sabrina fair,*
> *Listen where thou art sitting*
> *Under the glassy, cool, translucent wave,*
> *In twisted braids of lilies knitting*
> *The loose train of thy amber-dropping hair . . .*

and, in an instant, fifteen wearisome years had rolled away, and he had recaptured the poetic essence of that delightful period when, accompanied by Edward Noel Long, one of the dearest of his Harrow and Cambridge intimates, he had practised diving in the Cam's not very translucent waters for "plates, eggs, and even shillings." He remembered the landscape of the murky water-world, and a tree-stump in the bed of the river round which he used to cling, pleased with the strangeness of his sensations in the wavering half-light. Long had joined the Guards and had been drowned on the passage to Lisbon; and Byron had attempted, but had not had the heart to complete, his epitaph.

Three weeks later, his memories again attacked him—but from a completely different quarter. "What I feel most growing upon me [he wrote] are laziness, and a disrelish more powerful than indifference." He presumed he would end, like Swift, in madness, and was going on to observe that he did not "contemplate this with so much horror as he apparently did for some years before it happened" (though it was true at his present age "Swift had hardly *begun* life"), when he was interrupted by the music of a strolling barrel organ. ". . . A waltz, too [he exclaimed]. I must leave off to listen." For that very waltz he had "heard ten thousand times at the balls in London, between 1812 and 1815." Up rose the buried years of fame and fashion. In Byron's life the waltz had a special historic value: since the same year that brought the waltz to London dance floors, and saw the great world go gliding off to its lascivious measure, had introduced the wild beginnings of the Byron craze, the period of celebrity so intense and unparalleled that the poet's name formed the murmured background of every dinner party— *Byron—Byron—Byron*—in an incessant monotonous refrain.

"Music is a strange thing," he remarked concisely. Almost a decade had passed; on January 22nd, 1821, he had composed a mock epitaph to celebrate the extinction of his thirty-third year; yet certain undertones of feeling were still persistent, running through pleasure and satiety, the triumphs and the failures, haunting his middle age as they had haunted his youth itself. Between the mind and experience stood always a mysterious barrier. "Why [he wrote] at the very height of desire and human pleasure—worldly, social, amorous, ambitious, or even avaricious—does there mingle a certain sense of doubt and sorrow—a fear of what is to come—a doubt of what *is*— retrospect to the past, leading to a prognostication of the future?" The greater the elevation the mind achieved, the more vertiginous the "sentiment of the gulf" by which it was attended. "I feel most things [he concluded], but I know nothing, except"—and here with the point of his hurried and careless pen Byron broke into three long rows of impatient dashes, as if to symbolise the final hopelessness of the quest embarked on, from which the forces of the imagination fell back in disarray. He took up and threw down again a volume by

Frederick Schlegel. For all his wealth of words, the German meta-physician could tell him nothing.[1]

It was Byron's virtue, in the face of mystery, to remain unusually clear-headed. Self-deception he might indulge in with regard to his private problems; but, confronted by the large enigma of human destiny, his intellect was clear and honest, if his view was limited. To attempt to force an explanation, or to wring the confirmation of a theory from the facts of experience, was antipathetic to the nature of his instinctive genius. To systematise the material of life is to lose half its value: to concentrate on the destination, to which we may or may not be bound, entails inevitably some loss of the journey's interest. We are travellers and, in the condition of travellers, we must feel and speculate. Meanwhile, the world of appearance is beautiful, varied, inexhaustibly surprising; and, mingled with the doubts and cogitations, the regrets and memories, occur passages in Byron's journal of extraordinary descriptive brilliance, that reveal the sharpness of his eye and the strength and skill with which he sometimes handled the English language.

Came home *solus* [he wrote of Ravenna by moonlight]—very high wind—lightning—moonshine—solitary stragglers muffled in cloaks—women in masks—white houses—clouds hurrying over the sky, like spilt milk blown out of the pail—altogether very poetical. It is still blowing hard—the tiles flying, and the house rocking—rain splashing—lightning flashing—quite a fine Swiss Alpine evening, and the sea roaring in the distance.

Through these scenes he made his way to a *conversazione*. The women (he noted) were all frightened by the tempest and *"won't* go to the masquerade because it lightens! . . ."* He heard the customary talk of revolution and approaching war; but as the weeks went by, the prospects of a revolt appeared more and more unhopeful, and the behaviour of his fellow conspirators less encouraging. "I always had an idea [wrote Byron on February 24th] that it would be *bungled*; but was willing to hope, and am so still." Even the Gambas' conduct was indecisive; and on February 16th, without a syllable of warning, Count Pietro Gamba, having taken fright at a recent order prohibit-

[1] "I dislike him the worse . . . because he always seems upon the verge of meaning; and, so, he goes down like sunset, or melts like a rainbow, leaving a rather rich confusion. . . ."

ing the concealment of arms, sent his servant to Byron's house carrying "a bag full of bayonets, some muskets, and some hundreds of cartridges" which the poet had purchased at the request of his Carbonari friends. Luckily, Zambelli, his Italian steward, was there to receive them; for if they had been delivered to any other member of his household, except the steward, Tita the gondolier or William Fletcher, he would immediately have been denounced to the Papal police. Yet there was no bitterness or tendency to recrimination in Byron's attitude; and meantime he was delighted to learn of the success of the insurrectionary movement in the kingdom of the Two Sicilies, where the Neapolitans were reported to be "full of energy," to "have broken a bridge, and slain four pontifical carabineers." Unfortunately the sovereign of Naples appealed to Metternich; the constitution granted during the previous July was at once repealed; and in March the armies of Austria met the patriot forces. At the battle of Rieti and on the field of Novara (where a rising among the Piedmontese was promptly stifled) the monarchical system gained a crushing advantage over the Liberal vanguard.

Within a few weeks the plans of years had been reduced to chaos. There ensued throughout Italy a period of savage repression and methodical proscription; Byron's Milanese acquaintance, the poet Silvio Pellico, and a number of his associates, had been condemned to the dreadful fortress of the Spielberg (where Pellico was to remain for several years); and the high tide of persecution swept through the Romagna. Naturally the Gambas were not excepted; and, during July, both father and son, together with many other of all ranks, known to have been attached to the patriot cause, received an order of immediate expulsion from the Papal domains. They were hurried from their homes without process, without hearing, without accusation. As to the exact circumstances surrounding their departure we are a little vague (since Byron knew that his post-bag was carefully scrutinised, and did not wish to incriminate them when he wrote to England) but no doubt it was as dramatic and moving as befitted the Italian temperament, and accompanied by tears and vows and protests of eternal loyalty. From Ravenna, the Gambas and Teresa moved to Florence. But Byron, though his reasons for remaining in the Romagna were no longer operative and presumably he had given some promise that he would rejoin his mistress, clung to his comfortable quarters in the Palazzo Guiccioli. Whether from a determination to annoy the local authorities, who had struck at the rich and powerful Englishman through his unfortunate Italian friends; from a willingness (which an English visitor[1] had already noted) to give Teresa the slip if ever an occasion offered; or indeed from his habitual dread of change and movement, complicated by the indolence of an exceedingly selfish man, he treated the authorities' wishes and his mistress's feelings with equal disregard. The Gambas had been expelled in July; not until the end of October, 1821 had Byron (amid "all the sweat, and dust, and blasphemy of an universal packing . . . It is awful work, this love," he was to write to Moore) braced himself to take a further turn on the romantic treadmill.

[1] Sir Humphry Davy, writing to Tom Moore.

Chapter 19

DURING the previous months he was neither particularly unhappy nor by any means inactive. The fifth Canto of *Don Juan* reached a triumphant conclusion; and, in addition to his English rendering of the Paolo and Francesca episode from Dante's *Inferno* and a translation of a part of Pulci's mock epic poem, *Morgante Maggiore*, he produced during the period of his stay at Ravenna no less than three tragedies, *Marino Faliero*, *Sardanapalus*, *The Two Foscari* (works of which he himself was extremely proud but which Murray's "back-shop synod" persisted in condemning), *Cain*, *Heaven and Earth*, a couple of trifling satires, *The Blues* and *The Irish Avatar* and—best of all perhaps—the admirable *Vision of Judgement*, a brilliant and concentrated essay in poetic diatribe. It seemed that he had reached the topmost curve of his strength and genius. Shelley, who visited him at his invitation during the month of August to discuss the awkward question of Allegra's future, was again overwhelmed by a generous conviction of Byron's greatness. "I despair of rivalling Lord Byron [he wrote from the Palazzo Guiccioli], as well I may . . ."; and, though he distrusted the critical system that Byron advocated and thought that he recognised its "pernicious effects" in *Marino Faliero*, he was enchanted by the fifth canto of *Don Juan*, which fulfilled, he admitted, "in a certain degree, what I have long preached of producing—something wholly new and relative to the age, and yet surpassingly beautiful."

Once again, Shelley lost confidence in his own abilities. He wrote nothing, he informed Peacock, and probably would write no more. "It offends me to see my name classed among those who have no name. . . . The cup is justly given to one only of an age; indeed, participation would make it worthless. . . ." Shelley reached Ravenna on the 7th of August; and that night and the small hours of the day that followed went by in incessant absorbing conversation which revolved around the problems of verse and politics. Byron talked easily, boldly, gaily, with the worldly bias to which he was always inclined in earnest company—Shelley with his habitual enthusiasm and fevered brilliance. But beneath the surface of their renewed intimacy there were dangerous depths still. Shelley noticed that the influence of Teresa Guiccioli had been soothing and steadying: Byron was "greatly improved in every respect—in genius, in temper, in moral issues, in health, in happiness": but the "canker of aristocracy" had not yet been eradicated; while "between two persons in our situation" (he wrote to Mary) lurked always "the demons of mistrust and pride." Nevertheless, the slight *malaise*, moral or intellectual, from which he found that in Byron's company there was no escape, did not prevent him enjoying his stay at the Palazzo Guiccioli or appreciating the odder aspects of the poet's life there. Byron's household appealed to his love of fantasy. Besides Fletcher, Lega Zambelli, the steward and man of business, and Tita the gondolier, "a fine fellow with a prodigious black beard," it consisted at the time of "ten horses, eight enormous dogs, three monkeys, five cats, an eagle, a crow, and a falcon; and all these, except the horses, walk about the house, which every now and then resounds with their unarbitrated quarrels. . . ." Having compiled this list for Mary's benefit, he opened his letter again to add that his "enumeration of the animals in this Circæan palace" turned out to be defective: on the grand staircase he had just encountered "five peacocks, two guinea-hens, and an Egyptian crane. I wonder who all these animals were, before they were changed into these shapes."

Byron, like a true enchanter, preferred night to day. He did not rise till the afternoon, when he met Shelley (who got up at twelve) for a belated breakfast; after which they sat in conversation till the hour of sunset and then galloped, from six to eight, through the surrounding pine forest. Sometimes they would dismount and, using a pumpkin as a target, try their hands at pistol-practice, an exercise in which Shelley was almost Byron's equal. Returned home, they would dine together and sit up talking throughout the night. In the antiquities of Ravenna, apart from the tomb of Dante and the Mausoleum of Theodoric, Shelley showed singularly little interest. Though his education was far more complete than that of Byron and his æsthetic susceptibilities on the whole more acutely developed, he regarded the monuments of Byzantine civilisation as debased relics of a degrading and degraded dogma, and observed that it seemed to have been "one of the first efforts of the Christian religion to destroy the power of producing beauty in art." This generalisation is not easy to reconcile with his worship of Dante; but neither in his loyalties nor in his antipathies had he ever been consistent; for to the rational and generous indignation that he felt against society Shelley added a strain of irrational prejudice which caused him to divide the whole world into persecutors and persecuted, with parents, monarchs and priests upon the one hand and himself, devoted and forlorn, invariably in the opposite camp. For such a view of the universe, as soon as it has been firmly established, circumstances have a knack of providing a constant supply of fresh material; and the comparative tranquillity of his stay with Byron was presently overclouded by a fresh exposure of human baseness. Around him, as had happened so often during the course of his wanderings, opened infernal perspectives of guilt and infamy.

The fault was Byron's. Exposed to the strange charm of Shelley's character, his distrust of Shelleyan principles rapidly melted away. There might be times when he was stiff and silent and would surround himself with the attributes of mysterious melancholy; but at other times—not always well chosen—he was recklessly talkative. No doubt it was in such a mood, obeying some vagrant impulse of friendship and affection that, with complete disregard of the promise he had given Hoppner, he informed his companion of the scandal disseminated by Elise Foggi. Naturally, he did not add that he himself, on first hearing of it, had concluded that it was "just like" his former friends. Shelley's immediate response was one of disgust and horror—not so much, however, at the suggestion that Claire might have been his mistress as at the imputation that he had ill-treated Mary and discarded the child. Writing off to Mary on the 7th of August, he explained that Byron had acquainted him with a circumstance that had shocked him exceedingly "because it exhibits a degree of desperate and wicked malice for which I am at a loss to account." His patience and philosophy (he declared) had been "put to a severe proof"; and it was with difficulty that he refrained "from seeking out some obscure hiding-place, where the countenance of man may never meet me more." He thereupon proceeded to repeat the story. "Imagine my despair of good! imagine how it is possible that one of so weak and sensitive a nature as mine can run further the gauntlet through this hellish society of man!" But the remedy he proposed was typically businesslike. Mary must at once write to Mrs. Hoppner, contradicting the whole monstrous fabrication, and forward her denial to him to be sent on to Venice. His letter reached Mary at Pisa on the 20th of August; and she sat down, shaken and miserable, to compose a counterblast.

Of the depth and genuineness of her distress there could be not the slightest question—or of the honesty of the devotion that bound her to her husband. Having declared that the story was generally false and in certain minor details (such as the circumstances supposed to have surrounded Claire's confinement) palpably inaccurate, she wrote that she was forwarding the letter to Shelley at Ravenna and wished that Lord Byron might also read it, since "though he gave no credit to the tale . . . it is as well that he should see how entirely fabulous it is." By Shelley, Mary's communication was promptly handed on to Byron, who "engaged to send it with his own comments to the Hoppners." Byron's position (Shelley admitted) was a trifle awkward, "for the Hoppners [he told Mary] had extracted from Lord Byron that these accusations should be concealed from *me*. Lord Byron is not a man to keep a secret, good or bad; but in openly confessing that he has not done so, he must observe some delicacy, and therefore wishes to send the letter himself. . . ". Whether Byron posted the letter or quietly suppressed it, preferring to save himself the embarrassment of further complications, is a problem on which the controversy may never end.

We know, at least, that Mary's letter was found after his death, with the seal broken, among Byron's private papers. Are we to assume that it did not leave him, or that, having been read by the Hoppners, it was returned to Byron? And, if returned, for what reason did the Hoppners send it back? A rather naïve suggestion has been advanced that Byron may have requested that they should return the document because he was anxious to have the refutation of a scandal that concerned the mother of Allegra safely within his hands. Were that hypothesis correct, it is odd that he himself, in his letters to the Consul, should have assented so enthusiastically to the Hoppners' attack on Claire. It is not impossible that Hoppner may have sent back the missive, accompanied by a note that Byron did not preserve (though he was an inveterate hoarder of the smallest written trifle); but it seems more probable that Mary's protest was never despatched to Venice—certainly from Mrs. Hoppner Mary never received a reply.[1] Byron was annoyed at being "caught out": he was bored and lazy. Shelley's magnanimity irked him: he was exasperated by what he considered his friend's strain of moral humbug.

Yet Shelley's good nature was, as usual, invoked. Would he not write to the Countess Guiccioli (whom he had never met) proposing that, instead of going to Switzerland with her father and brother as she was at present anxious to do, they should fix their place of exile, more conveniently, in Tuscany or Lucca? Shelley wrote: Teresa agreed—but wound up with a further commission for the unknown Mr. Shelley: *Non partire da Ravenna senza Milord*. Next, there was the question of Byron's establishment. Supposing that he should at length decide to leave Ravenna, Byron would need an unfurnished house, of opulent proportions. Poor Claire must not be in the immediate neighbourhood; and Shelley, therefore, was disinclined to think of Florence, but favoured Pisa, where English tourists were much less numerous and a society might be established which would include his friends, the Masons, and his newer and even dearer friends, Jane and Edward Williams. But Shelley's first object had been to discuss Allegra. The little girl was no longer at her father's house; for on her fifth birthday, January 13th, 1822, Byron had at length done what he had often announced that he intended to do, and put her in charge of the sisters of a neighbouring convent.

The institution selected was the Capucine convent of Bagnacavallo, twelve miles beyond Ravenna. On learning of Allegra's fate, Claire had again begun to bombard Byron with petitions and remonstrances and it was in his usual rôle of mediator, or friend-of-all-work, that Shelley had agreed to visit the Palazzo Guiccioli. Having discussed the question, he was obliged to admit that, grave as might be the

---

[1] In later years, Mary Shelley cut Mrs. Hoppner on meeting her with her daughter in the street. Reasons for supposing that Byron may possibly have forwarded Mary's letter are ably set forth by the editor of *Lord Byron's Correspondence*.

disadvantages of a Catholic upbringing, Byron's intentions were good, and the motives that influenced him not injudicious. Her father's house would be no place for the child in times of revolution. Besides, while Byron declared that she was growing beautiful, he indicated that she had her full share of the Byronic temperament and was too vain, obstinate and imperious for any servant to manage. Nor did his own household, composed as it was "entirely of dissolute menservants," provide the domestic background that Allegra needed; and, when Shelley had ridden over to see her at the convent, he reported that, although she had become "tall and slight for her age," and was "much paler, probably from the effect of improper food," she appeared happy enough, if quieter and more obedient. "She yet retains [he wrote to Mary] the beauty of her deep blue eyes and of her mouth"; but she had acquired in the last year "a contemplative seriousness" which, combined with her "excessive vivacity," was strange and touching. The rule of the place was strict but not tyrannical; and Allegra, "prettily dressed in white muslin, and an apron of black silk, with trousers, seemed a thing of a finer and higher order," among the other children. At first she had been shy; but, reassured by Shelley's gift of a gold chain he had bought in Ravenna and a basket of sweets, she had conducted him at breakneck speed all over the garden and convent, and had shown him her bed and her playthings and her chair at the dinner table. "I asked her what I should say from her to her mamma, and she said—

> '*Che mi manda un bacio e un bel vestituro.*'
> '*E come vuoi il vestituro sia fatto?*'
> '*Tutto di seta e d'oro.*'

Her predominant foible seems the love of distinction and vanity. . . . Before I went away, she made me run all over the convent like a mad thing. The nuns, who were half in bed, were ordered to hide themselves and, on returning Allegra began ringing the bell which calls the nuns to assemble. . . . It required all the efforts of the prioress to prevent the spouses of God to render themselves, dressed or undressed, to the accustomed signal. Nobody scolded her for these *scappaturi*, so I suppose that she is well treated as far as temper is concerned. Her intellect is not much cultivated. She knows certain *orazioni* by heart, and talks and *dreams* of Paradise and angels and all sorts of things, and has a prodigious list of saints, and is always talking of the Bambino. This will do her no harm, but the idea of bringing up so sweet a creature in the midst of such trash till sixteen!"

With these misgivings and this report, Shelley returned home towards the end of August. Byron had been anxious that he should prolong his stay, and Shelley, notwithstanding his distrust of Byron, felt that his visit to Ravenna had done him good. He returned, nevertheless, "*senza Milord.*" But it had been agreed that, as soon as Byron could prevail upon himself to leave Ravenna, he should come to Pisa, and that he should be joined there by Teresa Guiccioli and her father and brother. Teresa and the two Counts Gamba reached Pisa during the latter days of August. Mary, who had expected perhaps a second Fornarina, was agreeably surprised; for Teresa, she discovered, was neither bold nor dissolute, but pretty, pleasant, sentimental and unassuming. Together they sat down to expect the poet; and within seven or eight weeks, in lordly travelling style—accompanied by servants, saddle-horses and domestic animals, basketed birds, caged monkeys and dusty enormous dogs—he swept out of Ravenna and took the road to Bologna. At one point Byron's equipage crowded off the highway the public coach in which Miss Clairmont was travelling to Florence; and at Bologna by previous arrangement he met Samuel Rogers, the parchment faced, bald-headed banking poetaster with whom he passed a day at Bologna and crossed the Apennines. They had been friends in London: they were strangers in Italy. Rogers was notorious for his savage tongue; and Byron, who had not seen him since 1816 and feared perhaps that Rogers must find him altered—he had been out of touch so long with the London great world, where the other in due course would repeat his story, among the Lambs and at Holland House, in the clubs and drawing-rooms—made a reserved and, it would appear, an unfriendly travelling companion. Rogers was devoted to the cult of "picturesque"; Byron had no love of sights or scenery; and "if there was any scenery well worth seeing [lamented Rogers], he generally contrived that we should pass through it in the dark." On October 31st, every window of the hotel in Florence was flung open to see Byron and his attendants leave for Pisa. . . . Rogers symbolised London at its worst and worldliest. Far more important to Byron, and far more moving, had been an earlier encounter—on the road between Imola and Bologna; and, if Byron when he met Rogers seemed unusually overcast, it may well have been because his heart and his nerves were both disordered.

For a few minutes he had come face to face with the past he loved. Some weeks previously, in his journal of *Detached Thoughts*, the second of the two journals he had kept at Ravenna, Byron had included a note on his Harrow friendships—"with *me passions* (for I was always violent)"—adding that he did not know of "one which has endured (to be sure, some have been cut short by death). . . . That with Lord Clare began one of the earliest and lasted longest. . . ." It was the hazard of separation, not coldness, that had finally parted them: "I never hear the word '*Clare*' without a beating of the heart even *now*. . . ." Seven or eight years had gone by. Suddenly they met on an Italian high road: "It was a new and inexplicable feeling, like rising from the grave, to me. Clare, too [Byron wrote], was much agitated—*more* in appearance than even myself; for I could feel his heart beat to his fingers' ends, unless, indeed, it was the pulse of my own which made me think so. He told me that I should find a note from him, left at Bologna." Their encounter was very brief—it lasted in all five minutes; and, though we cannot tell what was said, probably it was little enough, for deep emotion made Byron shy and hesitating; but those five minutes left behind them an ineffaceable imprint—"I hardly recollect an hour of my existence which could be weighed against them." Clare was the past; Clare was youth; Byron's devotion to him had gone far deeper than his love of women, by whom his instinctive unreasoning puritanism was often offended; Clare represented the ideal amalgam of love and friendship. But Clare was bound south and Byron westwards. They said good-bye and set out again upon their different journeys.[1]

Arrived in Pisa, Byron moved into the Palazzo Lanfranchi. A massive and dignified Renaissance building with a ghost on the floors above, a labyrinth of underground chambers beneath the water-level, in which it pleased Byron occasionally to spend the night, and a façade said to have been designed by Michelangelo, it looked across the yellow turbulent flood of the Arno to a smaller pile, the Tre Palazzi di Chiesa, where the Shelleys and the Williamses had

---

[1] "My greatest friend, Lord Clare, is in Rome; we met on the road, and our meeting was quite sentimental—really pathetic on both sides. I have always loved him better than any *male* thing in the world." *Byron to Moore*, March 1st, 1822.

taken separate flats. Byron's accommodation was suitably magnificent. Less to his taste, however, was the côterie he found expecting him. Of the second-rate, Shelley himself was always nobly tolerant: his personality was a lamp that attracted many curious insects which clustered in the light of genius. Not so Byron, more snobbish and more irritable, with fewer enthusiasms and a smaller fund of emotional gullibility. It was hardly to be expected that Lady Mountcashell would much amuse him—middle-aged, raw-boned and "democratical"—or Mr. Tighe, her retiring and bookish consort. In addition to the "Masons" and the Shelleys, there were also the Williamses—Edward Williams, a half-pay soldier of literary pretensions who was living with the deserted wife of a fellow cavalry officer, Jane, an unusually attractive woman with a pleasant singing voice. Other intimates were "Count" Taafe,[1] an eccentric Irish wanderer, and Tom Medwin, Shelley's cousin, that "perplexing simpleton," who wrote verse-tragedies which it fell to Shelley's lot to read and criticise. Then, in January, a new enthusiast joined the Shelley circle, a romantic, untrustworthy, mysterious personage, the former freebooter and professional adventurer, Edward John Trelawny.

Few men have been privileged more completely to look the part he played. A fine hawk-like nose, dark eyes—perhaps a little too close together—cold, shining and expressionless as those of a bird of prey, heavy bristling eyebrows and black moustaches, combined to make Trelawny the perfect image of a romantic hero. Had he stepped straight from the dream world of the *Corsair* or *Giaour*? As befitted his appearance, Trelawny's early life was enveloped in deep obscurity, and even to-day the cloud that covered it has not been dissipated. We know that he came of ancient Cornish stock: that he had hated his father, a ferocious despot: that he joined the Navy as a boy: deserted at Bombay after thrashing a superior officer, and had shipped with a privateer in the French service named Senouf or de Witt: and that in 1813 he had returned to England and contracted an unhappy marriage. So much at least it seems permissible to deduce

[1] John Taafe, described by Byron as "a very good man, with a great desire to see himself in print," was the author of a voluminous *Commentary on Dante*, which the poet endeavoured to persuade Murray to publish. "It will make the man so exuberantly happy. . . . we must give him a shove through the press . . . Besides he has had another fall from his horse into a ditch the other day. . . ."

from that strange mixture of distorted or magnified fact and melo-dramatic fantasy later published as *The Adventures of a Younger Son*. Though not an accurate record of the author's life, Trelawny's autobiography is a faithful impression of his personal temperament. Of such stuff are made soldiers of fortune, patriot guerilla leaders, sometimes great criminals. Trelawny was a man of passionate enthusiasms, strong appetites, fierce and lasting hatreds. He was also an inveterate, if not always a deliberate liar.

Engaging he might be: reliable or strictly honest at no time could Trelawny have ever seemed. Yet in one respect his mind was constant. For Shelley he had a jealous and protective love, compounded of a certain pity for Shelley's weakness, real attraction towards the central integrity of Shelley's nature, and a naïve confused appreciation of the poet's genius. In Switzerland he had been captivated by a chance reading of *Queen Mab*; and, when he reached Pisa on his way to shoot wild fowl in the marshes of the Maremma, he made haste to visit his friends, the Williamses. That they were Shelley's house-mates he already knew: but he was not prepared for the juvenile oddity of Shelley's looks. Across the threshold, from the shadows of the door where he had been lurking, until he was lured forth by Jane Williams with the reassuring exclamation: "Come in, Shelley, it's only our friend Tre . . . ," glided a tall slight adolescent figure, "habited like a boy, in a black jacket and trowsers," both garments shrunken and far too small for him. Blushing and embarrassed, he held out his hand. Only when Jane Williams, to relieve the awkward-ness, asked the name and nature of the book he carried, did his face clear and his utterance grow bold and lively, as he talked of the play by Calderon of which he was translating fragments. There followed a silence. Trelawny raised his eyes. The poet was gone again. "Where is he?" Trelawny demanded. "Who? Shelley!" said Mrs. Williams. "Oh, he comes and goes like a spirit, no one knows when or where."

It was not Trelawny's habit to lose the chance of improving an anecdote. No doubt the celebrated account of his meeting with Shelley, and of his call next day on Byron at the Palazzo Lanfranchi, were touched up in many details by the writer's dramatic sense; but they are too close to other existing records to be entirely fabulous. In both stories the bias is fairly evident. Almost from the first moment, Shelley's apparition was enspiriting and delightful; from the beginning his relations with Byron were far less easy. Shelley might disappear and appear at pleasure: Byron must be approached—and approached with circumspection. Escorted by Shelley, he ascended a gigantic staircase, passed through a spacious apartment above the hall and entered a smaller room containing books and a billiard table. Here they were welcomed by the growls of Moretto, the bulldog, which Byron posted to warn him of intruders' presence; and almost immediately its master joined them. His lameness was perceptible, but his step was quick; and though he was exceedingly pale—with the "moonlight pallor" so much admired by women—his whole appearance was "fresh, vigorous and animated." As an athlete, Trelawny admired his broad shoulders, compact well-proportioned body, "small highly finished head and curly hair." In person, his life at Ravenna had much improved him; the grossness of his Venetian period had dropped away; and there was not "a stain or furrow" on his transparent skin. As for his dress—that struck Trelawny as by no means singular: a blue velvet cap with a gold band, a braided tartan jacket ("he said it was the Gordon pattern," explaining that on his mother's side he belonged to the Gordon clan) and loose nankeen trousers carefully strapped down to conceal his feet. His manners, on the other hand, were decidedly disconcerting; for it was obvious that the great poet was extremely shy and did his best to conceal his embarrassment beneath an air of flippancy, the devil-may-care detachment of a Regency man of the world. In a light off-handed fashion, he asked for Shelley's advice on "the versicles I was delivered of last night, or rather this morning," and suggested that he and Trelawny should try a game of billiards.

Having once regained his composure, he began to talk; and his mode of talk was as unexpected as his former shyness. On and on, while he limped briskly around the table, flowed the stream of gossip and anecdote and chit-chat: "Old Bathurst" in whose frigate he had sailed to Greece: wigs and what he meant to do when he was obliged to wear one: the already hackneyed tale of how he had swum the Hellespont. Shelley's reappearance brought a different atmosphere; "he never laid aside his book and magic mantle; he waved his wand, and Byron, after a faint show of defiance, stood mute; his quick perception of the truth of Shelley's comments on his poem transfixed him. . . ." Trelawny was impressed, at the same time, by "Byron's

mental vivacity and wonderful memory; he defended himself with
a wealth of illustrations, precedents, and apt quotations from
modern authorities, disputing Shelley's propositions, not by denying
their truth as a whole, but in parts, and the subtle questions he put
would have puzzled a less acute reasoner than the one he had to
contend with." Towards his companion Byron's attitude was gay
and friendly, respectful and even deferential in questions of literary
judgment, on worldly subjects provocative and slightly teasing. His
nickname for Shelley (Trelawny discovered) was now The Snake:
Shelley reminded him (he said) of a serpent that walked on the tip of
its tail—so strange and rapid were his movements, so remote his
habits—glistening, ubiquitous and hard to capture. "I go on
[Shelley declared] till I am stopped: and I never am stopped." To
Byron's passivity and earth-bound fatalism there could have been
no sharper contrast.

Those characteristics were soon to appear, under their most
disastrous guise. The Shelleys had expected that, if he left Ravenna,
his daughter would accompany him; and, when he arrived alone,
they felt that Allegra had been deserted. Byron, however, was
reluctant to change his plans; and it is easy to understand, if not to
excuse, his obstinacy. On the whole, he felt that his behaviour had
done him credit. Again and again, to the Shelleys and to his friends
in England, he had expressed his intention of providing handsomely
for his natural daughter. He would see that she married well and
was properly educated—in the Catholic religion,[1] since it was the
faith he liked best; and now, when he had placed her in a decent
convent where some of the first families of the Romagna were glad
to board their offspring, it was intolerable that he should be thus
beleaguered and reproved and bothered. Claire's imprecations
merely increased his stubbornness; while the knowledge that the
entire Pisan circle were unanimous in their disapproval—Mr. Tighe
had made a personal visit to the convent of Bagnacavallo, and reported it unhealthy and damp and chilly: Claire wished Shelley to
challenge Byron, and implored her friends to rescue Allegra by force
of arms—merely helped to confirm him in the cynical and careless

[1] "I am no enemy to religion, but the contrary. As a proof I am educating my natural
daughter a strict Catholic in a convent of Romagna; for I think people can never have
enough of religion, if they are to have any." *Byron to Moore*, March 4th, 1822.

line that he had at first adopted. To Shelley's remonstrances he smiled and shrugged, until Shelley said that he had been tempted to knock him down. But Shelley held his hand; and nothing was done and nothing decided. Allegra remained at her cold and unhealthy convent. Then an epidemic rose from the Romagnol marshes and approached the convent walls. The good sisters took no steps to warn Allegra's guardians. Fever broke out, and on April 20th, ·1822, Allegra died.

Thus, at the age of five years and three months, expired the second (or possibly the third) of Byron's daughters, a queer, self-willed, vain, impressionable, nervous child, Mrs. Hoppner's difficult charge, the spoiled plaything of the Fornarina and Teresa Guiccioli. Byron had been carelessly and casually fond of her—never more so than when in her beauty and natural obstinacy he thought he recognised a resemblance to himself; but news of her death struck him a violent and numbing blow. Once again death was abroad in his immediate neighbourhood. All Byrons were ill-fated: most were short-lived. His first response, then, was acquiescent and even apathetic. "I do not know [he wrote to Shelley on April 23rd] that I have anything to reproach in my conduct, and certainly nothing in my feelings and intentions towards the dead. But it is a moment when we are apt to think that, if this or that had been done, such event might have been prevented—though every day and hour shows us that they are the most natural and inevitable. I suppose that Time will do his usual work. . . ." "A long letter from Lord Byron to-day [recorded Tom Moore in his diary, under June 21st]: he has lost his little natural daughter . . . and seems to feel it a good deal. When I was at Venice, he said, in showing me this child, 'I suppose you have some notion of what they call the parental feeling, but I confess I have not; this little thing amuses me, but that's all.' . . . Evidently . . . he feels much more naturally than he will allow."

Other troubles had preceded the news of Allegra's death. Already, after two or three months at Pisa, Byron's household was in bad odour with the ducal police, and the threat of banishment was again hovering over Teresa's family. Here, as at Ravenna, Metternich's spy-system was omnipresent; and it was hardly to be wondered at that the arrival of a famous modern poet, reputed to be mad, rich, revolutionary and atheistical, who was accompanied by a train of carriages and a horde of servants and carried on a regular and voluminous correspondence with foreign countries, should have been regarded with some suspicion by the established government. From Florence the local police received a reassuring report that the authorities were "well aware that Byron goes to Pisa solely for the beautiful daughter of Count Gamba," whose permit to reside at Pisa was in due course to be renewed. But Byron's own behaviour was more disturbing. Soon after his arrival he made through Lega Zambelli a request that he should be given leave to practise pistol-shooting in the gardens of the Palazzo Lanfranchi—a request that, since it was forbidden to carry arms, the governor of the town, the Marchese Niccolo Viviani, was obliged to decline in a categorical though courteous fashion. Secondly—an example of the faculty that certain characters have always possessed of incurring publicly while appearing to shun it—Byron commissioned Mr. Taafe to wait on the Grand Duke and beg his Highness to excuse him from paying his respects, his reason being that, as he had not yet been presented to any other of the reigning princes of Italy, it would be improper to make an exception for the Grand Duke Ferdinand. Finally, Byron's Italian servants were wild and quarrelsome. When they swaggered the streets, they had all the appearance of a private bodyguard.

For a time, however, the police, though they watched Byron carefully, could find little to complain of in his mode of conduct. But "at length [wrote the Cavaliere Torelli, a secret agent who reported directly to the Austrian Chancellor] Lord Byron, with his company of assassins, gave us a taste of the temper he had shown in other places." On the evening of March 22nd, a certain Sergeant-Major Masi, who had been dining in the country, was riding back towards Pisa whither his duties had recalled him. Not far from the gates of the city, he found that the road was blocked. Byron, accompanied by Pietro Gamba, Shelley, Trelawny, John Taafe and a Captain Hay, their servants and Teresa in her carriage, was riding in the same direction just ahead. As they did not make way, Masi endeavoured to push through. Taafe was a timid and incompetent rider. His horse shied and he lost his hat: whereupon, no doubt to cover his confusion, he called out to the others that he had been insulted. Immediately the English party rode forward, overtook Masi and demanded an apology; while Byron, who thought that he was an officer, pulled out his card. As the procession rolled on through the dust towards the city gates, tempers grew more explosive and voices higher; and, when the gates were reached, an attempt was made to arrest the Englishmen. Shelley tumbled from his saddle, struck by the flat of a sword; Captain Hay was wounded in the nose, endeavouring to parry a blow; Byron put spurs to his mount and gained the palace.

At once the Lung' Arno resounded with shouts and hoof-beats. Dismounting at the door of the Palazzo Lanfranchi, Byron hastened upstairs to call his steward, then descended and was returning to join his companions, when he encountered again the now thoroughly distracted soldier. Tita, who had the post of doorman, rushed from the palace and seized Masi's bridle. Byron ordered him to desist; but in the shindy that followed the Sergeant-Major was stabbed by one of the Gambas' servants. His helmet off, pale as a corpse, "his terrible face made more fearful by a mass of flaming red hair" which (according to an onlooker who described the incident many years afterwards) bristled upright on his head, Masi collapsed at the threshold of "Don Beppe's Caffé." Luckily, his wound, though serious, proved not fatal; and the governor took an indulgent view of the whole absurd affair. But Tita was arrested and ordered to shave off his beard,[1] since beards and whiskers were an indication of revolutionary sympathies; and a Gamba footman, suspected of delivering the blow, was also apprehended. The subsequent proceedings were long-drawn and inconclusive; but it was meanwhile signified to the Gambas that they would do well to leave the city.

During April, therefore, Byron took a villa belonging to the banker Dupuy at Montenero near Leghorn; and thither the two unfortunate Counts presently departed. Himself he was in no hurry to say good-bye to Pisa. He liked his life there. More important, it had become a habit; and habit was a drug to which he had always been addicted. Every day he would emerge from his bedchamber at one or two o'clock, breakfasting usually off "a cup of strong green tea, without milk or sugar," and an egg of which he devoured the yolk

---

[1] Tita was imprisoned for a time in Florence. "There [writes the police spy] he was ordered to shave off his long Asiatic beard. At first he thought it was to be given to his master, Lord Byron. But when he found that this was not the case, he wrapped up the hair very carefully in a sheet of paper."

raw. Medwin, Trelawny or Shelley was often in attendance; and when Medwin admired the abstemiousness of his meal, Byron would explain that his digestion was weak, that he was too bilious to eat more than once a day, and that just now he was living on claret and soda water. Next he petted his monkey or proposed a game of billiards; which continued until the horses and the carriage were ready. They were "very ordinary-looking horses," observed Trelawny, who, among his accomplishments, considered himself a judge of horse flesh; but "they had holsters on the saddles, and many other superfluous trappings, such as the Italians delight in, and Englishmen eschew." Byron did not mount before they had cleared the city—to avoid, he said, being stared at by the damned British tourists; and "after an hour or two of slow riding and lively talk— for he was generally in good spirits when on horseback—we stopped at a small *podere* on the roadside, and dismounting went into the house, in which we found wine and cakes. From thence we proceeded into the vineyard at the back. . . ." Pistols were produced and a five-paul piece, the size of a half-crown, was fixed as a mark in a split cane at a distance of fifteen paces. Byron's hand trembled but he was a practised shot. Each fired five or six bullets. Byron "pocketed the battered money and sauntered about the grounds." Evening fell; and they trotted slowly home down the road to Pisa.

At that distance, the prospect was unreal and enchanting. "With its hanging tower and Sophia-like dome," Pisa reminded Byron of an eastern city; and through the heavy smoke that drifted away from its roofs and ramparts appeared the massive configuration of golden evening clouds. Fine, said Byron, though not so fine as Venetian sunsets. "Ask Shelley." But Shelley, in his shrill, discordant, ecstatic voice, spoke with enthusiasm of the view from the Ponte Vecchio, when the river seemed on fire with the rays of the declining sun and "the graceful curve of the palaces," along its banks came to a full stop with the so-called dungeon-tower of Ugolino, which stood up solid and dark against the western sky. At the door of the Palazzo Lanfranchi, the party would disband. "It is impossible [declared Medwin] to conceive a more unvaried life than Lord Byron led at this period." His conversation, if not monotonous, was by no means various; and to an observer, who, like Trelawny, came fresh from England, it was clear that he lived on the memories of an earlier age. His talk was "anything but literary" except when Shelley was near him, "but seasoned with anecdotes of the great actors on and off the stage, boxers, gamblers, duellists, drunkards, etc., etc.," and embellished with slang and scandal that he alone remembered. Now and then, he would become conscious of his years of exile, aware that slang may alter and conventions change; and at such times he was particularly reluctant to join an English gathering and would fall back on the unpolished Trelawny for social guidance. "Does rank lead the way [he was anxious to learn], or does the ambassadress pair us off into the dining-room? Do they ask people to wine? Do we exit with the women, or stick to our claret?"

Worse was the suspicion that he might be losing his vogue. At Pisa, as at Ravenna, his days were desultory, and his evenings devoted to love and small talk; but the hours of darkness were busily occupied, often until dawn appeared. More and more he was possessed by a rage for writing; but much of the verse he produced is extremely uneven. His blank-verse dramas make particularly difficult reading. Yet these were the works on which Byron himself believed that his poetic reputation would eventually rest. Murray did not agree; and it presently occurred to Byron, when he noticed the reluctance his publisher showed to send his manuscripts to the printers the moment he delivered them, that, from Murray's point of view, he might perhaps be becoming a somewhat dubious commercial asset. But the row over *Cain* was at least encouraging; he had not forfeited his power to shock the public. That ponderous Biblical melodrama had produced a violent controversy; and, while Anglican clergymen thundered against the play, Lady Granville, an old acquaintance and offspring of "the Devonshire House set," informed a correspondent that she found it "most wicked," but confessed that hearing her husband read it aloud had reduced her to a paroxysm of helpless weeping and that she had "roared" until she could "neither hear nor see." Shelley and the aged Goethe both praised it warmly. Yet Murray still refused to admire its companion works; and Byron's mood grew more petulant as the year proceeded. If Mr. Murray had ceased to appreciate him, he would take his poems elsewhere.

Both his temper and his literary judgment suffered. Already, during the autumn of 1821, he had allowed his critical sense to be overridden by the claims of sentiment, and had promised Teresa that he would drop *Don Juan*. None of his poems had been composed with greater gusto; none of them had delighted him more; but the majority of two feminine readers thought the work "abominable." The resentment it aroused had at first diverted him. In these protests Teresa Guiccioli was not alone; and, soon after the appearance of the opening cantos, while he was still established at Ravenna, he had received a long scrawl signed by the notorious courtesan Harriette Wilson, whom he had once met at the zenith of her fame and fortune:

"Dear *Adorable* Lord Byron [wrote Harriette at 'exactly 20 minutes past 12 o'clock at night' from 64 Rue Neuve des petits Champs, whither she had retired since the failure of her attempt to marry Lord Worcester], *don't* make a mere coarse old Libertine of yourself. . . . When you don't feel quite up to a spirit of benevolence . . . in *gratitude* for the talent which after all must have caused you exquisite moments in your life, throw away your pen my love & take a little *calomel*. . . . Ecoutez mon Ange. It is not in my power or in my nature to forget any kindness shown me[1] (supposing I had not half loved you before) but I would not even to *you*, who in a wrong headed moment wrote it, lie under the imputation of such bad taste as to admire what in your cool moments you must feel to be *vulgar* at least and half destroys the effect of the most delicious beautiful poetry you ever wrote in your life. . . ." More sentimentally, Teresa expressed a similar prejudice—*Don Juan* was the literary antithesis of her private emotional creed; and Byron had been cajoled or blackmailed into complete surrender. In 1822, he obtained her permission to embark on the concluding cantos; but it was understood they were to be in a less immoral and a more romantic strain.

In Shelley's career such an influence was never operative. Painful and honest as were the feelings of diffidence that often overwhelmed him, wild and apparently haphazard as was the course he followed, he still rushed ahead, obeying his own convictions and propelled by his own velocity. But, though faith was not yet extinct, of hope he had little enough. Trelawny, with the anxious eyes of a new admirer, observed how careless was his hold on life, and how often and

---

[1] This letter—the last of several—had been preceded by a request for money: which Byron had gratified to the extent of a thousand francs.

eagerly he was apt to revert to the idea of suicide. Thus, when Trelawny, after "performing a series of aquatic gymnastics" in a deep pool of the Arno, suggested that Shelley would find it easy to swim, the poet plunged from the bank but immediately sank to the bottom, where he lay on the river bed extended "like a conger eel, not making the least effort or struggle to save himself. He would have been drowned if I had not instantly fished him out. When he recovered his breath, he said, 'I always find the bottom of the well, and they say Truth lies there. In another minute I should have found it. . . . It is an easy way of getting rid of the body.' " But "Don't tell Mary," he added, "—not a word!" On a later occasion, he begged Trelawny, who was visiting Leghorn, to procure him, if he should meet with any scientific person capable of preparing it, a small quantity of "the *Prussic Acid or essential oil of bitter almonds.* '. . . I would give any price for this medicine; you remember we talked of it the other night, and we both expressed a wish to possess it; my wish was serious, and sprung from the desire of avoiding needless suffering. I need not tell you I have no intention of suicide at present, but I confess it would be a comfort to me to hold in my possession that golden key to the chamber of perpetual rest. . . . A single drop, even less, is a dose, and it acts by paralysis.' "

His habits were as solitary and elusive as Byron's were unvaried. Once Trelawny pursued him into the depths of the Cascine forest. Mary Shelley, who had started out on the expedition, was presently defeated: "the loose sand and hot sun soon knocked her up"; but Trelawny skirted the forest and reached the sea, then turned back into the thickest shades of the pinewoods, shouting the poet's name as he wandered among stagnant meres from which herons rose flapping across the heavy silence. After a time he met an old peasant who was gathering pine cones and volunteered to show him that part of the accursed wood in which *l'inglese malinconico* was usually to be discovered. Beside a deep pool of dark glimmering water lay hat, books and scattered leaves of manuscript. "*Eccolo!*" said the old man; and for a second Trelawny supposed that he meant to indicate that Shelley was even now beneath the surface; for "the careless, not to say, impatient way in which the Poet bore his burden of life, caused a vague dread among his family and friends that he might lose or cast it away at any moment." But soon he caught sight of

him under the lee of a fallen trunk. When Shelley was called, he
turned his head; and, Trelawny having explained that Mary awaited
them, "Poor Mary!" he ejaculated, as he started to his feet and
bundled his books and manuscripts together into his hat and pockets,
"hers is a sad fate. Come along; she can't bear solitude, nor I society
—the quick coupled with the dead."

According to Trelawny, whose word at this and at every other
juncture can be accepted only with reservations, the manuscript that
lay scattered among the pine needles, beside the edition of Æschylus
and a volume of Shakespeare's plays, contained a rough draft,
scrawled and corrected and irascibly finger-smudged, of the celebrated verses on a musical instrument:

> *Ariel to Miranda:—Take*
> *This slave of Music, for the sake*
> *Of him who is the slave of thee.* . . .

Jane Williams was the Miranda to whom he addressed those lines, in
his emotional firmament the star that had followed Emilia Viviani,
the fascinating deceptive heroine of *Epipsychidion*, just as Emilia had
followed Sophia Stacey, and Sophia herself had succeeded to a galaxy
of earlier lights. Again, we meet the contrasted problems of Byron's
and of Shelley's character. Was Byron demonic, and Shelley angelic?
But, if Byron glowed with a dark destructive energy, hurtful to
himself and sometimes fatal to others, it must be allowed that angels
very often make dangerous house companions. They are dangerous,
that is to say, because, lacking the earthly virtues of common sense,
they wave their wings and scatter their gifts a trifle indiscriminately,
for the sheer joy of exercising their heavenly office. It is an angel's
business to love, and love he must. He does not remember that the
value of love depends to a very large extent upon the attention and
delicacy with which it is placed, and that love seriously misplaced
may be worse than hatred. Love can demoralise more quickly than
loathing. It gives trivial objects an importance they cannot sustain,
lifts weak spirits to an altitude from which they are bound to tumble,
envelops a Harriet and throws her at last into the suicide's graveyard.
Shelley believed in love with an abstract fervour. The sentiment
provided its own nobility and its own excuse.

The passion of love may be abstract: its results are concrete. A
Byronic rake, less concerned with theory than with practice, is

sometimes more merciful than a Shelleyan idealist—at least, the wounds he inflicts are more easily curable; and he embarks on each new adventure with wide-open eyes. In the first delirious trance of a new enthusiasm, Shelley was incapable of distinguishing the features of the person he loved; but that enthusiastic obliquity could not last for ever. From repeated disillusionments he learned little or nothing; and the fact that the heroine of *Epipsychidion* might afterwards turn out to be cold, conventional and calculating merely strengthened his belief that he was the victim of tyranny, and that the personified forces of Custom and Prejudice still rose to frustrate and harry him at every turn. And then, regarding the nature of love itself, Shelley's views were frequently somewhat hazy. Like all idealists who have contracted the insidious habit of discussing philosophy late into the night with attractive and susceptible young women, long after their wives had gone exhausted to bed, Shelley seems not always to have been very clear when philosophy withdrew from the field and passion replaced it. He was passionate; one may surmise that he was normally sensual. Whatever the exact colouring of his relationship with Claire Clairmont (who certainly advocated a community of wives and husbands) there is no doubt of the quality of his feeling for Jane Williams, and almost as little doubt that the heavenly love affair reached an earthly conclusion. At times the enthusiast's wife grew restive and miserable. Even the daughter of Mary Wollstonecraft was not proof against jealousy.

A regular social position, she had begun to understand, might produce positive benefits. Brought up in the dismal bohemianism of Godwin's household, swept as a young girl into Shelley's orbit and by him hurried through a succession of alien cities where sickness and weariness lay in wait for herself, and death for her children, Mary was already wearying of the rôle allotted her. Shelley had insufficient cynicism to be an acute psychologist. Well might he, with raised voice and pathetically extended arms, exclaim on the strange perversity of Byron's principles: "I do believe, Mary"—pausing as if reluctant to expose a friend—"I do believe, Mary, that he is little better than a Christian!" Mary's own unorthodoxy was somewhat suspect; and the worst happened when she threatened to give a party. It was to be a musical gathering, her husband informed Jane Williams: "there are English singers here, the Sinclairs, and she will ask them, and every one she or you know—oh, the horror!" By much diplomacy, Mary was persuaded to curtail her project and limit the guests to a few of their most intimate friends and some of the Gamba family; but it was clear that her high-minded independence was being gradually worn down. "Mary [Shelley concluded] is under the dominion of the mythical monster 'Everybody.' I tell her I am one of the Nobodies." But the shadow of the mythical monster was lengthening across Mary's spirit.

Hers was a limited mind and an inelastic nature. There was a hint of primness in those grey eyes and in that small but definite mouth; and it is a tribute to Mary's gift for devotion that she continued to bear with Shelley even when his moods and vagaries were most exasperating. During the latter part of April, soon after Allegra's death, the Shelleys moved at a few days' notice from their lodgings in Pisa, where Mary had been making tentative advances to the conventional English colony, and bundled themselves with Jane and Edward into a desolate seaside house, which Trelawny and Williams had discovered near Lerici on the gulf of Spezia. Their reason for making this sudden move was the necessity of breaking the news of her daughter's death to Claire Clairmont at a place where there was no immediate likelihood of seeing Byron; but it was also in accordance with a long established plan. Since early spring, Byron and Shelley had both been boat-owners; for, under Trelawny's influence, they had commissioned his friend Captain Roberts of the Royal Navy to construct them two craft in the shipyards of Genoa. By May, Shelley's boat, the *Ariel*, thirty feet in length and undecked, was delivered at Lerici; while Byron's yacht, the *Bolivar*, was ready a month later. Trelawny had been appointed captain of the *Bolivar*, which he pronounced to be fast and seaworthy and easy to handle; but regarding the other boat, constructed according to specifications Williams had brought out from England, he claimed afterwards to have been much less optimistic. "Fast, strongly built, and Torbay rigged," she was reported to be "a ticklish boat to manage"; and it had required "two tons of iron ballast to bring her down to her bearings." But Williams, who believed that he was a judge of boats, would hear no ill of her; and Shelley looked for unlimited delight from this new and romantic toy.

He was enchanted, moreover, with the house at Lerici. Nearer to the waves than any house he had yet inhabited, it was a plain two-storeyed building with an arcaded ground floor planted almost in the water. Above were a room for the Shelleys and a room for the Williamses divided by a passage. Otherwise it had few comforts; and when the sirocco blew up, as it did soon after their arrival, sheets of foam were flung against the white-washed housefront; the wind howled and the breakers crashed; and its shivering inhabitants imagined themselves passengers in a ship at sea. Then suddenly the storm would fall; and at their feet stretched the waters of the bay, smooth, tideless, radiant, enclosed to the east by the old castle of Lerici, to the west by the distant shape of Porta Venere. Behind Casa Magni ran up a precipitous hillside fledged with young trees, planted by the eccentric owner of the estate who had destroyed the olive yards to make way for his plantations and built the unfinished and now half-ruined house that crowned the summit. A rough and winding footpath lead to Lerici; but the country was trackless upon the other side; and the neighbouring peasants seemed as wild as the rocks they lived among. When the nights were hot they would frolic in the water, men, women and children, dancing and singing the refrain of loud and discordant ballads. Housekeeping, complained Mary, was extremely difficult: they could not have been more isolated had they been shipwrecked sailors. But Shelley with his passion for sea and solitude, and the passion for sympathy and beauty that fed on the sight of Jane, lived in a halcyon world of sensation and imagination, where Mary and the influence of her mythical monster could rarely penetrate.

This summer he would sail—and the scope of the voyages on which he intended to embark with Williams grew steadily more and more ambitious; but, before the summer was over, he expected Leigh Hunt and, with Byron's help, would strike a fresh blow in the cause of freedom. During the previous August, he had spoken to Byron of Leigh Hunt's plight, explaining that Hunt had been in poor health since his release from prison (where he had passed two years of not uncomfortable confinement after a particularly ferocious attack upon the present sovereign) and that he needed rest and sunshine and relief from financial cares. As a matter of course, Mrs. Hunt had invoked Shelley's assistance; and, during his stay at Ravenna, Shelley proposed that Hunt should be invited to Italy, and that the three of them should join forces in editing a liberal magazine. Byron liked the project and had promised to support the paper. With Hunt himself he had already some slight acquaintance; for he had visited him on several occasions at the Surrey Gaol and been received in the trellised, painted and flower-filled sitting-room into which Hunt had metamorphosed his prison chamber. Subsequently, he had called on him at his suburban lodgings. With gratitude, Hunt remembered the brisk, well-built, curly-headed young man, who would enter the room, carrying a couple of quartos that he hoped might provide hints for the *Story of Rimini*, or sit astride the children's rocking horse as he talked of literature. During his later visits, Lady Byron would remain below in the carriage; and, although Byron's expression was "not unmixed with disquiet,"—an effect presumably of the domestic trials he was then undergoing—"the turn of his head and countenance" was bold and spirited. "His dress, which was black, with white trowsers, and which he wore buttoned close over the body, completed the succinctness and gentlemanliness of his appearance."

He would find the democrat (Byron informed Trelawny) notwithstanding a taint of cockneyism that he owed to his Hampstead circle, unmistakably "a gentleman in dress and address." The idea of assisting Hunt appealed to his good-nature, though he knew that it might alarm Murray and infuriate Hobhouse; and he liked the idea that he would have a controlling voice on an important Liberal journal. To wield such influence would be a substitute for a career of action. Meanwhile, life at Pisa was calm and easy. Rogers reappeared, accompanied him when he rode out in the afternoons and was amused to note, on the face of a peasant girl said to be Byron's favourite, a look of pleasure and dignity as they passed her by. Early in June the poet removed to Leghorn. Described by Trelawny as a "new, flimsy-built villa—not unlike the suburban verandahed cockney boxes on the Thames"—Montenero proved "ten times hotter than the old solid palace he had left, with its cool marble halls, and arched and lofty floors. . . ." At this house he was delighted to be able to welcome Lord Clare, who paused briefly at Leghorn on his way back to England; and Teresa Guiccioli, in one of the more vivid passages of her otherwise almost unreadable memoirs, records the intense satisfaction with which Byron received his friend and the gloomy premonitions with which he saw him go.[1] For such companionship the society of the Gambas was indeed a poor exchange. He was attached to, but often exasperated by, Teresa's father and brother, that amiable, dignified yet incurably ineffective pair, who now regarded him as one of the family circle, with a relation's responsibility towards his helpless kinsmen. Either they would not, or they could not, control their servants; and the tranquil course of existence at Montenero—in spite of Trelawny's strictures, a pleasant enough seaside house, which looked out towards the islands of Elba and Corsica, across the dense or shimmering blue of the Mediterranean seascape—was presently interrupted by a succession of violent quarrels. Already suspicious of the household at Montenero, the authorities scored a further black mark against the Byron and Gamba names.

Very different was the atmosphere of Casa Magni. Like some strange aquatic creature that had never learned to swim, Shelley passed his days in or near the water, either helping Williams to sail the *Ariel*, which he did in a manner equally brave and inexpert, or alone at the oars of the light flat-bottomed dingy that Williams had constructed. This flimsy craft he would scull out to sea—"he felt independent [he said] and safe from land bores"; then let it drift with the current, till a rising breeze sent waves lapping over the gunwale and, slowly and regretfully, he was wafted to land again. As he disembarked, he would sometimes miss his footing and enter the house, leaving a puddle at every step, refreshed and radiant, his thick hair matted with sand and sea-salt. Once at least he distressed Mary by returning naked from a bathe, and in that condition gliding swiftly through the common dining-room where the party, which included a literary visitor, were all assembled. Jane Williams was still the emotional pivot around which his life revolved; and at night he would listen to her while she sang and played, or submit to experiments in what he believed to be "animal magnetism." Her hands on his forehead he found deeply soothing; but the old nervous troubles and the familiar hallucinations did not grow less persistent.

[1] "Lord Clare's visit also occasioned him extreme delight.... The day on which they separated was a melancholy one for Lord Byron. 'I have a presentiment that I shall never see him more,' he said, and his eyes filled with tears. The same melancholy came over him during the first weeks that succeeded to Lord Clare's departure whenever his conversation happened to fall upon this friend."

Byron in Italy

Between Shelley's nightmares and those of Byron there is a curious parallel; but whereas Byron's, from which he awoke sick and shaken and terrified, giving no hint of the experiences he had undergone, suggest the tormented dreams of an earth-bound giant, pinned under a rocky weight of fearful memories, Shelley's visitations seemed to explode from above like an Alpine thunderstorm. Late on a stormy night Jane Williams was aroused by a "weight . . . falling against her door and moaning." When Williams opened the door, "Mrs. Shelley, in her nightdress, tumbled into their room, helpless and tongue-tied by terror. The Poet, unconscious of everything, his eyes wide open . . . stood over her, upright and motionless, holding a lighted candle at arm's length. On Mrs. Shelley's recovering her senses she told Mrs. Williams she had been awakened by the glare of a light. . . . Opening her eyes, she beheld Shelley. . . . She spoke but he did not answer. His eyes were wide open, but misty; he resembled a statue. . . . Williams watched the sleep-walker; he stalked to the door leading out to the verandah, seemingly listening to the crashing of the waves, then walked into his room, put the candle on the table, and stretched himself on his bed." According to another account, also written by Trelawny, Shelley, as soon as he had returned to consciousness, explained that an image of himself had appeared before him, had beckoned him into the hall and there vanished with the question: "Shelley, are you satisfied?"

His affections, like his aversions, worked by a process of synthesis; and it was inevitable that Shelley's love of the sea and his love of Jane, with that impulse towards self-destruction which the sea evoked, should be woven into the same strand of romantic feeling. One hot evening, as Jane sat with her children on the beach, Shelley emerged from the house, dragging his boat. In his vehement, excited way, he invited her to join him and, as soon as she and the children were seated on the bottom, rowed them around a promontory into deep blue water. Here he rested on his oars and seemed to lose consciousness of his passengers' existence. They were alone: a single movement would have upset the boat. Suddenly his face brightened and he appeared to return to life, with the exclamation: "Now let us together solve the great mystery." Managing to control her terror, Jane replied in a firm yet gentle voice, and little by little was able to persuade him to return inshore; but once in shallow water she plunged overboard and scrambled to safety. That night, Shelley's expression was rapt and guileless, as he glided into the living-room to snatch a haphazard meal, which consisted as usual of grapes and a crust of bread. For the moment he was completely absorbed in the world of the Spanish drama.

It is not impossible that the entire incident had passed from his memory. Between his waking life and the life of dreams the distinction he made had always been indefinite; and earlier in the year, as they walked together on the terrace, observing the effect of the moonlight on the waters, Shelley had complained to Williams of being unusually nervous. ". . . Stopping short, he grasped me violently by the arm, and stared steadfastly on the white foam upon the beach under our feet. . . . I demanded of him if he were in pain. But he only answered by saying, 'There it is again—there!' He recovered after some time, and declared that he saw, as plainly as he then saw me, a naked child (Allegra) rise from the sea, and clap its hands as in joy, smiling at him. This was a trance that it required some reasoning and philosophy to awaken him from, so forcibly had the vision operated on his mind."

Yet his strong practical *flair* did not desert him. It was Shelley who had prepared the way for Leigh Hunt's visit, who had negotiated a loan from Byron when his own resources failed, and had arranged for his friend to occupy an apartment in the Palazzo Lanfranchi. On him, no doubt, would fall the main burden of preparing the magazine. What Shelley did not know, and Hunt did not explain until he had arrived in Italy, was that, some months since, he and his brother had ceased to own the *Examiner* (which the others had counted on to launch their project) and that he had left England penniless and empty-handed. In money-matters, as in all else, Hunt's was a complex character; and it was his misfortune that, although his virtues did not at once emerge, his shortcomings, personal and intellectual, were immediately evident. Buried in the depths of his nature were many admirable qualities; but, wherever they expanded into his public life, they were apt to fritter themselves away in gush and artifice. Thus, for social purposes, his real devotion to a host of friends was transmuted into sentimentalism and vapid côterie-talk, while his knowledge and intense love of art and literature tailed off in the attitudinising of a suburban *petit maître*. Such was the aspect of Leigh Hunt that had disgusted Keats who, after many pleasant evenings passed in the Vale of Health, in an atmosphere of puns and pleasantries and competitive verse-spinning, recoiled with the indignant energy of his honest and masculine spirit. "Hunt [he had written in 1818] does one harm by making fine things petty and beautiful things hateful—through him I am indifferent to Mozart . . . and many a glorious thing when associated with him becomes a nothing—This distorts one's mind—makes one's thoughts bizarre—perplexes one in the standard of Beauty." Under Hunt's touch, fancy was whimsy, and beauty prettiness. Yet the bounce that distinguished Hunt's talk and mannerisms, the air of complacency that irradiated his round-cheeked features and sparkled from his dark romantic eyes, were maintained against a constant pressure of work and worry. He was poor; he had a large family; his health was bad. While Hunt chirped or carolled among his busts and vases, wreathed verses in true-love knots or gaily hummed the *motifs* of an Italian opera, there were often tradesmen at the door, and always growing children to stamp or scream in the immediate background.

By temperament the innocent voluptuary was an inveterate optimist—his feeling for beauty and his taste for happiness had not declined; and it seemed merely natural that his friends in Italy should be anxious to effect his rescue. But even Hunt hesitated at the prospect of a long and expensive journey overland, burdened by six children and an ailing wife. He expressed his doubts: to which Shelley responded that they must come by sea. "Put your music and your books on board a vessel [he recommended], and you will have no more trouble." A delightful picture unfolded, bright with the colours of hope; and it was Shelley's visionary advice that Leigh Hunt followed. On November 16th, 1821, the whole family embarked at the port of London and by the 19th, "amidst rain and squalls," had passed the Nore. Rather less apparent now seemed the advantages of a winter sea-voyage. The cabin, in which Leigh Hunt and his wife were obliged to sleep upon the floor, while their children were packed tight in the bunks above, was small, wet and atrociously over-crowded. Let his readers imagine (wrote Leigh Hunt afterwards) "the little back-parlour of one of the shops in Fleet Street, or the Strand, attached or let into a great moving vehicle, and tumbling about the waves. . . ." Eventually the captain decided to make for

Ramsgate; and there they remained three tedious weeks. On December 11th they left the harbour "in company with nearly a hundred vessels, the white sails of which, as they shifted and presented themselves in different quarters," exhibited "a kind of noble minuet." Then the skies overclouded; a storm swept down; "and there ensued such a continuity and vehemence of bad weather as rendered the winter of 1821 memorable in the shipping annals" and strewed the coasts of Europe with wreckage from Jutland to Genoa. For ten hideous days they were battered and buffeted up and down the Channel. Twice they touched the Atlantic but were driven back again; one gale continued without respite for nearly sixty hours; the vessel "looked like a washhouse in a fit." Excepting Hunt, the whole party was incessantly seasick; but in nothing else that he ever wrote (save perhaps in three deservedly famous sonnets) did Hunt's literary virtues find better employment than in his account of their misery. Puking children, danger and cold and dark could not dull his dispassionate appreciation of all that he daily felt and suffered; and now he observed the even greater sufferings of the goat they had brought on board ("a present from a kind friend, anxious that we should breakfast as at home") which he lugged into the cabin and fed on biscuit; now admired the phantasmal appearance assumed by hanging garments which swayed and gestured mysteriously as the vessel laboured; now, when he had struggled up on to the slippery and reeking deck, gazed with delight and awe across a huge perspective of tormented sea space. "The sun [he remembered] rose in the morning, at once fiery and sicklied over; a livid gleam played on the water, like the reflection of lead; then the storms would recommence; and during partial clearing off, the clouds and fogs appeared standing in the sky, moulded into gigantic shapes, like antediluvian wonders, or visitants from the zodiac; mammoths, vaster than have yet been thought of; the first ungainly and stupendous ideas of bodies and legs, looking out upon an unfinished world. These fancies were ennobling, from their magnitude."

On December 22nd the Hunts' vessel reached the safety of Dartmouth. Exhausted and woebegone, they clambered ashore; and it was not until five months later, on May 13th, when further financial provision had arrived from Italy, that they again dared the perils of a voyage to the Mediterranean. That second voyage, comparatively speaking, proved swift and pleasant. Once more, Marianne Hunt was extremely ill; but Hunt, though his confidence was shaken, enjoyed the journey—the waters of the Bay of Biscay "heaving in huge oily-looking fields, like a carpet lifted" or "striped into great ribbons"; the "beautiful lone promontory" of Cape St. Vincent; or the burnished wings of "gold and yellow and rose-coloured, with a smaller minute sprinkle in one spot, like a shower of glowing stones from a volcano," which shone in the western sky over the hills of Spain as the sun descended. Incessantly he repeated the name of their destination: "the Mediterranean, the Mediterranean"—sea of Homer, Virgil, Catullus, with its 'Aνηριθμον γελασμα, its innumerable rippling smiles, and marmoreal expanses of unbroken dark blue. By June 13th, they were skirting the shores of the Gulf of Genoa and admiring groves and white villages that "looked as Italian as possible." On the 28th they left Genoa and set sail for Leghorn, where Hunt was to renew old friendships and begin his new life.

In the harbour of Leghorn, he discovered Trelawny, "dark, handsome and mustachio'd," standing on the deck of Byron's yacht. Leghorn itself appeared a commonplace seaport, a kind of "polite Wapping, with a square and a theatre"; and, having installed his wife and children in hotel rooms, Hunt's next move was to make a call at Montenero. The day was hot; the road led through hot and dusty suburbs; Montenero, when he arrived there, struck Hunt as the hottest-looking house he had ever seen. Its walls, washed a sultry salmon-pink, flared out in the sunshine across the surrounding countryside; but, once he had crossed the threshold, the atmosphere within doors was even more oppressive. A scene in the best Italian manner was rapidly boiling up. On June 28th, according to a report prepared by the local authorities, a violent quarrel had occurred between Byron's coachman and the Gambas' cook; during the dispute they had drawn their knives; the entire household was soon involved in meridional pandemonium; and a pitched battle had been fought beneath Byron's windows. Hurrying on to the balcony, with a brace of loaded pistols, he had threatened that he would shoot down all the combatants unless they immediately desisted; in spite of which it proved necessary to call the police. Into the aftermath of this teacup hurricane poor Leigh Hunt now stumbled. Pietro Gamba, unlucky as always, had received a knife-wound from one of his own servants. He was ruffled, extremely indignant and had his arm in a sling. Teresa, too, was in a state of the utmost perturbation. Her face was flushed; her eyes were bright; her long hair streamed round her shoulders. From an English point of view they were both unusual figures; but just as disconcerting to Leigh Hunt was the sight of the poet himself. Byron had changed considerably since 1816—so much so, that at a first glance he was scarcely recognisable.

In place of the "compact, energetic, and curly-headed person" whom Leigh Hunt had expected, stood a man fattish and no longer young, whose greying hair fell "in thin ringlets about his throat." His costume suggested a life of ease and lassitude—a loose nankin jacket, white trousers, an open neck-cloth; his manner was affable but vague and unconcerned, and he appeared anxious to make light of the whole ridiculous incident. Unfortunately the potential assassin was still outside. Leigh Hunt looked down from the casement; and there he lurked, "glaring upwards like a tiger," wearing a red cap and "a most sinister aspect, dreary and meagre, a proper catiff." Montenero was in a condition of blockade. Luckily, however, the hour had come when Byron and his friends were accustomed to take their evening ride; and it was resolved that this habit must not be interrupted. Byron, meanwhile, had assumed his velvet cap and a "loose riding-coat of mazarin blue," in which (observed Hunt) he looked "more lordly than before, but hardly less foreign"; and to-gether they began to edge towards the doorway. Pietro threatened; Teresa apostrophised; Byron, "metamorphosed, round-looking, and jacketed," did his best to damp down their southern fire "with his cool tones, and an air of voluptuous indolence." As they emerged—Teresa urging "*Bairon*" to hold back and "all squeezing to have the honour of being the boldest"—the besieger collapsed on a bench and burst into a flood of tears. "His cap was half over his eyes; his face gaunt, ugly, and unshaved. . . . To crown all, he requested Lord Byron to kiss him. The noble Lord conceived this excess of charity superfluous." But he excused the man; Pietro Gamba shook his hand; and Teresa looked on in a pitying sort. Before Byron's valet, who had been despatched for help, returned with a police officer, the scene had ended in dramatic repentance and equally dramatic pardon.

It was an exciting, but disturbing, preface to Hunt's Italian adventures. The following day Shelley arrived from Casa Magni, shrill, rumpled, enthusiastic, kind as ever—a welcome contrast to the affable but languid Byron—though Hunt noticed that he had "less hope" and that his hair was grey-threaded. Rapidly he whirled his friends off from Leghorn to Pisa, where he saw them installed on the ground floor of the Palazzo Lanfranchi, among furniture that he had bought with money supplied by Byron, and called in the physician Vacca to attend to Marianne Hunt. Vacca gave little hope of the patient's recovery. As usual, Shelley's task was to advise and comfort; but for the time being he had promised to return to Lerici, whither he intended to sail with Edward Williams; and after a day's sight-seeing he bade Hunt good-bye and set out for Leghorn. At Pisa he had found a letter from the Magnetic Lady, addressed to her "Dearest Friend" and concluding with a postscript that seems at least provocative. Why did he talk (inquired Jane) "of never enjoying moments like the past? Are you going to join your friend Plato, or do you expect I shall do so soon?" Drawn by the same lode-star, husband and friend were anxious to begin the journey. Byron, in the meantime, had left Montenero. The recent rumpus had given the authorities the excuse they needed—they had been thoroughly alarmed by Byron's suggestion that, as owner of the *Bolivar*, he should be allowed to embark or land passengers along the Tuscan coast wherever it pleased him; and an order of expulsion was pronounced against both the Gambas. Towards the end of June, they continued their flight to Genoa; while Byron and Teresa retired to the comparative quietude of the Palazzo Lanfranchi.

At Leghorn, the weather was sultry and stifling. "Processions of priests and religiosi," with prayers for rain, wound between the dusty housefronts bearing lights and images; but not a drop had yet descended from the unresponsive sky. On Monday, July 8th, Shelley visited his bankers accompanied by Trelawny, made some purchases at a store and finally embarked just after one o'clock. With the masters of the *Ariel* went a young English seaman, named Charles Vivian, whom Trelawny had engaged. The *Bolivar* was to escort them into the offing; but, when they were under weigh, the guard-boat boarded them to examine their papers, and, since Trelawny had not his port clearance, he was obliged to remain in harbour. Sulkily he gave orders to furl the sails, but did not leave the deck and continued to observe the *Ariel*'s progress out to sea, until it had vanished in the heat-mist that veiled the distance. The oppressive warmth and the unusual stillness had made him drowsy. He went below and fell asleep, to be aroused some hours later by the noise of his men getting up the cable chain. Though it was only half-past six, the heavens had darkened. "The sea was of the colour, and looked as solid and smooth as a sheet of lead, and covered with an oily scum. Gusts of wind swept over without ruffling it, and big drops of rain fell on its surface, rebounding, as if they could not penetrate it. There was a commotion in the air, made up of many threatening sounds. . . . Fishing-craft and coasting vessels under bare poles rushed by us . . . running foul of the ships in the harbour. As yet the din and hubbub was that made by men, but their shrill pipings were suddenly silenced by the crashing voice of a thunder squall that burst right over our heads. For some time no other sounds were to be heard than the thunder, wind and rain."

Within twenty minutes the storm had passed; but when Trelawny again examined the sea, the high sails of Shelley's boat had completely vanished. From the tower of the port, Captain Roberts had caught a last glimpse of the *Ariel*. It was then some ten miles out, and he noticed that Shelley and his companions were taking in their topsails. More significant is a story retailed by Taafe. Soon after they had put to sea, they were said to have been sighted by a vessel making for Leghorn, the captain of which, perceiving that they "could not long contend with such tremendous waves, bore down upon them and offered to take them on board." But "a shrill voice" returned a decisive "No." Astonished by their foolhardiness, the captain continued to follow them through his telescope. "The waves were running mountains high—a tremendous surf dashed over the boat which to his astonishment was still crowded with sail." A sailor, using a speaking trumpet, shouted to them to reef their sails or they would be lost. "One of the gentlemen [Williams, it is believed], was seen to make an effort to lower the sails—his companion seized him by the arm as if in anger."

On his own account, Shelley had now "solved the great mystery" —whether involuntarily or by an act of deliberate rashness it is impossible to determine; but the obscurity that surrounds his means of departure can never be cleared up. When *Ariel* was finally dragged from the sea-bed, there were indications that she had been run down by another vessel—for her "starboard quarter was stove in, evidently by a blow from the sharp bows of a felucca"—and, since the boat was undecked, had foundered instantly. That Shelley was the victim of a piratical onslaught by fishermen who believed that the rich *milord inglese* had embarked with a large sum in gold is also a suggestion that has been put forward;[1] but regarding none of these suggestions can we hope to arrive at certainty. It is plain, however, he had had such a death as he himself would have desired; and no doubt he sank as again and again he had announced that he intended to do—quickly, without protest or ignominious struggle. For nearly a fortnight nothing was heard at Leghorn of the *Ariel*'s crew; and on the third day Trelawny rode to Pisa, warned Hunt, then went upstairs to speak to Byron. "When I told him, his lip quivered, and his voice faltered as he questioned me." Soon afterwards a punt, a keg and some bottles that had belonged to the *Ariel* were salvaged along the coast. Ten days later two bodies were thrown ashore, one near Viareggio and the second three miles away at the Bocca Lericcio. The first Trelawny recognised as that of Shelley—not by the features, for both the face and hands were entirely fleshless, but by the tall slight figure, the schoolboy jacket, the volume of Æschylus in one pocket and the copy of Keats's poems, borrowed from Leigh Hunt and hastily turned back at *Lamia*, which had been thrust into another. Particularly horrible was the mutilation of Williams's body, which retained only sock, a boot, a black silk handkerchief knotted around the throat and the rags of a shirt pulled over the head, "as if the wearer had been in the act of taking it off." The body of the sailor Vivian was not found till three weeks after the *Ariel*'s disappearance and, like the bodies of Shelley and Williams, was given temporary burial where it had been discovered.

Trelawny at once undertook the problem of how they were to be disposed of. He it was—with the energy of a natural man of action—who had organised search parties and himself galloped along the coast, while Byron and Hunt remained at Pisa, helpless and dejected. It was Trelawny who now interviewed the Tuscan authorities and,

[1] In 1875, Trelawny, then living in retirement on the South Coast, received through his daughter in Rome a report that an old fisherman, who had died near Sarranza twelve years earlier, had confessed on his death-bed that he had helped to sink Shelley's boat. Trelawny accepted the story: and a correspondence on the subject took place in the columns of *The Times*.

to avoid any infringement of the strict quarantine laws, persuaded them to agree that the bodies should be disinterred and immediately cremated. By Trelawny's order an iron furnace was built at Leghorn; and on the morning of August 14th, Trelawny, Byron and Hunt met at Williams's grave, together with officials, a party of soldiers and some of the *Bolivar*'s crew. "A considerable gathering of spectators," including "many ladies richly dressed," hovered nearby. As the remnants of Williams's body were grubbed from the sea-sand, Byron looked on with horrified interest. "Is that a human body?" he demanded. "Why, it's more like the carcase of a sheep. . . . Let me see the jaw. I can recognise any one by the teeth, with whom I have talked. I always watch the lips and mouth: they tell what the tongue and eyes try to conceal." And later: "Don't repeat this with me," followed by a suggestion that they should try the strength of the water that had drowned their friends. Before they were a mile out, Byron was seized with cramp and vomiting, and reached land again, much to his annoyance, only by Trelawny's aid.

Next morning the same party assembled on the beach near Viareggio. It was a cloudless Italian day. On the horizon stood the island shapes of Gorgona, Capraja and Elba; behind the forest of stunted pine-trees that edged the shore rose the white marble crests of the distant Apennines. The sea was very blue and completely calm. As he thought how the prospect would have delighted Shelley, he felt (Trelawny remembered) a kind of reluctance at dragging his body from the deep yellow sand in which it had been briefly buried. For a time the gang of workmen continued to dig in vain; then they were "startled and drawn together" by the dull hollow sound of a mattock striking on the skull. Quicklime or the early effects of decay had discoloured what remained of the flesh a dark ghastly blue. Unlike Williams's, Shelley's limbs did not fall from the trunk when they were touched, and the corpse was lifted whole on to the funeral furnace. Then the wood was kindled; Trelawny threw frankincense and salt into the fire and poured wine and oil over the body. The oil and salt gave the flames a peculiar glistening and quivering brilliance. Watching from Byron's carriage which he had not had the strength to leave, Hunt observed the "inconceivable beauty" of the shimmering flame-sheet as it "bore away towards heaven in vigorous amplitude. . . . It seemed as though it contained the glassy essence of vitality."

So fierce was the combined radiance of fire and sun, that all around them the atmosphere waved and trembled. Meanwhile, the corpse had fallen open, disclosing the heart (which Trelawny claimed afterwards to have snatched from the brazier) and, the frontal bone of the skull having dropped away, Shelley's brains, cupped in the broken cranium on the red-hot furnace bars, "literally seethed, bubbled, and boiled as in a cauldron for a very long time." The last was a detail that deeply impressed Byron. But after a time the sight sickened him and he swam off to the *Bolivar*. That evening, as they drove homeward through the pine forests, both Byron and Leigh Hunt experienced one of those moods of hysterical gaiety which sometimes follow hard on the heels of an unbearably painful drama. They drank in the carriage, and sang and shouted like men possessed.

Chapter 20

WITH Shelley vanished the last possibility of an understanding between Byron and Leigh Hunt. Only Shelley could have succeeded in holding together two characters so inevitably antagonistic; and his extinction threw their differences into a sharper relief. Yet in the letter, if not always in the spirit of their compact, Byron's behaviour towards his friend's *protégé* was just and generous. After Shelley's death, his first move had been to request that Leigh Hunt would regard him "as standing in Mr. Shelley's place" and declare "that I should find him the same friend that the other had been." But already Hunt had experienced serious misgivings and, according to his subsequent account, written in a mood of retrospective rancour, "my heart died within me . . . I made the proper acknowledgment; but I knew what he meant, and I more than doubted whether even in that, the most trivial part of friendship, he could resemble Mr. Shelley. . . ." To Byron, nevertheless, he was indebted not only for the means of coming to Italy, but for his accommodation and furniture once he had arrived and various sums of money to help solve his immediate problems. Both men had suffered seriously from the shock of Shelley's death; and the effect on Hunt was to exaggerate some of his most unpleasing traits—to make him more than ever egotistical and vain and pettish. In his attitude to Byron he lacked dignity; and now he was so effusive and familiar as to overshoot the mark, now so distant and ceremonious as to appear absurd and stilted. In vain Byron addressed him facetiously as "Dear Lord Hunt," hoping thereby to limit the excessive frequency of his "Dear Lord Byrons." Hunt posed and prated, was tart or sulky, but found it utterly impossible to achieve composure.

Yet outwardly life at the Palazzo Lanfranchi was regular and placid. About the time Hunt began to think of bed, Byron, after a lazy sensuous day, would be marshalling his sluggish faculties to face the evening's work, and settling down to literature and gin-and-water. Byron drank heavily and wrote late: Hunt retired early and rose irritable. His study had been fixed in a small room overlooking the courtyard with an orange tree before the window; and from this refuge he would listen to the noises of the floor above, the *piano nobile*, where Byron and his household were established. He came to recognise them: in a short time he had come to hate them. The great man was a leisurely and languid riser, lounging aimlessly about his room while he read and breakfasted, gossiping with the English valet if his temper was good. More exasperating still, he loved to sing. To poor Hunt, rigid with annoyance at his table below—was he not conscious of his own superior musical sensitiveness?—would float the strains of a voice "at once small and veiled" rehearsing snatches of Rossini "in a swaggering style." Then he took a bath: then his valet dressed him. Finally, he would appear in the garden courtyard, handsome and prosperous-looking, blithe and self-confident. "Leontius!" he would shout at the study casement and limp up to the window-sill with some provocative pleasantry.

That Byron's behaviour may have been well-meant, though a little tactless, passed Leigh Hunt's somewhat limited comprehension. Grudgingly he left his books and his papers; reluctantly he descended into the garden, "very green and refreshing under the Italian sky." Chairs had been placed by the Italian servants; and there he found Byron, in his nankin jacket, his white waistcoat and trousers, his visored and gold-trimmed velvet cap, expecting him seigneurial and flippant as always. In the small feminine, heavily beringed hand (which otherwise played with a lace handkerchief) was the snuff-box which he carried to ward off hunger, and because he imagined that the taking of snuff helped to preserve his teeth. Presently they would be joined by the poet's mistress. She, too, had been late in getting up; and her blonde tresses, still glossy from combing and brushing, lay sleek and unbraided about her shoulders. Nostalgically Hunt remembered an English poet:

> *Yclothed was she, fresh for to devise.*
> *Her yellow hair was braided in a tress*
> *Behind her back, a yardè long, I guess:*

Byron in Italy

And in the garden (as the sun uprist)
She walketh up and down, where as her list . . .

Alas, the sun had risen many hours ago; and it was not an English
garden in which Countess Guiccioli walked, plucking at the orange
flowers and the oleanders and the other cribbed domesticated blooms
of that urban paradise, but an Italian *hortus conclusus* beneath a
meridional sky, so deeply blue as to seem oppressive and almost
hostile. No doubt she "was handsome and lady-like, with an agreeable manner . . ." But "none of her graces appeared entirely free
from art." Hunt would amuse her by "speaking bad Italian out of
Ariosto"; and she, good-naturedly enough, would "troll it over" on
her pretty patrician lips, "keeping all the while that considerate
countenance, for which a foreigner has so much reason to be grateful." There was no denying that, physically at least, she had many
good points; for "her hair was what the poet has described, or rather
blond, with an inclination to yellow; a very fair and delicate yellow.
. . . She had regular features . . . large . . . but without coarseness, and
more harmonious than interesting. Her nose was the handsomest of
the kind I ever saw; and I have known her both smile very sweetly,
and look intelligently, when Lord Byron said something kind to
her. I should not say, however, that she was a very intelligent
person. Both her wisdom and her want of wisdom were on the side
of her feelings, in which there was doubtless mingled a good deal of
the self-love natural to a flattered beauty. She wrote letters in the
style of the 'Academy of Compliments'; and made plentiful use, at all
times, of those substitutes for address and discourse which flourished
at the era of that polite compilation. . . ." At a closer glance, Hunt
discovered, she did not really please; and he was quick to notice, not
without a certain acid satisfaction, that, whereas her head and
shoulders were youthful and charming, her legs were abbreviated
and her figure was dumpy. He voted her calculating, self-conscious,
stilted in movement, "a kind of buxom parlour-boarder, compress-
ing herself artificially into dignity and elegance, and fancying she
walked in the eyes of the whole world, a heroine by the side of a
poet." She was the personification of showy Italian sentiment; and
more and more heavily as the days dragged by, all alike, all sunny, all
vacant and calm, the South had begun to weigh on Leigh Hunt's
spirit, until its sunshine and its quiet seemed to poison and suffocate

him. That Byron should appear so placid merely increased his anger. How dared he loll back in voluptuous ease, while Leigh Hunt, burdened by the cares of a family, tortured by solicitude for an ailing wife, himself in poor health, with indifferent prospects, accepted the odious rôle of literary pensioner! Was it for this that he had affronted authority and suffered imprisonment? With such a wealth of grievances beneath the surface, their conversation often hovered on the verge of acrimony; and when Byron in his casual and reckless fashion, having heard Hunt that morning "dabbling on the pianoforte," made some splenetic references to the art of music and suggested that musical interests implied effeminacy, Leigh Hunt was provoked to a snappish rejoinder. Who was this oiled and curled dandy that he should call him effeminate? "He, the objector to effeminacy, was sitting in health and wealth, with rings on his fingers, and baby-work to his shirt . . . just issued, like a sultan, out of his bath." Hunt replied, therefore, in a tone of carefully maintained reasonableness, that, although there was no question that the love of music might be overdone, he imagined that it would be "difficult to persuade the world, that Alfred and Epaminondas, and Martin Luther, and Frederick the Second, all eminent lovers of music, were effeminate men"; to which Byron did not attempt to produce an answer. He had been talking, as his habit was, for the sake of talking, in the spirit of moody contradiction that sometimes possessed him. He retired from the unequal contest baffled and irritated.

Towards noon Hunt would rise and go in to dine, Byron remaining behind in the courtyard or loitering upstairs to his books and his sofa. When the heat of the day decreased, the pair would again join company and ride out either on horseback or in Byron's open carriage, Trelawny, a heroic moustachioed figure, puffing at a thick cigar and bestriding his large and spirited horse, often cantering beside them as they entered the forest or turned into the vineyard of some peasant acquaintances. There they were greeted by a dark-haired girl whom Hunt had already encountered in the Palazzo Lanfranchi, and with whose whole family Byron was on intimate terms. In attendance were the favourite's younger sister, "delicate-looking and melancholy," an honest father who had difficulties with his landlord and heaved deep lugubrious sighs as he retailed his misfortunes, and a loud, hard-faced, swarthy-skinned peasant mother who served them ripe figs under a garden trellis, cracking (Hunt remembered) "some extraordinary jokes" which embarrassed him in so far as they were comprehensible. A patriarchal scene; yet he was glad to leave it. Like everything else he had observed of Italy, the landscape he explored on their rides round Pisa had "a certain hard taste in the mouth." Fondly conjured up from the steel-engraved embellishments to a favourite edition of the Italian poets, Hunt's ideal Italy continually failed to materialise. The real Italy he neither understood nor could learn to take delight in;—its mountains were "too bare, its outlines too sharp, its lanes too stony, its voices too loud, its long summer too dusty." He was "ill, uncomfortable, in a perpetual fever," longing for the greenness and neatness of the fields round London, from which one returned to one's own prettily appointed suburban parlour with the teacups, the rosewood piano-forte, the busts and vases, or for the snug appealing romanticism of the English Lake District. At home, in the Palazzo Lanfranchi, his consolations were few. Of the kind of inverted snobbery from which her husband suffered, Mrs. Hunt presented even severer symptoms; and she had reached Italy armed with the determination, on the one hand that she would not condescend to speak the language, on the other that her attitude towards Lord Byron should make it clear that his fame and title left her unimpressed. He was treated, therefore, to an alarming display of middle-class dignity, interspersed with occasional touches of feminine malice. Any suspicion of covert ridicule had always upset him. Educated in the school of Holland House (where manners, if not more Christian, were at least more accountable), he had had no experience of the acerbities of Hampstead; and by Mrs. Hunt and her acidulous sallies he was frequently dumb-founded. "What do you think, Mrs. Hunt?" he had once remarked, "Trelawny has been speaking against my morals! What do you think of that?" "It is the first time I ever heard of them," Mrs. Hunt replied, with a sniff or snicker not difficult to imagine. Byron (Hunt noted with some relish) was "completely dashed, and reduced to silence." On another occasion, when Byron had been talking dis-respectfully of various of Hunt's acquaintances, "criticising . . . their personal appearance, and that in no good taste," their injured friend carried the war into the enemy's camp by demanding if Byron had heard Marianne's *bon mot* to the Shelleys about the disdainful and romantic portrait that Harlow had drawn of him. Byron was too sensitive to decline a repetition; and Hunt thereupon explained with quiet gusto that Marianne had said that it "resembled a great school-boy, who had had a plain bun given him, instead of a plum one." Byron did not smile and "looked as blank as possible." But hence-forward he made no attempt to improve the relationship.

Incidentally, he had developed a violent dislike for his visitors' children. Hunt considered their behaviour above reproach. "They had lived in a natural, not an artificial state, and were equally sprightly, respectful, and possessed." But Byron thought them dirty, noisy and mischievous—they were a kraal of Hottentots, he said, a pack of Yahoos—and, since he expected them as soon as they arrived to proceed to the most monstrous acts of vandalism, he had posted his fierce bulldog on the main staircase, with strict orders to keep off "the little Cockneys," lest they should extend their depreda-tions to his first-floor rooms. The same bulldog savaged the Hunts' goat, a melancholy survivor of storm and shipwreck, and had bitten off one of its ears before the victim could be rescued. Hunt was devoted to his children and fond of animals (while Byron's feeling for both species was capricious and self-centred) and his touchiness grew more pronounced as his health deteriorated.

He had begun to suspect—and in this suspicion at least he came near the mark—that Byron's enthusiasm for their paper, now chris-tened *The Liberal*, was rapidly declining. Byron's London friends were furious when they learned of the association. It was not that they objected to Hunt's politics; but they considered that the poet's reputation might suffer irreparable damage if he linked his name with that of the leader of "the Cockney school." Thus Moore started a vigorous campaign against the journal; and Hobhouse (to borrow one of Leigh Hunt's most felicitous phrases) "rushed over the Alps, not knowing which was the more awful, the mountains, or the Magazine." In other words, Hobhouse, accompanied by his sisters, made an expedition through Italy during the summer months and paid a visit to Byron at the Palazzo Lanfranchi. There he met Hunt and was "very polite and complimentary," but, in private talk, "if his noble friend was to be believed, did all he could to destroy the connexion between us." Byron, however, refused to desert *The Liberal*; nor is it fair to suppose, as Hunt afterwards was at some pains to persuade his readers, that "from the moment he saw the moderate profits" that the magazine was likely to bring in, "he resolved to have nothing further to do with it in the way of real assistance." Hunt added the contradictory plaint, that Byron had made use of the paper "only for the publication of some things which his Tory bookseller was afraid to put forth." It was true that Byron had quarrelled with Murray—finally driven to despair by Murray's procrastination—but he would have had no difficulty in finding a new publisher. Within a week of his arrival at Leghorn, Leigh Hunt had applied for a loan on his brother's behalf; and Byron, since he was short of ready money, gave the Hunts, for publication either in *The Examiner* or in the new journal as they might decide, his *Vision of Judgment*, warning them that it contained actionable passages.[1] Among other works that he handed to the Hunts during Leigh's stay in Italy were *Heaven and Earth, The Age of Bronze* and nine cantos of *Don Juan*, from six to fourteen. The first number of *The Liberal* appeared on October 15th, 1822, and was received by the Tory press with wild invective. "Casting up the account," the *Literary Gazette* discovered "that Lord Byron had contributed impiety, vulgarity, inhumanity . . . ; Mr. Shelley, a burlesque upon Göthe; and Mr. Leigh Hunt, conceit, trumpery, ignorance and wretched verses. The union of wickedness, folly, and imbecility is perfect. . . ." The opening number, as it turned out, was not unsuccessful; but three numbers that followed it revealed a steady falling off.

Dogged already by the idea that his star was waning, Byron was in no mood to encounter a fresh defeat. Besides, he was exasperated by Leigh Hunt's helplessness—the side of his character that Dickens was to portray brilliantly and cruelly in the personage of Mr. Skimpole—and by Hunt's assumption that his friends' incomes were, as a matter of course, his own. ". . . You cannot imagine [Byron was to write to Moore in 1823] the despairing sensation of trying to do something for a man who seems incapable or unwilling to do anything further for himself—at least to the purpose. It is like pulling a man out of a river who directly throws himself in again." By the autumn of 1822, the relations of the collaborators had been severely tested; but, notwithstanding recurrent outbreaks of barely

---

[1] When John Hunt was prosecuted for the publication of this violent anti-monarchical satire, Byron provided the funds for his defence.

disguised hostility—Lord Byron making Marianne Hunt one of his cold and embarrassed bows; Mrs. Hunt snapping or sparking back, to the evident discomfiture of the haughty nobleman who, haughty though he might be, had little experience (she declared) of dealing with a "woman of spirit"; Moretto, the bulldog, worrying Mrs. Hunt's goat or growling on the marble staircase at her noisy children—intercourse between the two households was not entirely suspended. When, towards the end of September, Byron finally abandoned the Palazzo Lanfranchi and moved to the Casa Saluzzo, in the hilltop village of Albaro overlooking Genoa, he was accompanied, though in a different party, by the Hunts. With Mary Shelley they shared the neighbouring Casa Negroto. After the half-oriental existence of the house at Pisa, Hunt appreciated the "English welcome" that Mary gave them; but his dissatisfaction and dejection were now beyond repair.

At Albaro he spent "a melancholy time . . . walking about the stony alleys, and thinking of Mr. Shelley," and the more he regretted Shelley, the more he resented Byron, until the spiteful character-sketch he was to give to the world through the *Recollections* had become firmly imprinted on his mind. Warped by the author's self-pity, and tinged with envy, the portrait would be more amusing, and far more damaging, if the prejudice that informs it were less solemnly self-centred, and more convincing if it included a greater degree of human sympathy. But how should Hunt, impoverished, ailing, worried, feel sympathy for Lord Byron, rich, celebrated, care-free, pampered by his servants, adored by his mistress, spoiled, courted, admonished by his fashionable London friends? In fact, Byron's seeming placidity was the true measure of his disillusionment. At Venice there had been dissipation; at Ravenna, love: and, when love waned, the dreams of a united Italy. At Pisa and Genoa, there was nothing—neither love nor hope. Since the death of Shelley, to whom he was now prepared to pay a magnanimous valedictory tribute: "the *best* and least selfish man I ever knew"—he had had few associates whom he either respected or admired. Trelawny, of course, was a good fellow; but what a preposterous *poseur*! With his fierce eyes, his wild moustachios, the tall stories he was fond of telling about his early life, he bore an odd resemblance to one of Byron's own early heroes; and Byron was quick to grasp the situation's essentially comic side. Dramatist and character met face to face! The poet liked to tease Trelawny with his taint of Byronism; and presently some kind friend told Trelawny that Byron had said that it was a great pity he should ever have studied *Childe Harold*. Luckily, he did not learn that Byron, in a splenetic moment, had also declared that, if they could teach Trelawny to wash his hands and tell the truth, they would have some chance of turning him out a gentleman. Even so, he soon revolted against the poet's over-powerful influence, and derived a certain pleasure from the observation of his more blatant shortcomings—Byron's love of money, his physical bravado and nervous weaknesses. He was glad to note that, although proud of his patrician birth, among strangers Byron looked very often flushed and diffident, and that, although he delighted in his prowess as a swimmer, his reserves of strength were limited. Together they sailed and swam and shot and drank—Byron, Trelawny remarked, had an uncommonly light head: but the association was forced, and the friendship temporary.

Tom Medwin, another boon-companion, had already vanished. In his luggage he took a large sheaf of reflections and indiscretions, gathered (according to Shelley's widow) "when Lord Byron was tipsy." Byron had been warned that Medwin was Boswellising; but this revelation had by no means arrested his flow of confidences. Rather the reverse. When Byron was in the mood to talk, no considerations of ordinary prudence could hold him back, and a comparatively new acquaintance seemed as suitable an auditor as his oldest and dearest friend. Though possibly a fool, Medwin was an excellent listener: and, as they rode out to shoot or rode back in the cool of the evening or sat over their glasses in the Palazzo Lanfranchi, Byron's musical voice meandered irresistibly on and on, reckless of his own credit, unsparing, when an occasion prompted, of the credit of others. That Byron's talk was largely haphazard did not decrease its interest. Characteristic of his fluid and oscillatory temperament was the exuberance with which he gallivanted from theme to theme. Now women provided his subject, and now religion. Whereas on the latter, his opinions were vague and speculative—he loved the music of an English cathedral service, and had been "made very uncomfortable" by a little book that purported to prove the truth of Christian doctrine—on the former they had a positive and downright cast. Medwin could not imagine how it disgusted him to see a woman eat! European women were "in an unnatural state of society. The Turks . . . manage these matters better than we do. . . . Give a woman a looking-glass and a few sugarplums, and she will be satisfied." He had suffered from the opposite sex so long as he could recollect; and, besides a detailed analysis of Lady Byron's character and conduct, and of the motives that had induced her to become his wife—she had wished to befriend and reform a celebrated wrong-doer: "friendship is a dangerous word for young ladies"—he dwelt in passing on later and earlier love-affairs, on the autumnal charm of Lady Oxford, the crack-brained violence of Lady Caroline Lamb (concerning whom he repeated to Medwin some particularly savage verses[1]) and his unforgettable disappointment by the heiress of Annesley Hall. His memory was prodigious, both for joys and sorrows. But the joys had passed—"almost all the friends of my youth are dead"; and death, from childhood to middle age, had never been far away. Why, only that morning, he had heard of the suicide of poor foolish Polidori! "I was convinced something very unpleasant hung over me last night: I expected to hear that somebody I knew was dead;—so it turns out! Poor Polidori is gone! When he was my physician, he was always talking of Prussic acid, oil of amber, blowing into veins, suffocating by charcoal, and compounding poisons. . . . It seems that disappointment was the cause. . . ." He might have added that Polidori had expired of Byronism—too strong and too exciting a drug for weak and unbalanced natures, the excitant he had himself rejected but had not yet escaped from.

Yet escape he must, if he were to retain his integrity, and, perhaps, his sanity. Maybe he would purchase a stake in some younger and fresher continent. The idea of a flight to the New World was still attractive; and, before he left Leghorn in the spring of 1822, he received with warmth a cultured American traveller, Mr. George Bancroft, who followed in the footsteps of the Bostonian Mr. Coolidge, and had sat to an American painter, William Edward West, whose portrait was destined for the "Academy of fine arts at New

[1] The publication of these verses in Medwin's *Conversations with Lord Byron* did much finally to overset Lady Caroline's always precarious mental equilibrium.

York." During the same month, an American squadron reached the port of Leghorn; Byron was invited on board, where he was received "with all the kindness which I could wish, and *more ceremony than I am fond of.*" Commodore Jones was extremely courteous; Captain Chauncey showed him a "very pretty edition" of his poems published in the United States; and, as he took his leave, an enthusiastic feminine visitor asked him to give her the rose he happened to be wearing, "for the purpose, she said, of sending to America something which I had about me. . . ." Byron had returned home gratified, if a little exhausted. Plainly across the Atlantic there was none of that apathy towards his poems and dramas which he suspected, now and then, must exist in London; but, counterbalancing the attraction of the New World, was the idea of Greece.

The appeal that it exercised was largely an emotional one. He was dominated by images of the past; in the past lay happiness; and at no period of his existence had life been happier, had youth been more enjoyable and joy less transitory, than in the two rambling discursive years of Near-Eastern travel. The ideas of youth and freedom were closely intertwined. Now Greece, the country of his youth, was struggling to be free, just as he himself was struggling to throw off his servitude; and he listened eagerly to every report that arrived of the modern Grecian patriots. Those reports, it is true, were at best confusing. During 1822 Greece had flared up into open insurrection; and by the end of that year, with the exception of certain isolated and beleaguered points, including the Acropolis of Athens and various fortresses scattered along the Gulf of Patras, the whole of the Grecian peninsula had been overrun by the patriotic armies. It was only when the Greeks themselves sat down to form a government and frame a constitution that they faced an apparently insoluble problem. Such unscrupulous and bloodthirsty military chieftains as Odysseus and Kolokotronis, subtle Phanariot schemers from Constantinople, that nervous parliamentarian and friend of the Shelleys, Alexander Mavrocordato, dignitaries of the Orthodox Church and Western Philhellenes, proved among themselves at least as antagonistic as the Christian and the Mussulman; and no sooner had Greece been temporarily released from its oppressive Turkish masters than it split up into a multitude of warring political factions.

Yet behind this depressing spectacle loomed the conception of

Greece itself, glorious in history, further glorified by the associations of Byron's early manhood. Returning to Greece he might recapture hope. But, whether it was to Greece that he removed or to South America, one thing was evident—that he needed money; and the signs of avarice that were already noticeable while he lived in Venice, at Genoa became so exaggerated that there was no concealing them. The death of his detested mother-in-law in 1822 had not only entitled him to a second surname—henceforward he would sign himself always "Noel Byron"—but had brought him a share in the fortune of the rich Lord Wentworth, Annabella's uncle, who had died some years earlier[1]; and, from that moment his financial position had been secure. A converted spendthrift is as hard to deal with as a repentant profligate. Hour after hour he would sit over the steward's account-books, pen in hand, puzzling his way through Zambelli's figures, throwing his pen down with an expression of delight if he discovered that he could save a *scudo*. Pitiless in small accounts, he was generous in large sums. Never consistent, he no longer concealed his oddities; and the eccentric behaviour of his notorious Grand Uncle, "the Wicked Lord," who had shut himself up with his tame crickets among the ghosts of Newstead, found a mild reflection in the poetic recluse of the Casa Saluzzo. Teresa, of course, was still beside him; but hers was a declining light. In their relations Byron had now reached that particularly difficult stage where esteem, affection, gratitude upon the one hand are balanced by an intense emotional fatigue upon the other. Yet his attitude towards her was always mild and considerate. "Lord Byron [Medwin noted] is certainly very much attached to her, without being actually in love"; and among their acquaintances, when they were sitting together beneath the orange trees, he would address her as "*Piccinina*" or some other endearing diminutive, while she basked in the air of recovered intimacy that his casual phrase created.

Yet he was tired of her, as he had already hinted in his talks with Hobhouse, and of the whole existence of which she formed a part. From no point of view were his prospects pleasing. The failure of

[1] Contrary to the usual belief, Byron did not "marry an heiress." Annabella Milbanke, however, had expectations through her uncle, Lord Wentworth. On his death in 1815, he left his property for life to Byron's mother-in-law, Lady Milbanke, who thereupon took the name of "Lady Noel" and, much to Byron's indignation, survived till January, 1822.

The Liberal had done him little good; and during the spring of 1823 he remarked resignedly that he was now, he supposed, "as low in popularity and bookselling as any writer can be. . . ." Except for Scott, there were few contemporaries whom he could read with satisfaction: both on the field of literature and on the field of politics the Tories and their allies triumphed.

Byron was not alone in the despair he felt. Survivors of the "gigantic and exaggerated times" that had produced Napoleon, English Liberals watched their hopes of change growing steadily fainter and fainter. As the first impetus of the revolutionary movement appeared to have died down, so the first wave of Romantic poetry had broken and spent itself. By June 1822, when Shelley's featureless and decomposing body was scooped up from the sands of Viareggio, Keats had been dead for seventeen months. Coleridge and Wordsworth, however, had respectively twelve and twenty-eight years to live; and the decade that followed, for Coleridge at least, was distracted and inglorious. Yet, just as Keats, given different circumstances, might by his sheer poetic gift have bridged the gulf between the Augustan and Romantic traditions, so Coleridge, had his temperament been more happily constituted, and the conflict within himself less acute and prolonged, might have dominated the new literature by force of intellect.

Here, not for the first time, one is confronted by the observation that, although men make up an age, the age itself is contributory in making men. A poet may help to shape the future: he is shaped, nevertheless, by the immediate past and by the influence with which it bears down upon the present. Coleridge and Wordsworth belonged to the generation that had been excited, almost beyond endurance, by the events of 1789, troubled and horrified by the growth of the Terror and profoundly stirred by the astonishing spectacle of Napoleon's rise. Some had welcomed, some had shuddered at, the Revolution. But, in both instances, the shock went very deep, and the shocks that succeeded it were demoralising and, at length, disabling. Thus Wordsworth retired into a graceless conservatism, the youth and strength of his imagination gradually losing ground, enthusiasm giving way to arid prejudice. By 1822, and even earlier, he was regarded, along with Southey, as poetic arch-traitor to the

Liberal cause and the hireling representative of a Tory government whose principles he had adopted. In Coleridge's development, the effects of contemporary occurrences are perhaps somewhat less easy to discover; but he, too, after a burst of creation at the close of the century—practically all the poems that deserve to be remembered were written during 1797 and 1798—experienced a curious slackening of creative strength, until in 1801 he admitted that the poet was dead in him, while the opium-habit, to which he was already addicted, began to claim him more and more completely, soothing his sense of literary frustration and lulling his disordered nerves.

Yet opium was not the sole, nor indeed was it the main, cause of Coleridge's creative failure. Drug-addiction, like chronic alcoholism, is more often a symptom than the disease itself, though Coleridge's malady was of a type that baffles analysis and defies cure. In common with many other writers of the early nineteenth century, he suffered from that odd disease of the volition to which mystics have attached the name of *acedia*, a condition of spiritual despondency and mental paralysis that leaves the sufferer still lucid yet entirely impotent. And then, Coleridge had highly developed moral feelings. It is possible that, had those feelings been less highly developed, and his conscience not so squeamish, he might have given them fewer occasions to torment him. But his sense of duty intensified his sense of failure; and it was his sense of failure that, in spite of every prohibition, human or divine, he was obliged to lull by constant recourse to opium which, temporarily at least, reconciled him to his moral problem. Disintoxicated, he must justify himself by action. Intoxicated, he found no justification necessary: it was enough that he knew and felt and imagined. For Coleridge, in fact, as afterwards for Charles Baudelaire, opium provided an intensification, not so much of sensual as of spiritual experience. It procured the key to one of those *paradis artificiels* which are a visionary equivalent of the tree-embowered, rock-walled garden fastness, "enfolding sunny spots of greenery," where the pupils of the Old Man of the Mountain received their training. But he returned to the real world for the most part with empty hands. Alas, of the "two to three hundred lines" that formed the original *Kubla Khan* (a poem for which Byron expressed the deepest admiration), what with the insubstantial nature of such half-fixed reminiscences and the alleged arrival of the disastrous person from Porlock, only an imperfect recollection was ever salvaged; and the fate of *Kubla Khan* was typical of the fate of his other efforts. Remnants, husks, vestiges found their way to the reader; the essential substance remained with Coleridge to furnish his dream-life, just out of reach on the wrong side of the ivory threshold—huge epic poems, gigantic treatises, exhaustive commentaries, all unattempted though in the mind's eye vivid. Resolutions piled up till their magnitude terrified him. He groaned—moralised—then slipped back into ruinous reverie.

Yet Coleridge, notwithstanding the tragic diffusion and gradual dispersion of his creative gifts, had the kind of maturity to which Shelley could not aspire, and a critical clear-sightedness beyond the enthusiast's scope. The enemies that Coleridge dreaded were those within himself. Shelley's adolescent persecution-mania filled the world with bogeys, which assumed now the lineaments of Sir Timothy Shelley, now the pale murderous mask of wicked Lord Castlereagh (that domestic despot but singularly enlightened director of English foreign policy) and now emerged, crudely personified, as Priestcraft and Prejudice. Half the foes he engaged were of his own creation; half the sufferings he endured were self-provoked; and among real opponents he was a desperate but a random fighter. His verse has the same touch of sketchy enthusiasm. The orchestral accompaniment of *Prometheus Unbound* may be supplied by the spheres; but the celestial clockwork is not revolving very smoothly. The voice may be that of an archangel; but, now and then, it cracks on the top register; and the result is a singularly appalling dissonance.

Shelley confused ecstasy and imagination, just as in the field of politics he confused the hatred of "tyranny" (which may have a private psychological basis) with a defence of the intellectual principles on which freedom ought to be established. Indeed, his liberalism never quite outlived the period when, accompanied by the pretty stupid girl whom he had "rescued" from her boarding school, he attempted to launch an English revolution with the help of paper boats, handbills tossed into the street, and messages in bottles committed to the waves. His genius is most apparent when he is least declamatory, when he forgets the helter-skelter rush of rhetorical abstractions that went streaming through his mind, "Kings of suns and stars, Daemons and Gods, Aetherial Dominations," gleaming like meteors, blazing like planets, and comes home to the self and the self's perplexities, its loves and its disappointments, the beauty and the misery of a finite universe.

Keats's famous reproof was certainly merited. But then, Keats had already arrived at a balance between the imagination and the intellect—or between the creative and critical aspects of an artist's brain—that Shelley's temperament debarred him from ever achieving. It was his business (Keats knew) to create, not legislate. But nothing could be further from the selfish secluded æstheticism in which the deliberately non-political artist is supposed to pass his days than Keats's dedication of all his powers to the intellectual purpose that suited them best, and through which they could be exploited to the finest end. It is our misfortune, however, that the *Letters*, which outline his plan of campaign, should show him usually a step ahead of the campaign itself, and that even the *Odes* should strike us, here and there, as an anticlimax.

Yet few poets have accomplished such a remarkable process of self-clarification in so short a space of time. Sensibly, Keats refused to regret "the slipshod *Endymion*. That it is so [he told a correspondent only six months after its publication] is no fault of mine. No!— though it may sound a little paradoxical. It is as good as I had power to make it—by myself. Had I been nervous about its being a perfect piece, and with that view asked advice, and trembled over every page, it would not have been written; for it is not in my nature to fumble—I will write independently—I have written independently *without Judgment*. I may write independently, and *with Judgment*, hereafter. The Genius of Poetry must work out its own salvation in a man: I cannot be matured by law and precept, but by sensation and watchfulness. . . . That which is creatïve must create itself." *Endymion*, though evidently the product of an adolescent artist, in love with the idea of writing poetry and somewhat befuddled by an over-dose of the Elizabethans, has still movements of astonishing ease and amplitude:

> . . . *As when heaved anew*
> *Old ocean rolls a lengthened wave to the shore,*
> *Down whose green back the short-lived foam, all hoar,*
> *Bursts gradual with a wayward indolence.*

To re-read Keats's *Letters*, having not looked into them for several years, is an experience at once delightful and disconcerting. So much *naïveté* coexists with so much maturity, so much vulgarity with so much delicacy of imagination. Here is the suburban poetaster, prolific of schoolboy puns, who collaborated with his friend Brown in painfully facetious letters to Mrs. Dilke; and here, embodied in the same person—unselfconsciously sharing the honours upon almost every page—is a writer of adult seriousness and profound intelligence. His mind was peculiarly honest and utterly disinterested. "I never wrote one single line of Poetry [he declared in April 1818] with the least shadow of public thought." The most imperfect and irresponsible artists (he knew) are those afflicted with a strong sense of public responsibility or public self-importance; and, just as the individual must have begun to understand himself, and grasp his own limitations, before he can hope to interfere beneficially in the existence of others, so the artist must graduate through self-absorption into any extended sympathy with contemporary problems or the world around him.

There is a great gulf between the poet who, at the age of twenty-four, had decided that "the only means of strengthening one's intellect is to make up one's mind about nothing—to let the mind be a thoroughfare for all thoughts, not a select party," and poets who turned their minds into packed committee rooms, or, like Coleridge, into learned debating societies with a single speaker. Keats's nature was entirely innocent of the taint of salvationism; and for that reason alone his conception of poetry seems both more modern than the definitions attempted by many nineteenth-century critics, and also closer to the spirit of the previous age. No Augustan poet need have dissented from his view that "poetry should surprise by a fine excess, and not by singularity; it should strike the reader as a wording of his own highest thoughts, and appear almost a remembrance." And Johnson himself might certainly have agreed that "its touches of beauty should never be half-way, thereby making the reader breathless, instead of content. The rise, the progress, the setting of imagery, should, like the sun, come natural to him, shine over him, and set soberly, although in magnificence, leaving him in the luxury of twilight."

What happened to prevent the execution of so bold a design? The student of Keats's *Letters* feels that he is witnessing a tragedy where the enemies of perfection in art and of happiness in life, repulsed along the whole length of a poet's defences, suddenly re-emerge, disguised, behind the ramparts. To begin with, there is talk of the "sore throat" that followed the Scottish and Irish walking tours of 1818. Then there occurs a casual mention of the daughter of the lady who had moved in next door—her countenance attractive but wanting in "sentiment," her nostrils "fine—though a little painful," her mouth "bad and good," her profile "better than her full face," her entire personality fascinating but perplexing, "beautiful and elegant, graceful, silly, fashionable and strange." From that moment, death and love are seen working as malicious allies. The earliest letter to Fanny Brawne is dated July 8th, 1819; and, as death rapidly speeds up the tempo, the tone mounts in intensity and gains in bitterness. Yet Keats continued to fight a rearguard action. Again and again he affirmed his desire for that condition of moral and spiritual independence in which, he believed, great poetry must find its origin. Deliberately he would deny himself disturbing contacts and hurry through London without a visit to Hampstead because "I cannot resolve to mix any pleasure with my days. . . . I am a Coward, I cannot bear the pain of being happy. . . ." He saw life very clearly as it ought to have been, and only after a prolonged struggle did he abandon himself to his fate as it was. Finally, physical weakness had spoiled his triumph. Death had at once intensified the claims of life and made them impossible either to satisfy in terms of the body or relegate to their proper place in the world of the mind.

If Keats was a writer who, although not unconscious of the life of his time, was sufficiently strong to withstand its more malignant influences, Coleridge, Shelley, Wordsworth represent the plight of the artist in modern society from three widely separated but complementary points of view. Wordsworth is the type of intellectual who, after an early expedition into revolutionary experiment, allows himself to drift back towards conservatism once the tide has turned. His was the warm nature easily chilled, the magnanimous spirit strangely susceptible to specious argument, cursed with an instinctive appreciation of the main chance, that in every generation is held up to obloquy. Their former associates may revile such writers; but their pride increases. To the evasions and circumlocutions of middle age they still bring the obstinacy and the conceit of youth.

They are the arch-renegades who remain unaware of their own apostasy.

Very different was the spiritual doom of Coleridge, whose predicament seems to have reproduced in waking life an experience we have most of us undergone during the course of a nightmare. Then, as the necessity of executing some immediate and drastic move becomes more and more apparent, so does the sensation of complete impotence grow more and more powerful. All Coleridge's vices derived from his virtues. It was the fact that he could imagine with such lucidity, and analyse and discuss with such an easy strength, that made it at first difficult, and afterwards quite impossible, to desert the ideal world of reverie and speculation for the disturbing, imperfect world of action. As Shelley said, he had been blinded by an excess of light; as he himself remarked, his illustrations swallowed up his thesis; until every advance in thought became a retreat from reality, and every improvement in the theory of how books should be written a diminution of the ability to set pen to paper. Between his sensitiveness and a universe that, since the breakdown of his early revolutionary enthusiasms and the collapse of his existence as a husband and father, he had discovered that he could neither like nor understand, he raised the massive barrier of his intellect and his erudition.

Shelley no one could have accused of sparing his own sensitiveness; but, because he was enthusiastic rather than critical, and lacked any aptitude for self-discovery, he never succeeded in giving life and literature their respective dues. The connection of Shelley's love for his sisters, and consequent hatred of his father, with his detestation of Prejudice, Priestcraft, Tyranny, is so clear as to need little emphasis. A wrong-headed or foolish man may produce magnificent verse; but a poet who is both high-minded and muddle-headed, and feels the impact of emotion without admitting its origin, mistakes excitement for the faculty of inspiration, and romantic emphasis for the gift of poetic clarity. Shelley's revolt against the age he lived in —an age of industrial growth and political retrogression—would have been more effective had its origins been less confused and his view of the poet's functions been less didactic; had he been content (in Keats's phrase) to sit like Jupiter instead of constituting himself a kind of celestial busybody. His liberalism, though bold and generous in its expression, rested on a basis that was so insecure as to give a strained uneasy note to his poetic utterance. His choric verse has a breathless speed that is occasionally beautiful: it lacks the "comprehension and expansion" of the greatest literature.

At last the stage is cleared for the appearance of Byron. Wordsworth, Shelley, Keats, Coleridge were all of them devoted men of letters, unselfishly absorbed in their self-appointed task; Byron represents the intrusion of the brilliant amateur. It was at once the secret of his enormous popular success and the measure of his æsthetic limitations that he should rely so completely on the guidance of instinct. His capacity for deliberate reasoning was not impressive; but, as Goethe once observed, in an often-quoted passage of the *Conversations with Eckermann*, though he understood himself but dimly, he possessed "a high degree of that daemonic instinct and attraction which influences others independently of reason, effort or affection, which sometimes succeeds in guiding where the understanding fails." In life and literature he was an unrepentant, indeed an almost unselfconscious, egotist; but, whereas Keats might progress through a knowledge of himself to a love and understanding of the world around him, for Byron the self was circumambient— something he could no more escape from than he could escape from his destiny. Both his greatness and his littleness were on the same conspicuous scale; and it is our misfortune that his talents should have been sufficiently dazzling to lend a false dignity to the weaker side of his literary character. His conception of poetry was crude and straightforward. Verse, he said, was the "lava of the imagination"— its canalisation into literature prevented its overflow—and, elsewhere, that it was the "dream of his sleeping passions," the direct image of some experience he had actually lived through. The poet, in fact, above all other things, must be a personality!

It is to Byron's personal influence on modern literature that we owe the whole tribe of gifted exhibitionists who have attempted to "live" their poems as well as write them. Contrast Byron's deliberate exploitation of the poetic rôle with Keats's analysis of the artist's character. "As to the poetical character . . ." (Keats wrote during October 1818), "it has no self—It is everything and nothing. . . . It enjoys light and shade; it lives in gusto, be it foul or fair, high or low, rich or poor, mean or elevated.—It has as much delight in conceiving an Iago as an Imogen. What shocks the virtuous philosopher delights the chameleon poet. . . . A poet is the most unpoetical of anything in existence, because he has no Identity—he is continually . . . filling some other body. The Sun, the Moon, the Sea, and men and women, who are creatures of impulse, are poetical and have about them an unchangeable attribute; the poet has none, no identity —he is certainly the most unpoetical of all God's creatures . . ."

Had Byron's daemonic example been somewhat less overwhelming, and Keats's lonely voice more sustained and more powerful, how great might have been the benefit to modern poetry and how significant the results that it at length achieved! How different, perhaps, the whole face of twentieth-century Europe! Nationalism was essentially a romantic idea; and from nationalism sprang the half-baked racial theorist with his romantic belief in the superiority of Aryan blood and his romantic distrust of the use of reason.[1] So far-reaching were the effects of the romantic revival that they still persist even in shapes under which they are no longer recognised and among writers who have learned to profess themselves devoutly classicist. For romantic literature appeals to the strain of anarchism that inhabits a dark corner of every human mind and is continually advancing the charms of extinction against the claims of life—the beauty of all that is fragmentary and youthful and half-formed as opposed to the compact achievement of adult genius.

Not for Byron was that calm "autumnal felicity" which (in Gibbon's words) had fallen to the lot of "Voltaire, Hume, and many other men of letters," and which Gibbon himself by the accident of physical infirmity alone was prevented from enjoying. In Byron's career there could be no completeness. Or rather, there could be no completeness of the Augustan sort—a laborious triumph of intellect and art and will-power over the inevitable inequalities of human existence. Byron's peculiar genius depended as much on his weakness as on his strength, as much on what he failed to do—and on the splendid vigour of his unsuccessful efforts—as on any work that he was able to bring to maturity. Though his mind was more intuitive

[1] Perhaps the reader should here be reminded that this book was originally published in 1941.

than reasonable—his temperament had an extremely feminine side—
he possessed a strain of cool dispassionate candour; and through his
inward chaos, which he did not attempt to disguise, darted gleams
of brilliant prophetic insight.

Thus, he could not control his direction, yet could foresee his
destination. Looking back, he felt that his itinerary had been fore-
doomed and, looking on, he distinguished clearly enough the general
goal towards which it tended. More and more imperative became the
• claims of death. He did not run to it, however, with Shelley's
eagerness—like a stream to the ocean, a child to its parent—but
loitered casually, half reluctantly along the predestined path. His
mood might be tragic: it was not lugubrious. He had never been
afraid of appearing to trifle; and, with an enthusiasm so pronounced
as to be almost childish, he welcomed at the beginning of April, 1823
the company of a small and resplendent party of English visitors.
There had been other tourists at Genoa during the last few months,
both congenial and uncongenial: James Wedderburn Webster, an
old acquaintance, husband of the ill-fated Lady Frances, more
ridiculous than ever in a new glossy black wig of improbable
curliness; Lady Hardy, widow of Nelson's captain, an amusing,
observant, sharp-tongued woman, to whom Webster made violent
and ill-timed love; and Henry Fox the Hollands' second son to
whom Byron was attached for his father and mother's sake, and
because, like himself, Henry Fox had entered the world lame. But
the Blessingtons were an especially attractive pair. Lord Blessington,
Byron had known during his London period; and he preserved a
vivid memory of his fellow dandy and man-of-pleasure "in all the
glory of gems and snuff-boxes, and uniforms, and theatricals. . . ."
The former Lord Mountjoy seemed now to be "much tamed." Still
rich, pleasure-loving, indolent, incurably' good-natured, he was
slipping gradually into a condition of vinous sloth which would one
day degenerate into hopeless alcoholism. Meanwhile, in 1818, he had
married again; and Marguerite Blessington was an adventurous and
amusing personage. The daughter of a petty landowner in County
Waterford, at the age of fifteen she had been forced into a miserable
marriage with a certain Captain St. Leger Farmer of the 47th Foot.
After three months, Mrs. Farmer had left her husband; Lawrence had
painted her portrait in 1807; and she next re-emerges as the mistress

of a Captain Jenkins with whom for several years she had lived in placid domestic retirement. From Captain Jenkins's arms she had moved to those of the extravagant, fashionable Lord Mountjoy, and from Stidmanton in Hampshire to a grandiose London house. By falling while he was drunk out of the window of a debtor's jail, Captain Farmer had removed the last obstacle to his wife's good fortune, and from that moment she had swept onward with superb assurance. Lord Blessington, an indistinct but kindly figure, was as lavish as he was rich, and as complaisant, or unsuspicious as he was devoted. With the Blessingtons travelled that dazzling ephebus Count Alfred d'Orsay, paragon of elegance and model of manly grace, whom her circle accepted as Lady Blessington's lover.

At thirty-five, with her shining dark hair, neatly parted down the centre of the scalp and drawn back from the smooth white forehead, her delicate skin, noble brow and lustrous expressive eyes, Marguerite Blessington retained all her power of pleasing. To good looks she added a brisk intelligence, and to vivacity and curiosity some touches of literary aptitude. Naturally, she was anxious to visit Byron; and, though Tom Moore, when she met him in Paris, had alarmed her by the announcement that the poet was growing corpulent—"a fat poet is an anomaly in my opinion"—it was full of tremulous interest that she arrived at Genoa. To her diary she expressed her hopes and fears by means of a rhetorical question: ". . . Am I indeed in the same town with Byron? To-morrow I may, perhaps, behold him. I never before felt the same impatient longing to see any one known to me only by his work." Next day, with Lord Blessington's help, the longing was gratified; and following her first impressions came a minor pang of disappointment. Faithful to the conception of Byron's character that had been popularised by *Childe Harold*—and, for the vast majority of his admirers, not yet been qualified by *Don Juan*—she had imagined there would be some difficulty in obtaining access, and evidently must have promised herself the credit of overcoming his defences. But the citadel capitulated before she had had time to lay siege. Byron was delighted to receive his old friend. He was also delighted, yet evidently a little flustered, by the apparition of this talkative, brilliant, disarming creature who brought in her train the aroma of fashion and the sheen

Byron in Italy

of beauty. No reticence, if some trace of shyness, distinguished his almost effusive welcome. Ushered into a large plainly furnished chamber, Lady Blessington "looked in vain for the hero-looking sort of person" whom she had expected. She had imagined Byron "taller, with a more dignified and commanding air. . . ." The real Byron, on the other hand, was slight and nervous. Since a short but sharp illness during the previous autumn—the result of a long swim during a very hot day in the Gulf of Spezia—he had shed the excessive weight gathered at Montenero, and was now so emaciated as to seem frail and boyish. His coat—much too large for him—might have been several years old: his other garments induced a suspicion that they had been purchased ready-made. From a perpetual consciousness of his lame foot, he was abrupt and awkward. His reddish curls, darkened by macassar oil, were heavily grey-streaked.

"Were I to point out the prominent defect of Lord Byron [concluded the diarist], I should say it was flippancy, and a total want of that natural self-possession and dignity which ought to characterise a man of birth and education." Positively she found it hard to prevent him from talking; and if Lady Blessington had pictured herself in the attractive rôle of a woman of talent "drawing out" a man of genius or melting the cold reserve of a poetic misanthrope, those expectations were destined to be cut short. The confidences came unsolicited, and, accompanying them, a flood of gossip. Misfortune had saddened him; but he was rarely solemn. Their first talk revolved mostly round London friends; and, having handed the lady to her carriage with many elaborate courtesies—already her disappointment had begun to lose its edge, and she had decided that, though odd and foreign-looking, he was "remarkably gentleman-like"—he asked permission to call upon them the following day. Next morning, before they expected him, his card was brought up. Then Byron appeared in bubbling good-humour, and embarked once again on the subject of their English friends, concerning whom he spoke with affection, not untempered by badinage, in which "none of their little defects" was allowed to escape lightly. Nor was this all. When finally he took his leave, among profuse apologies for having stayed so long—he had lived so much out of the world, he explained, that he had forgotten its customs—he promised that Thursday to dine with the Blessingtons at their hotel, the Albergo della Villa. On the appointed day, he was announced an hour before the usual time. At first somewhat ruffled because he had found the passages and the staircase full of gaping English tourists, he very soon recaptured his previous gaiety, made a large meal which included two helpings of English plum pudding and, observing that he considered it a *jour de fête*, consented to drink several glasses of champagne. He hoped (he said) they would not be shocked by the extent of his appetite; but the truth was that for several months he had been living almost entirely on vegetables; "and now that I see a good dinner, I cannot resist temptation, though to-morrow I shall suffer for my gourmandise as I always do. . . ." In the meantime, he ate with appreciation and talked with gusto, provocative, malicious, gay, ingratiating.

On her side, Lady Blessington was both charmed and perturbed. Their relationship had a ludicrous but also a pathetic aspect: for whereas the admirer was repeatedly disillusioned and sometimes extremely shocked, until from blind admiration she had fallen back on a kind of tolerant affection, Byron was completely unaware of the effect he made and continued, as he thought successfully, to entertain his visitors. The flow of gossip that amused but disconcerted Lady Blessington was Byron's idea, somewhat falsified in memory, of English social small talk; but his conversation, like the cut of his coat, was a trifle out of date. London had changed considerably since 1816; manners were less licentious and conventions sterner; but Byron kept the pose and prattle of a Regency man of the world. It was as such, rather than as a mere versifier, Lady Blessington soon ascertained, that he liked to be regarded. Though savage in his criticisms of the London *beau monde*, its tedious crowded balls and stifling evening parties, about all its recent doings he still evinced the most compulsive interest. There was no doubt that he had a "decided taste" for aristocracy; and Lady Blessington, when she was conducted around his private apartments, raised her eyebrows at the oddity of the poet's bedchamber, where the bed itself was topped with coronets and wreathed with his family motto, ostentatious and richly gilt, but shoddy and gimcrack. Nothing could have been more "un-English" than his clothes and furnishings: they were extravagant but inexpensive, garish but well worn. Byron's taste might have passed without remark in a foreign nobleman. It was unlooked for—indeed horrifying—in a British peer!

Of these criticisms—or, indeed, of their possibility—the poet remained quite unconscious. But on other scores, he divined, he sometimes exposed himself; and when, as often happened, he felt that he had gone too far, he would do his best to efface the bad impression with a smile and a pleasantry. Lady Blessington was allowed to lecture him to her heart's content. No one (he declared) disliked being scolded by an attractive woman; and his new friend acquiesced in the compliment and readily accepted the privilege he offered. From time to time, it was true, she hurt his feelings; and then he would turn pale with anger or suddenly leave her presence, only to return a little later determined to "make it up." About their association hung a pensive autumnal radiance. The tired heart that had ceased to quicken its pace for Teresa Guiccioli broke into a sedate but pleasing flutter for Marguerite Blessington.[1] Life, long dull and automatic, became suddenly various and eventful. The quiet routine of vege-tarian meals and study and exercise—punctuated, if not enlivened, by visits to Teresa's rooms—was discarded in favour of a regular social round. When he rode out now in the afternoons, it was as one of a cavalcade. Byron (his friend noted) was a nervous rider; and the figure he cut on horseback was at least surprising, for his mount was "literally covered with various trappings, in the way of cavessons, martingales, and Heaven knows how many other (to me unknown) inventions. The saddle was *à la hussarde* with holsters, in which he always carried pistols." As for his costume—that was as outlandish as it was characteristic, combining a touch of inappropriate splendour with an indication of the wearer's economical habits. His nankin coat and trousers "appeared to have shrunk from washing," the jacket being "embroidered in the same colour" and embellished with "three rows of buttons; the waist very short, the back very narrow, and the sleeves set in as they used to be ten or fifteen years before." The *ensemble* was completed by a dark-blue velvet cap, with eye-shade, rich gold band and large gold tassel, a pair of blue spectacles

[1] His partiality was sufficiently pronounced to cause Teresa considerable unhappiness. On May 17th, Byron wrote to Lady Hardy that the association, innocent though it was, had plunged him into "a bit of domestic trouble . . . Mde. la Comptesse G., was seized with a furious fit of Italian jealousy and was as unreasonable and perverse as can well be imagined."

and nankin gaiters. Sometimes, in place of the white coat, he wore his Highland jacket, liberally befrogged, in the green tartan of his mother's clan.

Thus equipped, he would jog with the Blessingtons along the road to Nervi, usually talkative and (except when they encountered English sight-seers, and he blushed nervously and muttered irritably at the sound of their whispered comments) affable, entertaining, in high good-humour. Or he would spend the evening with them and, after tea, sit out on the balcony. From neighbouring balconies drifted the fragrance of southern night flowers; the blazing *fanale* cast fiery reflections upon passing sails; and fishing boats crossed the moonlit water, each with a flare at the prow. Beneath their windows "were crowded an uncountable number of ships from every country, with their various flags waving in the breeze, which bore to us the sounds of the various languages of the crews." But neither at this nor at any other time did Byron rouse the suspicion that he aspired to a lover's rôle. Love might colour his emotions: it did not cloud them. "I am worn out in feelings [he had told Marguerite Blessington].... Though only thirty-six, I feel sixty in mind...." Nowadays he was content with the pleasures of friendship.[1] He liked the sympathy of this attractive, experienced woman, whom he could shock, conciliate, then shock again, feeling all the while that he continued to hold her interest and perhaps to touch her heart. Moreover, she provided an excuse for his favourite mental indulgence. He could give way to the joys of recollection and incessantly remember aloud.

Not even to Marguerite Blessington did he uncover the whole of his past. But, as he talked, either in his flippant social manner or in the more serious and sententious style that he adopted when they were alone, name after name, and episode after episode, would come floating to the surface. For so self-conscious a man he was remarkably downright; and topics that his friend might have herself avoided were introduced and discussed by the poet at their earliest encounters. Lady Byron's conduct he was never tired of analysing and

[1] "Her slight acquaintance with me [Byron reassured Lady Hardy after the Blessingtons' departure] was of the most decorous description; the poor woman seemed deranged with ennui, entirely bored with her Lord and a little sick of her Parisian Paladin also, though why I could not perceive . . ." One suspects, however, that this account of the friendship was a trifle disingenuous.

describing. After eight years he could hardly forgive her for the blow she had dealt him; yet when he spoke of her it was usually in a respectful and sometimes an affectionate tone, as though he half admired, much as he resented, her inflexible righteousness. His daughter too, he mentioned often, and always regretfully. Her miniature portrait hung over his writing-desk. It was a kind of talisman—the symbol of permanence in a life that had been otherwise diffuse, overcrowded and chaotic. As he talked, how many were the names he mentioned! Lady Melbourne—there was a woman he had been really fond of. "She was a charming person—a sort of modern Aspasia, uniting the energy of a man's mind with the delicacy and tenderness of a woman's. . . . I have often thought that, with a little more youth, Lady Melbourne might have turned my head. . . ." And "Poor dear Lady Jersey!" Did she (he wondered) "still retain her beautiful cream-coloured complexion and raven hair?" Madame de Staël was the cleverest woman he had ever met. She had been kind to him, and given him good advice. But he could not forget how at a large London dinner party the famous blue-stocking had had trouble with her corset, and had appealed to the footman behind her chair to pull out an obtrusive whalebone! Madame de Lieven was another hostess for whom he felt affection and gratitude: she and Lady Jersey had rallied to his support during the separation scandal when the rest of the London *beau monde* conspired to cut him. "Of all that côterie, Madame de Lieven, after Lady Jersey, was the best. . . ." Then his reminiscences would slide back again to the more immediate past; and he would speak with tender regard of Teresa Guiccioli, her beauty and virtues, her exalted birth and the fortune that she had given up. ". . . She must know that I am sincerely attached to her; but the truth is, my habits are not those requisite to form the happiness of any woman. . . ." Through his references to his present mistress there sounded a hollow obituary note.

She belonged already to the past: she would have no share in his future life. It seemed to have been settled (he would sigh) that he must go to Greece; and, if he went there, he did not expect that he would return alive. But Hobhouse wished it, and the Greek Committee continued to bother him. . . . In fact, since February, 1823, when he had finally decided for Greece and against the Americas, Byron's feelings had been subject to considerable fluctuation. What had been attractive in fancy became alarming when it was translated to the plane of practical reality. Besides, there was an uncomfortable suspicion that he had perhaps been cornered! It was one thing to decide that he would go to Greece, and quite another to learn that the Greek Committee, a body of earnest Liberal gentlemen that included Jeremy Bentham, Hobhouse, Douglas Kinnaird and several others, had elected him to deputise for them on the field of glory. The idea of death might leave him calm: he shuddered, nevertheless, at the prospect of moving house. Heaped around him was the treasure-trove of so long a period! "Byron [Trelawny was to write] never sold or gave away anything he had acquired," and was surrounded by "all the rubbish accumulated in the many years he had lived in Italy, besides his men, women, dogs, and monkeys, and all that was theirs." He was usually "bedevilled for a week after moving": the removal from Pisa to Genoa had completely knocked him up; and it was now suggested that he should transplant himself to some far-off Grecian wilderness. Yet from every side his well-wishers appeared rapidly to be closing in. During 1823, a representative of the Greek patriots, Andreas Luriottis, had arrived in London. The Committee had held its first meeting on February 28; and Edward Blaquière had volunteered to travel to Greece and review the position. Blaquière and Luriottis had broken their journey to visit Byron, and he had welcomed them at the Casa Saluzzo. During May he learned that by unanimous vote he had been elected a member of the Greek Committee, to whom he responded that he was anxious to go to the Levant in person, and that the only difficulty was "one of a domestic nature." The obstacle he referred to was, of course, his mistress; but (as Trelawny noted) he did not "seem disposed to make a mountain of her resistance," and had promised that Pietro Gamba should bear him company.

From that point, there was no hope or possibility of turning back. But the more he thought of Greece, the more convinced he felt that this expedition was to be his ultimate journey. To Medwin he had already expressed the conviction that he would not survive it; and to Lady Blessington again and again he spoke of his approaching death. But in this, as in everything else, his attitude was disconcerting. Lady Blessington would have applauded an heroic pose. There was something (she mused) "so exciting in the idea of the greatest poet of his day sacrificing his fortune, his occupations, his enjoyments—in short, offering up on the altar of Liberty all the immense advantages which station, fortune, and genius can bestow, that it is impossible to reflect on it without admiration." But Byron gave his gesture of sacrifice a flippant and cynical cast, talked at length of the uniforms he meant to wear, of the loans he proposed to advance and of the worthlessness of the modern Greeks, "entering into petty details . . . always with perfect *sang froid*." In another mood, he would say that he longed to return to England, to bid good-bye for the last time to his wife and daughter, or speak of the "grey Greek stone" that might mark his burial place, lost in some wild valley of the Thessalian uplands, within sight perhaps of the snowy crest of unforgotten Olympus, where eagles screamed and wheeled against a brilliant Ægean sky. Lady Blessington was vexed and puzzled, then wondered and admired again. Byron seemed positively to flourish on her naïve discomfiture.

From April 1st to June 2nd their autumnal idyll lasted. Two long months went by in rides, visits, dinner parties, and in endless conversation. Hard as she tried to fix and romanticise it, Lady Blessington's portrait of Byron was still strangely nebulous: despite earnest attempts she had found it impossible to define his character. Generous yet avaricious, flippant yet tender-hearted, sceptical yet irremediably haunted by superstition—was there a single aspect in which he achieved consistency? But one thing was plain—that he believed in fate. "There was a helplessness about Byron, a sort of abandonment of himself to his destiny, as he called it, that commonplace people can as little pity as understand"; and when fate spoke to him clearly he always answered the call. With a certain reluctance, however, he took his leave of happiness. At the beginning of June, the Blessingtons made ready to depart; and on June 2nd for the last time he called at their hotel rooms, looking out from a flower-filled balcony across the harbour of Genoa. He wept and made no effort to conceal his tears. To each of them he presented a parting gift—to Lord Blessington, benevolent but indistinct: to "*le beau Alfred*," tall, splendid, Apollonian, who had done his pencil likeness to embellish a sketch-book: to Lady Blessington, still a little puzzled but no doubt deeply touched: to Miss Power, Lady Blessington's unmarried sister —and from each asked a corresponding *gage d'amitié*. Then he dried his eyes and uttered "some sarcastic observation on his nervousness," though at the same time his lip quivered and the words were tear-fogged. Behind him was a glimpse of the contentment he had always aspired to: it would pass away from him in the Blessingtons' travelling carriage on the road to Lucca. The hardest stage of his journey still stretched ahead.

Index

Index

Index

Index

Index

Index

Index